BMAT

Past Paper Worked Solutions (2003 – 2019)

Table of Contents

Year	Section	Value	
2011	Section 1	201	
	Section 2	214	
	Section 3	222	
2012	Section 1	225	
	Section 2	238	
	Section 3	249	
2013	Section 1	253	
	Section 2	265	
	Section 3	277	
2014	Section 1	279	
	Section 2	279	
	Section 3	279	
2015	Section 1	280	
	Section 2	296	
	Section 3	306	
2016	Section 1	309	
	Section 2	323	
	Section 3	331	
2017	Section 1	334	
	Section 2	349	
	Section 3	359	
2018	Section 1	362	
	Section 2	377	
	Section 3	386	
2019	Section 1	388	
	Section 2	403	
	Section 3	415	

If you believe that this book has helped you in your BMAT preparation, please leave a review on Amazon. This would be greatly appreciated!

For any queries, please email at: crackbmat@gmail.com

Even though I have taken great care to ensure that there are no errors in this book, if you do manage to spot any mistakes, please email, so that I would be able to assist you.

Please note that the information in this book is purely based on my knowledge and opinions. Therefore, the content of this book should only be considered as advisory. I do not accept any liability whatsoever, for any student's BMAT results or performance, the outcome of university applications or for any other loss. No liability is assumed for any damages due to any information contained within the book or for errors of any kind.

How To Do BMAT Past Papers?

It is crucial that you understand how to do BMAT past papers the correct way. Try to do as many past papers as you possibly can! The past papers are available for free on:
https://www.admissionstesting.org/for-test-takers/bmat/preparing-for-bmat/practice-papers/

Many students do very few past papers, which is not ideal! Doing many past papers will give you an idea of how the exam will feel like on the day.

Many students feel pressured by time on exam day, causing them to make all sorts of mistakes. So please ensure that you do the BMAT past papers under exam conditions as well. This means that you should do them in silence under timed conditions. Print the past papers and their respective response sheets.

Do the exam in order. Section 1 first, Section 2 next and Section 3 last.

Use the Response Sheets provided. Each response sheet is different for every past paper. So, make sure you do not print the same response sheet for every past paper.

Since the questions are mostly multiple choices, there cannot be any lenient or hard marking. You do not get marked for any calculations.

ANSWER ALL QUESTIONS!

After you have corrected your past paper, check the conversion tables to see which band you got for each section. The conversion tables are provided on the second page of the answer keys of each past paper.
The band conversion tables are different each year so make sure you check the correct answer key for the past paper you did.

How to Use BMAT Worked Solutions?

It is important that you know how to use BMAT worked solutions in the correct way.

For every question that you get wrong, check its worked solution. Understand how the answer was obtained and remember the process. You will see that many questions, especially in Section 2, require the same process.

2003 Section 1

1) E
Volume increases by a lot whilst the depth increases by a little amount at either end.
Our shape has a small increase in volume and a large increase in depth in the middle.
Therefore, the shape would have to be wider at the top and the bottom and narrower in the middle.

A – Wrong
The shape is not narrower in the middle.

B – Wrong
The shape is actually wider in the middle. So, this is definitely wrong.

C – Wrong
The shape is actually wider in the middle. So, this is definitely wrong.

D – Wrong
The shape is actually wider in the middle. So, this is definitely wrong.

E – Correct
The shape is wider at the top and bottom whilst narrower in the middle.

2) C
The argument is the first line of the paragraph where it states that ready meals should be labelled with health warnings. We must find a statement, which strengthens this argument.
A – Wrong
People not knowing how to cook is irrelevant to the argument that why ready meals should come with a warning.

B – Wrong
People not having the time to cook is irrelevant to the argument that why ready meals should come with a warning.

C – Correct
Since people are unaware of the unhealthy proprieties of the ready meals, they should come with labelled warnings. So, C is correct.

D – Wrong
Lack of exercise is not mentioned in the text and hence, this is irrelevant to the argument.

E – Wrong
This actually weakens the argument and states that a labelled warning would not have any effect on people.

3) B
Sum up all columns and rows. 1 row and 1 column would be incorrect. Where these meet, will be the incorrect value.

Summing the values in the year 8 column gives 150 (whilst it is 145 in the table) and summing the cars row gives 107 (whilst it is 102 in the table).

Where these meet is 33 on the table. Hence, year 8s going by car (33) is an incorrect value.

---

4) C
A – Wrong
The text does not state how interested students from poorer families are in entering university.

B – Wrong
There is no mention of universities not willing to help the government.

C – Correct
The text states that the government is planning to change the policy of grants into loans, which will cause the students to repay their debts. The last line of the paragraph says that this action will cause poor students to be deterred from entering university. So C is correct.

D – Wrong
The last line clearly specifies: "students from poorer families". So D is wrong.

E – Wrong
The paragraph does not say whether grants were too expensive for the government.

---

5) 109
1st scenario: Number of cabbages = $y^2 + 9$
2nd scenario: Number of cabbages = $(y+1)^2 - 12$
$y^2 + 9 = (y + 1)^2 - 12$
$y^2 + 9 = y^2 + 2y + 1 - 12$
$9 = 2y - 11$
$20 = 2y$
$y = 10$
Substituting, ($y = 10$) in ($y^2 + 9$) gives us:
$10^2 + 9 = 100 + 9 = 109$

---

6) D
The conclusion of the text is that "it may be undemocratic by favouring some political parties more than others".

A – Wrong
The text does not suggest in any way that a low turnout is endangering our democracy.

B – Wrong
Loss of secrecy is just one of the practical issues mentioned. However, we cannot say that this is the main conclusion of the text.

C – Wrong
The text does not mention whether any political parties object to internet voting or not.

D – Correct
The phrase "favouring some political parties" suggests that some sections of the societies would be favoured and the sections will be discriminated against.

E – Wrong
Even though this is a correct statement and may seem like the answer, you must consider the fact that this is not the conclusion of the text.

---

7) A
This is actually quite straightforward.
The average surgery session in 1997 lasted 140 min and the appointments are made 10 minutes apart.
Simple division $^{140}/_{10}$ gives us 14. The answer is A.

---

8) 27
Number of surgery sessions a week: 8.5
Minutes per surgery session: 140
Time spent in surgery per week: $140 \times 8.5 = 1190$
Time spent on home visits per week: 408
Total: $408 + 1190 = 1598$

1598 is approximately 1600 minutes
$^{1600}/_{60} = 26.6$ hours
26.6 is approximately 27 hours

---

9) C
$^{1 \times 10^7}/_{5000} = 2000$ patients per doctor
155 patients are seen in a week, therefore, $155 \times 50 = 7750$ visits per year
$^{7750}/_{2000} = 3.875$
3.875 is approximately 4 visits per year

---

10) D
The average length of a surgery session is 165 minutes. With a decrease in the number of doctors, this will have to increase. Hence, we eliminate options A, B and C. This leaves us with D and E.
Now,
$165 \times 5000 = 4500 \times$ new length of surgery required
New length of surgery = $^{165 \times 5000}/_{4500} = 183.3333\ldots$
Hence, 183 is the answer (D)

11) A

A – Correct

The average length of a surgery session increased by 25 minutes. Since this is the highest increase, A must be the answer.

B – Wrong

Length of a consultation in 1995 = 9:59 minutes
Length of a consultation in 2000 = 10:00 minutes
1 second extra per consultation will not contribute most to the rise. So B is not the answer.

C – Wrong

Average time spent on a home visit increased by 4 minutes from 1995 to 2000.

D – Wrong

The average length of a home visit is irrelevant because we already have the time spent on home visits per week.

12) A

The average number of patients seen per week is:
135 in 1995
155 in 2000
This is only shown by option A

13) B

Let number of people on bus = y
At the first stop, $\frac{2y}{3}$ people stay on, $\frac{4y}{9}$ on the second and $\frac{8y}{27}$ on the third.
$\frac{8y}{27} = 8$
$\frac{8y}{8} = 27$
y = 27

14) E

The text just transitions from the hours spent on internet by teenagers to isolation and obesity. This indicates that the text is trying to suggest that excessive use of the internet is causing isolation and obesity.

A – Wrong

The text is not focused on the benefits of Internet. So A is irrelevant.

B – Wrong

The text is meant to focus only on teenagers who use the internet excessively.

C – Wrong

It does not assume parents can enforce stricter controls. It just states that parents must enforce stricter controls. There is a difference between assuming and advising.

D – Wrong
TV and computer games are irrelevant as the text is meant to focus only on internet.

E – Correct
This identifies the flaw which is the causal link made by the text between internet and isolation and obesity.

---

15) C
Every team will play two matches against the other 5 teams in their pools. We must use the following process:
A plays B, C, D, E, F twice – 10 matches
B plays C, D, E, F twice – 8 matches
C plays D, E, F twice – 6 matches
D plays E, F twice – 4 matches
E plays F twice – 2 matches
SUM – 10 + 8 + 6 + 4 + 2= 30 matches in one pool
This gives a total of 60 matches in 2 pools. Since each team plays each of the other teams in other pool once, this gives us 6 x 6 = 36 matches. Finally, there is the final, which is 1 match.
Total number of matches: 60 + 36 + 1 = 97 matches

---

16) C
The line of y = 5 is only shown in A, B and C and out of these y=2x only in A and C.
If we compare A and C, only option C shows when y is greater than 2x, whereas A shows y is less than 2x.

---

17) B
A – Wrong
We cannot be sure whether the nematode worms cause a decrease in fertiliser residues or the decrease in fertiliser residues causes the increase in nematode worms. We cannot create a causal link between the two due to lack of sufficient information.

B – Correct
Option B just states that nematode worms and fertiliser residues are negatively correlated. It does not make a causal link and just states what the text tries to say. So this is correct.

C – Wrong
Again, with the same logic as A, we cannot infer a causal link between the two things.

D – Wrong
The text does not say anything about fertiliser residues interfering with reproduction of the nematode worms. This is definitely wrong. (Please understand that anything not written in the text will most likely be wrong).

---

18) 5

15 take the BMAT

13 take Biology

2 don't take Biology

Hence the 2 that do not take Biology must be taking Chemistry, Physics and Maths.

Now, 3 people take Chemistry, Biology, Maths and Physics. This gives us 3 + 2=5.

We can assume all 5 of these people are boys because we are looking to maximise the number of boys.

19) D

Julie put her clock 1 hour forward. Since she was meant to put her clock 1 hour back, difference between the actual time and her time = $1 - (- 1) = 1 + 1 = 2$ hours. So when her clock showed 11 am, the actual time must have been = $11 - 2 = 9$ am.

Clare did not interfere with her clock. So when the time is 11 am, her clock would have shown 10 am. So she would have arrived at 10 am.

So Julie arrives 1 hour before Clare.

20) B

The argument here is that "time and money spent…on persuading men…at an earlier stage would be easily offset by savings on treating advanced conditions". We must find a weakness in this argument.

A – Wrong

Even though men do not seek help until the condition becomes advanced, we cannot determine whether they are reluctant or they do not seek help for some other reason. So this is wrong.

B – Correct

The text gives an example of men not seeking help until their condition becomes advanced which causes the treatment to be more expensive and difficult. However, the text fails to consider that an early consultation for minor symptoms incurs high costs in doctor's time. So this is definitely a weakness in the argument.

C – Wrong

This statement does not find a weakness in the argument above which states that treatments become more difficult and expensive due to men not seeking help earlier on. Option C just focuses on women and why they seek help earlier on.

D – Wrong

Option D neither strengthens the argument nor weakens it.

E – Wrong

Involving other health professionals does not find a weakness in the argument stated above. In fact, this slightly strengthens the argument as it says that it would require more people to treat the advanced conditions.

21) 7.2 seconds
The cheetah runs 50 km/h faster than the Zebra. It is also 100 m (0.1 km) behind the Zebra.
We use the equation, Time = Distance ÷ Speed
$^{0.1}/_{50}$ = 0.002 hours.
0.002 x 3600 = 7.2 seconds

22) E
The latest date up to which the coins were used in was 157 AD.

A – Wrong
We cannot say that the occupation was abandoned before 157 AD as it was definitely occupied in 88 and 123 AD.

B – Wrong
We cannot infer that it was first occupied in 88 AD. It could have been occupied in 88 AD itself.

C – Wrong
It could have been occupied before as well but we just do not have any proof.

D – Wrong
Just because we have coin dating to 88 and 157 AD, we cannot assume that the site was only occupied during that period. It could have been occupied before and after as well, but we do not have any proof yet.

E – Correct
The site was definitely occupied till 157 AD. Therefore, it must have been abandoned in or after it.

23) B
The argument is that "the habitats of wading birds will, therefore, inevitable decline if gardening continues to be so popular".

A – Wrong
This does not necessarily need to be assumed as the text says that gardening has become the most popular. We need to find an assumption about the present and not the future.

B – Wrong
The text assumes that since gardening has become the most popular hobby, gardeners will ignore the encouragement to use alternatives which will inevitably cause wading birds to die.

C – Wrong
Nothing is mentioned about environmentalists ignoring the declining habitats of wading birds.

D – Wrong
Again, we cannot infer that garden enters cannot sell cheap alternatives to peat just from the information provided to us.

E – Correct
Nothing is mentioned about the habitats of other animals.

---

24) C
The Fair-E coefficient represents the degree of inequality in income distribution, and because this has increased, we can determine that income inequality has not been reduced. So C is the answer.

A – Wrong
We do not know about the overall income of people

B – Wrong
Chart 1 suggests an increase in household income of low earners

D – Wrong
We do not know about the standard of living

E – Wrong
We don't know anything about the 'real wealth'

---

25) D
A – Wrong
We cannot conclude for sure that the government's fiscal policy is definitely the cause of the rise in inequality. There could be other reasons or causes too.

B – Wrong
Again, B cannot be concluded, as it is a very general statement to make.

C – Wrong
We do not know what the phrase 'better off' could mean and hence we cannot reliably conclude this. It is too vague.

D – Correct
Chart 1 shows that there has been a net gain in the income of poorer people. However, chart 2 shows that the Fair-coefficient has risen at the same time. The only way both of these facts could go hand in hand is if the pre-tax income (income before tax) has increased for the richer people.

E – Wrong
This is wrong because the poor household has had a net gain in income according to Chart 1.

---

26) E
1 – Correct
1 is correct- the income increase of the poor is less than it could have been as seen in data

2 – Correct
2 could definitely be correct and we have already explored the idea that the incomes at the top end may have increased more than those at the bottom end

3 – Correct
3 could also increase the Fair-E coefficient while taxes and benefits change for the poor

Since all 3 statements are correct, E is the answer.

---

27) C
The Fair-E coefficient measures the degree of inequality.
Poland – 0.2,
Ruritania – 0.35
USA – 0.4
Panama – 0.6
So the correct order is: Poland, Ruritania, USA and Panama

---

28) B
In this question, the argument confuses cause with correlation. 2 factors could be correlated, but the causality can be either way around, or they may be linked by another factor. Hence, B is the correct answer.

---

29) E
Probability of it being yellow or blue = 70%
P (yellow) = $^{70}/_3$%
P (blue) = $^{140}/_3$%
We can say that there are 3 red, $^7/_3$ yellow and $^{14}/_3$ blue. However, we need whole numbers. If we multiply all of these by 3, we get the following numbers: 9 red, 7 yellow and 14 blue. This adds up to 30.

---

30) C
1 and 2 are correct.

1 – Correct
30% work, at least some of the time, in the commercial sector. This covers doctor working in both sectors together with the commercial sector alone. Thus some doctors must work in the public sector alone.

2 – Correct
Statement 2 is correct because 70% work solely in the public sector. On the other hand 30% work in either both or just commercial.

3 – Wrong
Statement 3 cannot be deduced, as we do not know how much time doctors spend at each service.

---

31) A & C
Express each one as an inequality:
A) $a \leq s$
B) $s < a$
C) $s \geq a$
D) $a \geq s$.

We can see that A and C are equivalent. Try considering whether Anne can be older than Susan, Anne can be the same age as Susan or Anne can be younger than Susan for each inequality.

---

32) E

Conclusion – the government must act quickly to plan for changes in holiday patterns.
Assumption- these changes will be more than short term

---

33) D

To start with, we have:

B > D and C > A.

D goes back 1 place so cannot start last whilst B goes up 1 place so cannot start first. Thus, we can deduce that originally, the order was CBDA. After the swap, the new order is BCAD.

---

34) C

Current ratio: 10 parts of water to 1 part concentrate. Therefore, we need to add more concentrate. Thus, we can rule out A and B.

Now, if we add 10cm concentrate, we now have 400cm water and 50cm concentrate, which is the correct 8:1 part dilution.

---

35) C

Firstly, we need to determine the net change for each year.

For example, 800 lost in the first year. We can use the process of elimination to rule out A, B and D as they began with an increase rather than a decrease. F does not decrease by 800 in the first year so is also wrong. E is incorrect because there is an increase between years 2 and 3. Hence C is correct.

---

36) B

455AD = year 9

72 − 9 = 63

Year 72 = 455 + 63 = 518 AD

---

37) C

Gildas was born in the year of the battle of Badon. If we knew his birth date we could confirm the date of the battle.

---

38) B

Year 93 = 539 AD in the Welsh Annals

However, if this was too late by 28 years, then the battle would have occurred in 511 AD.

---

39) 506 AD

Year of death of Kin Maelgwn was 549 AD

If Gildas was 43 at this date, the battle of Badon would be as late as possible, which means, 549 − 43 = 506 AD.

---

40) C

The Welsh Annals give information suggesting Gildas wrote his book after the King's death, which is only shown by C.

2003 Section 2

1) B
- Amylase in mouth partially digests starch
- Pepsin secreted in the stomach digests protein
- Small intestine is the location for the digestion of fats

Type of nutrient 1 represents starch
Type of nutrient 2 represents protein
Type of nutrient 3 represents fats

2) E
Mass of 8×10^6 U atoms = $4 \times 10^{-25} \times 8 \times 10^6$
(32×10^{-19}) kg = (32×10^{-13}) mg
Answer: 3.2×10^{-12} mg

3) a = 2, b = 9, c = 6

Carbon
3a = 6
Hence, a = 2

Hydrogen
6a = 2c
6 (2) = 2c
12 = 2c
c = 6

Oxygen
2b = 12 + c
2b = 12 + 6
2b = 18
b = 9

4) B
Pivot is located in the middle. So, ignore the weight of the
bar. Moments clockwise = Moments anticlockwise:
(500 x 0.2) = (0.4 x 200) + 200x
100 = 80 + 200x
x = 20 ÷ 200 = 0.1m = 10 cm

5) D
At pH 5:
Methyl orange would be yellow
Bromothymol blue would be yellow
Phenolphthalein would be colourless
So, yellow + yellow + colourless = yellow.

6) 76.8 kJ
Weight = mass x g
Horse's mass = 6000 ÷ 10 = 600 kg
Kinetic energy = $\frac{1}{2}mv^2$ = (0.5 x 600 x 16^2) = 300 x 256 = 76800 J = 76.8 kJ

---

7) B
Oestrogen reaches its highest level in the days prior to ovulation. So B is the answer (before ovulation).
NOTE: this is not in your specification anymore

---

8) A, C, B, D
Resistors in parallel have a lower overall resistance than the same resistors in series.
A has the lowest resistance. Now, B only has one resistor in each branch but C has two in the top branch. Hence, C has a lower resistance than B. All resistors in D are in series hence D will have the greatest resistance.
If you are still confused, let us assume that each resistor has a resistance of 2 Ω.

For A,
$\frac{1}{2} + \frac{1}{2} + \frac{1}{2} = \frac{1}{R_T}$
$\frac{3}{2} = \frac{1}{R_T}$
R (total) = $\frac{2}{3}$ Ω

For B,
Since 2 resistors are branched, we can use the formula,
$\frac{(R1 \times R2)}{(R1 + R2)} = \frac{(2 \times 2)}{(2 + 2)}$ = 4 ÷ 4 = 1 Ω
Add the resistor, which is in series.
Total resistance in combination B = 1 + 2 = 3 Ω

For C,
Resistors on top are in series so we can add them up, 2 + 2 = 4 Ω
$\frac{(R1 \times R2)}{(R1 + R2)} = \frac{(4 \times 2)}{(4 + 2)}$ = 8 ÷ 6 = 1.33 Ω

For D,
We just add everything
2 + 2 + 2 = 6 Ω

The order would be:
A → C → C → D

---

9) B
n(H_2) = 9 ÷ 2 = 4.5 moles
n(N_2) = 56 ÷ 28 = 2 moles
Ratio of H_2:NH_3 = 3:2

4.5 moles of Hydrogen react with 3 moles of Ammonia
We then use the formula:
Moles = mass ÷ Mr
Moles = 3
Mass = unknown
Mr = 14 + 3 = 17
Moles = m ÷ Mr
Mass = moles x Mr = 3 x 17 = 51 grams

---

10) B
For this question, you can substitute values into the variables 'y' and 'x'
So, when
x = 1, y = 2 (This eliminates D)
x = 0, y = 1 (This immediately rules out A & C)
(IT IS IMPORTANT TO UNDERSTAND THE POWER RULES)

---

11) A
Frequency remains the same in all of these phenomena. So A (0) is the answer. You cannot work this out.
This requires pre-requisite knowledge.

---

12) A
Fumaric acid is formed when succinic acid loses 2 hydrogen atoms. This is an oxidation reaction.

---

13) D
We need to rearrange this inequality so that we have 0 on one side and the other figures on the other side.

x^2 is equal to or more than $8 - 2x$
Shifting '8-2x' to the other side, we have:
$x^2 + 2x - 8$ is equal to or more than 0
Now we factorise the expression '$x^2 + 2x - 8$'
It is essential that you understand how to 'Factorise the middle term'
We get $(x + 4)(x - 2)$ is greater than or equal to 0
Solutions: x is less than or equal to -4 and x is greater than or equal to 2

---

14) i) 3, 4, 5   ii) E
i) Individual 7 has inherited the disease in an autosomal recessive fashion since individuals 4 and 5 do not have the disease. Therefore, individuals 4 and 5 must be heterozygous.
Since Individual 7 is affected, individual 3 must also be heterozygous.

ii) We now know that 3 and 4 are heterozygous.

	T	t
T	TT	Tt
t	Tt	tt

The only way for a person to be affected by a person is if they are homozygous and only have the recessive alleles i.e. 'tt'

Therefore, the probability of the child being affected by the condition is $1/4$.

Probability of a having a girl child = $1/2$

Probability of having a girl with disease = $1/2 \times 1/4 = 1/8$

---

15) 4 minutes

Initial count rate = 140 - 20 (background radiation) = 120

Final count rate = 35 - 20 = 15

We need to figure out the number of half-lives.

$120 \rightarrow 60$ = 1 half-life

$60 \rightarrow 30$ = 2 half-lives

$30 \rightarrow 15$ = 3 half-lives

There were three half-lives over the period of 12 minutes

Time per half-life = $12 \div 3 = 4$ minutes

---

16) C

The solubility of potassium chlorate (V) in 100g of water at 70°C is 78g.

Our sample was dissolved in 200g of water. Therefore, 136g of potassium chlorate (V) should have been dissolved.

However, we only added 80g. So, the full sample would have been dissolved.

So far: 80g of potassium chlorate (V) has fully dissolved in 200g of water.

Now, the solution becomes saturated when 80g of the potassium chlorate (V) dissolves in 200g of water.

Dividing by 2, the solution becomes saturated when 40g of potassium chlorate (V) dissolves in 100g of water.

From the graph, we can see that this happens at 46°C.

We know that the solution was cooled to 20°C from the question. Solubility per 100g of water at this temperature = 27g

Decrease in solubility (from 46°C to 20°C) = 40 - 27 = 13g per 100g water

Since our solution was had 200g water, we multiply 13 by 2 to get 26g.

---

17) E

You need to learn electricity equations which link power, current, voltage, energy and charge. Also, you need to learn the units of each measurement.

Let us look at the options:

A

Joules/coulombs = Energy/Charge

We know the formula, Energy = Charge x Voltage

Hence, Voltage = Energy/Charge

B

Amperes x ohms = Current x Resistance

We know V = IR which is Voltage = Current x Resistance

C

Watts/amperes = Power/Current

We know P = VI which Power = Voltage x Current

Rearranging, we get Voltage = Power/Current

D

$\sqrt{(\text{watts} \times \text{ohms})} = \sqrt{(\text{Power} \times \text{Resistance})}$

We know:

P = VI and I = V/R

If we substitute I = V/R in P = VI, we get:

$P = V^2 \div R$

$V^2 = PR$

$V = \sqrt{(\text{Power} \times \text{Resistance})}$

E

The given units cannot be used to manipulate equations.

---

18) E, B, C, A, D

It is essential that you know the direction of blood flow and the order of blood vessels that it flows in. Of course, ADH travels in blood.

I will use a flow chart to show exactly how the ADH will reach the kidney.

Pituitary Gland → Jugular Vein → Vena Cava → Right Atrium → Right Ventricle → Pulmonary Artery → Lungs → Pulmonary Vein → Left Atrium → Left Ventricle → Aorta → Renal Artery → Kidney

---

19) C

Frequency = $(5 \div 10^{-13}) = 5 \times 10^{13}$ (PLEASE LEARN THE POWERS RULES)

Energy = f x h = $5 \times 10^{13} \times 6.63 \times 10^{-34} = 33.15 \times 10^{-21}$

3.32×10^{-20} J

---

20) C

The number of electrons in the valence shell determines which group the atom belongs to.

The number of shells determines which period the atom belongs to.

4 outer electrons so the atom is in group 4

2 shells in total means that the atom is in period 2

---

21) E

The question gives you the types of levers. You just need to understand which one applies to the action of moving the load up and which lever is used to move the load down.

Imagine yourself doing a bicep curl in the gym!

You have the weight (load) in your hand, which acts downwards due to gravity. Using your elbow (fulcrum) and the biceps (the arm muscles which applies the effort), you move the load up.

So, the load (whose weight acts downwards), which is on the left, moves up, the effort is in the middle and the fulcrum, which is on the right, moves up. This is shown by lever 3.

For the downward action, the load is on your hand (left). Your fulcrum is in the middle. Your effort is to the right. This corresponds to lever 5.
You may be asking: Why is the fulcrum now in the middle? Position your arm as shown in the question.
Moving up action requires effort from your biceps whilst moving down action requires effort from your triceps. This is why the fulcrum is to the right when moving up whilst it is in the middle when moving down.

---

22) E
If the coil is rotated more quickly, frequency and amplitude will increase. Together with this, the total output e.m.f. will also increase.

---

23) E
As we go down group 1, the number of shells increases by 1. Since the number of shells increases, the atomic radius also increases. The attraction between the nucleus and the outer electron decreases. Therefore, it becomes easier to lose the outer electron as you go down group 1. Hence, the alkali metals become more reactive.
The other options are correct statements but they do not explain why the reactivity increases.

---

24) C
The process of exhalation or expiration is as follows:

1. The volume of thorax decreases (rule out options B and D)
2. The pressure in thorax increases since volume decreases
3. The diaphragm relaxes and becomes more convex (rule out option E)
4. The ribs come down and inwards (rule out option A)

If you face any confusion, try exhaling yourself and feel the movement of your ribs. Also, you will also notice that when you are about to exhale, the pressure inside your lungs increases. Since pressure is inversely proportional to volume, volume would decrease.

---

25) B
It is not possible for me to type the calculation on this blog. So I am attaching a picture of it.
Let us solve this question in portions.
$(2x^{3/2})^2 = 4x^3$
$(y^3)^2 = y^6$
$(\sqrt{z})^2 = z$

So the simplification would be:
$$\frac{4x^3 \, y^6}{z}$$

26) C

Y is relatively easy to figure out. The oxygen concentration greatly increases after blood passes through it. This is obviously the lungs. You can rule out options B, D, E and F.

Now, in organ X, carbon dioxide level increases, salt level decreases, glucose level decreases and oxygen level decreases. The only thing that stands out is the urea level. Urea level in blood only decreases after it has passed the kidneys. So C is the answer.

27) A

As soon as the parachutist falls from the aircraft, air resistance (drag force) immediately acts against him and starts to increase. Soon after, the drag force will become equal to the weight of the parachutist. They will reach a terminal velocity. As soon as the parachutist opens his parachute, the drag force increase greatly as air resistance acts on the parachute as well as the individual. As the velocity of the parachutist decreases, the drag force also decreases, reaching the same terminal velocity. Hence, A is the correct answer.

28) C

This is actually a pretty simple question. All of the compounds are electrically neutral i.e. they have no charge. We have been given the charges of the individual ions. We just need to calculate which of the options would give us an answer of 0.

A
$(2) + (-3) + (-1) = -2$

B
$(6) + (-6) + (-1) = -1$

C
$(10) + (-9) + (-1) = 0$

D
$(14) + (-15) + (-1) = -2$

29) This is no longer on the BMAT specification as this includes the use of sine rule.

1) You can discuss the following points:

- According to the article, an ethical market is one in which there would be no exploitation of people.
- The market would be restricted to a certain geopolitical area
- Only citizens from that area could be involved in the sale and purchase of organs
- There can only be one buyer who would buy all organs and distribute them in a fair manner
- This buyer could potentially be a government agency or organisation such as the NHS
- However, there is a possibility of a black market where organs are sold illegally for profits
- This black market can result in the exploitation of people who are in desperate need of money
- This black market would be the opposite of the ethical market discussed in the article
- Steps must be taken in order to prevent direct sales of organs
- The example of the US shows that there is a shortage of organs
- The government can play a big part in ensuring that the supply of organs increases and the number of donors also increases
- Policies can be formulated, for example, the 'opt-out' law instead of 'opt-in'
- It is important for the organ donor and the organ receiver to know what complications they may have after the donation
- This way, they can make informed decisions and choose whether they should go ahead with the donation
- Individuals should have the right to sell their organs if that is what they wish to do but only after having consulted with a doctor about any complications that can occur during transplant and after the transplant

2) You can discuss the following points:

- Alexander Pope is trying to say that it is better to have no knowledge than to have incomplete knowledge and act according to the incomplete knowledge
- Having incomplete knowledge can cause a person to be in danger and cause other to be in danger as they may form misconceptions about the subject
- e.g. there was a study which 'proved' that vaccines were correlated to autism. Due to this 'discovery', many parents did not vaccinate their children, potentially exposing them to danger. They did not know that the study was proven to be false. Their 'little knowledge' caused them to take actions which were totally wrong
- Other examples could include investing in stocks without having complete knowledge, an eleven-year-old child driving because they have seen their parents drive
- However, it is okay to have little knowledge if this little knowledge given to you by an experienced person

- For example, giving first aid can potentially help to save a life, even if the person giving first aid does not fully understand the mechanism. However, the person giving the first aid should first be taught by an expert in order to ensure what they are doing is correct
- It is important for one to have some knowledge of different subjects as long as they do not think they are experts in those fields

---

3) You can discuss the following points:

- The statement is trying to say that the living body is more than just a mechanism and it should not be simplified in such a way.
- Indeed, there are different systems in the body that work together in order to help the body survive. This can be thought of like a car, in which different parts of the car help the car to function (tyres, brakes, accelerator, steering wheel etc). If one of these parts fail to function, then the car would not work efficiently.
- Similarly, our body has different systems such as nervous system, circulatory system, respiratory system etc. We are taught about these systems in a general manner because the systems working a similar way for everyone.
- However, every person is different in his or her own respect. Everyone has different personalities and emotions, which is why it could be wrong to say that the living body is a mechanism. It should also be noted that treatments vary from person-to-person even if they have the same medical condition. Different approaches must be taken when treating different patients as every patient has different emotions, personalities and sentiments. It would be wrong to treat their bodies merely as a mechanism.
- The living body is a very complex structure and we have not even fully understood how it works. Therefore, the living body should be treated differently from person-to-person rather than generalising it as a singular mechanism.

---

4) You can discuss the following points

- Natural law here means a hypothesis. A proven hypothesis means a theory.
- Karl Popper tries to say that the best way to prove a hypothesis is to disprove other false hypotheses.
- By disproving other hypotheses, we get closer each to time to know that the original hypothesis is more likely to be correct.
- If we fail to refute the original hypothesis, we become more certain that it is likely to be a correct hypothesis.
- However, some scientists would argue that the best way to know if a hypothesis is correct or not is to directly prove it by experiments.
- By eliminating other hypotheses, we cannot be certain that the original hypothesis is actually correct or not.
- Therefore, in order to know whether a hypothesis is correct or not, it is better to prove it using, lab testing, experiments and evidence.
- For example, in the Meselson and Stahl experiment, results and evidence were obtained directly to prove the semi-conservative theory of replication.

- It is important to know whether a hypothesis is testable or not. Elimination of other hypotheses alone is not sufficient to know whether a hypothesis is correct. It is essential to do experiments and give evidence for a hypothesis before we can make it a theory and then a law.

1) C

A – Wrong

Halve the quadrilateral by using a diagonal. You end up with two triangles. Now halve each of these triangles from the middle. The tables can be used to make shape A.

B – Wrong

Halve the triangle from the middle. You end up with two triangles. Now halve each of these triangles.

D – Wrong

Divide the shape into two triangles and a quadrilateral by taking out the end triangles. Now divide the square into two triangles by using its diagonal.

E – Wrong

Shape E is placing shape B on A. Split E into the triangle and the quadrilateral. Then, halve the triangle from the middle and halve the quadrilateral diagonally.

If you look at C, you will notice that if you take out the two triangle ends and try to superimpose them on the quadrilateral, it will not work i.e. they will not be identical to the triangles the make up the quadrilateral.

2) C

The aim of this question is to strengthen the argument.
Statement C can greatly support the argument, as it is an example of something that has happened in the past. Since prices of cigarettes rose, the usage decreased. T
The paragraph suggests the same solution. Raise the prices of fatty foods and consumption should reduce. The analogy is the same.
All other options are irrelevant to the question.

3) B

We need to minimise our answer for each possibility.
There 60 cross-headed screws whilst the other 40 are slot headed.
70 of the screws are 3mm in diameter. In order to minimise this figure, we need to assume that all 40 slot headed screws are 3mm in diameter which leaves us with 30 cross-headed screws with 3mm diameter.
The other criterion is the length of screws. We have 80 screws that are 50mm long, 20 that are not 50mm long. We need to assume that the 20, which are not 50mm long, are all cross-headed.
Therefore, we have 30 - 20 = 10
The smallest number of cross-headed, 3mm diameter and 50 mm long is 10.

4) A

2 factors may be linked by another factor or the causality may be in the opposite direction to that stated. The whole class teaching is not necessarily the reason why the standards have improved.

Option B is not really relevant to the statement, C is not necessarily assumed. Options D and E could be incorrect.

5) C

Now, we know that Suki leaves 10 minutes before Tom and then Tom arrives 5 minutes before Suki. Therefore, we know that Tom takes 15 minutes (0.25 hr) less than Suki to travel 2km. Let us do this step by step.

Lets Suki's speed be 'N km/h'. Then Tom's speed must be '4N km/h'.

Let Suki's total time be 'T hours'. Then Tom's time would be 'T-0.25 hours"

Using distance = speed x time, we can get two equations:

a) $NT = 2$ km

b) $4N(T - 0.25) = 2$ km

If we manipulate the first equation to get N, we can see that $N = {}^2/_T$. Substituting the expression of N into the second equation, we can get:

${}^2/_T$ x $4(T - 0.25) = 2$km

${}^8/_T$ x $(T - 0.25) = 2$

$8 - {}^2/_T = 2$

$8 - 2 = {}^2/_T$ (Rearrange above equation)

$6 = {}^2/_T$

$T = {}^1/_3$ hours

Total time taken by Suki = 1/3 hours = 20 minutes

Suki's speed = $2 \div {}^1/_3$ = 6 km/hr

Essentially, the question is asking us to calculate the distance she has travelled when Tom leaves. So, at the speed of 6 km/h after 10 minutes (${}^1/_6$ hours), distance travelled by Suki:

Distance = 6 x ${}^1/_6$ = 1 km

6) E

A- Wrong

The sentence 'obviously this suggestion is not appropriate to people who are allergic to animals' suggests that the paragraph is not really assuming that people with allergies can NEVER have pets. The statement is just suggesting.

B- Wrong

There is nothing mentioned about having multiple pets.

C – Wrong

This option is irrelevant, as the paragraph does not mention emotions of pets

D – Wrong
This option is not necessarily assumed

E – Correct
This paragraph solely focuses on the fact that longevity is important. However, it just assumes that everyone should want to live longer. Therefore, this is the correct answer.

---

7) D
Profit gained from the job = £780 – £240 = £540
This figure is shared equally = £540 ÷ 2 = £270
Therefore Bill gets £270 and Alf gets £270. However, Bill must also pay Alf the price of the material, which is £240.
Hence, Bill owes Alf = £270 + £240 = £510, which is option D.

---

8) 12.0, 12.5, or 13.0
Use the graph to calculate the sum of episodes =
1.2 + 0.1 + 1.4 + 0.3 + 0.8 + 1.4 + 0.8 + 1.2 + 0.8 + 5 = 13
However, based on how you interpret the numbers in the graphs, your answer can vary from 12, 12.5 and 13

---

9) A
Simply divide the number of days by the number of episodes for cancer:
$(\frac{4,343,199}{1.4\ \text{million}}) \approx (\frac{4.2\ \text{million}}{1.4\ \text{million}}) = 3$ days ≈ 3.1 days

---

10) A
Find out one-sevenths of 1.4 million, you get 200,000.
Hence, A is the only option which is lower than 200,000.
However, if you still do not understand, we can use this method:
Let number of cases of women = 'n'
Therefore, number of cases in men = n + 0.5n = 1.5 n
Total number of cases = 1n + 1.5 n = 2.5n = 200,000
n= $\frac{200,000}{2.5}$ = 80,000
Number of cases in men = 80,000 + (0.5 × 80,000) = 120,000

---

11) A & C
A – Correct
A is obviously one of the correct options as it directly states that cancer treatments require shorter stays.

B – Wrong
B just says that the number of episodes or cases is twice that for cancer. However, it does not say anything about the stay of each of those episodes.

C – Correct
C says that circulatory system diseases require longer stays which is directly relevant to the question

D – Wrong
is irrelevant as death is not a factor, which relates to stay

---

12) B & C
The best way to answer this question is to multiply all of the options by 3 and see if the scores obtained by the remaining questions can be manipulated to give 18.

A: 5 x 3 = 15
This is 3 points less than 18. However, you only gain points by answering a question correctly. Since option A allows only 5 questions to be correct, John cannot get any more points. So this option is incorrect.

B: 6 x 3 = 18
We have already reached 18. Now it is a possibility that he did not answer the remaining questions and got 0 points. So this is one of the correct answers.

C: 7 x 3 = 21
Now, this is 3 points more than the required number 18. Also, there are 5 remaining question since the quiz only consists of 12 questions. It is possible that out of the 5, he got 3 incorrect and didn't answer the other 2. Final calculation:
Correct = $7 \times 3 = 21$
Incorrect = $3 \times (-1) = -3$
No answer = $2 \times 0 = 0$
Total = 21-3 = 18
So C can also be correct

D: 8 x 3 = 24
Remaining questions = 4
Points needed to get to 18 = -6
If he gets the remaining 4 questions incorrect, final points = 24 - 4 = 20
This does not lead to the required number 18, so D is incorrect

E: Same principle applies to E. It is not possible to obtain the number 18

---

13) B
This is a tricky question as the confusing options are B and C.
Obviously, the passage states that the unusual molecular structure of water is necessary. This immediately rules out options A and D.
The reason why C is incorrect is because life does not solely rely on the unusual molecular structure of water. It relies on other aspects as well, which is why this is incorrect and B is the correct answer.

---

14) B

It is very important you practise these types of questions as many times as you possibly can. These problems require very good visualisation skills and concentration. There is no other method of getting such questions correct.

This flat piece of cardboard can be folded in different ways and so, being able to visualise the answer will take up time. Therefore, aim to do such questions within 2 minutes.

---

15) D

A – Wrong

This obviously is not true and the passage does not suggest this in any way

B – Wrong

There is some relevance between this option and the passage, but the reason why this is not the conclusion is because it just says experimentation. It does not specify which type of experimentation.

C – Wrong

This is incorrect, as the passage does not justify all experimentation.

D – Correct

This is correct, reason being that the passage says "those experiments are morally acceptable". This phrase was used after the passage said that antibiotics help animal too. So, this is correct.

E – Wrong

The passage does not say anything about non-medical research so this option is irrelevant

---

16) A

This is a really simple question. We know that Colin has lost more than either Barbara or Annie.
Colin had started with 5 kg less than Barbara and hence, he cannot finish with a weight heavier than Barbara's. So, the answer is A.

---

17) A

Let us look at each of the other options first and then look at why A is the answer.

B – Wrong

This option is evidence that the worst has not happened yet and the damage is still being done. So, B is not the answer.

C – Wrong

This is not suggested by the passage and so, is irrelevant

D – Wrong

I understand why a lot of the people may think D could be the answer as the passage clearly states that the harmful effects are greater now than before. However, it does not summarise the entire passage as well as option A does. The passage tries to say that the worst is yet to come. D only says that the effects are greater now.

E – Wrong

This option only says the amount of time the oil will remain on the beaches. However, the passage is mainly focused on saying that the worst effects are yet to come.

---

18) C

Surface area of original marble chip = 6 x 1 x 1 = 6 cm²

Surface area of a single powder cube = 6 x 0.01cm x 0.01cm = 0.0006 cm²

Volume of original cube = 1 cm³

Volume of powder cube = 0.01 x 0.01 x 0.01 = 0.000001 cm³

Number of powder cubes = $^{1cm^3}/_{0.000001cm^3}$ = 10^6 cubes

Total surface area of powder cubes = 10^6 x 0.0006cm² = 600 cm²

Extra surface area = 600 – 6 = 594 cm²

---

19) D

The phrase "throughout their lives" is key here.

A – Wrong

This option is more of an assumption rather than a conclusion. It says that "developed countries WILL NOT be achievable" which is assumed.

B – Wrong

This is also an assumption

C – Wrong

This option actually does not make sense as people who exercise when they are young gain benefits

D – Correct

The passage clearly links lifelong exercise with good health, hence the correct option

E – Wrong

Again, this option does not make sense

---

20) D

Recommended intake = 6 grams/day

Percentage of men that took 6 grams or less = 15%

Total number of men = 567

Number of men that took 6 grams or less = 0.15 x 567 = 85.05 = 85

---

21) 7.6

$66 - 31 = 35\%$ have intake of between 6 and 9 grams per day. If we assume linearity, $^{19}/_{35}$ have between 6 and the median.

$^{19}/_{35} = 0.54$

$3 \times 0.54 = 1.62$

$6 + 1.62 = 7.62$

$7.62 \approx 7.6$

---

22) A

Subtract each cumulative percentage from the succeeding cumulative percentage.

3 or less = 4% (this should be on the graph for 3 or less)

6 or less = $15 - 4 = 11\%$ (this should be on the graph for 6 or less) 9 or less = $39 - 15 = 14\%$ (this should be on the graph for 9 or less)

12 or less = $60 - 39 = 21\%$ (this should be on the graph for 12 or less)

15 or less = $79 - 60 = 19\%$ (this should be on the graph for 15 or less)

18 or less = $91 - 79 = 12\%$ (this should be on the graph for 18 or less)

This is only shown by graph A. So, A is the correct answer.

---

23) B

The values are not evenly distributed across the age range and hence this calculation would be biased. The other options do not cause any bias.

---

24) 10 minutes

This is not a tricky question.

20 patients were booked but 2 did not turn up. So, 18 patients were present in the surgery. 1 of them took 12 minutes whilst the others took 5 minutes.

Total time so far = $(1 \times 12) + (17 \times 5) = 97$ minutes

An urgent call took 8 minutes = $97 + 8 = 105$ minutes

Emergency appointment took 5 minutes = $105 + 5 = 110$ minutes.

The surgery ended at 11 am. Surgery time is usually from 9 am to 11 am which 2 hours (120 minutes).

$120 - 110 = 10$ minutes

---

25) B

This passage is talking about the future.

Options A, C, D and E are not necessarily assumed. The assumption here is that gardeners will ignore the encouragement to use alternatives and will continue using peat.

---

26) A

Lighthouse 1 stays on for 3 seconds and then turns off. It stays dark for 8 seconds and then turns back on for another 3 seconds. Total time between 1st switch off and 2nd switch off = 8 + 3 = 11 seconds.

Lighthouse 12 stays on for 2 seconds and then turns off. It stays dark for 7 seconds and then turns back on for another 2 seconds. Total time between 1st switch off and 2nd switch off = 2 + 7 = 9 seconds

To answer this question, we must list all the times when the light from lighthouses disappear:

Lighthouse 1: 3, 14, 25, 36, 47, 58, 69, 70....
Lighthouse 2: 2, 11, 20, 29, 38, 47, 56, 65...
We now know that they both turn off together every 47 seconds. The last time they were in sync was 15 seconds off. Therefore, the next time they will be in sync would be 47-15 = 32 seconds from now.

---

27) B
Mass of container = 800g = 0.8kg
Mass of container full of water = 15.6kg
Mass of water alone = 15.6 - 0.8 = 14.8kg
The volume of cylinder = $\pi r^2 h$
If the diameter doubles, the radius also doubles. The question says the height also doubles.
New radius = 2r, New height = 2h
New formula = $\pi(2r)^2(2h) = \pi 4r^2 2h = 8\pi r^2 h$
Hence, the volume increases by 8 times. Therefore, weight increases by 8 times too. Volume of water = 14.8kg x 8 = 118.4 kg

Since the height and diameter double, the dimensions of the sheet also double.
Let us assume the original sheet had dimensions of 2mx2m. The area would be 4m². The new dimensions would be 4mx4m and the area would be 16m. Therefore, the area of the sheet increases by 4 times, meaning that the weight of the sheet also increases by 4.
Weight of new sheet = 0.8 x 4= 3.2kg
Total weight of new container full of water = 118.4 kg + 3.2 kg = 121.6 kg

---

28) C
The passage states, "30% of doctors in Great Britain work, AT LEAST some of the time for the commercial sector". The 'at least' suggests that the 30% of doctors mentioned consists of those who work in both sectors and in the commercial sector only. Therefore the remaining 70% of doctors work in public health service only.

1- this is true as 70% of doctors work in public service only
2 - this is correct as 70% work in the public sector only whilst the remaining 30% work either in commercial service only or both sectors.
3 - this cannot be verified from the information given.

Since statements 1 and 2 are correct, C is the answer.

---

29) E

Concentration of initial 250ml (0.25l) = 30g/l

Moles = concentration x volume = 30 x 0.25 = 7.5 mol

Volume after spillage = 0.2 l

Moles after spillage = 30 x 0.2 = 6 mol

Volume of new NaCl sol = 0.05 l

Concentration of new NaCl sol = 20g/l

Moles of new NaCl solution = 20 x 0.05 = 1 mol

Total moles = 6 + 1 = 7 mol

Concentration = moles/volume = $\frac{7}{0.25}$ = 28 g/l

---

30) B

Let us start with the flat section, which was 1 km long.

Runner's speed = 6km/h

Time = $\frac{1}{6}$ x 60 = 10 minutes

Cyclist speed = 30km/h

Time = $\frac{1}{30}$ x 60 = 2 minutes

Difference = 10 - 2 = 8 minutes

Only options B and C show that the cyclist is ahead by 8 minutes. This rules out options A and D

Muddy section which is 1.5 km long

Runner's speed: 4km/h

Time = $\frac{1.5}{4}$ x60 = 22 minutes 30 seconds

Total time for runner = 32 minutes 30 seconds

Cyclist speed: 3 km/h

Time = $\frac{1.5}{3}$ x 60 = 30 minutes

Total time for the cyclist so far = 32 minutes

This shows that the cyclist is still ahead by 30 seconds after 2.5 km of the whole race. Only B shows that. C shows that the runner gets ahead of the cyclist during the muddy race, which is not true.

---

31) A & C

The best way to solve this question is by expressing the four statements as inequalities.

A – Correct

Anne is not older than Susan. So Anne is either younger or is of the same age as Susan.

A ≤ S

B – Wrong

Susan is younger than Anne.

A > S

C – Correct

Susan is at least as old as Anne. So Susan is either older or is of the same age as Anne.

$A \leq S$

D – Wrong

Anne is not younger than Susan. So Anne is either older or is of the same age as Susan.

$A \geq S$

A and C have the same inequalities. So A & C are the answers.

---

32) 14%

The answer is in the last sentence.

The deaths decreased from 4900 to 4200. Decline = 700

Initial number of deaths = 4900

Percentage decrease = $\frac{700}{4900} \times 100 = \frac{1}{7} \times 100 = 14.3\% \approx 14\%$

---

33) B

"By 1992, sprains and strains had risen to 83% and all other injuries had fallen to 40%' means that some of the claims for the sprains and strains came together with claims for all other injuries.

---

34) 22

Let the number of claims be 'C'

The increase was 33% and 'C' rose to 29.

$[C + (0.33C)] = 29.3$

$C(1 + 0.33) = 29.3$

$C(1.33) = 29.3$

$C = \frac{29.3}{1.33}$

$C = 22$

---

35) B & C

A – Wrong

A does not give any explanation so, is incorrect.

B – Correct

B says that lawyers have introduced a policy in which they will not charge the claimants if they do not get the claim money. This could be a reason why the number of claims increased.

C – Correct

C says that people do not claim if there is no damage.

So both B & C are the answers.

---

1) B
1 is the Aorta
2 is the pulmonary vein
3 is the left atrium
4 is the left ventricle
5 is the right ventricle
6 is the right atrium
7 is the vena cava
8 is the pulmonary artery

From the lungs, the blood will flow into the heart via the pulmonary vein (2)
From the pulmonary vein, the blood will enter the left atrium (3)
From the left atrium, the blood will enter the left ventricle (4)
From the left ventricle, the blood will flow to the rest of the body via the aorta (1)
From the body, the blood returns to the heart via the vena cava (7)
From the vena cava, the blood will enter the right atrium (6)
From the right atrium, the blood will enter the right ventricle (5)
From the right ventricle, the blood will flow to the lungs via the pulmonary artery (8)

So the order is:
2 3 4 1 7 6 5 8
The answer is B.

2) B
Area of a right angled triangle = 0.5 x base x height
$0.5 \times (4 + \sqrt{2}) \times (2 - \sqrt{2})$
$0.5 \times [4 (2 - \sqrt{2}) + \sqrt{2} (2 - \sqrt{2})]$
$0.5 \times [(8 - 4\sqrt{2}) + (2\sqrt{2} - 2)]$
$0.5 \times [8 - 4\sqrt{2} + 2\sqrt{2} - 2]$
$0.5 \times [6 - 2\sqrt{2}]$
$(3 - \sqrt{2})$ is the answer

3) q = 3, r = 12, s = 3, t = 6
There are a total of 12 Hydrogen atoms on the RHS and that is unchangeable.
Hydrogen is only present in HNO_3 on the LHS.

Therefore, to balance the Hydrogen atoms on both sides, **r = 12**.

Copper is present on its own on LHS and in $Cu(NO_3)_2$ on RHS.
So q = s

Let us form algebraic equations.
For Copper,
q = s

For Oxygen,
3r = 6s + 6 + 2t
36 = 6s + 6 + 2t
30 = 6s + 2t-------- (1)

For Hydrogen, r
= 12

For Nitrogen, r
= 2s + t
Since r = 12
12 = 2s + t ------ (2)

Using simultaneous equations,
6s + 2t = 30
(2s + t = 12) x 2

6s + 2t = 30
4s + 2t = 24

2s = 6
s = 3

Since (q = s) and (s = 3),
q = 3

Using equation (2),
12 = 2s + t
t = 12 - 2s
t = 12 - 2(3)
t = 12 - 6
t = 6

q = 3, r = 12, s = 3, t = 6

4) E
The perpendicular distance from the midpoint of pivot to the midpoint of the pedal = 16 + 4 = 20 cm
Force applied to the pedal = 60 N
Moments = F x d = 60 x 20 = 1200 N cm

The perpendicular distance from the midpoint of pivot to the midpoint of the piston= 4 = 4 cm

Let Force applied to the piston = P
Moments = F x d = P x 4 = 4P N cm

Moment on pedal = Moments on piston
1200 = 4P
P = 1200 ÷ 4 = 300 N

---

5) 0.32 A
Total number of ions per second = 10^{18} ions
Total charge = $2 \times 1.6 \times 10^{-19}$ C
Current = $(2 \times 1.6 \times 10^{-19}) \times (10^{18})$
$(2 \times 1.6 \times 10^{-19}) \times (10^{18})$
$(3.2 \times 10^{-19}) \times (10^{18})$
$(3.2 \times 10^{-19 + 18})$ (3.2×10^{-1})
0.32 A

---

6) E
The easiest one to figure out is Y. During expiration, the diaphragm relaxes and curves upwards.
The pressure Z increases to force the air to move out of the thoracic cavity.
The intercostal muscles also relax to allow expiration.

---

7) E, B, A and C
i) E
A giant molecular structure would have a very high melting and boiling point. Also, it would not conduct electricity.

i) B
A metal would have a moderate melting and high boiling temperature and would conduct electricity when solid or molten.

i) A
An ionic compound would only conduct electricity when molten.

iv) C
Room temperature = 25° C.
The only substance that would be a liquid at room temperature would be the one, which has a temperature lower than 25° C. This is only C.

---

8) E
Round up the percentage mass of tungsten = 80%
So percentage mass of oxygen = 20%
We know Moles = Mass / Mr
Moles of W = (80 ÷ 184) = 0.44

Moles of O = (20 ÷ 16) = 1.25

Ratio = 0.44 : 1.25
This gives us an approximate ratio of 1 : 3
So the answer is WO_3

---

9) 7.2 m
Kinetic energy = $0.5mv^2$
Potential energy = mgh

Since Kinetic energy = Potential energy,
$0.5mv^2$ = mgh
0.5 x 144 = 10 x h
h = 72 ÷ 10 = 7.2 m

OR

We can just use a SUVAT equation
$v^2 - u^2 = 2as$
144 - 0 = 2 x 10 x s
s = 144 (2 x 10) = 7.2 m

---

10) A & B
This is no longer on the BMAT specification.

---

11) B
Counting the number of atoms of each element of both pyruvic acid into lactic acid, we can see that lactic acid has 2 more Hydrogen atoms than pyruvic acid.
The addition of hydrogen atoms to a molecule is called reduction.

---

12) D
Individual 1 has a recessive X allele. Since individual 1 is a male, he must have X and Y chromosomes. Only his daughters can receive his recessive X chromosome. So 4 and 5 will receive it by 6 will not.

Since 5 does not have any offsprings, she cannot pass on the X chromosome.
4 will pass on her X chromosome to her offsprings. So 8 and 9 will obtain the X chromosome.
So 4, 5, 8 and 9 will inherit this allele.

---

13) D
We need to use the inequalities given in the options to solve this question.
$x^2 \geq 8 - 2x$

Rearranging, x^2
$+ 2x - 8 \geq 0$

40

Factorising (x + 2x - 8),
$x^2 - 2x + 4x - 8$
$x(x - 2) + 4(x - 2)$
So we have, $(x - 2)(x + 4) \geq 0$

Writing them down individually,
$x - 2 \geq 0$
$x + 4 \leq 0$

Rearranging, x
≥ 2
$x \leq -4$
So the answer is D.

---

14) D
Lighter molecules diffuse faster than heavier molecules.
Since the mass of an ammonium molecule is less than that of a hydrogen chloride molecule, it will diffuse across the tube more than the hydrogen chloride molecule.
Hence, the white ring is formed near the concentrated hydrochloric acid.

---

15) i) False, ii) False, iii) True, iv) False, v) False
i) False
Since the circuit is in parallel, the voltage in the voltmeter and the bulb will remain the same.

ii) False
The voltmeter and the bulb will have the same voltage. Due to Ohm's Law, current will also remain the same.

iii) True
Closing S2 will open a new pathway for current to flow in the bulb in the lowest branch. This will cause the total resistance of the circuit to fall. Since current is inversely proportional to resistance, current will increase.

iv) False
The voltage and current across A3 will remain the same.

v) False
If S3 is closed; there will be negligible resistance in the ammeters. So the reading in ammeter A2 will definitely NOT increase.

---

16) B
Tree diagrams are really helpful in solving such probability questions.
Let Y represent a person having the illness and let N represent a person not having the illness.
There can be three possibilities of exactly one person having such an illness.

YNN, NYN, NNY

41

25% of the people of Wales have reported such an illness.
We only need to find he probability on of the possibilities first.
Let first person have the illness and the next two persons not have the illness.

Probability of first person having the illness = ¼
Probability of second person having the illness = ¾
Probability of third person having the illness = ¾

$\frac{1}{4} \times \frac{3}{4} \times \frac{3}{4} = \frac{9}{64}$

Since there are 3 possibilities, we need to multiply this probability by 3.

$\frac{9}{64} \times 3 = \frac{27}{64}$

---

17) D

Since the parachutist has reach terminal velocity; the resultant force (i.e. sum of forces acting on the parachutist) will be zero.
The forces acting on the parachutist would be the weight and air resistance.
Weight = 90 x 10 = 900 N
Since resultant force is zero, weight = air resistance
So air resistance = 900 N

---

18) D

Let us take an alkane: Butane. Butane is C_4H_{10}
The $-NH_2$ group will be joined by taking out a hydrogen atom from the butane.
So the formula would be $C_4H_{11}N$. This amine has one extra hydrogen atom and one nitrogen atom compared to the original butane.
So the general formula would be $C_nH_{2n+3}N$

---

19) A, D & E

An egg always has only the X chromosome. So A is correct but B and C are wrong.
A sperm could either have X or Y chromosome (but not both). So D and E are correct but F is wrong.

---

20) C

A is a measure of electrical power. P = VI

I = Q ÷ t
Substituting (I = Q ÷ t) in the equation P = VI,
P = (Q ÷ t) x V = QV ÷ t

B is a measure of electrical power.
P = IV
V = IR
Substituting (V = IR) in the equation P = VI,

$P = I \times IR = I^2R$

C is not a measure of electrical power.
There is no way to equate $P = (Q^2R / t)$

D is a measure of electrical power.
$P = VI$ is the most basic formula for power and it something that needs to be learnt.

E is a measure of electrical power. P =
IV
$I = V \div R$
Substituting $(I = V \div R)$ in the equation $P = VI$,
$P = V \times (V \div R) = (V^2 / R)$

---

21) D
The Hepatic portal vein is the only blood vessel, which carries nutrient rich blood from one organ to another (gut to liver). So it has capillaries at both ends.
Other vessels do not do the same.

You probably could have figured this out by the process of elimination. (No problem if you couldn't. Now you know!)

---

22) F
In the first decay, the atomic number is increased by 1 but the mass number remains the same. This can only be beta decay. In beta decay, a fast moving electron is emitted, the mass number remains the same but the atomic number increases by 1.

In second decay, the atomic number decreases by 2. (This may seem confusing as it says there Z-1. However, you must remember that from Z+1, it went to Z - 1.
Overall change = [Z - 1 - (Z + 1)] = [Z - 1 - Z - 1] = (-2)
This means that this must be alpha decay.
In alpha decay, a helium nucleus is emitted. This means that the mass number decreases by 4 and the atomic number decreases by 2. So X = A - 4

---

23) E
The order is clearly given by the paragraph.
The third sentence says that in the presence of air, the last water molecule is displaced by oxygen.
So water is weaker than oxygen.
In the last sentence, it says that in the presence of carbon monoxide, oxygen is displaced. So oxygen is weaker than carbon monoxide. Therefore, water must also be weaker than carbon monoxide.
We get the order:
water, oxygen, and carbon monoxide.

24) C
This is no longer on the BMAT.
In the picture, you can see that the person is straightening their leg. To straighten your leg, you need to contract your quadriceps (upper front thigh = R) and relax your hamstrings (upper back thigh = P).
The glutes (Q) must also contract to provide maximum force to get a good start to the race. You can see that at the ankle, the person is pointing their toes out more in position 2. The gastrocnemius (T) must contract and the anterior tibialis (S) must relax.

Muscles that contract = R, Q, T
Muscles that relax = P, S

25) D
We first need to square both the LHS and RHS. We get:
$$T^2 = 4\pi^2 \frac{(k^2 + h^2)}{gh}$$

Move the gh from the RHS to the LHS.
$$T^2 gh = [4\pi^2 (k^2 + h^2)]$$

Move the $4\pi^2$ from the RHS to the LHS.
$$\frac{T^2 gh}{4\pi^2} = k^2 + h^2$$

Move the h^2 from the RHS to the LHS
$$\frac{T^2 gh}{4\pi^2} - h^2 = k^2$$

Root both the LHS and RHS k
$$= \frac{\sqrt{(T^2 gh - h^2)}}{\sqrt{(4\pi^2)}}$$

26) i) mitosis, ii) both, iii) meiosis, iv) meiosis, v) both
i) Mitosis
In mitosis, the daughter nuclei are always genetically identical to the parent cells or nucleus.

ii) Both
In order to carry out nuclear division, both processes must involve all chromosomes being replicated.

iii) Meiosis
Gametes can only be produced by meiosis. Since gametes are haploid, they must be formed by meiosis as mitosis only forms diploid cells.

iv) Meiosis
Haploid nuclei are only formed by meiosis.

v) Both
Genetic material always appears as distinct chromosomes in both processes.

---

27) C
To solve this, we need to use the equation:
$(x - a)(x - b) = (x^2 - xb - xa + ab)$, where a and b are the solutions.
$x^2 - xb - xa + ab = x^2 - x(b + a) + ab$
We know that the sum of the roots of the quadratic equation is 7 and the product is 9.
I.e. $(a + b) = 7$ and $(ab) = 9$.
So, we need to substitute these values in. We get the equation:
$x^2 - x(b + a) + ab = (x^2 - 7x + 9)$
Hence the answer is C.

2004 Section 3

1) You can discuss the following points:

- The statement is trying to say that laws and regulations cannot coexist with a person' freedom. If there are laws, then a person's freedom cannot be complete and their life would be restricted in some way, shape or form.
- There are numerous ways in which laws can limit a person's freedom.
- Some examples may include: laws for women and men are mostly equal in some countries whilst other countries have put certain restrictions based on a person's gender.
- Abortion laws vary in different countries. In UK, most abortion cases occur before 24 weeks. They can be carried out after but only if there are some complications e.g. if the mother's life or health is at risk. In Sweden, however, the abortion law restricts this time period to 18 weeks.
- Other than that, over-the-counter drugs vary between different countries.
- However, other may argue that laws are made in order to allow everyone to live in harmony. They are created in a way so that everyone is given ample and equal opportunity to do what they want as long as it is reasonable and does not affect anyone else in a bad way.
- The statement exaggerates that fact that individual freedom and rule of law are mutually incompatible. There have been many instances where freedom was gained without crossing the boundary of the rule of law e.g. Martin Luther King against racism.
- The main reason for laws and regulations to be present is that it allows everyone to be equal. Laws prevent people from committing crimes and offences and if they do occur laws provide justice for those who were affected. Laws are also created with caution in order to minimise their interference with a person's freedom.

---

2) Science is the basis of everything. Science provides an explanation for all events happening around us although some events still require more research e.g. cancer and how the universe came to existence.

Predictions are made first. Then experiments are carried out to prove whether the predictions are correct or not. Based on the results obtained, further research is carried out to know why such results have been obtained. Then they are repeated by fellow scientists and doctors to ensure that they obtain similar results. If they do, then the theory is accepted.
Alternative treatments must also be created because not every patient is the same. Different patients with the same condition may require different treatments because they may have different lifestyles and allergies.

It is true that there is more to healing than just the application of science. People can argue that doctors just give the treatment and "nature does the healing".

Together with this, a patient must have belief that they are feeling better. This can only happen if they have trust in their doctor and feel comfortable. Doctors are required to do more than just apply their scientific knowledge. They must take into consideration the social and psychological aspects of the treatments to allow patients to feel as comfortable as possible. There are treatments, which have little to no scientific explanation but help to improve a patient's health. A clear health benefit can be seen.

You can give the example of the Deep Brain Stimulation treatment for Parkinson's disease. Even though we would prefer to know how the mechanisms for such treatments work, it is not absolutely necessary as long as the patient's health is not affected in an undesirable way.

---

3) The statement is trying to say that since our genes are adapted for the Stone Age, it would be ideal for us to revert to the Stone Age lifestyle in order to have optimal health.

It is not necessary that just because we have 'Stone Age' genes, we cannot live an optimal life in a time other than the Stone Age.

Returning to the Stone Age lifestyle would mean little to no dependence on the recent technological inventions such as automobiles, internet, mobile phones and the most important of all, electricity. Our way of living would change drastically and this can be advantageous and disadvantageous.

It would be advantageous mainly because everyone would have to do a substantial level of manual work in order to survive. This includes hunting, running, farming with manual tools and swimming. This would help to keep everyone fit and healthy. However, the advantages are very limited.

There are numerous disadvantages with this ideology. We would lose thousands of years of progress and human development. Our technological advancements have enabled us to fulfil our needs.

Firstly, our technology has played a huge role in providing safer and faster medical treatments. The introduction of electron microscopes has allowed humans to study life at the atomic level. By using this knowledge, we have been able to come up with treatments that would not have been possible thousands of years ago. X-rays and MRI scans have allowed us to study different parts of the body and devise treatments according to our findings.

Other than that, farming inventions such as tractors and harvesters have allowed farming on a much larger scale. We are able to keep food demand and supply at approximately the same level. It would be impossible to get sufficient food supply for 7 billion people thousands of years ago. This would only cause widespread famine and chaos.

To conclude, I think that the disadvantages of adopting Stone Age habits outweigh the advantages by a big margin. The statement tries to make an intelligible point but fails to consider the consequences of adopting Stone Age habits.

---

1) C

Counting the number of each type of tiles can help solve this.

Number of black tiles = 9

Number of white tiles = 9

Number of grey tiles = 20

Ratio = 9 : 9 : 20

This is approximately 1 : 1 : 2

2) D

The argument is that schools should revert to traditional sports days. The reason for this is that adult life involves competition.

A – Wrong

The text does not assume that children are not naturally competitive. It just says that they should let children be part of competitions to prepare them for adult life.

B – Wrong

This statement makes an unnecessary correlation between children losing races and being unsuccessful in adulthood. The text does not assume this at all.

C – Wrong

Schools have introduced non-competitive games to prevent damage to losers' self-esteem. It does not necessarily assume that non-competitive games, however, will boost children's self-esteem.

D – Correct

The text assumes that since sports days are competitive and adulthood is competitive, competitions in sports will help prepare children for adult life.

3) B

We know birds have 2 legs and sheep have 4 legs.

Let number of sheep = S

Let number of Birds = B

Total number of animals = 13 = S + B

Total number of sheep legs = 4S

Total number of bird legs = 2B

Total number of legs = 4S + 2B = 36

Using simultaneous equations,

4S + 2B = 36

[S + B = 13] x 2

$4S + 2B = 36$
$2S + 2B = 26$

$2S = 10$
$S = 5$

---

4) A

"why these two statements are not incompatible" means why these two statements are compatible.

A – Correct

A suggest that the individual movement of galaxies is not related to the overall expansion of the universe. So e.g. galaxies can move at different velocities and directions, meaning that galaxies could move apart but can collide.

B – Wrong

This is too specific and we do not know how fast the Andromeda galaxy is moving towards us.

C – Wrong

This statement does not explain why galaxies collide against each other.

D – Wrong

If spots on a balloon move apart is analogous to galaxies moving apart form each other, then this again, does not explain why galaxies collide against each other.

E – Wrong

The text never says that the Big Bang occurred in the universe. it says the matter of the universe was created in the Big Bang. Also, this does not explain why galaxies move apart from each other and collide with each other.

---

5) 30 to 49

We are told that in only age categories 30-54 cancer death rate for females is more than males. So we only need to look for the answer within those categories.
In age group 30-34, there were more female deaths than male deaths for all the time periods.
In age group 35-39, there were more female deaths than male deaths for all the time periods.
In age group 40-44, there were more female deaths than male deaths for all the time periods.
In age group 44-49, there were more female deaths than male deaths for all the time periods.

However, in age group 50-54, there were more male deaths than female deaths in some time periods. So 50-54 cannot be part of the answer.
So the answer is 30 - 49

---

6) B

The argument is that "our health is at much greater risk from natural pesticides than from synthetic ones."

A – Wrong
This actually strengthens the argument as it says natural pesticides can harm animals (humans are also animals).

B – Correct
This weakens that argument. If humans have become tolerant of such natural pesticides, then they cannot harm us, meaning our health will not be at greater risk.

C – Wrong
This again strengthens the argument. The last line suggests that we consume a vast amount of natural pesticides compared to synthetic ones. C states that natural pesticides can be harmful.

D – Wrong
This is not relevant for the argument, which states natural pesticides can harm us.

---

7) £10,500

£350,000 is in the £250,000 to £499,999 category. So 3% tax needs to be paid.

$(\frac{3}{100})$ x £350,000 = 3 x 3500 = £10,500

---

8) C

Let us discuss why A, B and D are wrong.

The easiest way to solve this is by calculating the tax for £800,000 (upper limit on the x-axis).
The tax on a house costing £800,000 = 4%
4% of £800,000 = £32,000

The graphs of A, B and D do not look like they are going to reach £32,000 for £800,000. Only C looks like it can do so. So C is the answer.

---

9) B

The tax on the first £120,000 is free.

The maximum limit on the next band = £250,000
Difference = 250,000 – 120,000 = £130,000
Tax on this £130,000 = 1% = £1,300

Next band limit = £500,000
However, the price of the house is only £300,000
Difference between 300,000 and 250,000 = £50000
So the tax of 2% would be on this amount.

3% of 50000 = £1500
Total tax = 1300 + 1500 = £2800

---

10) £3300
If no cheating was not taking place,
Original tax would be = 3% of £260,000 = £7800

After cheating,
The tax would be = 1% of 249,999 = £2499.99 ≈ £2,500
The buyer agrees to pay an extra £2,000
So total money buyer would have to pay = 2500 + 2000 = £4,500

Buyer would save = 7800 – 4500 = £3,300

---

11) A
All students who study Spanish also study French. This means that there must be a small circle representing Spanish inside a big circle representing French.

Hence, the small circle, which is inside the large circle, represents Spanish and the big circle represents French.

Some students who study German also study Spanish. This is represented by the intersection between the second big circle and small circle. The second big circle represents German.

The shaded area represents those who study both French and German but not Spanish.

---

12) E
The text argues that since the incidence of schizophrenia has remained stable and the use of cannabis has increased, it cannot be true that smoking cannabis causes schizophrenia. **This is effectively saying that cannabis does not cause schizophrenia.**
We need to find a weakness in this conclusion.

A – Wrong
This actually supports the argument as it says that cannabis does not cause schizophrenia.

B – Wrong
Cancer is not related to the argument.

C – Wrong
This is irrelevant to the argument, as it does not mention either cannabis or schizophrenia.

D – Wrong
Tar and tobacco is irrelevant to the argument.

E – Correct
If under 15 year olds have only recently started smoking, then we would have to wait for some time to see the correlation between cannabis and schizophrenia.

---

13) B
Through the first sheet of glass, 80% of the light will pass through to the second sheet.
Through the second sheet of glass, 80% of the 80% will pass through.

80% of 80% = 0.8 x 0.8 = 0.64
0.64 = 64%.

However, out of the 80% that passed through the first sheet, the (0.15) light reflected from the second sheet will be reflected again (0.15) towards the second sheet. 80% out of this light that is reflected again will pass through.
So extra light passing through = (0.8 x 0.15 x 0.15 x 0.8) = 0.0144 = 1.44%
64 + 1.44 = 65.44
To the nearest 1%, this will be 65%

---

14) E
Argument of the text: "So although nuclear power is seen as problematic…it will have to continue to be used in 2050".
We need to find a weakness in this argument.

1 – Correct
If the government's economic growth is not achieved, then the energy consumption may not have increased and hence a lot of energy production would not be needed. So, this is a weakness.

2 – Wrong
The argument is about the continuation of using nuclear power and not about storing its waste.

3 – Correct
The text suggests that development of wind, tidal and solar power will be unable to meet the shortfall in supply. However, it fails to consider that the development of such sources of energy can speed up.

Since statements 1 and 3 are correct, E is the answer.

---

15) D
Let price of 1 biscuit = P
So price of 3 biscuits should be = 3P
Price of 4 biscuits = 4P
Since the shop has an offer price of 4 biscuits = 3P

Price of 1 biscuit = $(^{3P}/_4)$ = 0.75P
Decrease in price = P – 0.75P = 0.25P
Percentage decrease in price = $(^{0.25}/_P)$ x 100 = 25%
Since price decreased by 25%, profit will also be decreased by 25%.

Let original profit = M
Profit after offer = M – 0.25M = 0.75M
Since the shop is still making a profit of 20%,

$0.75M = 120\%$

$M = (^{120}/_{0.75}) = 160\%$

So profit = 60%

---

16) D

Before filling 500 l of oil, the height of the dipstick was 0.15 m. According to the graph, 0.15 m is 400 l of oil.

After filling the 500 l of oil, the tank would contain = 400 + 500 = 900 l

900 l, according to the graphs is 0.6 m.

---

17) E

The text says that its wrong to say that we are ruining the countryside's natural beauty by wind farms because many other factors have already caused the British countryside to change.

A – Wrong

Nothing is mentioned about the industrial areas.

B – Wrong

This actually states that wind farms will cause the areas to not be beautiful. So B is wrong.

C – Wrong

Carbon dioxide emissions are not relevant to the argument.

D – Wrong

The text does not say that any form of energy production has an impact on the environment.

E – Correct

The argument is that there were other factors that have already contributed to the change in the countryside appearance over the last 800 years.

---

18) C

The text tries to say that in order to prevent dissent towards the referee; footballers should immediately banned for the next 3 games.

Therefore, the assumption is that a ban would reduce such incidences of dissent in the future. This is paraphrased only by option C.

---

19) 3200 (allow 3100)

In the division column, the figure of overall crime for the year up to the installation of CCTV would be in the 'start' column.

This is 37838. Since this is the annual figure, we need to divide this value by 12.

37838 ÷ 12 = 3150

---

20) F

We need to identify which factors could decrease the significance of CCTV in decreasing crime.

1 – Correct

Improved street lighting could have been a reason for the decrease in crimes.

2 – Correct
An anti-burglary initiative could have caused the fall in crime levels.

3 – Correct
A decrease in number of cars parked in the target areas could have reduced the vehicle crimes. So this could have led to a fall in overall crime levels.

Since all 3 statements are correct, F is the answer.

---

21) 9%
Change in Target area = 131 − 161 = -30

% change in Target area = $(^{-30}/_{161})$ x 100 ≈ $(^{-30}/_{160})$ x 100 ≈ 18.75%

Change in Division area = 6442 − 7164 = -772
% change in Division area = $(^{-772}/_{7164})$ x 100 ≈ 10%
Percentage difference = 18.75 − 10 = 8.75 ≈ 9%

---

22) 22%
Target Start
Start with vehicle crime = 1526
Vehicle crime = 279
Start without vehicle crime = 1526 − 279 = 1247 ≈ 1250

Target End
End with vehicle crime = 1098
Vehicle crime = 126
End without vehicle crime = 1098 − 126 = 972 ≈ 970

Decrease = 970 − 1250 = -280
Percentage = $(^{280}/_{1250})$ x 100 = 22.4% ≈ 22%

---

23) E
1 – Correct
Since the target area had been installed with CCTVs, it is important to see whether the criminals had shifted their location of crimes to nearby areas.

2 – Wrong
Statement 2 is irrelevant to the buffer area idea.

3 – Correct
The data from the buffer area would help us to understand whether the CCTV had caused the fall in crime or if it was more of a general trend.

Since only statements 1 and 3 are correct, E is the answer.

---

24) A & C

There were not too many people getting very low marks, indicating that the easy questions were too easy.

Also, a lot of people got high marks, indicating hard questions were too easy.

---

25) C

A – Wrong

C is not directly connected to X. It first has to go to I and then to X. So, there cannot be a direct line from C to X.

B – Wrong

A is not directly connected to I. It first has to go to C and then to I. So, there cannot be a direct line from A to I.

C – Correct

E is directly connected to G. So, there must be a direct line from E to G.

D – Wrong

F is not directly connected to G. It first has to go to E and then to G. So, there cannot be a direct line from E to G.

E – Wrong

J is not directly connected to X. It first has to go to I and then to X. So, there cannot be a direct line from J to X.

---

26) A

The text says that only female birds have the medullary bone. So in order to prove that a fossil is male, then it is necessary for it not have the medullary bone.

However, the text also says that the medullary bone can deplete in females, meaning that if a fossil without a medullary bone is found, then it can either be male or female.

So it is a necessary but not a sufficient condition.

---

27) B

1 – Correct

Percentage of 17-34 year olds = 30%

Percentage that travel by walking or public transport = 10 + 15 = 25%

Even if we assume that all those who travel by walk/cycle are 17-34 year olds, then the remaining 5% must travel by car and 5% is ($1/6$) of 30%.

2 – Correct

Half of percentage of under 16s = $30/2$ = 15%

Number which travel by public transport = 15%

If we assume that all those who take public transport are under 16, then the maximum that can use the public transport is 15% of under 16s which is no more than half of the total 30%.

3 – Wrong

Percentage of 60 and above = 15%

Percentage 60 and under = 100 – 15 = 85%

Percentage which are not walking or cycling = 100 – 10 = 90%

Since 85 % can fit in 90%, we cannot know for sure that some 60 and under people either walk or cycle.

---

28) B

Starting from RIGHT to LEFT, we need to find the latest sequence of numbers, which can add up to 14.

This sequence is 4, 2, 5 and 3. (4 + 2 + 5 + 3 = 14)

After this sequence, we have the numbers 5 and 5. This adds up to 10 so far. Since 4 numbers need to add up to 14, the next number cannot be 4 as that would mean three numbers add up to 14. (5 + 5 + 4 = 14)

We are also given the information that the device never generates 5 consecutive odd numbers. So far, the latest numbers have been 5, 3, 5, 5. This means that the next number cannot be odd. The only remaining number, which is even is 2. So option B is the answer.

---

29) F

The conclusion of the text is that "global travel helps to immunise the population".

1 – Correct

According to the conclusion, global travel helps to immunise the population. However, since majority of the British residents are not global travellers, this would mean that they will not be immune to bird flu.

2 – Correct

All infectious diseases are different. So even though we may be immune to some diseases, this would not mean that we could be immune to the bird flu as well.

3 – Correct

Good nutrition is dependent on other factors as well such as environment, pollution etc. and not just the strength of the economy.

---

30) D

So the buyer will definitely not buy the first car.

So probability of buying it = 0

If the second car is bought, probability of it being the best = 1

If the third car is bought, probability of it being the best = ½ (car 2 could have been better)

If the fourth car is bought, probability of it being the best = ⅓ (car 2 or 3 could have been better).

Adding up these probabilities = $1 + (1/2) + (1/3) = {}^{11}/_6$
However, we now need to multiply $({}^{11}/_6)$ by $(1/4)$ since each option had a $(1/4)$ chance of occurring. We get a probability of $({}^{11}/_{24})$

---

31) A

1 – Correct
Aspiring can reduce the risk of further trouble after heart attack but it can also induce internal bleeding and carries a slight risk of cerebral haemorrhage. So it is a matter of balancing risks and benefits.

2 – Wrong
80% reach the threshold by 50. The other 20% do not. so we cannot conclude statement 2.

3 – Wrong
No information is given about the relative risk of heart attack in men aged 40 compared to men aged 50.

Since only statement 1 is correct, A is the answer.

---

32) D
According to the information given the equation for the sequence of elements given:

The first element will be multiplied by the following elements until a smaller element is reached.
The first element is 2. The next is 5. So we have (2 x 5).
The third is 5. So we have (2 x 5 x 5).
The fourth is 5. So we have (2 x 5 x 5 x 5).
The fifth is 3. So we need to add what ever is after the (2 x 5 x 5 x 5).
The sixth is 5. So we have (3 x 5)
The seventh is 1. So we need to add 1 to whatever we have so far.

We get:
(2 x 5 x 5 x 5) + (3 x 5) + 1
250 + 15 + 1
266

---

33) B
One in three out of 247 million went to alternative medical practitioners = $({}^{247}/_3)$= 82 million
Total number of visits made to alternative medical practitioners = 425 million
Average visit per patient = $({}^{425}/_{82})$ = 5

---

34) C
A – Wrong
Nothing is mentioned about conventional doctors not being concerned about the overall well-being of their patients in paragraph 3 and 4. We are jsut given the information that doctors are

getting frustrated because it is difficult to get the time to listen to their patients and counsel them.

B – Wrong
The sentence "On obstacle to better understanding is the lack of agreement on a central definition of 'alternative' therapies. So we cannot infer for sure whether alternative medicine does not claim to treat or cure any individual diseases.

C – Correct
The sentences "the time it takes…at a premium" and "this is the void that alternative medicine appears to be filling" suggest that time pressure on doctors is one of the factors which has increased the popularity of alternative therapies.

D – Wrong
The sentence "alternative medicine appears to be the belief in the body's ability to heal itself" does not suggest that doctors do not believe in the same. So we cannot conclude D to be correct.

E – Wrong
We cannot say that all alternative therapies have no side effects so we cannot say that they score over conventional medicine.

35) D
A – Wrong
Paragraph 3 is not mainly focused on invasive procedures and anyway this statement is too bold to say that invasive procedures do not cure diseases.

B – Wrong
Nothing in paragraph 3 suggest that doctors support alternative techniques.

C – Wrong
Nothing about the influence of pharmaceutical companies is given in paragraph 3.

D – Correct
The frustration of doctors due to time pressure has contributed to the increased popularity of alternative therapies.

2005 Section 2

1) A

A – Correct
Tidal volume is the volume of air displaced in the absence of extra respiratory effort.

B – Wrong
B represents the total lung capacity.

C – Wrong
C represents Inspiratory reserve volume.

D – Wrong
D represents Residual volume.

E – Wrong
E represents Inspiratory capacity.

2) B

A – Wrong
Bromine water is the test for the presence of alkenes.

B – Correct
A burning splint makes a popping sound in hydrogen, goes out in carbon dioxide and then the glowing splint relights in oxygen.

C – Wrong
Limewater turns milky in the presence of carbon dioxide. However, no observations are made in the presence of hydrogen and oxygen.

D – Wrong
This is the test for acids. Blue litmus turns red in acid.

E – Wrong
This is the test for alkali. Red litmus turns blue in alkali.

3) D
We need to calculate the difference in mass numbers and atomic numbers.
Mass number of U = 238
Sum of mass number of products Sr and Xe = 95 + 139 = 234

Atomic number of U = 92
Sum of atomic numbers of products Sr and Xe = 38 + 54 = 92

Atomic number is same, meaning that no protons are emitted. Since the mass number decreases by 4 and no protons are given off, 4 neutrons must have been emitted.

---

4) C

No calculations needed for this question.
Current follows the path with least resistance.

A – Wrong

If resistance of p and q becomes lower, then the current will only flow through the top branch. It will not go down to the ammeter from the top branch.

B – Wrong

If resistance of p and q becomes lower, then the current will split equally between top and bottom branch. It will not flow through the ammeter.

C – Correct

If resistance of r and q becomes lower, then the current will flow through the top branch first. It will then go down to the ammeter from the top branch in order to reach r.

D – Wrong

If resistance of r and s becomes lower, then the current will only flow through the bottom branch. It will not go up to the ammeter from the bottom branch.

---

5) D

Emphysema is a condition in which lungs and air sacs are damaged, causing breathlessness. Therefore, D is the answer, which states that alveoli (air sacs) are ruptured.

A – Wrong

Emphysema is not caused by reduced oxygen carriage by red blood cells.

B – Wrong

Emphysema is not caused because cilia are temporarily paralysed.

C – Wrong

Rapid growth of cells is called cancer not emphysema.

E – Wrong

Irrelevant to breathlessness and inhibited oxygen transport.

---

6) C

$z = xy^2$

$1.2 \times 10^{13} = 3 \times 10^6 (y^2)$

$y^2 = \dfrac{1.2 \times 10^{13}}{3 \times 10^6}$

$y^2 = 0.4 \times 10^{19}$
$y^2 = 4 \times 10^{18}$
$y = 2 \times 10^9$

---

7) A

You will realise that the number of hydrogen atoms do not add up to the original 12.
There are 4 hydrogen atoms in each molecule of pyruvic acid. Since there are two molecules, total number of hydrogen = 4 x 2 = 8

So 4 atoms of hydrogen are lost. When hydrogen is lost, the molecule becomes oxidised. Since one big molecule is broken into two smaller ones, decomposition occurs.
So the answer is A: oxidation and decomposition.

---

8) A

If the long lashes were caused by being homozygous recessive then A and her mate would have to be homozygous recessive. If both were homozygous recessive, then all of their offsprings would also have to be homozygous recessive and have long lashes.

However, that is not the case. So the long lashes are caused by the presence of a dominant allele. So even if a person were heterozygous, they would still have the long lashes.

If A and her mate were homozygous dominant, then all of their offsprings would also be homozygous dominant and have long lashes. Since A can neither be homozygous recessive nor homozygous dominant, she has to be heterozygous.

C could either be homozygous dominant or heterozygous.

D and E have to be homozygous recessive since they have short lashes and the only way to have short lashes is to be homozygous recessive.

---

9) C
Increase by 40% = 140% = 1.4

$A \propto \dfrac{1}{(1.4B)^2}$

$A \propto \dfrac{1}{1.96B}$

The fraction ($^1/_{1.96}$) is just above 50% (50% of 1.96 = 0.98)
So the decrease in percentage terms of A must be just under 50%. So C is the answer.

---

10) 39 cm
The problem requires the knowledge of Moments.
Length of beam = 60cm
The weight always acts on the centre of an object. In this case, the centre is (60 ÷ 2) = 30cm.

Weight of beam = 10N
Distance of pivot from centre = 30 − 10 = 20cm
Since the beam is in equilibrium, Clockwise moment = Anti-clockwise moment
Clockwise moment = 10 x 800 = 8000 N cm
Anti-clockwise moment = (X cm * 200N) + (10N x 20cm) = 200X + 200 N cm

8000 = 200X + 200
7800 = 200X
X = 7800 ÷ 200 = 39cm

---

11) D
Sodium carbonate = Na_2CO_3
Decahydrate means 10 moles of water. (Deca = 10)

So the formula of sodium carbonate decahydrate = $Na_2CO_3.10 H_2O$

Mr of sodium carbonate decahydrate = (23 x 2) + (12 x 1) + (16 x 3) + (2 x 10) + (16 x 10)
(23 x 2) + (12 x 1) + (16 x 3) + (2 x 10) + (16 x 10) = 46 + 12 + 48 + 180

Since there are 10 moles of water, mass of water = (2 x 10) + (16 x 10) = 180

So the equation for the percentage by mass of water of crystalline in sodium carbonate decahydrate:

$$\frac{180 \times 100}{46 + 12 + 48 + 180}$$

So the answer is D.

---

12) B
Don't worry if you do not know the answer to this, as this is no longer on the BMAT specification.
When looking away, you need to cover more area. The suspensory ligaments tighten to make the lens less convex so you can do so and the ciliary muscles relax.
So the answer is B

---

13) A

$$y = \left[\frac{x^2 + 2ax}{b}\right]^{1/2}$$

$$y^2 = \frac{x^2 + 2ax}{b}$$

$$by^2 = x^2 + 2ax$$

This is a bit tricky. ($x^2 + 2ax$) is part of $(x + a)(x + a) = x^2 + 2ax + a^2$

$(x + a)(x + a) = x^2 + 2ax + a^2$
$x^2 + 2ax = (x + a)(x + a) - a^2$

So we get,
$by^2 = (x + a)(x + a) - a^2$
$by^2 + a^2 = (x + a)^2$

Rooting both LHS and RHS,
$(by^2 + a^2)^{1/2} = x + a$
$x = (by^2 + a^2)^{1/2} - a$
So the answer is A.

---

14) B
Distance of transmitter from abdomen = 10 cm = 0.1 m
Time taken to reach the abdomen = Distance ÷ Time = 0.1 ÷ 500 = 0.0002 s

Since the receiver is adjacent to the transmitter, distance from the abdomen to receiver must also equal 0.1m

Therefore, the time taken for the pulse to travel from the abdomen to the receiver must be equal to 0.0002 s.
Total time = 0.0002 + 0.0002 = 0.0004 s
0.0004 s = 0.4 ms

---

15) D
Number of $N \equiv N$ bonds in reactants = 1
Total energy of $N \equiv N$ bonds in reactants = 1 * x = x
Number of H − H bonds in reactants = 3
Total energy of H − H bonds in reactants = 3 x y = 3y

Number of N − H bonds in products = 3 x 2 = 6
Total energy of N − H bonds in products = 6 x z = 6z

Since the reaction is exothermic, Energy of products must be greater than energy of reactants. Therefore, we get the inequality:
6z > x + 3y

---

16) This is no longer on the BMAT syllabus.

---

17) A
We know the general quadratic formula $(a - b)^2 = a^2 - 2ab + b^2$

So we have,
$(\sqrt{5} - \sqrt{2})^2 = (\sqrt{5})^2 - [2 (\sqrt{5}) (\sqrt{2})] + (\sqrt{2})^2$
$(\sqrt{5})^2 - [2 (\sqrt{5}) (\sqrt{2})] + (\sqrt{2})^2 = 5 - 2\sqrt{10} + 2 = \underline{\mathbf{7 - 2\sqrt{10}}}$

We know the general quadratic formula $(a + b)^2 = a^2 + 2ab + b^2$

$(\sqrt{5} + \sqrt{2})^2 = (\sqrt{5})^2 + [2 (\sqrt{5}) (\sqrt{2})] + (\sqrt{2})^2$
$(\sqrt{5})^2 + [2 (\sqrt{5}) (\sqrt{2})] + (\sqrt{2})^2 = 5 + 2\sqrt{10} + 2 = \underline{\mathbf{7 + 2\sqrt{10}}}$

So we have:
$(\sqrt{5} - \sqrt{2})^2 (\sqrt{5} + \sqrt{2})^2 = (7 - 2\sqrt{10}) (7 + 2\sqrt{10})$
$7(7 + 2\sqrt{10}) - 2\sqrt{10}(7 + 2\sqrt{10})$
$49 + 14\sqrt{10} - 14\sqrt{10} - 40$
$49 - 40 = 9$

---

18) B
Total number of parts = 7 + 1 = 8
The maximum age would be when the rock contained 8 parts of ^{235}U.

Here are the half-lives:

Half – life	^{235}U	^{207}Pb
0	8	0
1	4	4
2	2	6
3	1	7

So it was after 3 half-lives that the ratio became 1 : 7

Half-life = 7.1×10^8 years
So maximum age of rock = $3 \times 7.1 \times 10^8 = 21.3 \times 10^8 = 2.13 \times 10^9$ years

---

19) B
Volume of NaOH = 50 cm³ = 0.05 dm³
Moles of NaOH = c x v = 2 x 0.05 = 0.1 mol
Molar ratio of NaOH : H_2X = 2 : 1

So moles of H_2X = 0.1 ÷ 2 = 0.05 mol
Mr of acid = Mass ÷ Moles
Mr = 4.5 ÷ 0.05 = 90

---

20) C
Oxygen is only required for active transport. Active transport is the movement of molecules from a region of lower concentration to a region of higher concentration (Opposite of diffusion)

A – Wrong
Cytosine will move from L to K from a region of higher concentration to lower concentration. So movement of cytosine from L to K would not require active transport and hence no oxygen.

B – Wrong
Glucose will move from K to L from a region of higher concentration to lower concentration. So movement of glucose from K to L would not require active transport and hence no oxygen.

C – Correct
Magnesium ions will move from L to K from a region of lower concentration to higher concentration. So movement of magnesium ions from L to K would require active transport and hence would require oxygen.

D – Wrong
Nitrate ions will move from K to L from a region of higher concentration to lower concentration. So movement of nitrate ions from K to L would not require active transport and hence no oxygen.

---

21) A
The third side of the **equilateral triangle** is the diameter of the semi-circle.
Therefore, diameter of semi-circle = 'x' cm. Radius = ½x = $(\frac{x}{2})$

We first need to find the area of the equilateral triangle. In order to do this, we need to find its height using Pythagoras theorem.

Divide the equilateral triangle into two right-angled triangles.
Hypotenuse = 'x'
1st side = ½x
2nd side (height) = A

$x^2 = (½x)^2 + A^2$
$x^2 - ¼x^2 = A^2$
$¾x^2 = A^2$
$A = \sqrt{(¾x^2)} = \dfrac{x\sqrt{3}}{2}$

Area of equilateral triangle = 2 x area of right-angled triangle

Area of 1 right-angled triangle = $\frac{1}{2}$ * $\frac{(x\sqrt{3})}{2}$ * $\frac{x}{2}$ = $\frac{x^2\sqrt{3}}{8}$

Area of equilateral triangle = 2 * $\frac{x^2\sqrt{3}}{8}$ = $\frac{x^2\sqrt{3}}{4}$

Area of semi-circle = $\frac{1}{2}\pi r^2$
$\frac{1}{2}$ * π * $\frac{x^2}{2^2}$ = $\frac{\pi x^2}{8}$

Total area = area of triangle + area of semi-circle
$\frac{x^2\sqrt{3}}{4}$ + $\frac{\pi x^2}{8}$

$\frac{2x^2\sqrt{3} + \pi x^2}{8}$

$\frac{2x^2\sqrt{3} + \pi x^2}{8}$

$\frac{x^2 (2\sqrt{3} + \pi)}{8}$

So, the answer is A.

22) D
Acceleration on Earth = 10 m/s²
¼ of Earth's acceleration = 2.5 m/s²

u = 0
a = 2.5
s = 20
v = ?

$v^2 - u^2 = 2as$
Since u = 0,
$v^2 = 2 (2.5) (20)$
$v^2 = 5 \times 20 = 100$
v = 10 m/s²

23) B
Butane would always have 4 carbon atoms.
Mr of 4 carbon atoms = 12 x 4 = 48

80% = 48
1% = 48 ÷ 80 = 0.6
100% = 0.6 x 100 = 60

So the mass of butane = 60

Mass that must be made by deuterium and hydrogen = 60 – 48 = 12
Mass of deuterium = 2 x mass of hydrogen

Let number of hydrogen atoms = H
Let number of deuterium atoms = D

H + 2D = 12

Sum of number of hydrogen and deuterium atoms = 10
So H + D = 10

Using simultaneous equations,
H + 2D = 12
H + D = 10
D = 2

Since H + D = 10
H = 10 – 2 = 8

So the formula must be $C_4H_8D_2$

---

24) A
If the foramen ovale does not close, the deoxygenated blood from the right atrium will mix with the oxygenated blood in the left atrium.
This will cause the aorta (which carries oxygenated blood from left ventricle to the body) to carry some deoxygenated blood.

There would be no major effect on the heartbeat so B is wrong.
The amount of blood pumped will also not drastically change. So C is wrong.
The pulmonary vein would not be affected since it comes from the lungs.
There will be little to no change in the blood pumped to the lungs.

---

25) B
760 mm Hg has a force of 100kPa.
152 m Hg would have a force of = $[(^{152}/_{760}) \times 100] = [0.2 \times 100] = 20$ kPa = 20×10^3 Pa
2.0 cm² = 0.0002 m²

Pressure = Force ÷ Area

20×10^3 Pa = Force ÷ 0.0002

Force = 20×10^3 Pa x 0.0002 = 4 N

26) D

This requires you to remember the reactivity series off by heart as such question do often come up.

Na is the most reactive and it will require the most energy to break its oxide. Hence reaction D would enquire the highest temperature.

---

27) 0.8

Let the center of the circle be O.

Here is how the diagram should look like:

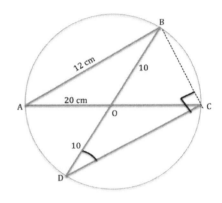

AO = CO = 10 cm

Since D is opposite B, BD is also a diameter of the circle, meaning:

BO = DO = 10 cm

We know that triangle ABC is a right-angled triangle. We can find out BC using Pythagoras theorem.

$AC^2 = AB^2 + BC^2$

$20^2 = 12^2 + BC^2$

$400 - 144 = BC^2$

$BC^2 = 256$

BC = 16 cm

We know triangle DBC is also a right-angle triangle with the hypotenuse being AC.

Sine $\angle BDC = \frac{Opposite}{Hypotenuse} = \frac{BC}{BD} = \frac{16}{20}$

16 ÷ 20 = 0.8

---

1) The statement is not necessarily saying that animals do not feel physical pain as humans do. The word 'feel' can be used for emotional pain too. Therefore, the statement can interpreted as animals do not feel emotional pain in the same way as us.

Now, we cannot determine how much pain an animal is suffering from. Pain is a sensation that only an individual can feel. (Therefore it is difficult to answer the second question).

We can surely understand if an animal is feeling pain, either emotional or physical. It is often observed that a dog becomes depressed when they do not see their owners for a long time. They tend to eat less and can often be seen sitting in one area waiting for their owners to return. We can therefore argue that some animals do feel emotional pain. Humans also feel a similar kind of emotional pain when we lose someone really close to us.
If physical pain is inflicted on an animal, they try to escape or retaliate. These behaviours can hence help to argue against the statement.

It is impractical and unreasonable to think that all animals have the same nervous systems. Therefore, others may argue that some animals may not feel pain since they have a different brain physiology. They may not have the part of the brain that we have that senses pain.

2) Pronouncements sounds very similar to announcements (which mean to declare something). Pronouncement actually means a formal or authoritative declaration. Therefore, pronouncements in sciences would refer to any evidence or findings that have been obtained as a result of studies and researches, which have been declared authoritatively.
In the second part of the statement, Sir James Jeans tries to convey the message that many scientific pronouncements have been proven wrong.

The most famous biomedical pronouncement that was proven to be false was the link made between MMR vaccines and autism by Andrew Wakefield. This link was later debunked by science as no research or study could prove that MMR vaccines were linked with autism. This pronouncement, however, caused lots of parents to refuse the MMR vaccination for their children. This resulted in many deaths due to measles, mumps and rubella.
This case highlights the importance of taking precautions before making an official biomedical pronouncement.

Others may argue that without pronouncements, we would not have the technology that we have now. Take the case of Dr Edward Jenner, the father of immunology.
His research involved exposing people to cowpox (which was harmless) to immunise them against smallpox. If Dr Edward Jenner had not pronounced his findings and evidence, our knowledge of vaccines would not be possible. Similarly, Sir Alexander Fleming would not have discovered antibiotics.
Making pronouncements may motivate other scientists and doctors to follow in the footsteps of the likes of Dr Edward Jenner and Sir Alexander Fleming.

3) The population of the world is ever growing and has been doing so for hundreds of years. As a result, the number of patients, as expected, is increasing proportionally. The statement is trying to say that with shortage of resources, doctors' main concern in the future would be whether to provide treatment or not. The doctors must then make decisions about who requires the treatment more.

The most obvious factor, which will contribute to the increasing demand, is the growing population. This occurs when the birth rate exceeds the death rate. Due to overpopulation, there will be shortage of food supply, which will cause malnourishment on a wide scale. These people will require immediate medical attention. Similarly, the amount of pollution, whether it is air, noise or water, will increase. This will lead to people being affected by diseases such as lung cancer, cholera or typhoid.
The resources required to treat an increasing number of patients will fall short. Such resources include medical tools, machinery (such as X-ray machines or MRI) and even the medical workforce.

Others may argue that a doctor 'should always act in a patient's best interests'. Denying a treatment to a patient will certainly not uphold this statement. This would be opposing the very principle of the NHS. Refusing a treatment because someone else needs it more can be considered as passive euthanasia.

There are a lot of ethical and moral issues with this situation. The government can play an important role in ensuring cost-effectiveness in the medical field. Equal consideration should be given to all patients no matter their condition.

2006 Section 1

1) C

Let us use numbers instead of the ratio.
Let us say there are 80 birds and 1 person on the island.

Let population of seabirds 20 years ago = 's'
Let population of people 20 years ago = 'p'

$s - 60\%(s) = 80$
$p + 25\%(p) = 1$

$s - 0.6s = 80$
$p + 0.25p = 1$

$s(1-0.6) = 80$
$p(1+0.25) = 1$

$0.4s = 80$
$1.25p = 1$

$s = 200$
$p = 0.8$

Ratio = 200 : 0.8
We need to increase the ratio of persons to 1.
$0.8 + 25\% = 1$
We increased 0.8 by 25%. Hence we also need to increase 200 by 25%. This equates to 250.
Hence the ratio is 250 : 1. The answer is C.

---

2) E

The last line of the text is the conclusion. E paraphrases the last line of the text correctly.

---

3) B

The four sections shown in the picture are the four tables. You can use the sections and try to make the shapes given.

You will realise that it is not possible to make shapes 2 and 4.
OR
You can even use scissors and cut out shapes similar to the shape of the table. There are no rules against cutting shapes from the question paper.

---

4) C

The argument is that "political journalists are not doing job properly".

A – Wrong

The text does not suggest that the journalists are doing it deliberately. So we cannot say that it is an assumption.

B – Wrong

Nothing written in the text suggests that voters believe everything they see in the newspapers.

C – Correct

The text says that journalists are not doing their job properly because they include all details of the minister's incompetence and omit any alternative views. However, the text assumes what the job of political journalists is. It assumes that it is the job of the journalists to inform the voters.

D – Wrong

This is neither true nor an assumption

E – Wrong

The text does not assume that journalists aim to destroy the careers of politicians. It just highlights that journalists tend to focus on the incompetence of the minister.

5) 62 seconds

Let us first convert the speed given into m/s

$$\frac{45 \times 1000}{3600} = 12.5 \text{ m/s}$$

Since the trains need to COMPLETELY emerge from the tunnel, the distance they need to cover must be the sum of the length of the tunnel and length of the train itself.

Since we need to find out the time taken for BOTH trains to emerge from the tunnel, we only need to find the time taken by the train that is going to take the longest to emerge.
Since the speed of both trains would be the same, we need to find out which train needs to cover the most distance.

1st Train:
Distance that must be covered = 80 + 615 = 695

2nd Train:
Distance that must be covered = 40 + 120 + 615 = 775

Since the second train needs to cover the most distance, we just need to find the time taken by it to emerge from the tunnel.

Speed = 12.5 m/s
Time = $\frac{775}{12.5}$ = 62 seconds

6) C

A – Wrong
We cannot infer whether women are more influenced by photographs or not based on the information given in the text.

B – Wrong
We cannot infer whether the print media is aware or unaware.

C – Correct
Since the media takes photographs of thin models and then talk about anorexia, we can deduce that they are clearly inconsistent in their approach to the problem of eating disorders.

D – Wrong
Firstly, we cannot deduce what the public is interested in. Secondly, you must realise that this statement is too strong since it uses the word 'only'.

E – Wrong
The dangers of anorexia and bulimia are not relevant to the question at all.

---

7) B
We need to look at the TOTAL row and the TOTAL column. In the '% with 5 A* to C' sub-column, the figure for white is 55.1% and the figure for Asians is 58.7%
Difference = 58.7 – 55.1 = 3.6 ≈ 4%

---

8) E
We need to look at the 'TOTAL ROW' and in the 'KS 2-4' sub-column in the 'Other than English as a first language.'
The ethnic group Chinese has the highest figure (1036.0) which means E is the answer.

---

9) D

A – False
In the 'KS 2-4' sub-column in the 'TOTAL' column, you can clearly observe that girls have shown a bigger improvement than boys.

B – False
In the 'TOTAL' row and the 'Eligible pupils' sub-column of the 'Other than English as a first language' column, you can see that the figure for Asians is higher than Chinese.

C – False
To answer this question, we need to look at the '% with 5 A* to C' sub-column of the TOTAL column.
We can see that difference between performance of boys and girls = 60.2 – 50.3 = 9.9%
The difference is smaller in the Chinese ethnicity: 85.1 – 77.1 = 8%

D – True

This ethnic group is mixed. The figure for '% with 5 A* to C' sub-column in the 'English as a first language' is 54.7% whilst the figure for their equivalents in the 'Other than English as a first language' column is 55.0%

In all other ethnics groups, the figure for 'English as a first language' is higher than 'Other than English as a first language'

---

10) D

1 – Wrong

If they were innately more intelligent, then it perfectly explains why they improve more between ages 11 and 16 than boys.

2 – Wrong

If girls mature earlier than boys, then that also explains why girls improve more at ages 11 and 16 than boys.

3 – Wrong

This also explains why girls improve more academically than boys.

4 – Correct

The question clearly says "for all ethnic groups". Whether Asian girls improve more or not does not matter and is irrelevant.

---

11) E

1 – Correct

Those who had been taking cannabis for 15 years recalled fewer words than those who had been taking it for 7 years. Also, those who had been taking cannabis for 7 years recalled fewer words than those who had never smoked cannabis. This shows that long-term smoking had an impact on the ability of a person to learn and remember.

2 – Correct

Another explanation could be that cannabis' effect lasts for more than 24 hours, which explains the results that we got.

3 – Correct

This could also be true. Difference in IQs could be the reason why such results were obtained, independent of cannabis smoking.

Since all three statements are correct, E is the answer.

---

12) A

The offer: 3 boxes for the price of 2
Price of 2 = $1.50 x 2 = $3.00
Since 3 boxes are sold at $3.00, price of 1 box = 3.00 ÷ 3 = $1.00
Price reduction = 1.50 – 1.00 = $0.50
Since the supermarket always makes 40% gross margin, they always pay the suppliers 60% of the cost of the cereal.

Price the supermarket paid before the offer = 0.60 x 1.50 = 90 c
Price the supermarket pays during the offer = 0.60 x 1.00 = 60 c
Difference = 90 – 60 = 30c

13) 68 p
23p (there is a stamp worth 23p)
32p (there is a stamp worth 32p)
37p (there is a stamp worth 37p)
49p (there is a stamp worth 49p)
50p (there is a stamp worth 49 p and another worth 1p. So 49 + 1 = 50)
68p (we cannot make 68p with the prices of stamps available)

---

14) C
The argument is that "we should not doubt its reliability..examiners are the experts..they all agree that is completely reliable method of identifying criminals".

A – Wrong
It does not matter whether expert sometimes fail when they try to apply their methods. We are not interested in how they apply their method. This statement is too general and does not relate back to fingerprinting.

B – Wrong
Not knowing about something does not mean that it is unreliable. Also, this statement is paraphrased in the first line of the text already. So we cannot say that this is a weakness as it has already been considered.

C – Correct
Experts' opinion does not always have to be correct. Also, this statement says that experts have an opinion and opinions are not facts.

D – Wrong
We are not interested in how long a technique has been used for.

---

15) C
It is easier to start with the villages that appear more than once in the description.

Ruilick
Wellbank is due east of Ruilick
Aultviach is due north of Ruilick.
(Due means directly)

The only letter on the map which has villages directly north and east of it is E.
So Wellbank is F and Aultviach is A.

Clashandarran
Rheindown is due south of Clashandarran.
B is the only village, which has a village directly south of it. B is Clashandarran and D is

Rheindown.

B also satisfies the sentence "Clashandarran is south an east of Aultviach".

This leaves us with letters F, G and C.

We must satisfy the statement "Beauly is south and west of Windyhill".

F does not have anything south and west of it.

G does not have anything south and west of it.

So C is the answer.

---

16) B

1 – Wrong

We do not know for sure whether the less developed countries have set targets or not, so we cannot consider this statement as an assumption.

2 – Wrong

The text does not mention whether developed countries are prioritising alleviating poverty or reducing global warming.

3 – Wrong

We do not know whether levels of prosperity in developing countries are improving or not.

4 – Correct

The text gives two options: either reduce global warming or alleviate levels of poverty in developing countries. So it must be assuming that we cannot alleviate poverty without contributing to global warming. So the assumption is that developing countries can only improve their economies by activities, which generate greenhouse gases.

Since only statement 4 is correct, B is the answer.

---

17) B

Total number of children = 1 + 9 = 10

She had enough money left to buy 10 children a packed of bubble gum each.

Amount of money left = 0.25 x 10 = £2.50

So total money spent = 125 – 2.5 = £122.5

Two chose to go on the Apocalypse. Since they chose Apocalypse, they must have gone on the Carousel. Amount spent on these two kids = 2 (9 + 3.5) = 2 (12.5) = £25

Money left = 122.5 – 25 = £97.5

All the other kids must have chosen the Armageddon as their main ride.

Let number of kids that chose Armageddon + Dodgems = d

Let number of kids that chose Armageddon + Helter Skelter = h

Amount spent by d = d (7.5 + 5) = 12.5d

Amount spent by h = h (7.5 + 4.5) = 12h

We know that two people went on the Apocalypse. Therefore all the other 8 kids must have chosen the Armageddon.

So, d + h = 8

12.5d + 12h = 97.5

d + h = 8
Using simultaneous equations, we get:

12.5d + 12h = 97.5
12d + 12h = 96

0.5d = 1.5
d = 3

d = number of children that chose Dodgems + Armageddon
Hence, the answer is 3. Option B is correct.

18) C
The argument is that people do not have the right to criticise farmers for their use of pesticides. We must find a flaw in this argument.

A – Wrong
Statement A is not true. The argument only says that people should not complaint about farmers' use of pesticides since they choose supermarkets according to price.

B – Wrong
It is not necessarily contradicting itself. The use of pesticides has advantages and disadvantages but you cannot correlate maximum yield and damage to environment. Giving advantages and disadvantages of something does not necessarily mean that you are contradicting yourself.

C – Correct
The text says that farmers make a loss because the public chooses the cheaper supermarket, which leads to farmers bringing their prices down. This forces farmers to use pesticides to increase yield and hence avoid loss. However, the text does not consider other options for avoiding loss and assumes that using pesticides is the only solution.

D – Wrong
Farmers selling directly to the public is not relevant to the question and the conclusion.

E – Wrong
Since we do no know if people living near farms are affected or not, we cannot classify this as a flaw of the argument.

19) E
She only loses her fitness when she misses a SCHEDULED session. This means that we do not need to take the session that she misses on Saturdays, as they are not scheduled.
Number of scheduled sessions between 8th to 15th April: 6 (8th and 15th are Saturdays so there are no scheduled sessions)
For each session she misses, it will take her three sessions to regain her fitness. So 6 x 3 = 18 sessions
We know that two weeks after she came back (came back on 16th as she was on holiday on

15th), she had a sore shoulder. 2 weeks after 16th = 30th.

By the 30th, she would have completed 12 scheduled sessions, meaning that she would have recovered 4 days worth of fitness. She still needs to recover the fitness from 2 more days.

She missed 4 sessions due to the sore shoulder. She missed the sessions on 1st, 2nd and 3rd and 4th. In order to recover her original fitness, she needs to do (2+4) x 3 = 18 sessions.

Starting from the 5th, we need to count 18 sessions (remember to not count Saturdays). This would give us the answer Wednesday 24th May.

So the answer is E.

---

20) B

In 2004, total number of GPs = 31250

Number of female GPs = 12500

Percentage = (12500 ÷ 31250) x 100 = 40%

This is closest to 36%

---

21) C

Percentage of female GPs working part time = 48% ≈ 50%

50% of 12500 = 0.5 x 12500 = 6250

This is closest to C (6000)

---

22) D

Number of GPs in 1994 = 27500 ≈ 28000

Percentage working part time = 12% ≈ 10%

Number working part time = 10% of 28000 = 2800

Total working hours = 10(28000 − 2800) + 5(2800) = 252000 + 14000 = 266000

Number of GPs in 2004 = 31250 ≈ 32000 (not exactly a correct estimation but we need good figures)

Percentage working part time = 25%

Number working part time = 25% of 32000 = 8000

Total working hours = 10(32000 − 3200) + 5(3200) = 288000 + 16000 = 304,000

Percentage difference = (304000 ÷ 266000) x 100 = 114.3%

This its an increase by 14% which is closest to a rise of 10%.

You must remember that we have always rounded up the figures in our calculations. Therefore, we must round down the final answer.

---

23) B

Let us first calculate the average = (40 + 37 + 26 + 19 + 9 + 4) ÷ 6 = 22.5 cwt

Suzie's guess was nearer than Wally's. Average of Wally's and Suzie's guesses = (40 + 4) ÷ 2 = 22 cwt

Since Suzie's guess is nearer, the actual weight of the bull would be between 4 and 22.

However, the information given to us says that the average (22.5) is closer than any of the guesses.

The closest guesses to 22.5 are 19 and 26. Since it cannot be more than 22, it cannot be 26.

Looking at the options, it cannot be 20 as it is closer to 19 than 22.5

It can be 21 as this is closer to 22.5 than 19.

It cannot be 22 as this is the average of Suzie's and Wally's guess.
So the answer is B (21 cwt).

---

24) C
The conclusion of the text is that "it cannot be transmitted easily between people. Influenza virus can mutate and thus possibly change the way in which they infect victims".

A – Wrong
The text clearly says that it cannot easily be transmitted from one person to another. So saying that many more people will catch the strain is wrong.

B – Wrong
We cannot say for sure that it will cause an epidemic. Also we are not sure that it will spread easily even if it mutated.

C – Correct
The only way for the strain to spread more easily is by mutation. So unless it mutates, the chance of an epidemic is unlikely.

D – Wrong
The text just says that is cannot be transmitted **easily** between people. So it can still be transmitted. Also, this is not the main idea of the text.

---

25) B
Let us say the period of time is 1 hour.
In one hour, the minute hand will sweep the entire 360°
The hour hand will sweep = 360 ÷ 12 = 30°
Let us say the minute hand is the radius of a circle. Radius = 8.4cm ≈ 8cm
Area of the circle = πr^2 = $(8)^2\pi$ = 64π
Since the minute hand will sweep the entire 360°, the area it will sweep would be 64π
Let us say the hour hand is the radius of a different circle. Radius = 6.3 cm ≈ 6
Area of the circle = πr^2 = $(6)^2\pi$ = 36π
Since the hour hand will only sweep the 30°, the area it will sweep would be $^1/_{12}$ x 36π = 3π
Ratio = $^{64\pi}/_{3\pi}$
The πs cancel out, giving: 64 ÷ 3 = 64:3
Hence, B is the answer.

---

26) D
The argument made in the text is that "no new nuclear plants..they will not be needed".
We must find a reason why not building new nuclear power plants could prove to be unsafe.

1 – Correct
If the demand for electricity goes up, new nuclear power plants would be needed.

2 – Correct
If the green technologies start to become inefficient in producing electricity, then new nuclear plants will be needed.

<u>3 – Wrong</u>
Storing nuclear waste is irrelevant to the argument and to the question.

Since statements 1 and 2 are correct, D is the answer.

---

27) 5 hours
Distance covered forward journey = Distance covered reverse journey = $20 \div 2 = 10$ km

Let distance covered on flat = F
Let time taken to cover flat surface = f
Speed on flat = 4
$F = 4 \times f = 4f$

Let distance covered uphill = U
Let time taken to cover uphill surface = u
Speed on uphill = 3
$U = 3 \times u = 3u$

Let distance covered downhill = D
Let time taken to cover downhill surface = d
Speed on downhill = 6 (which is twice the speed on uphill)
$D = 6 \times d = 6d = 10$ km

We know that the distance covered uphill = distance covered down hill

Hence, we get the equation:
$U = D$
$3u = 6d$
$u = 2d$

Forward journey + reverse journey = 20km
$4f + 3u + 4f + 6d = 20$
$4f + 6d + 4f + 6d = 20$
$8f + 12d = 20$
$4(2f + 3d) = 20$
$2f + 3d = 5$

Hence the answer is 5 hours.

---

28) B
Let us start by understanding the graph first.
As population in year n increases, population in year n+1 also increases.
However, there comes a point where the population of snaffles in year n + 1 starts to decline as population of snaffles in year n increase.

A – Wrong
If births = deaths, then the population would be constant.

80

B – Correct
Since population of snaffles in year n increases, food demand overtakes food supply causing some of the snaffles to die out in the following year.

C – Wrong
We cannot work out number of cubs produced. This is completely irrelevant.

D – Wrong
There is no information regarding time of the year.

E – Wrong
At the start of the graph, populations of snaffle in year n and n+1 are low.

---

29) D

1 – Correct
The acrylamide itself is not harmful but its product glycidamide is. Since humans produce less glycidamide, acrylamide is not as harmful to humans as animals.

2 – Wrong
Cooking over 120°C causes glycidamide to be produced, which is harmful.

3 – Correct
Cooking at lower temperatures causes more fat to be ingested meaning that it is harmful.

So 1 and 3 are correct. The answer is D.

---

30) A
The wooden puzzle itself is a cube.
The surface of the cube is made up of 3cm cubes and 1cm cubes.
Length of 1 side of puzzle = 3 + 3 + 1 + 1 = 8cm
Volume = 8 x 8 x 8 = 512 cm³

There are 8 cubes with side 3cm.
Volume = 8 x 3 x 3 x 3 = 8 x 27 = 216 cm³

Number of 1cm cubes which are adjacent to two sides = 24
Volume = 1 x 1 x 1 x 24 = 24 cm³
Number of extra 1 cm cubes on each side = 20
Number of sides = 6
Number of extra 1 cm cubes = 6 x 20 = 120
Volume = 120 x 1 x 1 x 1 = 120cm³

Volume taken by 1cm and 3cm cubes = 120 + 24 + 216 = 360 cm³

The 2cm cubes must cover the remaining volume.
Remaining volume = 512 – 360 = 152cm³

Volume of one 2cm cube = 2 x 2 x 2 = 8cm³
Number of 2cm cubes = 152 ÷ 8 = 19 cubes

---

31) B

A – Wrong
This cannot be deduced from the paragraph. It states that Microsoft does not want anyone repeating on the internet what it achieved but this does not mean that Google is achieving what Microsoft already has.

B – Correct
The sentence "the three, who recently looked down on Google" suggests that the three used to look down on Google but not anymore.

C – Wrong
It is not certain that an alliance will be able to stop Google. The line "the three…**wonder** if they can forge alliances to combat it." suggests that they are considering an alliance but they are not certain.

D – Wrong
This cannot be inferred from the passage.

---

32) B
The information given suggests that the value exceeds 2 billion pounds. Therefore, we cannot confirm the exact value. Therefore we cannot set a limit (i.e. the value is more or less than a certain value).
Options A, C and D suggest that the value could be a less than certain number which we cannot decide.

---

33) C

A – Wrong
The cartoon does not show the knight (Google) is winning against the three headed dragon (Microsoft, Yahoo and E-bay).

B – Wrong
Even though a knight portrays Google, it is not in comparison with the other companies.

C – Correct
The cartoon shows that Google may be forced to combat against an alliance consisting of Microsoft, Yahoo and E-bar (Each head of the dragon represents each of the three companies).

D – Wrong
The cartoon does not show the knight (Google) is losing against the three-headed dragon (Microsoft, Yahoo and E-bay).

E – Wrong
This is clearly wrong, as the cartoon does not show this.

34) C

1 – Correct

If Google had not struck a corporate link with another company, Microsoft would have benefitted. Instead, Google was benefitted so this could be a reason for 'Google making the pace'.

2 – Correct

If Google is making large profits, then a possible reason could be that it is gaining a large share of the advertising market.

3 – Wrong

This statement is not related to the conclusion given in paragraph 3.

Statements 1 and 2 are correct. So C is correct.

35) A

A – Correct

Competition is the general focus of the passage. The last sentence "the jockeying offers…opportunities for consumers" suggests that competition is good for consumers.

B – Wrong

'Have' is a very strong verb and hence, this is wrong.

C – Wrong

This is not a rule that mature companies cannot compete with emerging ones.

D – Wrong

The passage only suggests that the other three companies could form an alliance. There is no guarantee that none of the three companies will not merge with Google.

E – Wrong

There could be other companies that pose a threat to Microsoft.

2006 Section 2

1) E
Remember that insulin converts glucose to glycogen so it can be stored in the liver and in the muscles.
Therefore, when insulin levels drop in the blood, glycogen synthesis will also decrease. This can be seen in time periods 3 and 5; when glycogen levels are decreasing, meaning that insulin concentration is below normal.

2) C
The melting temperature and boiling temperature are normal and the fact that they lack of conductivity of its solution is reasonable.
However the property of solubility in water is not normal as simple molecular structures are usually insoluble in water.

3) F
Number of half-lives after 8 years = 8 ÷ 4 = 2 half-lives
Number of atoms of X left after 8 years = $32 \times 10^{20} \div (2 \times 2) = 8 \times 10^{20}$

We know all of the X atoms decay into isotope Y.
Number of X atoms that decay = $32 \times 10^{20} - 8 \times 10^{20} = 24 \times 10^{20}$
We know that initial number of Y atoms present was 4×10^{20}
Number of Y atoms present after 8 years = $24 + 4 = 28 \times 10^{20}$

4) B
Always remember that when water needs to be kept in the body, the urine produced will be concentrated. This eliminates A, C and F.
Since, water needs to be kept in the body, more water must be reabsorbed from the nephrons.
In order to reabsorb more water, ADH production must increase. Only option B shows this.
ADH (Anti-Diuretic Hormone) reabsorbs water from kidney

5) C
As you go along a period, reactivity of non-metal increases since their electronegativity increases. Therefore, the halogens are the most reactive non-metals within each period.
Noble Gases ARE NOT the most reactive since they are inert.
As you can see from the periodic table below, reactivity increases across a period and up a group for non-metals. Therefore, Fluorine is the most reactive non-metal.
The electronic configuration for Fluorine is 2,7. Hence, C is the answer

6) A

This is no longer in your BMAT specification.

If you do not know how to do it, then skip the question and move on! You cannot afford to waste time in the BMAT, especially in Section 2.

Draw the triangle out first. A visual representation always helps.

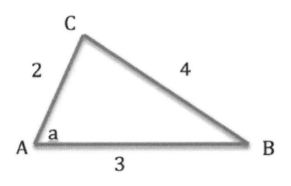

$a = BC = 4$
$b = AC = 2$
$c = AB = 3$
$A = \angle BAC$
$a^2 = b^2 + c^2 - 2bc \cos A$
$4^2 = 3^2 + 2^2 - 2(2)(3) \cos A$
$16 = 9 + 4 - 12 \cos A$
$16 - 13 = -12 \cos A$
$^3/_{12} = -\cos A$
$^1/_4 = -\cos A$
$-^1/_4 = \cos A$

---

7) A

Microwaves are transverse waves. So 1 is not correct.
Microwaves travel at the speed of light. So 2 is correct
For pre-natal scanning, ultrasound is used. So 3 is not correct
Infrared is used for thermal imaging. So 4 is not correct.
Microwaves along with other EM waves travel in vacuum.

---

8) C

Upper quartile means 75% to 100%.
Difference = 100 - 75 = 25%
Probability of a person having a heart beat of 165 or more = 25% ÷ 100% = ¼

<u>4</u> members were chosen. 3 would have probability of ¼ and the fourth would have probability of ¾.

Possibilities of the order of people = YYYN, YYNY, YNYY, NYYY

Y = person has a heart beat of more than 165

N = person has a heart beat of less than 165

So there are 4 possibilities.

Probability of 3 members having heart beat 165 or more = ¼ x ¼ x ¼ x ¾ x $^4/_1$ = $^{12}/_{256}$

The question says **at least** 3 people. So we can also obtain 4 people with a heart beat of more than 165.

Probability of this = ¼ x ¼ x ¼ x ¼ = $^1/_{256}$

Probability of at least 3 people having a hear beat of more than 165 = $^{12}/_{256}$ + $^1/_{256}$ = $^{13}/_{256}$

---

9) B

Firstly, catalysts do not affect the equilibrium position and so, 1 is incorrect. This rules out options A, D and F.

Adding more ammonia will favour the forward reaction, which desirable. So 2 is correct. This rules out option C.

Increasing the pressure will favour the forward reaction, which will increase the yield of salt. So, 3 is correct.

Increasing the temperature will favour the backward endothermic reaction and hence, the salt yield will decrease. So 4 is incorrect and this rules out option E.

---

10) D

Let 'T' be the dominant allele and let 't' be the recessive allele.

	T	t
T	TT	Tt
t	Tt	tt

We know that recessive allele prevents seed development, which is why all seeds, which had genotype 'tt' (¼ x 1000 = 250), are dead. The remaining 750 seeds developed.

Out of these 750 seeds, some have genotype 'TT' whilst others have the genotype 'Tt'
From the table, we can see that 2 out of three plants are Tt whilst $^1/_3$ are TT.
Number of heterozygous plants in the 750 mature plants = $^2/_3$ = 66.666% ≈ 67%

---

11) C

No calculations required for this question. The pressure applied at X will remain the same at Y.

---

12) E

We need to get rid of the 1 from the right hand side first.

So we get:

$$r - 1 = \frac{(-)\, 6\, \Sigma d^2}{n\,(n^2 - 1)}$$

We need to get rid of the (-) sign from RHS,

$$1 - r = \frac{6\, \Sigma d^2}{n\,(n^2 - 1)}$$

Solving $n\,(n^2 - 1)$, we get $= n^3 - n$
We need to get rid of $(n^3 - n)$ from the RHS.
$(1 - r)\,(n^3 - n) = 6\, \Sigma d^2$
We need to get rid of the 6 from RHS

Answer:
$$\Sigma d^2 = \frac{(1 - r)\,(n^3 - n)}{6}$$

---

13) B
Mr of $2KHCO_3 = 2(39 + 1 + 12 + 48) = 200$
Moles of $KHCO_3 = m \div Mr = 50 \div 200 = 0.25$
Moles of $K_2CO_3 = 0.25 \div 2 = 0.125$
Mass of $K_2CO_3 = 0.125 \times 138 = 34.5g$
The loss in mass is calculated as the mass of the gases (H_2O and CO_2) produced.
Loss in mass = Mass of $KHCO_3$ - Mass of $K_2CO_3 = 50 - 34.5 = 15.5g$

---

14) $x = 3$; $y = 1$

$2x - y = 5$
$y = 2x - 5$
Substitute this value of 'y' into the first equation.
$4x^2 + (2x - 5)^2 + 10\,(2x - 5) = 47$
$4x^2 + (4x^2 - 20x + 25) + (20x - 50) = 47$
$4x^2 + 4x^2 - 20x + 25 + 20x - 50 = 47$
$8x^2 - 25 = 47$
$8x^2 = 72$
$x^2 = 9$
$x = 3$

Substitute this value of 'x' into the second equation.
$y = 2\,(3) - 5$
$y = 6 - 5 = 1$

---

15) E

When the concentration of glucose is high, it gets converted to glycogen and stored in the liver. This is why glucose concentration must be high in the blood vessel connecting stomach & intestines and liver (2). This leaves us with options C and E.

Urea is a waste product produced by the breakdown of protein in the liver. Since the liver produces it, it must go back into the blood vessel leaving the liver (3). This leaves us with option E only.

16) 2m/s²

Downward force (Weight of object) = 20 x 10 = 200N
Upward force = 120 + 120 = 240 N
Resultant force = 240-200 = 40 N

Force = mass x acceleration
40 = 20 x a
a = 40 ÷ 20 = 2 m/s²

17) E

The mass number is given as 40. So the nucleus' relative mass must also be 40. Therefore, 1 is incorrect.

Noble gases have full outer shells. This element has an atomic number of 20.
So the electronic configuration of this element is 2, 8, 8, 2. This element does not have a full outer shell. So 2 is incorrect.

This element has 2 electrons on its outer shell. So, it will lose 2 electrons to become stable forming a positive ion. It will not form a negative ion. So 3 is not correct.

This element has 2 electrons on its outer shell. The number of electrons in an element's outer shell determines which group it belongs to. So this element is in group 2. Hence, 4 is correct.

Since it is in group 2, it must be a metal. 5 is not correct.

18) C

Volume of air inhaled in 1 minute = 500 x 14= 7000cm³ = 7dm³
Volume in 4 minutes = 7 x 4 = 28dm³
Volume of oxygen inhaled in 4 min = 0.21 x 28 = 5.88 dm³
Volume of oxygen exhaled = 0.16 x 28 = 4.48 dm³
Volume of oxygen absorbed by lung capillaries = 5.88 - 4.48 = 1.4 dm³

19) C

This is no longer on the BMAT syllabus.
However, you should have been able to at least eliminate options A and D.
This is because when levels of light are reducing, the pupil would get bigger (dilated) to allow more light to enter the eye.

To allow the pupil to dilate, the radial muscles need to contract and the circular muscles need to relax.

---

20) E
Parallel circuits rule: Voltage is equal in all branches.
Hence the two branches of the given circuit must have the same voltage.

Circuits rule: 'Resistance in series is always greater than resistance in parallel'

In branch 1, the resistors are in series. In branch 2, resistors are in parallel. Hence, branch 1 has more resistance than branch 2.
Since current is inversely proportional to resistance, branch 1 would have less current than branch 2.
Since voltage is directly proportional to current, voltage in branch 1 would be less than voltage in branch 2.
Hence V1 < V2

Branch 2 splits into two more branches. Hence, voltage splits into two more branches.
V2 = ½V3
R2 has double the voltage of R3. Hence, V2 > V3

Compared to R3, R1 has a higher voltage, as there are only 2 resistors in branch 1 whilst there are 3 resistors in branch 2.
V1 > V3

Order: V3 < V1 < V2

Hence, E is the answer.

---

21) 9
If you are not sure about solving powers, click here.
Let us solve the values given in the problem individually.

$32^{1/5} = \sqrt[5]{32} = 2$
$9^0 = 1$
$81^{3/4} = (\sqrt[4]{81})^3$
$\sqrt[4]{81} = 3$
$(\sqrt[4]{81})^3 = (3)^3 = 27$

So we have:
$^{2 \cdot 1}/_{27} = {}^3/_{27} = \frac{1}{9}$

We also have a $^{(-1)}$ power too.
So $(\frac{1}{9})^{1} = 9$

89

22) D

Let us start by identifying what the letters are.

The reaction is endothermic (energy is absorbed during the reaction) since products have more energy than reactants.

U represents the energy of the reactants

Z represents the energy of the products

V + W = activation energy

V represents the difference in energy between products and reactants

W is the part of the activation energy.

Y represents the activation energy needed if a catalyst was used.

X shows the route taken without a catalyst.

A:

Reaction is endothermic - Correct

V is the heat of reaction - Correct

X is the activation energy - Wrong

So, A is wrong.

B:

Products (Z) have more energy than the reactants (U) - Correct

X shows the route taken when a catalyst is present - Wrong

W is the activation energy - Wrong

So B is wrong.

C:

Y is the route taken when a catalyst is present - Correct

V is the heat of reaction - Correct

The reaction is exothermic overall - Wrong

Hence C is wrong

D:

X shows the route taken without a catalyst: Correct

V + W is the activation energy: Correct

V (the heat of reaction) has a positive sign: Correct

So, D is correct.

___

23) C

The equation for speed (c) with relation to wavelength (λ) and frequency (f) is:

$c = f \times \lambda$

$f = c/\lambda$

Speed of red light in glass = $\frac{2c}{3}$

Now, wavelength is directly proportional to speed. Since speed decreases, wavelength also decreases by the same amount.

Wavelength of red light in air = λ

Wavelength of red light in glass = $\frac{2\lambda}{3}$

Frequency = $(\frac{2c}{3}) \div (\frac{2\lambda}{3}) = \frac{2c}{3} \times \frac{3}{2\lambda} = \frac{6c}{6\lambda} = \frac{c}{\lambda}$

Since blue light refracts more than red light, speed of blue light in glass must be smaller than

speed of red light in glass.
c (blue light) < c (red light)
c (blue light) < $\frac{2c}{3}$
Hence, C is the answer

---

24) E

1 - Correct

The statement itself is correct. This requires pre-requisite knowledge of aerobic respiration and anaerobic respiration.

2 - Wrong

Anaerobic respiration does not require oxygen therefore causing an oxygen debt.

3 - Wrong

Water is also formed as a waste product by aerobic respiration.

4 - Correct

Active uptake (or active transport) requires ATP to work. ATP is formed by aerobic respiration. If aerobic respiration is reduced, then there will less active transport.

5 - Wrong

Since there is still some oxygen, aerobic respiration together with anaerobic respiration will occur.

6 - Correct

The statement itself is correct. This require pre-requisite knowledge of anaerobic respiration

1, 4 and 6 are correct. Hence, E is the answer.

---

25) B

The equations are made to confuse you.
Helium has a mass number of 4 because it has 2 protons and 2 neutrons.
We are given the information that 4 protons are used to make Helium.
Since a Helium atom has 2 protons and 2 neutrons, 2 out of the original 4 protons would have to be converted to 2 neutrons.
Therefore, $2p \rightarrow 2n + 2e^+$
Hence, B is the answer.

---

26) A

'a' is inversely proportional to 'b²'.
$a \propto \frac{1}{b^2}$
In order to turn this inequality into an equation, we need to use a constant (let us say 'k')
$a \propto \frac{1}{b^2}$

$a = k/b^2$

When a = 9, b = 4
$a = k/b^2$
$9 = k/4^2$
$k = 9 \times 4^2 = 9 \times 16 = 144$

When a = 4, b = ?
$a = k/b^2$
$b^2 = k/a$
$b^2 = 144/4$
$b^2 = 36$
$b = 6$

---

27) 5 seconds

Current (I) = Charge (Q) ÷ time (t)

$I = Q/t$

We know charge density = charge per unit surface area

Charge density (0.25) = charge ÷ unit surface area (0.04)
Charge (Q) = 0.25 x 0.04 = 0.01 C

$I = Q/t$

I = 2mA = 0.002 A
Q = 0.01 C
t = ?

$t = Q/I = 0.01/0.002 = 5$ seconds

---

1) For Knowledge (not part of the essay):
zeal means enthusiasm
anthem in this statement means success
epitaph in this statement means failure

In this statement Bryan is trying to say that our constant desire and enthusiasm to make things better will lead not our success but to our failure. Since this statement was made with reference to modern technology, I think Bryan is trying to say that technology has more disadvantages than advantages.

Certainly, technology has made our lives much easier and more comfortable. Some of the things that we are now capable of include: use of vehicles for transport, contact someone thousands of miles away in seconds, access the internet and increase farm produce using advanced machinery.
However, this has reduced our capability to do more manual work. More comfortable lives have led to an increase in diseases such as obesity and diabetes. The trend of a fast paced lifestyle is spreading. This causes people to suffer from stress, high blood pressure and mental health issues.
The use of technology such as vehicles and industrial machinery produces large amounts of carbon dioxide which is a greenhouse gas and contributes to global warming. Global warming is a major world issue which is causing the climate change. This will ultimately lead to the extinction of many species of animals and plants.

On the other hand, advancements in technology have allowed us to provide much safer and faster medical treatments. The invention of the electron microscopes allowed us to study life at the molecular level. We were then able to study DNA and how the cells of the body work together to keep us alive. X-rays and MRIs have enabled us to provide non-invasive treatments. Being able to look inside the body without surgery is truly remarkable. This has reduced chances of complications and treatments going wrong.

The most effective way to tackle the disadvantages of technology is to use technology only when we need it. Also, we can use renewable sources of energy to limit carbon dioxide emissions and bring global warming under control. Proper treatments should be provided for those who suffer from sever stress and blood pressure problems. The use of machinery in agriculture has allowed us to provide food supply for the growing world population.
Space exploration for all humans can also be made possible in the coming years, allowing us to find new habitable planets.

Our reliance on technology has increased over the years and without it, we would be unable to do a number of daily tasks. In my opinion, it would be impractical to think that we can stop the use of technology completely.

2) In this statement, Nietzsche is trying to say that higher education is not compatible with a greater number of students. According to Nietzsche, the word 'higher' in 'higher education' indicates that only those who are exceptional in academics should be allowed to continue higher education.

Higher education in today's world usually means going to university to get a degree. The government tries to ensure that every student gets equal opportunity to go to university. Based on merit, the university may or may not select a student for a particular course. However, it is ensured that every student in A levels has a right to at least apply for a place in university.

Higher education is different from further education. In the United Kingdom, further education is compulsory until the age of 18. Schooling is compulsory until the age of 16. After the age of 16, individuals may take up A levels or do vocational courses in colleges. Higher education, on the other hand, is optional and students who want to have careers in medicine, dentistry, law, business etc. need to take higher education.

Some people may argue that the ratio of number of students and lecturers is too great. These lecturers often feel overworked which is not ideal, as they have to teach hundreds of students everyday. Therefore, Nietzsche may be right in the sense that universities right now are overcrowded and the students there may not be as intelligent or talented.

Other may debate that many students just view higher education as a way to have a career and lead a comfortable life in the future. This certainly is inarguable and every person wants to have a secure life. Even though they may not be academically strong as other students in their group, they have a right to study whichever subject they wish to study if they meet all the required criteria to be enrolled in that course.

It may be possible to provide higher education for a large proportion of the population by opening more universities and higher education institutions. There should be sufficient staff to allow students to get ample support and guidance so that no one feels left out or isolated. This will also prevent staff members from feeling stressed and overworked. Since there has been a rise in tuition fees, this extra money can be used to provide students with all the facilities that they require throughout their higher education journey. This will allow the students to improve intellectually and academically.

---

3) The statement is trying to say that if a patient has given permission for a treatment and if the treatment does not go according to the plan, then it is not the doctor's fault.

There is a limit to how true this statement is. If the treatment has gone wrong due to the carelessness of a doctor, then it must be their responsibility. If a treatment was going well and an unexpected event caused the treatment to go wrong, then the doctor should not be blamed for this. A treatment always involves a team of medical staff, ranging from doctors to nurses.

The principle of consent is an important part of medical ethics. It must be voluntary, informed and the patient must be capable of giving the consent. The consent can be given either verbally or in writing.

A meaningful consent is one in which the clinician provides all the details of the treatment. This includes all the procedures, length of procedures, side effects, and possible complications and how their life would be after the treatment. This way, the patient can truly decide whether to accept the treatment or not. This respects their autonomy and is one of the benefits of patient consent.

The patient must be in the right state of mind and must be fully informed before a treatment can be given. Only the patient can give the consent and this consent must not be given due to pressure from the medical staff, friends or family. In some cases, parents may need to give consent for a child up to the age of 16.

Consent is not meaningful when a patient gives it due to pressure placed on them by medical staff, family or friends.

Clinical decisions should be made after the patient and their family have been fully consulted. The junior doctors must also consult a senior doctor. This will ensure whether the treatment being given to the patient is ideal or not. Once all the possible treatments have been discussed and the patient has given consent, the treatment can be started.

Ultimately, if patients have been fully informed about the treatment, complications, side effects and procedures, then it is their wish if they want to continue on with the treatment.

2007 Section 1

1) B

If height path the end of first year = 1m, then height at start of second year would also = 1m

Maximum theoretical height of tree = 30m
Difference between 30 and 1 = 30 - 1 = 29m
Since the growth will be 10% of the difference, growth in second year = 10% of 29 = 2.9 m

Height at the start of third year = 1 + 2.9 = 3.9m
Difference = 30 - 3.9 = 26.1m
10% = 2.61m

Total height = 3.90 + 2.61 = 6.51 m
To the nearest 10 cm, this will be 6.5 m

So the answer would be B

2) C

The text tries to compare WMD with other weapons and methods of war. We need a phrase that can fit a comparison.

A - Wrong
The text does not mention anything about morality of bombs and weapons. However, it is obvious that WMD are morally unacceptable since "200,000 people were killed".

B - Wrong
Again, we know that WMD is a serious threat, so this is wrong.

C - Correct
The text tries to say that there are other methods of war such as 'conventional bombing' which cause more widespread death than WMD.
Therefore, the correct phrase would be "But any idea that 'WMD' are unique dangerous is easily disproved".

D - Wrong
We know they are necessarily devastating given the statistics given.

3) C

Increase in sales:
Increase in sale of Asquith = 300,000 - 240,000 = 60,000
Increase in sale of Burton = 420,000 - 380,000 = 40,000
Increase in sale of Coleridge = 400,000 - 350,000 = 50,000
Increase in sale of Darwin = 250,000 - 150,000 = 100,000
Increase in sale of Elgar = 630,000 - 580,000 = 50,000

Main features of the pie chart:
Darwin will have the largest proportion (100,000 is the biggest) of the pie chart. This rules out D and E.

Coleridge and Elgar will have equal proportions (both have 50,000) of the pie chart. This rules out A and B.

We are only left with C. So this is the answer.

---

4) A
The argument made in the paragraph is "To reduce this loss of young life...the driving test should require a much higher level of mastery". We must find a statement which weakens this argument.

1 - Correct
The text says that the driving test should be made more difficult. However, it does not take into consideration that the young drivers may already be very skilled.

2 - Wrong
Having passengers in car during the accident is irrelevant to the argument made above.

3 - Wrong
The argument made is related to the difficulty of the test and not how much experience the drivers have.

Since only statement 1 is correct, A is the answer.

---

5) B
It would be easier if we round the number up or down.
Percentage occupancy:
Acute = $(^{90,000}/_{110,000})$ x 100 ≈ 81%

Geriatric = $(^{24,000}/_{27,000})$ x 100 ≈ 88.9%

Mental illness = $(^{28,000}/_{32,000})$ x 100 ≈ 87.5%

Learning disabilities = $(^{4100}/_{4900})$ x 100 ≈ 83.6%

Maternity = $(^{5700}/_{9100})$ x 100 ≈ 62.6%

The highest percentage occupancy is in Geriatric ward. So the answer is B.

---

6) B
Argument: "The best way to reverse the trend towards increasing violence...encourage more young men to take up boxing". The text makes a casual relationship between boxing and lack of violence. We must find a weakness in this statement.

A - Wrong
The text does not suggest that boxers are never aggressive. It just says that "Boxing is not primarily

about aggression" which means that boxing is not only about aggression.

B - Correct
The text makes a link between boxing and violence. It does not take into account the other leisure activities that could have caused a reduction in violence.

C - Wrong
The text just states that boxing can keep young men occupied during their leisure time. It does not, in any way, suggest that most young men lack discipline and self-restraint.,

D - Wrong
This is irrelevant as it does not matter why people take up boxing. This statement does not find a weakness in the argument.

---

7) E
P (first one being red) = $^3/_6$ = $^1/_2$
P (second one being yellow) = $^3/_5$
P (third one being red) = $^2/_4$ = $^1/_2$
P (fourth one being yellow) = $^2/_3$
P (fifth one being red) = $^1/_2$
P (sixth one being yellow) = $^1/_1$

$^1/_2$ x $^3/_5$ x $^1/_2$ x $^2/_3$ x $^1/_2$ x $^1/_1$ = $^6/_{120}$ = $^1/_{20}$

There are two situations which can satisfy our need:

R - Y - R - Y - R - Y
Y - R - Y - R - Y - R

Since there are two situations we need to multiply the probability we obtained by 2.
So probability of having alternate coloured flowers = 2 x $^1/_{20}$ = $^2/_{20}$ = $^1/_{10}$

---

8) C
The first line of the paragraph is the main line that will help to get the answer. It states that people who are unable to explain certain occurrences claim such occurrences to be paranormal. The writer. however, criticizes this thinking and gives examples of occurrences which were thought to be paranormal until explanations were given.

A - Wrong
This statement is too strong as the phrase "no truly" is used.

B - Wrong
This is too strong as well as the word "everything" is used.

C - Correct
This statement correctly summaries the paragraph. Since the author criticises the thinking of people, this is correct.

D - Wrong
We cannot infer this from the information given to us.

---

9) E
Cat weighs 2kg
Bodyweight (bw) = 2kg

Using the formula (30bw + 70), we get: (30 x 2) + 70 = 130

The cat has sepsis
Factor = 1.6
Using the formula for maintenance energy requirement, we get 130 x 1.6 = 208 kcal/day

The cat does not have hepatic or renal failure.
Using the 3rd table, we get that the cat needs 7g of protein per 100 kcal of energy.
The cat we are talking about needs 208 kcal of energy.

Protein needed = $7 \times (^{208}/_{100}) = {}^{1456}/_{100} = 14.56$ g of protein.
To the nearest 0.1g, we get 14.6g. So the answer is E.

---

10) C
Bodyweight (bw) = 1kg

Since the cat has a weight less than 2kg, basic energy requirement = 70 kcal

The cat is in post trauma.
So maintenance energy requirement for post trauma = 70 x 1.3 = 91 kcal/day

It is being fed CCFR which has 1 kcal/ml. Since the cat requires 91 kcal, it is being fed 91 ml of CCFR.
Protein in 91 ml CCFR = 0.06 x 91 = 5.46 g
The cat's protein intake is 5.46 g/day

Since the cat does not have hepatic or renal failure, its protein intake should be the maintenance level, i.e. 7 g/100 kcal
Recommended level = $7 \times (^{91}/_{100}) = 7 \times 0.91 = 6.37$ g

Difference = 6.37 - 5.46 = 0.91g

The cat's intake is 0.9 g too little.

---

11) C
A cat suffering from renal failure requires 4g/100kcal

FCH - 1.4g/1.3 kcal ≈ 107g/100kcal - This is far too high
CCFR - 0.06g/1 kcal = 6g/100kcal - This is far too high
ES - 0.04g/1 kcal ≈ 4g/100kcal - This is correct
OHN - 0.05g/1.1 kcal ≈ 4.5g/100kcal - This is high

99

EMF - 0.08g/2.1 kcal ≈ 3.8g/100kcal - This is little too low

---

12) C
Firstly, the ratio of protein to energy of CCFR = 0.06 : 1 = 6 : 100

Let volume of ES added = E

100 (0.09) + 0.04E = 100 (0.06) + 0.06E
9 + 0.04 E = 6 + 0.06 E
3 = 0.02 E
E = 150 ml

---

13) C
Let us use the bar for all ages which is about 18%.
Now remember, the graph is for x days **or more.**

If x = 3
The bar would be for 3 days or more.
Percentage should be = 10 + 6 + 4 + 3 + 11 = 34%
This is higher than 18%.

If x = 4
The bar would be for 4 days or more.
Percentage should be = 6 + 4 + 3 + 11 = 24%
This is higher than 18%.

If x = 5
The bar would be for 5 days or more.
Percentage should be = 4 + 3 + 11 = 18%
This is equal to 18% so this is correct.

If x = 6
The bar would be for 6 days or more.
Percentage should be = 3 + 11 = 14%
This lower than 18%.

So x = 5 and hence, C is correct.

---

14) A
The argument made in the text is the last line "...dogs' hearing abilities, the most likely explanation is that dogs can hear sounds...".
The answer would be a statement that strengthens this sentence.

A - Correct
The text says that almost 50% of the dogs were observed to be more active and anxious. If the other dogs had hearing impairment, they could not have heard the sound waves and hence did not show increase in anxiety.

B - Wrong
If this was true, then it does not explain why dogs showed an increase in anxiety.

C - Wrong
This does not strengthen the argument.

D - Wrong
This weakens the argument as this suggests that there are no sounds produced before an earthquake.

---

15) D
Let total number of votes = V
Ann received = ⅓V
Paul received = 116 votes
Elaine received = 116 ÷ 2 = 58 votes

We can form the equation:

116 + 58 + ⅓V = V
174 = ⅔V
V = (174 x 3) ÷ 2 = 261 votes

Ann received = ⅓ x 261 = 87 votes

So Paul won, Ann came second and Elaine came third
Paul won by = 116 - 87 = 29 votes

D is the answer.

---

16) A
The argument made in the text is the last line. "So it's clear that someone who is awarded a PhD in Sweden will live longer...if they had not studied for a higher degree".
We must find a flaw in this sentence.

A - Correct
The census is only for people aged 64. The above argument generalises people aged 64 with 'someone'. Hence this is the flaw.

B - Wrong
No mention of healthy lifestyles in the text.

C - Wrong
No mention of other countries in the sentence above. It specifies Sweden.

D - Wrong
Nothing mentioned about the health of people who are awarded PhD.

---

17) B

The argument: "It would not be surprising...that today's smokers find it harder to give up...inhaling more nicotine"

1 - Wrong
Even if the cigarettes burn at the same rate, the inhaler would take in the full amount of nicotine present in the cigarette. If there is 11% more nicotine now than before, this does not weaken the argument.

2 - Correct
If this is true, and a smoker smokes less cigarettes, then the amount of nicotine inhaled does not necessarily increase. This weakens the argument that smokers are inhaling more nicotine".

3 - Wrong
Irrelevant to the argument

Since only statement 2 is correct, B is the answer.

18) B

Number of slabs that can be bought with £140 = 140 ÷ 2.80 = 50 slabs

Dimensions of one slab = 70cm x 70cm = 0.7m x 0.7m
Area of 1 slab = 0.7m x 0.7m = 0.49 m²

Area that can be covered with 50 slabs = 50 x 0.49 = 50 x (49/100) = 49/2 = 24.5 m²

We know that the length covered is twice the width. Let the width be W. So length is 2W.
We can form the following equation:

2W x W = 24.5
2W² = 24.5
W² = 12.25
W = 3.5m

So we know the width covered by the slabs = 3.5m
Width of the whole patio= 5m
Width of flower garden = 5 - 3.5 = 1.5m

19) B
Let faster driver be A
Let slower driver be B

Time of A = 1 minute 6 seconds = 66 seconds
Time of B = 1 minute 10 seconds = 70 seconds

Lapping means that the faster driver covered 1 more lap than the slower driver.
Let number of laps covered by B = n
Number of laps covered by A = n + 1

After lap 1, A would be 4 seconds ahead, after 2 laps, A would be 8 seconds ahead etc.

In order for A to lap B, we need the following equation to be satisfied:

66 x (n + 1) = 70 x (n)
66n + 66 = 70n
66 = 4n
n = 16.5 laps

So number of laps covered by A = n + 1 = 16.5 + 1 = 17.5
Time taken by A to cover 17.5 laps = 17.5 x 66 = 1155 seconds
1155 seconds = 19 minutes 15 seconds.

---

20) D
Total number of men that were screened positive = 85 + 21 = 106 (Doesn't matter true or false. 106 were screened positive)
Percentage screened positive = ($^{106}/_{1000}$) x 100 = 10.6%

---

21) C
Percentage of men that have an abnormal PSA = 10% = 0.1
It is mentioned that of those with abnormal PSA, 26% will have cancer = 0.26
Men that will have cancer with abnormal PSA = 0.1 x 0.26 = 0.026 = 2.6%

Percentage of men that have normal PSA = 90% = 0.9
It is mentioned that of those with abnormal PSA, 26% will have cancer = 0.008
Men that will have cancer with normal PSA = 0.9 x 0.008 = 0.0072 = 0.72%

Total percentage = 2.6 + 0.72 = 3.32%
Hence the answer is C

---

22) A
PSA
Amount of false positives = 10% x 74% = 0.1 x 0.74 = 0.074
Amount of false negatives = 90% x 0.8% = 0.9 x 0.008 = 0.0072

DRE
Amount of false positives = (85 ÷ 1000) x 100 = 8.5% = 0.085
Amount of false negatives = (16 ÷ 1000) x 100 = 1.6% = 0.016

So PSA gives fewer false positives and fewer false negatives than DRE. So 1 is correct and A is the answer.

---

23) B
Probability of false positive on PSA = 0.1 x 0.74 = 0.074
Probability of false positive on DRE = (85 ÷ 1000) x 100 = 8.5% = 0.085

Probability of false positive on both = 0.074 x 0.085 = 0.00629

This gives us a percentage of 0.6% which is 6/100.
So B is the answer.

---

24) D
The conclusion is the last line: "So what really drives globalisation is the availability of cheap air travel and cheap shipping".
For the answer, we must look at the line "But globalisation must involve...which **is possible without** the communication provided by the internet".
From this, we can infer that internet is neither a necessary nor a sufficient condition for globalisation.

---

25) B
Total area of land required to produce 35 billion gallons of ethanol = 54000 + 334000 = 388,000 km^2 ≈ 390,000
Production per km^2 = (35 x 10^9 ÷ 390,000) = (35 x 10^5 ÷ 39) ≈ (35 x 10^5 ÷ 40) = 9 x 10^4 gallons
Production right now = 54000 x 9 x 10^4 = 486 x 10^7 = 4.86 x 10^9 ≈ 4.9 billion gallons

---

26) C
Let us look at the possible combinations:

M   N   P   ( )   ( )   O : First possibility of seats vacant next to each other

O   ( )   ( )   P   N   M : Second possibility of seats vacant next to each other

M   N   ( )   P   ( )   O : No seats vacant next to each other

O   ( )   P   ( )   N   M : No seats vacant next to each other

Total number of combinations = 4
Number of possibilities in which there are 2 seats vacant next to each other = 2
Probability = $^2/_4$ = $^1/_2$

---

27) C
Number of chickens that had metal rings = 50

The next day, number of chickens that had metal rings = 6
Probability = $^6/_{50}$
This probability must be used to find the total number of chickens.

The farmer must keep rounding the chickens up until one day, all 50 of the chickens rounded up have metal rings on them.
So the numerator will become 50 whilst the denominator will be the total number of chickens.
Let total number of chickens = C

$^6/_{50}$ = $^{50}/_C$
C = $^{(50 \times 50)}/_6$ = $^{2500}/_6$ = 416.66666 ≈ 417 chickens

28) A

The arguments made in the text is the correlation between light at night being left on and myopia. We must find a reason why this correlation could be wrong or unreliable.

A - Correct

This shows that myopia in children could have been caused by genetic inheritance instead of the light being left on.

B - Wrong

Irrelevant and does not give an explanation why the correlation could be unreliable.

C - Wrong

This statement does not discuss about the correlation made between night light and myopia.

D - Wrong

We cannot discuss about children from other parts of the world.

29) C

The argument the first line: "A conflict diamond..to finance the military rebellion of groups...and internationally recognised government". The conclusion suggests that human-cost for the war-torn countries is high. Therefore, we must find a weakness in this statement.

A - Wrong

It does not weaken the argument that the human cost for the war torn countries is high.

B - Wrong

This statement does not mention anything about the sale of diamonds.

C - Correct

This weakens the argument as it states that sales of diamonds actually brings revenue for the governments. This suggests that the sale of diamonds is actually beneficial to the governments.

D - Wrong

This highlights an irrelevant significance of diamonds and is out of context.

30) E

There is not particular method to solve these types of questions. It is advisable to skip these types of questions and not waste too much time trying to visualise each of the options.
When you have finished all of the other questions and have some time left, then cut the nets out of the question paper. (You can bring scissors to the exam but **please check with the exams officer first!!**)

OR

If you have unbelievable visualisation skills and you are sure that you can obtain the correct answer in a reasonable amount of time, then go ahead and answer the question.
When you cut the nets out, you will realise that nets Q and S can form squares but not P and R.

31) B
Step 1 : Using the Miller formula, we get the MHR = 217 - (0.85 x 60) = 217 - 51 = 166
Step 2 : Since the person is 55+, we need to add 4 beats. So we get 166 + 4 = 170
Step 3: Since the person is a swimmer, we need to subtract 14 beats. So we get 170 - 14 = 156 bpm

32) D
A - Wrong
We cannot confirm what are the exact values of wages. We are only given proportions of wages relative to the wages obtained by 15 year olds **for each sex**.

B - Wrong
Again, we do not know the exact wages.

C - Wrong
Not necessarily.
e.g. Wage proportion of women in education after 21 shows a downward trend.

D - Correct
The downward trend in the graph suggest this.

E - Wrong
We only have proportions of wages compared with the wages of 15 year olds. We are not given information about wages relative to people leaving education at 18.

33) C
The text and graph suggests a correlation between extra education and higher wages. However, this doesn't necessarily mean that the extra education **is the cause** of higher wages. A correlation cannot be confused with a change in factor 1 causing a change in factor 2.
The higher wages could have been caused by something else.
Hence, the assumption its that the higher wages are due mainly to the extra education.

34) B
The statement in the question suggests a correlation between trade union members and less financial returns for a degree.
Since we have the correlation, we need a cause for this link.

A - Wrong
Trade union membership is irrelevant

B - Correct
Since trade union members are graduates in low paying jobs, there is less financial return for a degree.

C - Wrong
This statement talks about people without degrees whist trade union members do have degrees.

D - Wrong
Age is irrelevant.

E - Wrong
Again, the number of trade union members is not a cause for the correlation.

---

35) D
Since older people left education **earlier** and earned more, our correlation is weakened.

A - Wrong
It would not have no effect. There would be some change in our graph since our correlation is weakened.

B - Wrong
The weakening of our correlation would not cause only part of the graph to change.

C - Wrong
The entire graph would not shift up for any reason as there has to be a point on 0%. This is to show wage proportions as compared to wages of 15 year olds.

D - Correct
Since our correlation is weakened, the gradient of the graph would be lower.

2007 Section 2

1) B
A - if it was A, there would be some protein present.
Water is reabsorbed and glucose is completely reabsorbed as we progress through the kidney. This would lead to an increase in the percentage of urea in the fluid. Since the percentage of urea is only a little, the sample must have been taken from an initial part of the nephron. Therefore, the answer is B.

---

2) B
This is quite an obvious answer. The answer is only asking for 1 statement which is correct. We know that 'x' is in period 2. This means that it has 2 shells with the first being completely full. Since, 'y' has six more electrons, it must have more than 1 shell as well. This means its first shell must also be full. First shell of any atom can only contain 2 electrons. Therefore, both 'x' and 'y' must have 2 electrons their first shells. Hence, they have the same number of electrons in the first shell.

---

3) α = 220, ß = 40
Background radiation = 20 units
α + ß = 280 - 20 = 260
We know that when the paper is placed, all α radiation will be blocked.

So,
ß + background radiation = 60
ß + 20 = 60
ß = 40
α + ß = 260
α + 40 = 260
α = 220

2007 Section 2 Q4

$$\frac{\left(1.5x + 1.5y\right)^2 \times 0.8z \cdot \sigma}{2P}$$

$$\frac{1.5^2 \left(x+y\right)^2 \times 0.8z \times \sigma}{2P}$$

$$\frac{1.5^2 \times 0.8}{2} = \frac{2.25 \times 0.8}{2} = 2.25 \times 0.4$$

$2.25 \times 0.4 = 0.9$
$0.9 = 90\%$
Hence, the percentage change is:
$90\% - 100\% = -10\%$
10% decrease

108

4) A

'x' increases by 50% = 1.5x
'y' increases by 50% = 1.5y
'z'decreases by 20% = 0.8z
'P' is doubled = 2P
'Q' remains the same = Q

5) E

Exhale now! You will notice that when you breathe out, your ribs come inwards and downwards. So 1 is correct.

However, the diaphragm does not contract while exhalation. It only contracts when you inhale. So 2 is incorrect.

Think about statement 3. Air goes from high pressure to low pressure. Since air comes out of your lungs into the surrounding air, it must be going from high pressure to low pressure. Therefore, pressure in lungs must be high when you exhale.

6) A

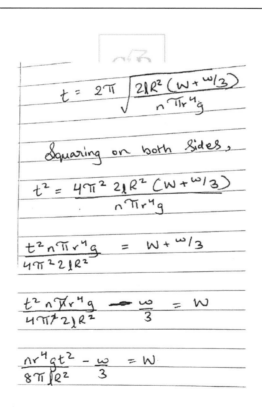

$$t = 2\pi \sqrt{\frac{2lR^2 (W + w/3)}{n\pi r^4 g}}$$

Squaring on both sides,

$$t^2 = 4\pi^2 \frac{2lR^2 (W + w/3)}{n\pi r^4 g}$$

$$\frac{t^2 n\pi r^4 g}{4\pi^2 2lR^2} = W + w/3$$

$$\frac{t^2 n\pi r^4 g}{4\pi^2 2lR^2} - \frac{w}{3} = W$$

$$\frac{nr^4 g t^2}{8\pi lR^2} - \frac{w}{3} = W$$

7) 300

Let number of turns on primary coil be = N1 = 1500
Let number of turns on secondary coil be = N2

Input voltage = V1 = 250V

Output voltage = V2 = $^P/_I$ = $^{(0.5 \times 1000)}/_{10}$ = 50 V

Formula:

$$\frac{N1}{V1} = \frac{N2}{V2}$$

$$\frac{1500}{250} = \frac{N2}{50}$$

N2 = 300

---

8) $^1/_3$

Oxidation number of O in Fe_3O_4 = (-2) x 4 = -8

Oxidation number of Fe = +8

Possible number of Fe^{2+} and Fe^{3+} atoms = 8 = (3 x 2) + (2)

So there are 2 Fe3+ atoms and 1 Fe2+ atom.

Fraction = $^1/_3$

---

9) B

You must remember that valves on both sides of the valves open and close at the same time. E.g. the left atria-ventricular valve closes at the same time as the right atrioventricular valve.

To pump blood to the lungs, the blood must be pumped by the right ventricle into the pulmonary artery. In order to do this, the atrioventricular valve on the right must close first. So, the left atrioventricular valve closes since they always close together. To pump blood to the pulmonary artery, the semilunar valve must open on the left must open, which means that the right semilunar valve must also open.

So we have:

Left and right atrioventricular valve open

Left and right semilunar valve closed

This corresponds to option B

---

10) D

To solve this question, we need to find out the moles of lead nitrate solution and add this value to the moles of potassium iodide solution.

Formula:

Moles = Volume x Concentration

Just by looking at the values given in the table, we can see that D would give the largest value. However, we will do the working to show you how to obtain D.

A = n[lead(II) nitrate sol] + n{2 x potassium iodide sol]

(0.005x2) + (0.01 x 2 x 2) = 0.03 mol

B = (0.0025x5) + (0.0025 x 2.5 x 2) = 0.0375 mol

C= (0.0075x3) + (0.005 x 5 x 2) = 0.0725 mol

D= (0.005x4) + (0.0075 x 5 x 2) = 0.095 mol

---

11) E
1 - Correct
A substance can lose heat energy without its temperature decreasing by changing state.

2 - Correct
Heat energy from the sun reaches Earth via vacuum.

3 - Correct
Intermolecular bonds between molecules of water are still unbroken at 100°C whilst they are broken in steam at the same temperature. This causes steam to have more heat energy than water at 100°C.

4 – Correct
Cooling or heating of water will always setup a convection current.

Hence, all statements are correct.

12) E
Mean number of steps (line in the box) = 50% = 850
Upper quartile value = 75% = 1000 steps

Percentage difference = 75 - 50 = 25%
So 25% (¼) of the people have taken steps between 850 and 1000.

Probability of first person being within the range = ¼
Probability of second person being within the range = ¼
Probability of third person being within the range = ¼

Probability of all three members being within the range = ¼ x ¼ x ¼ = □₆₄

---

13) C
Since they are standing on their toes, the point at which movement occurs is the the toes. Hence the fulcrum would be the toes.

The effort is made by the muscle. In this case, the muscle making the effort is the calf muscle.
The load is in between the effort and the fulcrum.
So C is the answer.

---

14) A
Reactivity increases down Group 1. So Caesium is most reactive element in group 1 that is given in the options.
Reactivity increases up Group 7. So Fluorine is most reactive element in group 7 that is given in the

options.
The reaction between Caesium and Fluorine will be very violent and hence, this will be the most exothermic reaction.

---

15) B
Infra**red** has a longer wavelength than ultra**violet**. You can know this by looking at the electromagnetic radiation.
Since, frequency does not change during refraction and $c \propto \lambda$, we can know that speed of red light would be higher than violet light in the air bubble. This means that red light will refract less than violet light.

Let us use elimination now.

Both red and violet light will follow the same path after they exit the bubble. Hence, C and D are wrong.

Since the incidence occurs at the top half of the bubble, the refraction will also occur in the top half of the bubble. Hence, E and F are wrong.
Since red light will refract less than violet light, B is the answer.

---

16) C
Substitute the values given in the options into the inequalities.

A - Wrong
When $x = -1$, and $y = -6$
$y \geq x^2 + 3$
$-6 \geq -1^2 + 3$
$-6 \geq 1 + 3$
$-6 \geq 4$
This is definitely wrong.

B - Wrong
When $x = 2$, and $y = -1$
$y \geq x^2 + 3$
$-1 \geq 2^2 + 3$
$-1 \geq 4 + 3$
$-1 \geq 7$
This is definitely wrong.

C - Correct
When $x = 1$, and $y = 6$
$y \geq x^2 + 3$
$6 \geq 1^2 + 3$
$6 \geq 1 + 3$
$6 \geq 4$
This is definitely correct. However, we also need to ensure whether the values can be substituted

into the second inequality or not.

$x \geq 1/y$

$1 \geq 1/6$

This is also correct. Hence C is the answer.

D - Wrong

When $x = 2$, and $y = 2$

$y \geq x^2 + 3$

$2 \geq 2^2 + 3$

$2 \geq 4 + 3$

$2 \geq 7$

This is definitely wrong.

---

17) D

This requires the knowledge of genotypes and the X and Y chromosomes.

Let the gene that causes the condition be X^a and the good gene be X^n

We need to starts with the male with NPS in the first generation. Since he has the condition, he must have the bad gene X^a.

He passes this gene to his daughters, 8 and 9. Since his daughters do not have NPS, the man's wife (6) must be have provided the good gene. Therefore, 8 or 9 have to be heterozygous.

The only pairs given with 8 and 9 are D and E. We now need to find out who out of 4 and 5 are heterozygous.

We know 3 does not have the condition. So he must have X^n. Since one of his sons has the condition, the mother (4) must have provided the faulty gene. She could not be homozygous with the faulty gene as this would cause her to have the condition. She could not be homozygous with the good gene as she would not have been able to get an offspring with a condition (but she does have a offspring with NPS). So 4 must be heterozygous.

D is the answer.

---

18) D

Mr of water in ice = (1 x 2) + (16 x 1) = 18

Moles = Mass ÷ Mr

Moles = $^6/_{18}$ = ⅓ moles

Moles of steam would be the same = ⅓ moles

1 mole of steam at R.T.P. has a volume of 24 dm³ (24,000 cm³)

⅓ moles would have = ⅓ x 24,000 = 8,000 cm³

---

19) 700 N
This requires the knowledge of Moments.

In order for the bar to be in equilibrium, Moments clockwise = Moments anticlockwise

Moments = F x perpendicular distance

Moments anticlockwise = 1.5 x 1000 = 1500 Nm
Moments clockwise = 100 x 4.5 = 450 Nm
Moments required = 1500 - 450 = 1050 Nm

Total length of the bar = 1.5 + 4.5 = 6 m
Since the weigh of the bar acts on the middle, the weight would act at (6 ÷ 2) = 3 m

Distance of weight from the pivot = 3 - 1.5 = 1.5m

Moments required = 1050 Nm
1050 = F x 1.5
F = 700 N
Hence weight = 700 N

---

20) A
This is a simple Pythagoras question.
Let long side = A = (6 + √5)
Let shorter side = B = (3 + 2√5)
Let third side = C

$A^2 = B^2 + C^2$
$C^2 = A^2 - B^2$
$C^2 = (6 + √5)^2 - (3 + 2√5)^2$
$C^2 = [6^2 + (2x6x√5) - √5^2] + [3^2 + (2x3x2√5) + (2√5)^2]$
$C^2 = (36 + 12√5 + 5) - (9 + 12√5 + 20)$
$C^2 = (41 + 12√5) - (29 + 12√5)$
$C^2 = 41 - 29 + 12√5 - 12√5$
$C^2 = 12$
$C = √12$
$C = √2 x 2 x 3$
$C = 2√3$

---

21) E
Platelets' role is in blood clotting. Since there is low blood platelet count, blood clotting would be low.

White blood cells play a role is in disease resistance. Since there a high percentage of white blood cells are abnormal, disease resistance would be low. Note that the question does not say that there is a high percentage of white blood cells. It says that a high percentage of white blood cells are abnormal.

Oxygen transport would be normal as there is nothing mentioned about red blood cells (which carry oxygen) in the question.

---

22) D

1 - Correct
I always remember it like this: Ammonia has fewer letters (in the word Ammonia itself) than Ammonium.
So Ammonia is NH_3 (1 less Hydrogen since it has fewer letters) and Ammonium is NH_4.
But everyone has different ways of remembering things!

2 - Wrong
Ammonia in water is a weak alkali. So the pH would be slightly higher than 7.

3 - Correct
Ammonia has a molecular structure.

4 - Wrong
Again, you must come up with things which help you remember concepts like these.
I remember it like this:
Acid has four letters and blue has four letters. So an acid turns blue litmus red.
So Alkali must be the other way round. Alkali turns red litmus blue.

5 - Wrong
Ammonia is a gas at room temperature.

6. Correct
Nitrogen atom covalently bonds to 3 Hydrogen atoms to form Ammonia.

Statements 1, 3 and 6 are correct. So D is the answer.

---

23) E
It is important that you understand that the artery is in a shape of a cylinder.
The cross-sectional area would be the area of the circle in the cylinder:

◎

Let us first list the information that we are given:

Length of artery = x
Speed of cell = V
Time taken by cell to travel length of artery = T
Let cross sectional area = A

Volume of blood flowing through the artery in one second = (Ax ÷ T)

So A = (VT ÷ x)

The units for this would be ml/mm. We know 1 ml = 1 mm³

So A = (VT ÷ x) x 10³

Hence, E is the answer.

---

24) A
Firstly, it is important that you realise that radius of cylinder = radius of hemisphere.

Volume of solid = Volume of cylinder + volume of hemisphere

Volume of cylinder = $\pi r^2 l$
Volume of hemisphere = $\frac{2}{3} \pi r^3$

$\pi r^2 l + \frac{2}{3} \pi r^3 = \pi r^2 (l + \frac{2}{3} r)$

If you multiply the whole thing by 3, you will get

$\pi r^2 / 3 (3l + 2r)$

Hence, A is the answer.

---

25) A
The top of the column is the location where the compound with the lowest boiling point separates. This needs to be 68°C.

The temperature in the flask should neither be 68°C nor 98°C. If it was 68°C, then this would mean that hexane would just start boiling. However, this cannot be true as we have obtained some distillate. It cannot be 98°C as this would mean that heptane would start boiling. This is not true. So it has to be 83°C.
Hence the answer is A.

---

26) C
Oestrogen - thickens the lining of the uterus.
Progesterone - maintains lining of uterus
If there is fall in progesterone, the lining of uterus would break down.

So the order must be:

Rise in oestrogen   High conc. of progesterone   Fall in progesterone conc.

So the answer is C.

---

27) D
1 - Correct
Since Cobalt-60 decays by beta, its atomic number increases by 1 and mass number stays the same.
Radiation by gamma does not affect the mass number nor the atomic number.
So after beta decay, the atom's mass number would be same = 59
Atomic number would be +1 = 27 + 1 = 28.
So Cobalt-60 is converted to $_{28}$Nickel.

2 - Correct
Since Cobalt - 60 decays by gamma, the tumour is attacked by gamma.

3 - Wrong
The radiation attacks all the cells and not just the malignant cells.

Since statements 1 and 2 are correct, D is the answer.

_____

2007 Section 3

1) With this statement, Sigerist is trying to say that new technological advancements in medicine are being rejected by certain parts of society. There could many reasons for this e.g. cultural or personal beliefs.

Our technology has allowed us to carry out blood transfusions with ease. However, Jehovah's Witnesses refuse any treatments that involve blood transfusion from one person to another. There are many ethical and legal issues involved in a situation where a patient, whose condition is life-threatening, is refusing a blood transfusion. The physician may be in a dilemma. In such a case, GMC's rule "make the care of your patient your primary concern" may contradict its other rule "you must respect a competent patient's decision to refuse an investigation or treatment, even if you think their decision is wrong or irrational".`
The use of embryonic stem cells is also rejected by some people as it involves destroying an early embryo which means potentially destroying a human life. On one hand, you can help treat diseases like diabetes but on the other hand, you are destroying human life. There is much controversy regarding this.

To address such problems, scientists, doctors and researchers must find new methods of solving ethical problems such as the ones mentioned above. Researchers have been studying ways to obtain embryonic stem cells without interfering with the life of the embryo. In order to tackle the problem of blood transfusion, doctors have looked towards methods such as cell salvage and vasoconstriction. Together with this, erythropoietin is used which stimulates red blood cell production for patients who are in need of blood transfusion due to anaemia.

Alternatives to such treatments must be found so that the rule "make the care of your patient your primary concern" is upheld.

---

2) Our intense medical researches and studies have enabled us to provide treatments which defy nature and have increased our life expectancy. This 'revolution' in medicine has changed our lifestyles and cause us to look at life and death from a different perspective.

These researches have not only allowed us to treat diseases but to also prevent them. Immunisation techniques are used to prevent people from being infected to dangerous diseases such as malaria or typhoid. These diseases were responsible for countless deaths before their vaccines were introduced. Other than this, the introduction of chemotherapy has cured many cancer patients. Even though cancer at its most dangerous level is not curable yet, we can still manage to save patients who have cancer at an early stage.

However, there are many negatives associated with longevity. Longevity is causing an imbalance between birth rate and death rate, resulting in overpopulation which is an unwanted situation. This overpopulation puts pressure on the limited resources that we have such as land and water. The trend of famines, droughts and poor quality of life is increasing in many parts of the world today. This also puts pressure on the government to provide free treatments for the increasing number of people suffering from medical conditions. Some may argue that the ageing population, which is a result of longevity, may also be seen as a burden on medical resources.

Attitudes towards life and death have also changed drastically after the 'revolution'. People are now more ensured that they will be able to recover if their medical condition deteriorates. The trend for carrying out dangerous activities such as skydiving and bungee jumping is increasing. Such activities may have been deemed ridiculous hundreds of years ago.

On the other hand, other may argue that longevity has not really shaken the foundations of societies. Our fears of falling fatally ill still exists even though we have treatments and vaccines. We still view death as something unwanted and scary. Longevity has not changed our normal behaviour and way of life. We still need basic necessities such as food and water to survive. People in third world countries still suffer from many problems so we cannot definitely say that their attitudes have changed towards life and death like people from first world countries.

---

3) This is a statement which relates to epistemology. This basically means a theory of knowledge with regards to its validity.
Let us break down the statement. "Irrationally held truths" means something that is probably factual but lacks proof that this truth is based on evidence and hence, cannot be justified. By "reasoned errors", Huxley is trying to say that if an individual has wrongly reasoned something, their logic is open to review for other researchers and scientists who can correctly give the accurate reasoning. Huxley, in this statement, is trying to convey the message that 'something that is probably factual but lacks evidence' is more dangerous than 'something that is wrongly reasoned but is open to criticism'.

With regards to medicine, there are and have been many cases where the treatment given to a patient lacked evidence to prove that it is effective. Homeopathy is classic example of this. It is widely regarded as 'natural medicine', mainly in the eastern part of the world. They are not yet proven to be effective by science. However, some people do claim that it has worked for them and hence, should work for everyone. Such claims could prove to be fatal for some patients. Homeopathy can probably just have a placebo effect on some people but it is not necessary that it will do the same on others. Therefore, some may argue that it is inappropriate to treat someone with a serious illness with homeopathy since there is no evidence that it is effective.

The contrary argument could be that 'it is better to arrive at the correct answer without any method or incorrect method than to arrive at a wrong answer using the correct method'. This would be preferable in many cases in medicine. Some would argue that it is better to treat a patient with an invalid method with little evidence if no valid treatments work for them.
An example of this is the Deep Brain Stimulation to treat Parkinson's disease. Even though we do not know the exact mechanism behind this treatment, we can see positive results in patients. Therefore, the argument here is that as long as treatments repeatedly produce positive results on patients, we do not really need to know how they work.

In order to turn something irrational to rational, scientific researches need to be carried out. This allows evidence to support any claim. The work of many scientists in the past had been disregarded because there were other 'explanations' for the phenomena occurring around us e.g. religious explanations. However, later on, those works of scientists were later found to be true using rigorous and logical scientific experiments and studies.

1) D
Let Malgons = X
Let Zanders= Y
Let Tvints = Z

Some of X are Y and all of Y are Z

A – Wrong
Only some the X are Y. So we cannot conclude that all of Y are Z. So All Zanders are Malgons is wrong.

B – Wrong
Some of X are Y and all of Y are Z. So SOME of X must be Z. However, we cannot say that ALL of X are Z.

C – Wrong
All of Y are Z does not mean that all of Z are Y. Similarly, we cannot conclude that all of Z are X.

D – Correct
Some X are Y and all Y are Z. So the section of Y that are X must also be Z. So we can conclude that Some of X are Z.

E – Wrong
Something definitely can be said. We described the relationship between X and Z in option D.

---

2) C
A – Wrong
Nothing is mentioned about humans in the text.

B – Wrong
The text does not say that traditional evolutionary theory is discredited. Some exceptions are seen when some birds carry out reciprocal altruism in order to receive paybacks in the future.

C – Correct
Some birds carry out reciprocal altruism in order to receive clear paybacks in the future from other birds. Therefore, the birds that do carry out reciprocal altruism do it for their own benefit. This is compatible with the traditional evolutionary theory, which suggests that animals are never altruistic.

D – Wrong
The paragraph is not only about birds. It just uses birds as an example of reciprocal altruism.

E – Wrong
'Survival of the fittest' is not relevant to this text.

---

3) B
Total number of screws = 68 + 10 + 2 + 22 + 20 + 18 + 10 + 54 + 46 = 250.
Number of 4 mm screws which have length of either 35 mm or 45 mm = 20 + 18 = 38
Probability = $^{38}/_{250}$ x 100 = 15.2 ≈ 15%

---

4) A
It is important to understand the text clearly.
The first line suggests that animal testing is justified because it has been involved in the major discoveries of drugs.
However, later on it says that every new drug requires animal testing and hence, every major discovery must have had to use animal testing at some stage.

The last sentence effectively tries to ask the question:
Is animal testing necessary for checking effectiveness of drugs or for being involved in major drug discoveries?

A – Correct
This completes the question above.

B – Wrong
We are not given any information about what the wonder drugs can cure.

C – Wrong
Nothing is mentioned about whether laws about animal experimentation need to change or not.

D – Wrong
Scientists ill-treating animals is not mentioned in the text.

E – Wrong
Nothing is mentioned bout drug testing on humans.

---

5) E
On the conventional die, the face opposite to 2 would be 5 (2 + 5 = 7).
We can conclude that the black die is conventional. The orientation of 6 compared to 4 and 3 shows that 4 and 3 are on opposite sides. Since 4 + 3 = 7, the black die must be conventional.
On the white die, the orientation of 6 compared to 4 and 5 shows that 4 and 5 are on opposite sides.
The faces around 6 are 5, 3, 4 and 1. The face opposite 6 must be the only remaining number: 2.
So face 2 is opposite face 6.

---

6) D
1 – Correct
The headline says that there is a growing **digital divide**. However, the survey is only for social networking sites. The survey may not support the headline because the older age group may be using other digital appliances.

2 – Correct
Results from one survey cannot be generalised for the whole population. Also, in order to show a increase in gap, we need results from an earlier survey for comparison.

3 – Wrong
Statement 3 doe not mention anything about the headline and the contents of the survey.

Since statements 1 and 2 are correct, D is the answer.

---

7) D
Total area of patio = 5 x 4 = 20 m²

Area of 1 big square tile = 0.6 x 0.6 = 0.36 m²
Number of big black tiles = 6
Total area of big black tiles = 6 x 0.36 = 2.16

Area of 1 small square tile = 0.4 x 0.4 = 0.16 m²
Number of small black tiles = 2
Total area of big black tiles = 2 x 0.16 = 0.32

Area of a rectangular tile = 0.4 x 0.6 = 0.24 m²
Number of small black tiles = 6
Total area of big black tiles = 6 x 0.24 = 1.44

Total black area = 1.44 + 2.16 + 0.32 = 3.92
Percentage of black area = $\frac{3.92}{20}$ x 100 = 3.92 x 5 = 19.6%

---

8) 39%
Relative risk in non-left-handed women = 1
Relative risk in left-handed women = 1.39
Increase = 1.39 – 1 = 0.39
Percentage increase = $\frac{0.39}{1.00}$ x 100 = 39%

---

9) B
Total number of incidences of breast cancer = 361 + 65 = 426 cases
We can use approximate values for the estimated person-years lived.
So total number of person-years lived = 153400 + 20000 = 173,400 years
Number of 1000 years = $\frac{173300}{1000}$ = 173.4 ≈ 170

$\frac{426}{170}$ ≈ $\frac{425}{170}$ ≈ 2.5

---

10) A

Total number of cases = 144 + 20 = 164

Total number of person years = 57500 + 7500 = 65,000 years

Number of 1000 years = $^{65000}/_{1000}$ = 65

$^{164}/_{65}$ = 2.5

11) D

We need to identify a reason, which can cause the increase in cancer risk in left-handed women as compared to right-handed women.

A – Wrong

This is actually a correct technique to use. The value for cancer risk in left-handed women will be relative to 1.

B – Wrong

This is not related to left-handedness

C – Wrong

We need to identify why cancer risk in left handed women is higher than risk in right-handed women. This does not give us a cause of the increased risk.

D – Correct

D gives us a cause for the correlation observed in the study.

E – Wrong

The relative risk takes into account the number of people present in the group so this does not cause any bias.

12) A

Total money gained in first football match = £1560

Let price of admission = P

So number of adults = $^{1560}/_{P}$

Price is reduced by 25% = 0.75P

Number of adults now = 140% of previous number of adults = 1.4 x $^{1560}/_{P}$ = $^{2184}/_{P}$

Total price = Admission fees x number of adults = 0.75P x $^{2184}/_{P}$

Price = 0.75 x 2184 = £1638

13) E

1 – Wrong

Even though the text mentions pressure groups, we cannot be certain that they have influenced some people's opinions.

2 – Correct
Some people clearly are mistaken. 40% of the people think that air travel contributes more to air pollution. However, that is certainly wrong as the statistics given in the first line clearly tell the opposite story.

3 – Correct
The last line proves this sentence correct. 47% think that air travel should be limited. However, only 15% are ready to travel less often. This means that 32% think that air travel should be limited but they do not want to travel less often.

Since statements 2 and 3 are correct, E is the answer.

---

14) A
Steve Cram broke the World Record and set a new world record of (3:29.67) in 07/1985.
The person who broke the record next is the one who got a faster time than him just after him. This is Said Aouita (in 08/1985).

The person who broke the record next is the one who got a faster time than Said just after him. This is Noureddine Morceli (in 07/1995).

The person who broke the record next is the one who got a faster time than Noureddine just after him. This is Hicham El Guerrouj (in 07/1998).

No one has got a faster time than Hicham after.
So the world record was broken 3 times after.

---

15) D
A – Wrong
The text does not specify whether the increases and decrease in proteins has a negative effect on human health. So A is wrong.

B – Wrong
The first and second lines do say that radiation from mobile phones are not strong enough (low level) but may affect cell behaviour. So we cannot say that there is negligible reaction.

C – Wrong
We cannot deduce this just from the fact that cell behaviour is affected. We do not know whether the changes in cell behaviour are harmful or not. So we cannot conclude that people should keep conversations to less than an hour or not.

D – Correct
The first and second lines do say that radiation from mobile phones are not strong enough (low level) but may affect cell behaviour.

---

16) D

The tank is cone shaped.

For the first part of the cone, for every increase in measurement on the dipstick, the volume of liquid is greater. So the first part of the graph would be accelerating.

As the dipstick goes down further, the volume of liquid would be fairly constant relative to the measurement of the dipstick (straight line).

However, at the final part of the cone, an increase in measurement on the dipstick would result in a lower increase in volume (decelerating part of the graph).

---

17) A

1 – Correct

The writer gives us numerous reasons as to why pop stars and celebrities should not promote awareness. However, if they are more influential than other people, then they should be the ones to do so. So this poses a challenge to the position taken by the writer.

2 – Wrong

Artists becoming more aware of themselves and raising more awareness does not necessarily challenge what the writer says.

3 – Wrong

Artists being paid was not one of the reasons why the writer takes such a position. The writer says that artists do a lot of things, which contribute to damage done to the environment. So this does not pose a challenge to what the writer says.

Since only statement 1 is correct, A is the answer.

---

18) A

Since volume of water is rounded to nearest 10 cm^3,

Minimum volume of water = 5

1% of 5 = 0.05

Since volume of each droplet is 0.02 rounded to the nearest 0.01, maximum volume of droplets = 0.025

To ensure we do not have more than 1%, we would need = $^{0.05}/_{0.025}$ = 2 droplets

---

19) 79

In the second to last paragraph, it states "those who took on more intense exercise – equivalent of running half an hour a day – extended their lives on average by **3.6 years**".

So we must add 3.6 to 75:

75 + 3.6 = 78.6 years

To nearest year, this is 79.

---

20) C

Running for 30 minutes = 3.6 years extra

Walking for 30 minutes = 1.4 years extra

Difference = 3.6 − 1.4 = 2.2 years
Percentage increase = $^{2.2}/_{1.4}$ x 100 = $^{220}/_{1.4}$ = 157%

---

21) C
Franco's study does not specify exactly when people started exercising.

A – Wrong
This is not a conclusion as there is no mention of when people started exercising.

B – Wrong
The statement cannot be a reason for the conclusion.

C – Correct
The evidence given in the passage does not support about when people start exercising.

D – Wrong
The statement given in the question does not explain anything

E – Wrong
The statement given in the question does not counter Franco's study

---

22) D
The conclusion is that people live longer if they exercise regularly.

A – Wrong
In order for he conclusion to be drawn, it is not necessary to assume that elderly and middle aged people have exercised throughout their lives.

B – Wrong
The passage does not indicate that people walk vigorously. So it is not necessarily needed to assume this.

C – Wrong
The passage does not assume that being overweight reduces lifespan. The passage just indicates a positive correlation between exercising regularly and longer lifespan. It does not necessarily need to assume a positive correlation between being overweight and reduced lifespan.

D – Correct
The text assumes that exercising is the main factor, which extends lifespan and does not consider other factors.

E – Wrong
Nothing is suggested about exercising delaying heart disease.

---

23) D

This one is a bit tricky, as you need to figure out the number of flashes for each of the letters first.

However, it is actually easier than you think.

The first two letters only require one flash each. There are only two lights, Red and Blue. So there can only be two combinations of single flashes.

The next four letters require two flashes each. There can be four combinations of two flashes: RB, RR, BR, and BB. So this will cover C, D, E and F

There can be eight combinations of three flashes: RRR, BRR, RBR, RRB, BBB, BBR, RBB, BRB.
So this will cover G, H, I, J, K, L, M and N.

For the remaining 12 letters, four flashes will be required.

Since each flash takes one second, total number of seconds:

$(1 \times 2) + (2 \times 4) + (3 \times 8) + (4 \times 12) = 2 + 8 + 24 + 48 = 82$ seconds

Between each of the 26 letters, there will be 25 one-second gaps. So time for gaps = $25 \times 1 = 25$ seconds
Total number of seconds = 82 + 25 = 107 seconds

---

24) D

A – Wrong
Option A unnecessarily makes a correlation between Standard of play in Britain declining and commitments outside the sport. Also, we cannot deduce that just because Young British competitors are affecting their own chances of wining, standard of play in Britain is declining.

B – Wrong
No information in the text suggests that British players are more interested in money.

C – Wrong
The text gives information about the friendliness of current players. However, we cannot deduce what the friendliness of past British players was.

D – Correct
The first line of the second paragraph is key to answering this question. It suggests that in the past, you could barely make a living by WINNING competitions. However, now you can make millions just by competing. Earning millions is more that what a person needs for a living.

E – Wrong
We have not information of outside commitments hindering British players' performances.

---

25) 245
Let number of representatives of Blue Party prior to General Elections = R
Number of representatives of Red Party prior to General Elections = 2.5R

In order for the lead to be reduced by 56, 28 seats must have gone to the only other Party, the Blue Party. The Blue Party will gain 28 seats and the Red Party will lose 28, decreasing the lead by 56.

So number of representatives of Blue Party after General Elections = R + 28
Number of representatives of Red Party after General Elections = 1.5 (R + 28) = 1.5R + 42

Total number of representatives will be the same prior to and after elections. So we get the equation:
R + 2.5R = 1.5R + 42 + R + 28
R + 2.5R − 1.5R − R = 70
R = 70
Total number of seats = R + 2.5R = 3.5R = (3.5 x 70) = 245 seats

---

26) D
1 – Correct
The last line of the texts suggests that only those who have committed crimes will commit sexual and violent crimes in the future and hence, only the DNA of those who have committed crimes should be kept. It does not take into account that some cases of sexual and violent crimes are first offences.

2 – Correct
The argument is that only the DNA of criminals should be kept because only they will commit sexual and violent crimes in the future. However, if a person is found not guilty and actually, they have committed it, then their DNA should be kept according to the writer's logic.

3 – Wrong
It does not matter how the crimes are solved. According to the writer's logic, criminals' DNA should be kept regardless.

Since statements 1 and 2 are correct, D is the answer.

---

27) C
Let speed of courier = S
Let speed of convoy = P

Tine taken to go back = 30 seconds = 1/2 x 1/60 = (1 / 120) hours
Time taken to come to the front = 3 minutes = (1 / 20) hours

Going back
we have to add the speed of convoy and courier to get the net speed.
1 km = ($^1/_{120}$) x (S + P)
S + P = 120

Return to front

Obviously, the speed of the courier must be more than speed o convoy.

We need to subtract the speed of convoy from speed of courier to get the net speed.

$1 \text{ km} = (^1/_{20})(S - P)$

$S - P = 20$

$P = S - 20$

Using simultaneous equations,

$S + P = 120$

Substituting value of P,

$S + (S - 20) = 120$

$2S - 20 = 120$

$2S = 140$

$S = 70$

---

28) E

Argument made in the text: "We…are facing a future of limited geographic mobility which will have social and economic consequences".

1 – Correct

The third sentence suggests that as climate change increases, flooding will also increase. So 1 is assumed.

2 – Correct

The last sentence suggests that we will face a future with less geographic mobility. This sentence assumes that no action will be taken to prevent flooding.

3 – Correct

The second sentence suggests that no one will buy homes, which are built in flooded areas. So this assumes that people will not want to move to areas, which are at risk of flooding.

All statements are correct, so E is the answer.

---

29) C

73 is not an option.

Two 37s is not an option. (Repetition cannot be a possibility)

By dividing the sequence multiple times, we can get the following:

34, 37, 4, 27, 33, 7

So 37 is the highest.

---

30) E

The argument is: "The road safety campaigners should turn their attention to finding ways of helping young people to drive safely...".

1 – Correct
The traps are placed in order to stop accidents. It doesn't matter whether or not it focuses on the most common cause of accidents.

2 – Wrong
This cannot be correct, as the fact that most common cause of accidents is driver under the age of 25 still remains a fact.

3 – Correct
Th last sentence of the text suggest that safe and responsible driving does not include obeying the speed limit.

Since 1 and 3 are correct, E is the answer.

---

31) B

Draw out F and G joined together. Check which one out of the remaining 5 options can be used to make a 3 x 2 x 2 cuboid.
The only piece capable of doing so is B.

---

32) E

The first bullet point says that cycling accounts for 1% of all trips.
The second bullet point says that a person makes 14 cycling trips per year.

1% = 14
100% = 14 x 100 = 1400 trips.

This is **per year** though.
We need divide this by 52 to get **per week**.

$$^{1400}/_{52} \approx {}^{1400}/_{50} = 28 \text{ trips}$$

This is approximately 27.

---

33) D

A – Wrong
We know 85% cycle less than once a week but we do not know what distance.

B – Wrong
We know an average person makes 14 trips a year. This equates to more than 1 per month. However, this is clearly wrong, as we cannot say this for every UK resident.

C – Wrong
We do not have enough info to conclude this.

D – Correct
15% cycles at least once a week
8% cycles at least once a month. Minimum 12 trips
69% cycle less than once a year. Maximum 1 trip
Remaining = 100 – 15 – 69 – 8 = 8%
So the remaining 8% must travel between 1 and 11 times a year.

---

34) C
Graph suggests that having more cars results in less cycling. The text indicates that having more income means you cycle more.
So income and cars have a negative correlation.
C is the only option, which gives an explanation for this negative correlation.

---

35) B

1 – Wrong
Males between 21-29 travel 78 miles every year and make 27 trips.
Number of miles per trip = $^{78}/_{27} \approx 2.6$ miles per trip

Males between 11-16 travel 74 miles a year and make 46 trips
Number of miles per trip = $^{74}/_{46} \approx 1.5$ miles per trip

Twice of 1.5 is 3. So 2.6 is not more than twice as much as 1.5

2 – Correct
Trips taken by males between 11 and 16 = 46
Miles travelled = 74
Miles per trip = $^{74}/_{46} = 1.5$ miles per trip

Trips taken by males between 17 and 20 = 29
Miles travelled = 59
Miles per trip = $^{59}/_{29} = 2$ miles per trip

So males aged 11-16 make more trips than males aged 17-20 but travel less miles per trip.

2008 Section 2

1) D
Active transport is the movement of molecules from an area of lower concentration to an area of higher concentration. This requires energy.

A – Wrong
CO_2 moves into the alveoli via diffusion. Carbon dioxide moves from an area of higher concentration (in blood in capillary) to an area of lower concentration (alveoli).

B – Wrong
This occurs via diffusion.

C – Wrong
This is the easiest to discard. There is little to no sweat on the skin surface, meaning that the higher concentration is in the sweat gland and lower concentration is on the skin. So this could occur by diffusion.

D – Correct
Reabsorption of glucose from kidney tubules requires movement of glucose form an area of lower concentration to an area of higher concentration. This requires energy; hence, active transport is used.

E – Wrong
Loss of urine occurs due to change in pressure.

F – Wrong
Same concept as A. Oxygen moves from an area of higher concentration (in alveoli) to an area of lower concentration (blood in capillary).

---

2) C
The (-3) charge on Y suggests that an atom of Y requires 3 electrons to fill its outer shell.
The ion Y^{3-} has an electronic configuration of 2, 8, 8.

Since Y has gained 3 electrons to form Y^{3-}, Y must have an electronic configuration of 2, 8, 5 (8 – 3 = 5)
The number of outermost electrons (in this case there are 5) determines which group the element belongs to. Y belongs to group 5.
The number of shells (in this case there are 3: 1st that holds 2 electrons, 2nd that holds 8 electrons and the 3rd which holds 5 electrons) determines which period the element is in. Hence, Y is in period 3. So the answer is C.

3) B

X decays into Y. Therefore, as time progresses, the mass of X will decrease and mass of Y will increase.

Half-life of X is 20s. After every 20s, mass of X will halve whilst mass of Y will double.

The question is asking us to identify how the mass of **Y** varies with time.

Graphs A, C and E show that as time progresses, mass decreases. Hence these are wrong.

Since all graphs show that there are 100g of X; after 20s, there should be 50g (half of 100g).

B
Mass at 20s = 50g (Correct)

D
Mass at 20s = 75g (wrong)

E
Mass at 20s = 100g (wrong)

---

4) D

$P = 2r^2t$

$P = 2 (3 \times 10^3)^2 (2.5 \times 10^4)$

$P = 2 (9 \times 10^6) (2.5 \times 10^4)$

$P = 5 \times 10^4 \times 9 \times 10^6$

$P = 45 \times 10^2$

$P = 4.5 \times 10^1$

---

5) C

Let the dominant allele be (T) and the recessive allele be (t)

	T	t
T	TT (33%)	Tt (66%)
t	Tt (66%)	tt (dead)

There can only be two genotypes present in live offspring. The foetus with genotype (tt) will die.

Possibility of homozygous dominant (i.e. TT) = 1/3 = 33%

---

6) E

Most efficient way: make equations.

Equation for CI

b = a + 2a + 2y

b = 3a + 2y

Let us check which of the options can satisfy the equation above.

A – Wrong

$8 \neq 3 + 6$

B – Wrong

$8 \neq 3 + 8$

C – Wrong

$4 \neq 3 + 2$

D – Wrong

$16 \neq 6 + 12$

E – Correct

$16 = 6 + 10$

---

7) B

n^{th} term = $\frac{n}{n + 1}$

So, $(n + 1)^{th}$ term is:

$$\frac{n + 1}{n + 1 + 1}$$

$$\frac{n + 1}{n + 2}$$

Difference between $(n + 1)^{th}$ term and nth term:

$$\frac{n + 1}{n + 2} - \frac{n}{n + 1}$$

$$\frac{n + 1 (n + 1) - n (n + 2)}{(n + 2)(n + 1)}$$

$$\frac{n^2 + 2n + 1 - n^2 - 2n}{(n + 2)(n + 1)}$$

$$\frac{1}{(n + 2)(n + 1)}$$

134

8) A

Speed of lift = 0.4 m/s

Time the load is lifted for = 5s

Distance (height above ground) = 0.4 x 5 = 2 m

Potential energy = m x g x h = 100 x 10 x 2 = 2000J

Hence statement 1 is correct.

In order to lift the load the tension in the cable at point P must be equal to the weight of the load.

Weight of the load = 100 x 10 = 1000N

Hence tension at P = 1000N

So statement 2 is wrong.

The question states that the load is being lifted at a constant speed. This means that there is not change in speed. So there is no acceleration at all. Statement 3.

___

9) D

A – Wrong

Oxygen demand is more than oxygen demand. Since there is a lack of oxygen, anaerobic respiration must be taking place. However, there is still some aerobic respiration taking place as oxygen is present. Therefore, this is wrong as both aerobic and anaerobic respiration is taking place and not only anaerobic.

B – Wrong

This is clearly wrong as the line for oxygen demand is higher than oxygen supply.

C – Wrong

Again, both anaerobic and aerobic respiration is taking place. This is wrong.

D – Correct

Both aerobic and anaerobic respiration always take place.

___

10) C

A – Wrong

This is methane (a type of alkane). This can be produced.

B – Wrong

This is ethene (a type of alkene). This can be produced.

C – Correct

This is not a possible product or a molecule. 6 carbon atoms cannot be attached to 16 hydrogen atoms. The maximum number of hydrogen atoms that can bond with 6 carbon atoms is 14.

D – Wrong

This is octene (a type of alkene). This can be produced.

E – Wrong
This is dodecene (a type of alkene). This can be produced.

---

11) D
Remember! A beta particle is a fast moving electron. A neutron turns into a proton and an electron.
The proton stays in the nucleus and the fast moving electron is emitted.

1 – Wrong
The electron comes from the nucleus.

2 – Wrong
A neutron (not a proton) turns into a proton and a electron.

3 – Wrong
A neutron turns into an electron and a proton.

4 – Correct
The mass number is changed. A neutron changes into an electron and a proton. The proton remains in the nucleus. Since the mass number is proton + neutrons, it remains unchanged.

Hence D is correct, as only statement 4 is correct.

---

12) E
We must first identify the products that will be formed due to the enzyme action.

Carbohydrase will break down carbohydrates to form sugars such as glucose
Protease will break down proteins to form amino acids
Lipase will break down lipids to form fatty acids and glycerol

Sugars such as glucose will not cause a change in pH because it is neither basic nor acidic.
Amino acids have an acidic element to their molecule structure so they will cause the pH to decrease.
Fatty acids will also cause the pH to decrease.

So products of protein and lipid will cause a change in pH.
Hence the answer is E.

---

13) D
Try drawing out graphs on the question paper to identify which of the combination will transform PQR to LMN.

You will realise that the triangle only needs a rotation of 270° about the origin

The answer is 2 followed by 5.

Rotation of 90° followed by a rotation of 180° will cause it to be rotated by 270°, which is what is needed.

---

14) D

A – Wrong
The addition of a catalyst never affects the equilibrium of a reaction.

B – Wrong
Number of moles of gas on left side = Number of moles of gas on right side. Hence, decreasing pressure will produce no change.

C – Wrong
Number of moles of gas on left side = Number of moles of gas on right side. Hence, decreasing pressure will produce no change.

D – Correct
Decreasing temperature will favour the exothermic reaction (forward reaction which reduces amount of CO)

E – Wrong
No nitrogen is involved so it would have no effect on this reaction.

---

15) F
Graph Z is the easiest one to identify.
There are two options given to us for Z: kinetic energy and weight.
Kinetic energy depends on velocity. As velocity changes, kinetic energy changes.
However, weight remains the same no matter what.
Since Z has a straight horizontal line (there is not change), Z must be weight.

Since the car reaches a terminal speed after a while, Y must be velocity. The graph Y becomes flat after a while.

X could either be resultant force or acceleration. However, the only combination possible is option F. Therefore, X must resultant force.

So the answer must be F.

---

16) A
This is rather an easy question.
Since the triangle is right-angled, we can use the formula: Area = 1/2 x base x height

Area = $0.5 \times (4 - \sqrt{6}) \times (6 + \sqrt{6})$
Area = $0.5 \times [4 (6 + \sqrt{6}) - \sqrt{6} (6 + \sqrt{6})]$ (Multiply $(4 - \sqrt{6}) \times (6 + \sqrt{6})$ together first)
Area = $0.5 \times [24 + 4\sqrt{6} - 6\sqrt{6} + 6]$

Area = 0.5 x [18 – 2√6]
Area = 9 – √6

---

17) B
- In order to produce a reflex, a stimulus must be present. So 1 is the stimulus.
- Receptors sense the stimulus. So 2 must receptor.
- The receptors send electrical impulses to CNS via sensory neurones. 3 must be CNS.
- CNS then relays these electrical impulses to the muscles via motor neurones. 4 must be muscle.
- Muscle then contracts to produce a movement (response). 5 must be response.

Hence B is correct.

---

18) F
1 Hydrogen atom is removed and replaced with -$CONH_2$ group.
Formula with 1 less hydrogen atom = C_nH_{2n+1}
When the -$CONH_2$ group is added,

The number of carbon atoms increases by 1
Number of Hydrogen atoms increases by 2
Oxygen atom is added
Nitrogen atom is added

New formula would be:

$C_{(n+1)}H_{(2n+3)}ON$

Hence F is the answer.

---

19) C
A bearing is an angle measured clockwise from the north direction.
It is much easier to draw a diagram to show the situation.

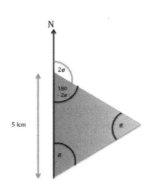

138

The original bearing is 'ø' and when the person walks 5 km towards the north, the bearing becomes 2ø.

The angle inside the triangle adjacent to the 2ø, must be equal to 180° – 2ø

The sum angles inside the triangle, which are opposite to the 2ø, must be equal to 2ø (Exterior angle rule).

Since the initial bearing was ø, the third angle = 2ø – ø = ø

Since there are two angles, which are the same in a triangle, the triangle must be isosceles.

2 equal sides = 5 km

Let the third side = T

Split the isosceles triangle in to two right-angled triangles. The third side must be 0.5 T

Cos ø = $\frac{adjacent}{Hypotenuse}$ = $\frac{0.5T}{5}$

5 cos ø = 0.5 T

T = 10 cos ø

---

20) F

Since the switch is now closed, current is likely to flow through the wire with the switch rather than through resistor Y. Current always flows where there is least resistance.

Current in Y = 0

Hence voltage in Y = 0

Now voltage is shared amongst two resistors (X and Z) instead of three.

Since X and Z are identical resistors, they would have the same resistance as well.

Voltage in Z = 12 ÷ 2 = 6V

Voltage in Y when switch was open = 12 ÷ 3 = 4V

Current in Y when switch was open (given) = 20mA = 0.02A

Resistance in Y when switch was open = V ÷ I = 4 ÷ (0.02) = 200Ω

Each resistor therefore has a resistance of 200Ω.

When the switch is closed, there are two resistors. Hence total resistance = 200 x 2 = 400Ω

When switch is closed, Current = 12 ÷ 400 = 0.03 A = 30mA

Hence F is the answer.

---

21) B

1 – Correct

Blood from lungs flows to the heart. The heart then pumps the blood to the rest of the body. From the body, blood then flows back to the heart followed by the lungs. So the blood from lungs flows through the heart twice before coming back to the lungs.

2 – Wrong

Lungs receive all the blood from the heart. When the heart then pumps blood to the body, it is distributed to different parts. Hence, kidneys do not receive all of the blood that flows to the lungs.

3 – Correct

Lungs receive all the blood that flows in the liver.

4 – Wrong
The liver can obtain blood from two ways.

Statements 1 and 3 are correct. Hence, B is correct.

---

22) D
A – Wrong
Diamond does not have any intermolecular forces. It only has intramolecular forces which are strong covalent bonds between carbon atoms.

B – Wrong
In graphite, each carbon atom is only bonded to 3 other carbon atoms.

C – Wrong
Diamond is the hardest material on the planet whilst graphite is really soft.

D – Correct
All of these allotropes have only carbon atoms. They do not have any other elements. Therefore, they will react with O_2 to give the same products.

E – Wrong
Graphite can conduct electricity.

---

23) C
We first need to find the work done by the braking force. The work done would be equal to the energy of the lorry. Since the lorry was moving, its energy would be kinetic energy.
So work done by braking force = KE of lorry
Work = $\frac{1}{2}(mv^2)$
We know that work done = force x distance
Force x distance = $\frac{1}{2}(mv^2)$
Distance = $mv^2 \div 2F$
Hence, C is correct.

---

24) A
$(x = a)$ and $(x = b)$
$x - a = 0$
$x - b = 0$

We can write: $(x - a)(x - b) = 0$
$x^2 - xb - ax + ab = 0$

We know $(ab) = 3$
$x^2 - xb - ax + 3 = 0$
$x^2 - x(a - b) + 3 = 0$

140

We know (a + b) = 5 [since we have (a − b), the sign on 5 becomes negative]
$x^2 - x(-5) + 3 = 0$
$x^2 + 5x + 3 = 0$

Hence A is correct.

---

25) D
The man has chromosomes X and Y. He must have received the Y chromosome from his father and the X chromosome from is mother.
Since the condition is only carried on the X chromosome, his mother must carry the recessive allele.
His daughter must have the chromosomes X and X. The daughter must have received one X chromosome from her father (the man in the question) and one from her mother. Therefore, she must also carry the recessive allele.
So D is correct.

---

26) C
Volume of sulphuric acid = 12.5 = $0.0125 dm^3$
Concentration of sulphuric acid = 2 mol/dm^3
Moles of sulphuric acid = concentration x volume = 0.0125 x 2 = 0.025 mol

Molar ratio (XOH: H_2SO_4) = 2:1
Moles of XOH = 0.025 x 2 = 0.05 mol
Mass of XOH = 2.8g ≈ 3

Mr of XOH = mass ÷ moles = 3 ÷ 0.05 = 60
Ar of H = 1
Ar of O = 16
Ar of X = 60 − 1 − 16 = 43

This is closest to 39. So C is the answer.

---

27) C
Time taken by sound to travel in steel = t
Let time taken by sound to travel in air = t + 1.5
The distance travelled by the sound in steel would be the same as distance travelled by sound in air.
Distance travelled by sound in air = (t + 1.5) x 300
Distance travelled by sound in steel = t x 4800

300t + 450 = 4800t
450 = 4500t
t = 0.1 s
Distance of train = 4800 x 0.1 = 480 m

141

1) The statement made by Lord Kelvin is suggesting that any qualitative knowledge that cannot be quantified is not sufficient, as knowledge should have both qualitative and quantitative aspects.

This applies to medicine and biology quite well. Whilst doing experiments in school, we make a link between an independent variable and a dependent variable. We then measure the dependent variable using apparatus such as a stopclock, measuring cylinder or water baths. This way, we obtain quantitative data to prove our hypothesis. Without the results, we would not be able to provide sufficient evidence for the link that we made between the independent variable and the dependent variable.

A good example of this is the yeast experiment to measure the rate of respiration. We use a stopclock to measure the time taken for methylene blue to change colour. We can then use the times to calculate the rate of respiration.
In medical treatments, the use of blood reports is important for the identification of certain conditions. We need to quantify the RBC count, platelets count etc. to be able to recognise the condition a patient is suffering from.

However, we are still unable to quantify many results in medicine. This mainly applies for psychiatric disorders such as depressive disorders, neurodevelopmental disorders and personality disorders.

2) This statement is easier to understand compared to some of the previous Section 3 questions.

Life always has a natural end. If one or more of a patient's systems fail to function effectively and are in critical condition, then there is a high chance that they are getting closer to death. The statement is just trying to say that it is better if doctors, medical staff, the patient's friends and family realise this fact.

Firstly, it is the duty of the doctor to inform a patient fully about how critical their condition is as it is vital for the patient to know how ill they actually are. Patients must be informed about what complications or suffering they may face during and after the treatment. This will allow them to make an informed decision.

A patient's desires, quality of life, treatment burdens and cost of treatment must be taken into consideration to ensure which is the best course of treatment.

Some may argue that if there are no benefits to the patient or if the suffering and burdens outweigh the benefits, then doctors may decide to prevent the patient from enduring pain unnecessarily. Not being aware of this will only cause pain to the patient.

There are many ethical issues related with such situations. "Make the care of your patient your primary concern" is contradictory. The treatment may have a low chance of being successful but there is still hope. If, however, the patient is suffering throughout this treatment, then this would not be caring for them, keeping in mind that the treatment has a high chance of being unsuccessful. This causes the medical staff and the family to be in a state of dilemma and confusion.

In such cases, some people may say that if the patient is capable of making an informed and calculated decision regarding their life, then everyone should respect that decision because ultimately, it is their life.

---

3) Enthusiasm and superstition in this statement refers to an individual's personal beliefs and faith. Smith is trying to convey the message that science has the power to disprove any superstitions that a person may have.

Science is based solely on proof and evidence. Results of decades of rigorous research and studies have provided evidence for most of the phenomena that occur around us. Science is rational and logical because it does not involve any emotions or enthusiasm.

Superstitions, on the other hand, are irrational because they arise from a person's emotions and feelings. There is no evidence to prove their existence. They often cloud a person's mind and personality, which results in irrational behaviour and actions.

An example of this could be why people get diseases. Science proved that a person gets a disease either due to an infection, genetics or lifestyle. Superstitious people on the other hand believe that people get sick due to their wrongdoings, which is not backed by any evidence. Therefore, science acts as an antidote against enthusiasm and superstitions.

Others may argue that science cannot prove everything and there is an extent to what science can explain. For example, how the universe began is still a mystery to us. In such cases, science is limited.

---

1) 15 monarchs
From the graph, you can see that 20 on the x-axis corresponds to 20 on the y-axis. 40 on the x-axis corresponds to 35 on the y-axis. In total there were (35-20 = 15) 15 monarchs that reigned for 20 years or more but less than 40 years.

2) B
A – Wrong
The passage does not suggest whether the Health secretary is right or wrong. They just gave their opinions.

B – Correct
This is correct according to what is mentioned in the last paragraph.

C – Wrong
Nothing related to costs is mentioned in the text so this is irrelevant.

D – Wrong
This option is too strong and cannot be justified. "Strongly opposed" is too strong as opposed to "whether childbirth should take place away from the hi-tech environment."

E – Wrong
This cannot be proven and there is no mention of progress of mothers and their babies.

3) D
To solve this, we need to compare each graph with other graphs.
Let's start with graph A. Compare A with B, C, D and E. A has 2 bars different than B, 3 bars different than C, 2 bars different than D and 4 bars different than E.

Since the graphs cannot have more than 2 different bars, A, C and E cannot be the correct graphs.
Comparing B with E, 4 bars are different. Hence B cannot be the correct one either.

This leaves us with D. If we compare D with the other options, we will see that:
D has 2 different than A, 2 different than B, 2 different than C and 2 different than E.
D is the only graph which has no more than 2 different bars when compared to the other options.

4) B
A – Wrong
Even though the statement in option A is correct, the passage mainly focuses on the heavy snowfall. Therefore, this option is incorrect as it is irrelevant.

B – Correct
It is clearly implied in the text that the government needs to take into consideration the

probability of an event happening. Since the probability of heavy snowfall is low, the government was right not to spend large amounts of money into preventive measures.

C – Wrong
This is irrelevant and an easy option to eliminate. The last sentence clearly states that pandemics and asteroids are considered "low risk but high cost" and hence, the government should not be spending lots of money on these issues.

D – Wrong
The text clearly says that likelihood of a prolonged period of heavy snow in the UK is very low. So the government should not have spent more on the precautions.

E – Wrong
There is no mention of any compensation that should be made by the government.

5) E
1 birthday each calendar month = 12 x 1 = 12
3 pairs of twins only in April = 3 x 2 = 6
2 pairs of twins not in April = 2 x 2 = 4
We must take into consideration that the two pairs of twins that are not born in April must have been born instead of a single grandchild's birthday in the other months.
The year COULD be as follows:
January – one of the pair of twins = 2
February – second pair of twins = 2
March – 1
April – three pairs of twins = 6
May – 1
June – 1
July – 1
August – 1
September – 1
October – 1
November – 1
December – 1

This gives us a total of 19 birthdays. However, if we look at the third paragraph, it says "twice as many granddaughters as grandsons"
We cannot divide 19 into a ratio of 1:2
We cannot divide 20 into a ratio of 1:2
However, we can divide 21 into a ratio of 1:2
Hence 21 is the answer. (14 granddaughters and 7 grandsons)

6) G
1 – Correct
Since there are campaigns, young people are more informed of the harms of ecstasy. If there were no campaigns, more young people would start using ecstasy. Hence, this is correct.

2 – Correct

This is correct as it compares ecstasy only to horse riding. It assumes that since horse riding is not dangerous and still causes so many deaths a year, it should be compared to ecstasy as ecstasy causes fewer deaths per year. It assumes the horse riding is not dangerous even though it still is slightly dangerous.

3 – Correct

This is the easiest weakness to identify. Let us say 60 people take ecstasy. The passage states that 30 people die from ecstasy. This means that 50% die by using ecstasy.
On the other hand, let us say 1000 people do horse riding out which 100 people die. This percentage is quite small compared to the percentage of deaths caused by ecstasy. Hence, this option is correct.

Since all three statements are correct, G is the answer.

---

7) C

It is clearly stated that the total cost would be the same regardless of whether they choose Gold membership or Silver membership.
Let the number of times the equipment is hired = 'N'

For Gold membership, total cost would be = £100 + (0.50N)
For Silver membership, total cost would be = £80 + (1N)
100 + 0.5N = 80 + 1N
20 = 0.5N
N = 40 times

Total cost for either Gold or Silver membership = 80 + 40 = £120
If the person had continued their Bronze membership, their total cost would have been:
70 + (3 x 40) = £190
Savings = £190 – £120 = £70
Hence, C is correct.

---

8) B

Number of people that witness a crime = 1119 ≈ 1100
Number of people that did not report = 421 ≈ 420
Number of people that do not think the crime is unimportant = 133 ≈ 130
0.75 x 420 = 315
0.50 x 420 = 210
0.25 x 420 = 105
Since 105 < 130 < 210, then probability is greater than 0.25 but less than 0.33

---

9) G

1 – Wrong

We cannot determine what the percentage would be next year

2 – Wrong

The statement does not state that the residents have witnessed or experienced crime. Hence, we cannot say anything about the thinking of those who did not witness or experience crime.

3 – Wrong
We cannot determine the number of people that gave more than one reason for being dissatisfied with the police.

No statements are correct. Hence G is the answer.

---

10) A

A – Correct
If the police had been unsuccessful at dealing with crimes in the past, then the public would lose their trust and cause them to not report crimes.

B – Wrong
It does not matter whether there is a high level of crime or low level of crime. The level of crime should not influence why the public does not report any crime.

C – Wrong
There is no mention of drug related crime in the text.

D – Wrong
There is no mention of crimes against criminals.

E – Wrong
There is no mention of paperwork and bureaucracy in the police force in the text.

---

11) D
There are 2 ways to solve this:
a. Imagination
b. Cutting the shapes out from the paper (as long as you don't need the back page anymore). However, PLEASE ask your admissions officer before bringing a pair of scissors to the exam. Options A, B and C cannot be folded in half to form a right-angled triangle.

---

12) B
The argument made in the text is the last line "The government should act now…make slimming pills object to the same strict controls as medicines"
Our answer must be a statement, which weakens this argument.

A – Wrong
People wasting their money on many products besides slimming pills does not weaken the argument that the government should take action.

B – Correct
If the government **is** introducing legislation then it weakens the argument that the government **should** take action.

C – Wrong
Even if the statement that the demand for slimming pills is likely to grow was true, it does not weaken the argument that the government should take action.

D – Wrong

Even if this was a cost to the taxpayer, the government would be saving people's money from being wasted on ineffective slimming pills.

E – Wrong

This statement cannot be correlated with the argument made.

---

13) E

Instead of going straight into the answer, let us examine each of the options given.

A – Wrong (1 and 2)

Even if both bags each started off with more than two marbles, it would still be possible to obtain the results that we got. 1 marble from the left bag was put into the right bag and then one from the right bag was put into the left. **A is wrong.**

B – Wrong (1 and 3)

Let us say the left bag starts with 4 marbles and all of them were green.
Let us say that the right bag starts with 2 (both red) marbles.
If one green was taken from the left bag and placed in the right bag and then one red from the right bag was placed in the left, we can still obtain the results that we did. Option **B is wrong.**

C – Wrong (1 and 4)

Let us say the left bag starts 4 marbles in (2 green, 2 red)
Let us say the right bag starts with 2 red marbles.
If one green was taken from the left bag and placed in the right bag and then one red from the right bag was placed in the left, we can still obtain the results that we did. **C is wrong.**

D – Wrong (2 and 3)

Let us say the left bag starts 4 marbles in (4 green)
Let us say the right bag starts with 4 marbles. (2 red, 2 green)
If one green was taken from the left bag and placed in the right bag and then one green from the right bag was placed in the left, we can still obtain the results that we did. (Right can have 2 green and 2 red). **D is wrong.**

E – Correct (2 and 4)

Let us say the left bag starts 2 marbles in (1 green, 1 red) [It doesn't matter how many there are in the left]
Let us say the right bag starts with 4 marbles. (4 red) [more than 2 and same colour]
If one green was taken from the left bag and placed in the right bag and then one red from the right bag was placed in the left, we cannot obtain the results that we did. There won't be half green and half red. **E is correct.**

F – Wrong (3 and 4)

Let us say the left bag starts 2 marbles in (2 green) [same colour]
Let us say the right bag starts with 2 marbles. (2 red) [same colour]
If one green was taken from the left bag and placed in the right bag and then one red from the

right bag was placed in the left, we can obtain the results that we did. There will be half green and half red in the right bag. **F is wrong.**

---

14) A

The focus of the text is that the colour of the interrogation room can **help** the police to be more successful during interrogation. However, there is **no guarantee** that it **will** make an interrogation more successful.

A – Correct

An interrogation is successful when the truth is extracted from people. The first sentence "A Welsh police station…. intention of improving the success of interrogation" suggests that colour which can help people to be more at ease can improve success in interrogation.

B – Wrong

It is not implied that psychologist have full knowledge of what happens in an interrogation but the text just says that psychologists know which colours help people to be more relaxed. More relaxed people will tend to speak more truthful.

C – Wrong

Colour psychology can aid the interrogation process but it is in no way implied that it is the **best way.**

D – Wrong

This is not an assumption.

E – Wrong

The text clearly does not assume that a good interrogation technique is less useful than colour psychology. It only suggests that colour psychology can help people to be more relaxed.

---

15) D

The easiest way to solve this is by identifying the squares, which are not connected to any other squares with names on them (vertically, horizontally or diagonally)

The first row (at the top) does not have any such squares.
The second row does not have any such squares.
The third row has two such squares (the fifth and the last squares). Let us call them A and B.
The fourth row has one square (the last square). Let us call it C.
The fifth has one (the last square). Call it D.
The sixth has none.
The seventh has two (the third and the fourth squares). Call it E and F.
The eighth has one (the seventh square). Call it G
The ninth has none.
The tenth has none.

We must also now remember that the two squares that will be chosen must not touch each other.

149

Pairs available:
1. A and B
2. A and C
3. A and D
4. A and E
5. A and F
6. A and G
7. B and D
8. B and E
9. B and F
10. B and G
11. C and E
12. C and F
13. C and G
14. D and E
15. D and F
16. D and G
17. E and G
18. F and G

(E and F), (B and C) and (C and D) cannot be pairs as these squares touch each other.

So there are 18 pairs available.

16) s = 38, b = 36
Number of gold medals won by US = 36 (first graph)
Number of total medals won by US: 110 (second graph)
Number of bronze and silver medals = 110 − 36 = 74 medals
If gold (g) = 3, silver (s) = 2 and bronze (b) = 1
US has a score of 220
We can get the following equation:
3g + 2s + 1b = 220
(36 x 3) + 2s + 1b = 220
2s + 1b = 112

We know that s + b = 74
Using simultaneous equations, we get:
2s + 1b = 112
s + b = 74

s = 38
Since s + b = 74, b = 36
s = 38
b = 36

17) 13
Australia is not plotted on the first graph. This means that they must have won less gold medal

than Germany. Since we need the minimum silver medals, we must assume that Australia won 1 less gold medal than Germany. So Australia won = 16 – 1 = 15 gold medals.

$g + s + b = 46$

If a gold media equates to 3, silver medal equates to 2 and one bronze medal equates to 1

$3g + 2s + 1b = 89$

Using simultaneous equations, we get:

$3g + 2s + 1b = 89$
$g + s + b = 46$

$2g + s = 43$

Since number of gold medals = 15, we get:

$2(15) + s = 43$
$s = 13$

---

18) B
Number of gold medals won by China = 51
Total number of medals won by China = 100
Ratio = 51 : 100 ≈ 1:2

Number of gold medals won by US = 36
Total number of medals won by US = 110
Ratio = 36 : 110 ≈ 1:3

Number of gold medals won by Russian Federation = 23
Total number of medals won by Russian Federation = 72
Ratio = 23 : 72 ≈ 1:3

Number of gold medals won by GB = 19
Total number of medals won by GB = 47
Ratio = 19 : 47 ≈ 1 : 2.5

GB would still be ranked 2nd above US and Russian Federation.

---

19) F
1 : Correct
3 gold + 5 silver = (3 x 3) + (5 x 2) = 19
Population of Norway = 4.6 million
Medals per million = 4.5
19 ÷ 4.6 = 4.5 per million

2 : Wrong
Population of Iceland = 0.3 million
Even if all 3 medals were bronze, weight = 3
Number of medals per million = 3 ÷ 0.3 = 10
The figure given is 6.8 which is wrong

3 : Correct
Population of Slovenia = 2 million
Number of medals per million = 4.5
Total weight of medals won = 4.5 x 2 = 9

Medals won by Slovenia = 6
1 gold medal = 3
Weightage of the other 5 medals = 9 -3 = 6
This could be 1 silver, and 4 bronze
(2 x 1) + 4 = 6

So this scenario could be correct.

Statements 1 and 3 are correct. So F is the answer.

---

20) C
Total weightage won by GB = 98
Population of GB = 62 million
Weightage per million of GB = 98/62, which is more than 1 but less than 2
Total weightage won by US = 220
Population of US = 306 million
Weightage per million of US = 220/360, which is much less than 1
Total weightage won by Russian Federation = 139
Population of Russian Federation = 142 million
Weightage per million of Russian Federation = 139/142, which is less than but very close to 1

1 : Correct
GB has a value less than Slovenia's value but more than US's value

2 : Correct
Russia has a value less than 1 (1 is the value of a bronze medal)

Both statements are correct. So C is the answer.

---

21) 50 g
Maria takes a drink which has a volume of 500 ml and 4.0 Joules
100 g of the powder has 2.0 Joules
So Maria's drink out have 200 g of the powder (2 x 2 = 4 J)

The nurse has 2 drinks (let us say A and B)
A has 1.5 Joules = $^3/_4$ of 2 Joules

$^3/_4$ of 100 g = 75 g
A has 75 g of the powder.

B has 2 Joules in 400 ml
Since B has 2 Joules, it must have 100 g of the powder.
Concentration = 100 g per 400 ml = 1 g per 4 ml
Since the Nurse pours 300 ml of B into A, mass of powder transferred = $(^{300}/_4)$ x 1 = 75 g

Total mass of powder in new drink = 75 + 75 = 150 g
Since Maria needs 200 g, the Nurse must add = 200 – 150 = 50 g

---

22) A

1 – Correct
The line "The most valuable kind of praise is that which the recipient knows to be appropriate." suggests that the recipient is able to assess which kind of praise is appropriate and deserved and which praise is not.

2 – Correct
The line "Praise should only be given to the extent that it is deserved" suggests that the person giving the praise can also assess whether praise is deserved or not.

3 – Wrong
This is neither implied nor assumed by the text. The paragraph does not mention anything about any duty.

4 – Wrong
The text does not say that self-esteem benefits anyone. Hence this is irrelevant.

Statements 1 and 2 are correct. So A is the answer.

---

23) E
Let us first figure out what each digit means.
The first three digits meant the month of operation of the clinic.
The 4th and 5th digits mean which date of the month the sample is taken. In the example given, 04 in 12404360 means the 4th of September.
So, 04 = 4th

The 6th and 7th digits mean the number of samples taken in that month.
36 in 12404360 means 36th sample.

The last digit is a digit, which makes the sum of the eight digits a multiple of 10.
The sum of the first seven numbers in 12404360 = 1 + 2 + 4 + 0 + 4 + 3 + 6 = 20. This figure is already a multiple of 10 and hence the last digit must be 0.
In 25431438, the sum of the first seven digits = 22
In order to make this a multiple of 10 (30), we need to add 8 to 22 in order to make 30.

Let us find out which month's reference number is given in the options.

Since, 124 is September,

A – 254 must be July. July has 31st
B – 264 must be May. May has 31st
C – 274 must be March. March has 31st
D – 284 must be January. January has 31st
E – 294 must be November. November does not have 31st. Hence, this is the correct answer.

---

24) E
1 : Wrong
We only have the stats for teenage pregnancies. We do not have the statistics for sexual activity of those who do and do not drink. There is a difference between sexual activity and teenage pregnancies.
2 : Wrong
Teenage pregnancies will still occur even if there was stricter control on alcohol sale to young people. However, we cannot assume that teenage pregnancies will be fewer or more.

3 : Wrong
We do not know how many girls have consumed alcohol before the age of 16. We only know that 40% of teenage girls **who became pregnant** had consumed alcohol.

No statements are correct. So, E is the answer.

---

25) A
Firstly, there are no two points of the same value on the same axis. Hence, neither of the axes can be 'Number with special education needs' since there no two 12s.
So D definitely cannot be the answer.

Option A: If x-axis was absenteeism rate and the y-axis was percentage with 5 or more A* to C.
The highest value for absenteeism is 9.1 meaning it would be the furthest right point on the x-axis. Percentage with 5 or more A* to C with an absenteeism rate of 9.1 is 40.
There are 3 points higher than this point on the graph whilst there are 3 values higher than 40 56, 70, 76) in the column 'percentage with 5 or more A* to C'.
So A could potentially be correct.
Let us look at the other options.

Option B: If x-axis was number of pupils and y-axis was percentage with 5 or more A* to C.
The highest value for number of pupils is 202 meaning it would be the furthest right point on the x-axis.
Percentage with 5 or more A* to C with 202 pupils is 56.
However, there are 3 points higher than this point on the graph whilst there are 2 values higher than 56 (70, 76) in the column 'percentage with 5 or more A* to C'. So B is wrong.

Option C: If x-axis was number of pupils and y-axis was absenteeism rate.
The highest value for number of pupils is 202 meaning it would be the furthest right point on the x-axis.
Absenteeism rate for 202 pupils is 8.3.

However, there are 3 points higher than this point on the graph whilst there are 2 values higher than 8.3 (8.8, 9.1) in the column 'percentage with 5 or more A* to C'. So C is wrong.

Hence the answer is A.

---

26) E

The main conclusion of the passage is the first line of the second paragraph "But these surprising…make them their slaves." The next line indicates that the butterfly, which is an endangered species, can survive by exploiting the ants.

A – Wrong

No sentence in the text indicates that making sounds will eventually cause them to become extinct or die out.

B – Wrong

The Rebel's large blue butterfly is an example used in the text to show how the ants can get exploited. However, it is not mentioned that it is the most notable species to exploit ant colonies.

C – Wrong

It is mention that ants even slaughter their own young to feed the caterpillars when food is scarce. However, they do not always slaughter their own young. They only do it when food is scarce. Also, this is not the main focus of the text. The main focus is that some insect species can exploit ants.

D – Wrong

There is no mention of threats from parasites.

E – Correct

From the information given, we can deduce that some species, which are endangered, can exploit ant colonies in order to aid their own survival.

---

27) B

The first thing we need to find out is how many tokens does it take to get a free meal.

Since Tim receives 7 tokens **every** day, the cost of a free meal must definitely be more than 7 tokens otherwise he would never run out.

If the cost of a free meal is 8, then the net number of tokens lost each day = 8 – 7 = 1
If the cost of a free meal is 9, then the net number of tokens lost each day = 9 – 7 = 2

Since Tim had 20 tokens on Monday 1st and the cost of each meal is 8, he would have had 12 tokens by next Tuesday which means he would have had enough for a meal. However, this is not the case, as he did not have enough tokens to get a meal on Tuesday.

If the cost of a meal was 9 tokens, he would have had 8 tokens left. This would not be enough for him to buy a meal. Hence cost of a free meal = 9 tokens.

On Wednesday next morning, he would have 8 + 7 = 15 tokens.
After free meal = 15 − 9 = 6 tokens

On Thursday morning, he would have 6 + 7 = 13 tokens.
After free meal = 13 − 9 = 4 tokens

On Friday morning, he would have 4 + 7 = 11 tokens.
After free meal = 11 − 9 = 2 tokens

On Monday morning, he would have 2 + 7 = 9 tokens.
After free meal = 9 − 9 = 0 tokens

On Tuesday morning, he would have 0 + 7 = 7 tokens.
Since he does not have 9 tokens, he would not be able to get a free meal.

Hence the next day of the week in which Tim cannot get a free meal is Tuesday.
So B is the answer.

---

28) B
The main condition to sustain life, according to the text, is that the Earth-sized planets should be at the right distance from their star. The conclusion of the text is the last sentence "So if the Kepler…life on planets other than Earth". The flaw in the argument is that the text assumes that, Earth-sized planets that are at the right distance from their star, is the only condition needed in order to sustain life.

A – Wrong
Earth-sized planets is not the complete criteria for life. The right distance from the star is.

B – Correct
The text assumes that the right distance from the star is the only criteria needed in order to sustain life.

C – Wrong
This is a fact rather than an assumption. The Kepler telescope will definitely help to find planets that are the right distance away from their star.

D – Wrong
This is a fact rather than an assumption. Highly sensitive equipment is needed to detect the existence of planets.

E – Wrong
The presence of liquid water is definitely not sufficient for life to exist. So this is not an assumption.

---

29) D
Starting from left to right on each row, let us label each of the tiles.

A	B	C	D
E	F	G	H
I	J	K	L

1. A is unique
2. B is similar to F and H
3. C is similar to E and G
4. D is unique
5. I is similar to J
6. K is unique
7. L is unique

So there are 7 different patterns. So D is the answer.

---

30) D

The conclusion is in the last sentence "…the more systematic and organised…produce more valid explanations…to support decisions".

A – Wrong
The text does not discard common sense explanations and does not say that no decisions should be made based on common sense explanations.

B – Wrong
The text does not specifically suggest that Human nature has always preferred informal observation to scientific study. It only says that people have always been curious to explain the things happening around us.

C – Wrong
It is not suggested that scientists discount all common sense explanations. It only suggests that observations carried out by scientists are often more valid than common sense explanations.

D – Correct
This statement neither totally discounts common sense explanations nor does it say that common sense explanations are better than scientific ones. Hence, this is correct.

E – Wrong
The text does not suggest that scientific explanations support common sense explanations.

---

31) D

The lift is currently on floor 7. Floor 4 and 10 are equal distance from the lift. However, there are more stops requested on floor 10 side. So the lift moves in the direction of floor 10. As soon as the lift moves, a request for floor 7 comes.

However, the lift will carry on moving towards floor 10. When it stops on floor 10, the closest stop will be floor 7. So it moves towards 7.

After 7, 4, then 0 then towards 14 and then 16. So 16 will be the last stop.

All floors visited before 16 = 10, 7 (again), 4, 0, and 14

It will visit 5 stops before 16. So the answer is D.

32) C
For the first stage, we can round up or down the decimals to nearest unit.
Cattle: 440 − 490 = -50
Percentage change = $(^{50}/_{490})$ x 100 ≈ 10%

Pigs: 70 − 90 = -20
Percentage change = $(^{20}/_{90})$ x 100 ≈ 20%

Potatoes: 117 − 81 = 36
Percentage change = $(^{36}/_{81})$ x 100 ≈ 50%

Wool: 7.4 − 7.7 = -0.3
Percentage change = $(^{0.3}/_{7.7})$ x 100 ≈ 4%

Vegetables: 38.3 − 34.5 = 3.8 = 4
Percentage change = $(^{4}/_{34})$ x 100 ≈ 12.5%

So the biggest percentage change is seen in potatoes.

33) C
On the graph, you can clearly see that the closest pairs of bars are (1994, 1997) and (1995, 1996). The bar for 1998 can be seen discreetly as being small compared to all other bars.

Farm crops:
The figures of 1994 and 1997 are fairly far apart so this cannot be correct.

Horticulture:
The figures of 1994 and 1997 are fairly far apart so this cannot be correct.

Livestock:
The figures of (1994,1997) and (1995, 1996) are fairly close so this can potentially be correct.

Products:
The figures of all 5 years are very close, meaning that all bars should roughly be the same height. However, the bars shown on the graph show that not all 4 bars are of the same height. Hence this cannot be correct.

34) D
A – Wrong
If this were true, the output of flowers should have been more than vegetables in 1998. However, this is not true.

B – Wrong
We do not know the price of pigs and cattle. We only know the total output of these livestock. The difference between values could have been purely due to the amount of each livestock bought.

C – Wrong
We cannot infer that the pound was definitely stronger in 1980 than in 1998 based on the information provided to us.

D – Correct
There was a decrease in output of Farm crops during the time period but a large increase in output of horticulture. Since 'volumes of production have not changed', this suggest that a higher percentage of farm crops than horticulture must have been sold overseas.

E – Wrong
We are unable to infer the other factors, which could have influenced the output (such as volume of potatoes produced).

35) E

Output change from 1997-1998 = 237.4 – 245.1 = (-) 7.7 ≈ 8

Percentage change = $(8/245) \times 100 \approx 1/30 \times 100 = 3.3\%$

Percentage of sheep exported = $(3.3/5) \times 100 = 66\%$

This is closest to 63%. Hence, E is the answer.

2009 Section 2

1) C
Firstly, we must find out what D is.

	R	R
r	Rr	Rr
r	Rr	Rr

There is 100% chance that D is heterozygous.
Now if E is homozygous recessive, this would be the case:

	R	r
r	Rr	rr
r	Rr	r

There is a 50% chance that F would be homozygous recessive

If E was heterozygous, this would be the case:

	R	r
R	RR	Rr
r	Rr	rr

There would be a 25% chance that F would be homozygous recessive.
Hence, this corresponds to option C in the given table.

2) E
Only molecules that contain a double bond can participate in addition polymerisation. Such molecules have twice as many other atoms as there are carbon atoms. e.g. C_3H_6 , C_4H_8
The only molecules that contain twice as many other atoms as carbon atoms in the molecule are $C_{24}H_{48}$, $C_4H_6Cl_2$ and $C_8H_{12}Cl_4$

3) C
Resultant force = 900N - 600N = 300N upwards
Direction would be upwards as the drag force (upward force) is greater than weight (downward force).
We know that Force = mass x acceleration; Acceleration = Force/Mass

Force = 300N
Mass = 60kg (given in question)
Acceleration = Force ÷ Mass = 300 ÷ 60 = 5 m/s^2

---

4) C
Total number of balls = $(x + y + z)$

Probability of the first ball being red $= \dfrac{x}{x + y + z}$

Since the ball is replaced, the total number of balls will remain the same, i.e., $(x + y + z)$

Probability of the second ball being blue $= \dfrac{y}{x + y + z}$

Probability of first ball being red and second ball being blue:

$$\dfrac{x}{x + y + z} \times \dfrac{y}{x + y + z}$$

$$\dfrac{xy}{(x + y + z)^2}$$

---

5) E
A - Wrong
Clones will not always have identical external features due to the environment.

B - Wrong
This is not necessarily true as twins show some differences between each other. They can also be non-identical

C - Wrong
Clones can occur naturally in the environment too in asexual reproduction.

D - Wrong
If mutation did occur, there would be some sort of variation in their DNA and genes. Mutation is the complete opposite of clones.

E - Correct
Clones contain identical DNA and show no variation whatsoever.

---

6) B
Out of all the options, SiO_2 is the only molecule, which can form a giant structure. Silicon is a large molecule as has more diffuse valence orbitals. This allows it to form giant structures.

7) E

A - Wrong

Voltage = current x resistance = amp x ohm. Hence amp/ohm is wrong.

B - Wrong

We cannot prove voltage = coulomb per joule

C - Wrong

joule/second is the unit of power

D - Wrong

We cannot prove voltage = newton per coulomb

E - Correct

We know power = voltage x current. Voltage = power/current = watt/amp = watt per amp

---

8) B

Let the dashed line be called L.

Let length of each side = 1

We first need to calculate the length of half of the diagonal of one of the faces.

Let diagonal be = D

Using Pythagoras,

$D^2 = 1^2 + 1^2$

$D^2 = 1 + 1 = 2$

$D = \sqrt{2}$

Half of D = $\sqrt{2}/2$

Imagine the dashed line forming a triangle with the vertex just below.

Using Pythagoras,

$L^2 = 1^2 + (\sqrt{2}/2)^2$

$L^2 = 1 + 2/4 = 1 + 1/2 = 1.5$

$L = \sqrt{1.5} = \sqrt{3}/2$

So dashed line = $\sqrt{3}/2$

---

9) D

A - Wrong

The table shows that when number of mutant alleles increase from 0 to 1, the risk value also increases from 1.0 to 1.5 in the light drinker category, and from 4.0 to 4.5 in the heavy drinker category.

B - Wrong

There is a positive correlation between heavy drinking and light drinking. Risk values are much higher for heavy drinkers than for light drinkers.

C - Wrong
Addition of a mutant allele increases the risk factor by 0.5. Heavy drinking increases the risk factor by 3.0.

D - Correct
Heavy drinking is the main factor for increasing risk as discussed in option C.

E - Wrong
Presence of 2 mutant alleles in light drinkers increases the risk factor by 0.8.
Presence of 2 mutant alleles in heavy drinkers increases the risk factor by 2.0.

---

10) E
Mass of CO_2 produced = 4.77 g
Mr of CO_2 = 12 + 16 + 16 = 44
Moles = Mass ÷ Mr = $\frac{4.77}{44}$ ≈ 0.1

Molar ratio of $(C : CO_2)$ = 1 : 1
Moles of C = 0.1 mol

Mass of C = 0.1 x 12 = 1.2 g

Percentage = $\left(\frac{1.2}{2}\right)$ x 100 = 60%

This is closest to 65% which is option E.

---

11) C
The detector 2 graph shows us that the background radiation is 20 counts.
In order to find the half-life, we need to find the initial count rate of the source.
This is = 220 - 20 = 200
The half-life of the activity would be the time taken for the count rate to become $\left(\frac{220}{2}\right)$ + 20 = 120

This is 2.4 hours.
α - radiation stops after 1-2 cm of air. Therefore, this radiation cannot be α.
ß - radiation stops after 1m of air. Since detector 2 is 1m away and does not pick up any radiation, the type of radiation must be ß.
γ - radiation is not stopped by air.

Type of radiation = ß
Half - life = 2.4 hours

---

12) C
From the given information about the symbol, we can form the equation:
$2 \diamond 3 = 2^3 \div 3 = \frac{2 \times 2 \times 2}{3} = \frac{8}{3}$

$(^8/_3) \diamond 2 = (^8/_3)^2 \div 2 = (^{64}/_9) \div 2 = {}^{64}/_9 \times {}^1/_2 = {}^{32}/_9$

---

13) B

The key to solving this question is to find out which of these processes are passive and which one is active.

Passive processes do not require energy to occur

Active processes require energy to occur, meaning they need ATP. ATP can only be formed in the presence of oxygen.

So we must find out which of these processes require ATP to occur.

A - Wrong
CO_2 diffuses into the alveoli and diffusion is passive.

B - Correct
Glucose absorption is an active process, which would require ATP. If the concentration of oxygen were low, ATP production would decrease. If ATP production decreases, glucose absorption would also decrease.

C - Wrong
O_2 diffuses into the blood and diffusion is passive.

D - Wrong
This process is passive.

E - Wrong
This process is osmosis and osmosis is passive.

F - Wrong
This process is osmosis and osmosis is passive.

---

14) B

1 - Wrong
T is less reactive than M. This means that it will not displace M to form TCl_2.

2 - Correct
J is more reactive than M. This means that it will displace M to form JSO_4.

3 - Correct
Q is more reactive than T. This means that it will displace T to form QO.

4 - Correct
J is more reactive than Q. This means that it will displace Q to form JO.

5 - Wrong
T is less reactive than J. This means that it will not displace J to form TSO_4.

6 - Wrong
Q is less reactive than M. This means that it will not displace M to form QO.

Reactions 2, 3 and 4 can occur. Hence C is correct.

---

15) D
We know that the total distance travelled = area under the graph.
However, remember to always convert the minutes into seconds as the speed is given in metres/second

Let us split the graph into a trapezium, a rectangle and a triangle.
Area under trapezium = [h (a + b)] ÷ 2
[60 seconds (15+20)] ÷ 2 = (60 x 35) ÷ 2 = 30 x 35 = 1050m

Area under rectangle = (240 - 60) x 20 = 180 x 20 = 3600 m

Area under triangle = ½ b x h = ½ x 180 x 20 = 1800 m

Total distance = 1050 + 3600 + 1800 = 6450 m = 6.45 km

However, you must remember that the triangle is not really a triangle as one side is curved. Since it is curved towards the x-axis, the area will actually be smaller than the one we obtained.
Hence distance = < 6.45 km
The answer is 6.00 km. Option D is the answer.

---

16) F
Let us break down such a complicated problem into smaller parts.

(2×10^3) = 2000
(8×10^2) = 800
So, $(2 \times 10^3) + (8 \times 10^2)$ = 2000 + 800 = 2800

$\dfrac{1}{2500}$ = 0.0004 = 4×10^{-4}

$(4 \times 10^{-4}) + (3 \times 10^{-4}) = 7 \times 10^{-4}$

$\dfrac{2800}{7 \times 10^{-4}}$ = 400×10^4 = 4,000,000

$\sqrt{4,000,000}$ = 2000

---

17) F

1 - Correct

Competition between individuals of the same species is known as intraspecific competition. Intra-specific competition is a part of natural selection.

2 - Correct

Competition between individuals of different species is known as inter-specific competition. Inter-specific competition is a part of natural selection.

3 - Correct

Natural selection can lead to evolution when individuals with certain characteristics have a greater chance of survival as compared to individuals who do not have those characteristics. When such individuals reproduce, they pass their advantageous characteristics on to their offsprings.

4 - Correct

Natural selection can lead to extinction when individuals do not have certain advantageous characteristics. This causes them to have a lesser chance of survival, eventually leading to extinction.

Since all statements are correct, F is the answer.

---

18) D

Let us form an equation for the number of O atoms present in the reaction equation.
Equation 1: $3b = 6a + c + 2$

Let us form an equation for the number of H atoms present in the reaction equation.
Equation 2: $b = 2c$

Let us form an equation for the number of N atoms present in the reaction equation.
Equation 3: $b = 2a + 2$

Using the second and third equations,

$b = 2c = 2a + 2$
$2c = 2a + 2$
$2(c) = 2(a + 1)$
$c = a + 1$

Submitting this expression of 'c' into the second equation,
$b = 2c$
$b = 2 (a + 1)$
$b = 2a + 2$
$3b = 3 (2a + 2) = 6a + 6$

Substituting the expression for 3b into the first equation,

3b = 6a + c + 2
6a + 6 = 6a + c + 2
6 = c + 2
c = 4

Substituting the value of 'c' into the second equation
b = 2c
b = 2 (4)
b = 8

19) B
From rest indicates the initial velocity (u) = 0
Final velocity (v) = 20 m/s
Mass = 5 kg
Acceleration (g) = 10 m/s²

Using SUVAT equation,
v = u + at
t = (v - u) ÷ a
t = (20 - 0) ÷ 10 = 20 ÷ 10
t = 2 seconds

s = ut + ½at²
s = 0 + ½ x 10 x 2²
s = 5 x 4 = 20 m

20) D
Diameter of sphere = r x 2 = d
Height (or length) of cylinder = d
Radius of cylinder = r
Volume of cylinder = πr²h = πr²d
We need to find the fraction of space taken by the sphere

$$\frac{\frac{4}{3}\pi r^3}{\pi r^2 d}$$

$$\frac{\frac{4}{3} r}{d}$$

Since d = 2r,

$$\frac{\frac{4}{3} r}{2r}$$

$$\frac{\frac{4}{3}}{2}$$

$4/3 \div 2 = 4/3 \times 1/2 = 4/6 = 2/3$

---

21) D

We know that at the alveolus, oxygen diffuses out of the alveolus and carbon dioxide diffuses into the alveolus.

Since oxygen diffuses out of the alveolus and into the capillary, its concentration must be high in the alveolus since diffusion is the movement of particles **from** high concentration **to** low concentration.
So first column must be high.

Since oxygen diffuses into, its concentration must be low in the capillary since diffusion is the movement of particles **from** high concentration **to** low concentration.
So second column must be low.

Since carbon dioxide diffuses into the alveolus, its concentration must be low in the alveolus since diffusion is movement of particles **from** high concentration **to** low concentration.
So third column must be low.

Since carbon dioxide diffuses out of the capillary, its concentration must be high in the capillary since diffusion is movement of particles **from** high concentration **to** low concentration.
So fourth column must be high.

So D is the answer.

---

22) D
1 - Slow
H-H and I-I bonds are broken. Molecules H_2 and I_2 split to form 2HI. Since bonds are broken, this will be a relatively slow reaction.

2 - Fast
No bonds are broken. Ag+ and Cl- just react to form AgCl.

3 - Fast
Again, 2 molecules of CH_3 just bond together to form C_2H_6

4 - Slow
The C-Br bond is broken meaning this will be a relatively slow reaction.

Reaction 2 and 3 are the fastest so D is the answer.

---

23) A

Total mass of the train = 20000 + 5000 + 5000 = 30000 kg
Ratio of masses = 20000 : 5000 : 5000 = 4 : 1 : 1

Initial thrust = 15000 N
Total parts in the ratio above = 4 + 1 + 1 = 6
15000 ÷ 6 = 2500N
Thrust on engine = 2500 x 4 = 10000 N
Thrust on individual carriage = 2500 x 1 = 2500 N

So A is the answer.

---

24) A

We first need to remove the (-10) from the RHS

$$y + 10 = 5 \left(\tfrac{x}{2} - 3\right)^2$$

We need to remove the 5 and the 4 from the RHS

$$\frac{(y + 10)}{5} = \left(\tfrac{x}{2} - 3\right)^2$$

Square rooting on both sides,

$$\pm \frac{\sqrt{y + 10}}{\sqrt5} = \tfrac{x}{2} - 3$$

Removing the 3 from the RHS

$$\pm \frac{\sqrt{y + 10}}{\sqrt5} + 3 = \tfrac{x}{2}$$

Removing ½ from RHS,

$$2 \left[\pm \frac{\sqrt{y + 10}}{\sqrt5} + 3\right] = x$$

$$x = \pm \frac{2\sqrt{(y + 10)}}{\sqrt5} + 6$$

---

25) F

1 - Wrong
Insulin helps to control the glucose content in the body.

2 - Wrong
Homeostasis also depends on the nervous system and not only hormones.

3 - Correct

Pancreas secretes the hormone insulin, which helps to control the glucose content of the blood.

4 - Correct
Both the nervous and the hormonal systems play a role in homeostasis

5 - Correct
The skin can help to control the body temperature because it has an immense blood supply. Dilated vessels allow for heat loss while constricted vessels help to retain heat.

Since statements 3, 4 and 5 are correct, F is the answer.

---

26) C
We are not sure which isotopes of chlorine and bromine are present in the molecule.
Let Ar of Br in the molecule = M
Let Ar of Cl in the molecule = N
Mr of CH_2BrCl = 128

$128 = (12 \times 1) + (1 \times 2) + (M \times 1) + (N \times 1)$
$128 = 12 + 2 + M + N$
$114 = M + N$

The only possible combination of isotopes that can be present in the molecule is: Cl = 35 and Br = 79

Chlorine isotope 35 is three times more common as isotope 37.
Ratio = 3 : 1
Total parts = 3 + 1 = 4
So probability of having isotope 35 in the molecule = ¾

Bromine isotope 79 is equally as common as isotope 81.
Ratio = 1 : 1
Total parts = 1 + 1 = 2
So probability of having isotope 79 in the molecule = ½
Probability of having Chlorine isotope 35 and Bromine isotope 79 = ¾ x ½ = ⅜

---

27) E
Time taken for three complete oscillations = 0.6
Time taken for one complete oscillation = 0.6 ÷ 3 = 0.2
Time taken for two complete oscillations = 0.2 x 2 = 0.4

Distance covered by two complete oscillations = 60m

Speed = Distance ÷ Time
Speed = 60 ÷ 0.4 = 150 m/s

2009 Section 3

1) The statement is stated in the Good Medical Practice, 2006 which means that it is directed towards medical professionals.

The statement tries to say that it is important to be truthful and a good doctor is one that provides all information to patients with good faith and morals.

It is important to be honest to patients as it allows them to become knowledgeable about their condition and helps them to understand what their treatment would entail. A doctor should be able to give information about any alternative treatments that would be suitable for the patient. All details of side effects, complications and treatment burdens should be given to the patient. This will enable the patient to make an informed decision about which treatment would be best for them. This respects their autonomy.

On some occasions, doctors may need to be flexible with their morals. An example would be when a patient is being aggressive towards the staff and other patients. In such cases, a doctor may need to break the doctor-patient relationship by calling a senior member of staff who will be more competent to handle the situation. In other cases, a doctor may wish to not disclose the results of a test to a patient immediately. It would be desirable to do the test again to ensure that the result is not a false positive. If a patient has stolen something from the clinic or hospital, then it is the duty of a doctor to inform the seniors.

A doctor should always seek to have the attributes highlighted in the Good Medical Practice handout. However, the most important thing is the welfare of patients and a doctor should ensure that this is their foremost priority.

---

2) Fooling yourself means being convinced about something and thinking it is factual when in reality, it is false. Scientists are the people who carry out researches and find evidence to explain the events that occur around us. They are able to convert hypotheses into theories and theories into laws.

It is important for scientists to be objective. They cannot allow their researches to be influenced by emotions or personal beliefs. Their experiments must be reliable, valid and controlled so that the results they obtain can also be reliable.

It is easy to make mistakes whilst carrying out researches that last decades. Committing mistakes whilst carrying out experiments and studies might cause the results to be inaccurate. If a scientist does not recognise the fact that he/she is making a mistake then they may convince themselves that the results they obtained are reliable. They will be "fooling themselves".

The easiest way of eliminating such mistakes is peer review. If another group of scientists carry out the experiments and obtain different results, then there must be something wrong.

171

This allows scientists to identify any faults in their methods. Scientific bodies must ensure that all experiments are carried out under a controlled environment. Doing this will remove other factors that could be affecting the research, hence increasing the reproducibility of a scientific experiment.

---

3) The statement is rather clear in what it is trying to say. "Rich people can buy better medical treatment than poor people" is an argument that people have different opinions on. In this case, 'better medical treatment' refers to private treatment.

It is true that rich people often prefer private treatment. Some may argue that people have the right to spend their money on anything they desire. If they wish to spend money on private treatment then it would be improper to say that it is obscene that they have access to better medical care.

An obvious assumption here is that private treatment is better than public treatment. All doctors study the same course and hence, they have the same scientific knowledge and skills to provide any treatment, which a patient needs. The NHS is one of the best healthcare systems around the world and it is respected by everyone in the country. Also, even poor people are able to afford private treatment nowadays with the help of health insurance.

The main advantage of private clinics is that it has shorter waiting times. Some appointments in the NHS are given for 6 months later, which is a long time for someone who is receiving a treatment, which requires regular check-ups e.g. orthodontic treatment.

However, if an individual prefers shorter waiting times and is willing to spend the money, then they have full right to do so. Prohibiting them from spending money on private treatments is a breach of their rights and is unethical. Together with this, the presence of private healthcare is actually beneficial for the NHS. It relieves a lot of burden and pressure put on the NHS due to the increasing number of patients.

To conclude, the statement itself may not actually be true as no one can definitely say that private healthcare is better than public healthcare or vice-versa. In fact, both of them are necessary as they provide options for the public and allow them to choose what is best for them.

1) A

Identify the weight of Jay. Since Jay is 150 cm tall and has a BMI of 22, their weight must be 49 kg.

Identify the weight of Charlie. Since Charlie is 156 cm tall and has a BMI of 24, their weight must be 58 kg.
Combined weight = 172
Let Alex's weight be = A
A + 49 + 58 = 172
A = 172 − 49 − 58 = 65 kg
Since Alex is 162 cm tall and has a weight of 65 kg, their BMI must be 25.

2) C

The argument made is the last line: "if we want to live in the most democratic…we should demand that the government subsidies the arts to a level which enables them to flourish". It makes a correlation between democracy and the arts sector. However, the flaw is that the paragraph thinks that the cause of a democratic society is flourishing art sector.
REMEMBER: **Correlation is not the same as causation.**

A – Wrong
A does not discuss anything about the correlation made in the text

B – Wrong
People's physiological health is irrelevant to the text.

C – Correct
This correctly identifies the flaw. The text tries to say that in order to make a robust society, the arts sector must flourish. Hoover, it could be the other way around, i.e. a robust society could be the reason the arts sector flourishes.

D – Wrong
This differentiates between different types of arts, which is irrelevant to the text and the question.

3) C

The diamond, which is to the far right must represent the student who scored the highest on test 1. That must be Hazel.
Moving backwards from the far right, the white diamond must represent the person who got the fifth-highest mark on test 1. The order of scores is: 94, 88, 74, 73, and 63. The person who scored the fifth highest on test 1 is Erin (63).

4) C
A – Wrong
The text just says to fight spam at the source. It does not suggest that it is **always better** to fight problems at the source.

B – Wrong
The text does not make any comparison between reducing spam and easing congestion on the road. So we cannot conclude which one is a higher priority.

C – Correct
This discusses the link made between spam and global warming. Also, the second line of the text suggests that reducing spam can take off 2.3 million cars off the road, meaning less global warming.

D – Wrong
This does not discuss the link made between global warming and spam.

E – Wrong
'Never' is too strong and also, global warming is not mentioned in this statement.

---

5) D
Number of batches = 72 / 12 = 6 batches
40 minutes to prepare 1st batch
25 minutes in the oven (this time is used to prepare the 2nd batch).
5 minutes to cool.
Total time taken for 1st batch = 40 + 25 + 5 = 70 minutes
Since we started at 1 pm, the first batch will be ready by 2:10.
We can start preparing the second batch as soon as we put the first one in the oven, i.e. 40 minutes after 1 pm, i.e. at 1:40.
The second batch will take 40 minutes to prepare. Preparation finishes at: 1:40 + 0:40 = 2:20
Since the first batch was made at 2:10, and 5 minutes were required to cool the first batch, only 15 minutes extra were inquired to prepare the second batch.
Baking time = 25 minutes
Cooling time = 5 minutes
Total time for second batch = 25 + 15 + 5 = 45 minutes.
All of the following batches will require 45 minutes as well.
Total time needed to make 6 batches = 70 + 5(45) = 70 + 225 = 295 minutes
295 minutes = 4 hours 55 minutes
Since we started at 1 pm, we will finish at 5:55 pm

---

6) B
1 – Wrong
The text makes an argument based on the fact that the world suddenly stopped burning fossil fuels. So statement 1 is irrelevant.

2 – Correct
The text's assumption is that in fifty years' time, the carbon dioxide levels would be double of what was present pre-industrial level. However, it fails to recognise that carbon dioxide levels can be decreased significantly in fifty years' time.

3 – Wrong
Past predictions cannot be generalised with this prediction. So statement 3 is irrelevant.

Only statement 2 is correct. So B is the answer.

---

7) B
Only the first digit (8) was faulty and three lights were permanently on.
So we need to look at which numbers can be formed from 8.
0 can be formed if we take out 1 light from 8.
2 can be formed if we take out 3 lights from 8.
5 can be formed if we take out 3 lights from 8.
6 can be formed if we take out 3 lights from 8.
9 can be formed if we take out 3 lights from 8.

However, the maximum score is 505.
So the actual score could have been:
005
205
It could not have been 505, 605 or 905.
There could have been 2 different values for the actual score.

---

8) A
The first part of the first paragraph says that children's peers encourage them to play with different types of toys.
However, at the end of the paragraph, the writer challenges the view that social factors influence the types of toys children play with.

A – Correct
At the end of the first paragraph, the writer challenges the view that social factors influence the types of toys children play with.

B – Wrong
The author does not challenge the fact that boys and girls play with different types of toys. The author challenges the reason given for this kind of behaviour.

C – Wrong
This is clearly wrong. This is correct according to the writer so is not challenged.

D – Wrong
D is completely irrelevant to the argument made in the first paragraph.

9) A

The inference made in the study is that male monkeys naturally showed more interest in masculine toys and female monkeys naturally showed more interest in feminine toys.
We need a statement that can either prove this inference unreliable or wrong.

A – Correct
Firstly, it does not matter which sex is more dominant. To put this simply, the more dominant sex took all the attractive toys for themselves and left the less attractive ones for the other sex. This means that there is not necessarily a gender preference.

B – Wrong
Irrelevant as we are not sure how long is 'quickly'.

C – Wrong
Preference for different kinds of foods is completely unrelated to preferences in different kinds of toys.

D – Wrong
Studies on monkeys are more reliable than studies on other species as monkeys are more relatable to humans. So this is not a strong challenge.

E – Wrong
Preferences for different kinds of toys is not related to signs of social behaviour.

10) A

The second paragraph says that "assessed the monkeys' preference for each toy by measuring how much time they spent with each. So clearly, in order to prove that sex preference does occur in monkeys, the time spent with each toy must be an indicator of how much they are interested in the toy.

A – Correct
A paraphrases the assumption mentioned above correctly.

B – Wrong
Genetic makeup being alike in both species is not assumed in the text.

C – Wrong
A doll and a cooking pot were chosen only because they were stereotypically feminine toys.

D – Wrong
This is not necessarily assumed.

E – Wrong
This is not necessarily assumed.

11) D

1 – Wrong

Showing a female monkey playing with a doll and a male monkey playing with a car does not show that they respond in the same way as humans.

2 – Wrong

Even though this could be true, we cannot be 100% sure that this was the case. The monkeys could have been given the toys just for the photo.

Neither of the statements can be reliably inferred.

---

12) C

We know that only 4 out of these 5 tiles are to be used to make the floor.
For now let us add up all the number of black, white and grey squares on all 5 tiles.

Number of black tiles

A = 2
B = 1
C = 3
D = 4
E = 5
Total = 15

Number of white tiles
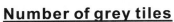

A = 3
B = 6
C = 4
D = 3
E = 0
Total = 16

Number of grey tiles

A = 4
B = 2
C = 2
D = 2
E = 4
Total = 14

We need to remove a tile which can satisfy this equation:
Black tiles = white tiles = grey tiles

If we remove A, we get:
Black tiles = 15 – 2 = 13
White tiles = 16 – 3 = 14

Grey tiles = 14 − 4 = 10
So, A is wrong

If we remove B, we get:
Black tiles = 15 − 1 = 14
White tiles = 16 − 6 = 10
Grey tiles = 14 − 2 = 12
So, B is wrong

If we remove C, we get:
Black tiles = 15 − 3 = 12
White tiles = 16 − 4 = 12
Grey tiles = 14 − 2 = 12
So, C is correct

If we remove D, we get:
Black tiles = 15 − 4 = 11
White tiles = 16 − 3 = 13
Grey tiles = 14 − 2 = 12
So, D is wrong

If we remove E, we get:
Black tiles = 15 − 5 = 10
White tiles = 16 − 0 = 16
Grey tiles = 14 − 4 = 10
So, E is wrong

C is the answer.

---

13) E
The last line "since there will be negative stories in the press..we should ignore them and not worry about them" is the argument of the text. We need to find a flaw in this argument.

A – Wrong
The argument is not about the examinations. It is about the negative stories that will be published either way.

B – Wrong
Even though it may be true, attacking the press is not the flaw of the argument.

C – Wrong
Again, it may be true. However, the argument is not about predicting what the press might say when examination results are out. The argument is that there will be negative stories and that we should just ignore them. C does not find a flaw in this argument.

D – Wrong
The argument is not about the examinations being easy.

E – Correct
The flaw is that we should ignore negative stories. So E is the answer.

---

14) D
The most number of elements that would need to change would be from the digit that has the least elements to the digit that requires the most changes from the digit that has the least elements.

The digit which has the least elements = 1
1 has two elements.

To change 1 to 0, we need to add 4 elements
To change 1 to 2, we need to change 5 elements
To change 1 to 3, we need to add 3 elements
To change 1 to 4, we need to add 2 elements
To change 1 to 5, we need to change 5 elements
To change 1 to 6, we need to change 6 elements
To change 1 to 7, we need to add 1 elements
To change 1 to 8, we need to add 5 elements
To change 1 to 9, we need to add 4 elements
Hence the maximum number of elements that change from one number to another is 6 (from 1 to 6).

---

15) D
A – Wrong
The statistics we have are those for the number of child cyclists **killed or seriously injured**. We do not have the statistics for the number of children that **own** bicycles.

B – Wrong
We do not have the statistics for the number of girls and boys that were pedestrians unsupervised by adults.

C – Wrong
C could be counteracted simply by the fact that there probably are more boy cyclists than girl cyclists.

D – Correct
Number of boy pedestrians and cyclists killed or seriously injured = 1300 + 400 = 1700
Number of girl pedestrians and cyclists killed or seriously injured = 700 + 100 = 800
1700 is more than twice that of 800. So D is the answer.

E – Wrong
No. There are also a large number of females that are either killed or seriously injured. We need lessons in road safety designed for males and females. So E is wrong.

16) D

This can only be solved by visualisation.

We can eliminate A and C easily though. Look at the original die. The orientation between 5 and 6 is different in the original die as compared to A and C.

B has the same orientation of 3 as it is in the original die. This is only possible when the die is rotated in the same direction twice. Since it was rotated in a different direction, B is worn.g

In E, none of the original numbers are present on the die. At least one of the original number should have remained after 2 rotations, no matter the direction. So E is wrong.

We are left with D.

17) C

The argument made in the text: "By keeping these treasures at the British Museum..safety is ensured for the whole world". It also gives the example of the Standard of Ur and how it would have gotten stolen if it were not kept in the British Museum.

A – Wrong

Although this may be true, it does not find a flaw in the statement that keeping artefacts in Britain instead of their home country ensures safety to the whole world.

B – Wrong

Although this may be true, it does not find a flaw in the statement that keeping artefacts in Britain instead of their home country ensures safety to the whole world.

C – Correct

The text assumes that giving an example of one country means that the same thing will happen to the artefacts of other countries too.

D – Wrong

This is irrelevant as the argument is related to the safety of the artefacts and not who will get to see them.

E – Wrong

The argument is not about the safety of the British Museum. It is about the safety of the artefacts if they were returned to their home countries.

18) D

We need to calculate the maximum number of cards needed. So we need to use most of the space available on each rectangular card.

2 ends of the H (2 cm each) can fit in the centre of another H (4 cm each).

Please draw them out, as it will take longer to visualise.

Soon, you will realise that we can have 6 rows of 3, 2, 3, 2, 3, and 2.

Drawing them out:

1	1	1
1	1	
1	1	1
1	1	
1	1	1
1	1	

This gives us = 3 + 2 + 3 + 2 + 3 + 2 = 5 + 5 + 5 = 15 H shaped cards.

---

19) 217

Total number of air passengers in 2005 = 228 million
The text says that 9 in 10 passengers were international. So 1 in 10 must be domestic.
Number of domestic passengers = 0.1 x 228 = 22.8 million passengers.
Since each domestic passenger was counted twice, we need to divide 22.8 by 2.
So number of domestic passengers = $^{22.8}/_2$ = 11.4 million.
Total number of passengers (international + domestic) = (228 − 22.8) + 11.4 = 216.6 million
To the nearest million, this is 217 million.

---

20) C
Number of passengers travelling to Spain = 34 million
Total number of passengers = 228 million
Proportion = $(^{34}/_{228})$ = $(^{17}/_{114})$ ≈ $(^{17}/_{119})$ = $(^1/_7)$

Total number of passengers in 1980 (according to the graph) = 60 million
$^1/_7$ of 60 = 8.57 million
This is closest to C (9 million).

---

21) F
1 – Correct
Increase from 1955 to 1980 = 60 − 5 = 55 million

181

Increase from 1980 to 2005 = 228 – 60 =168 million
168 million is more than three times that of 55 million.

2 – Correct
Total number of passengers in Gatwick and Heathrow = 68 + 33 = 101 million passengers
Total number of passengers = 228 million
4 out of 10 means 0.4
0.4 x 228 = 91.2 million
101 million is more than 91.2 million

3 – Correct
Increase predicted by Department of Transport = 500 – 228 = 272 million
Number of years = 2030 – 2010 = 20 years
Increase needed = $^{272}/_{20}$ = 13.6 million
This figure is more than 10 million per annum.
Since all three statements are correct, F is the answer.

---

22) D
This is pretty simple. The data has been correctly interpreted with the help of previous results and an informed conclusion has been made. So D is correct.

---

23) E
In order for the number to consist of 3 digits, one of the numbers must be a two-digit number and the second number must be a single digit number.
All single digit numbers = 1, 2, 3, 4, 5, 6, 7, 8, 9
All double digit numbers = 10, 11, 12, 13, 14, 15
Remember that ALL DIGITS MUST BE DIFFERENT. So 1 cannot be matched with 10, 11, 12, 13, 14 or 15 as they all have 1. Similarly, 11 cannot be matched with anything as it has two 1s.

2 can only be matched with 10, 13, 14, 15
3 can only be matched with 10, 12, 14, 15
4 can only be matched with 10, 12, 13, 15
5 can only be matched with 10, 12, 13, 14
6 can only be matched with 10, 12, 13, 14, 15
7 can only be matched with 10, 12, 13, 14, 15
8 can only be matched with 10, 12, 13, 14, 15
9 can only be matched with 10, 12, 13, 14, 15

Total number of possibilities of having three digits all different = (4 x 4) + (5 x 4) = 16 + 20 = 36

Now we must look at total number of possible pairings.1 can be matched with 14 other numbers.
2 can be matched with 13 other numbers. (13 because 2 and 1 would have already had 1 pair).
Similarly, number of possibilities:
14 + 13 + 12 + 11 + 10 + 9 + 8 + 7 + 6 + 5 + 4 + 3 + 2 + 1 = 105

So probability = $(^{36}/_{105})$ = $(^{12}/_{35})$

24) C

The text presents us with two possible explanations for the extinction of dinosaurs: space impact and super-volcanic activity. The text says that since it cannot be volcanic activity, space impact is the only plausible explanation.

However, the text fails to recognise that there could be other explanations as well. So the assumption is that there are no other possible explanations for the extinction of the dinosaurs.

A – Wrong

This statement just focuses on volcanic activity, which means that this cannot be the answer.

B – Wrong

Cooling of the atmosphere and acid rain is just an observation that would have been seen if volcanic activity had actually happened. It wouldn't directly have made dinosaurs extinct. So this is not necessarily an assumption.

C – Correct

This correctly identified the assumption that I discussed above.

D – Wrong

This may seem like the answer. However, scientists must take this statement as a fact and not as an assumption.

E – Wrong

Changes in the ecosystems are not mentioned in the text so is irrelevant.

25) A

Score of the person right now = 2 + 7 = 9
Score of first friend = (4 + 7) x 2 = 22
Score of second friend = 5 + 8 = 13
Score of third friend = 2 + 9 = 11

Highest position possible for the person is 1st.

In order to finish first, the person would have to swap their lowest value card with the highest value card from friend 1 to break the friend 1's pair.

So the person would swap their 2 with friend 1's 7.
Now the person has a score of = 7 + 7 = **14**

They will be first because:
Friend 1 has a score of = 4 + 2 = 6
Friend 2 has a score of = 5 + 8 = 13
Friend 3 has a score of = 9 + 2 = 11

26) A

This is one of the easiest questions on the test.

The conclusion is the first line of the text "the behaviour of the public has contributed…to do out of hours work".

A – Correct

This correctly paraphrases the conclusion which is mentioned above.

B – Wrong

The text does not mention anything about what the government is planning to do to tackle the problem.

C – Wrong

The text just says that the public expects 24-hour medical care, no matter how trivial their medical problem is. However, the text does not specify whether the patient knows how serious their problem is.

D – Wrong

This is clearly wrong. We do not have any data or any statement from which we can infer that doctors running out of hours surgeries see more patients with non-urgent than urgent medical problems.

E – Wrong

Wrong! Patients have full right to obtain treatment no matter how urgent or non-urgent their problems are. The text does not say that doctors should turn away patients who come to out of hours surgeries with non-urgent medical problems.

---

27) C

Phil's score so far = 12 + 8 = 20

He is confident that his dart will not land further away from one of the two neighbouring sections from the one he is aiming at.

For example, if he aims for 6, his dart could either go to 9, 6 or 11.

A – Wrong

If he aims at 4, he has the possibility of getting 1. So his total score would be 21. After this, he would have to aim for a number, which has a value of 9 or higher.

If he gets 1 and for his 4th dart:

If he aims for 9, he has a possibility of getting 4 or 6 (so total score would not be 30)

If he aims for 10, he has a possibility of getting 5 or 8 (so total score would not be 30)

If he aims for 11, he has a possibility of getting 2 or 6 (so total score would not be 30)

B – Wrong

If he aims at 7, he has the possibility of getting 3. So his total score would be 23. After this, he would have to aim for a number, which has a value of 7 or higher.

If he gets 3 and for his 4th dart:

If he aims for 7, he has a possibility of getting 5 (so total score would not be 30)
If he aims for 9, he has a possibility of getting 4 or 6 (so total score would not be 30)
If he aims for 10, he has a possibility of getting 5 or 8 (if he lands on 5, the total score would not be 30 and if he lands on 8, he would get eliminated).
If he aims for 11, he has a possibility of getting 2 or 6 (so total score would not be 30)

C – Correct
If he aims at 9, he has the possibility of getting 4 or 6. So his total score would be 24. After this, he would have to aim for a number, which has a value of 6 or higher.
If he gets 4 and for his 4th dart:
If he aims for 6, he has a possibility of getting 9 or 11 (so total score would be above 30).If he gets a 6 on his 3rd dart, his total score would be 26. He can then aim at 5, which will guarantee him a win.

D – Wrong
If he aims for 10, there is a possibility of landing on 8. If he lands on 8, he will automatically be eliminated.

E – Wrong
Using the same principle as A and B, E is wrong.

---

28) A
Argument made in the text: "…the name alone had influenced public opinion and prevented members of the public from having sympathy for the child". The argument is that ONLY the name had influenced public opinion.
We need to look for statements, which can strengthen this argument.

1 – Correct
If the media had reported the child's background accurately, this would have reduced bias and hence ensure that there were not any other factors that influenced public opinion except the name.

2 – Wrong
If the newspaper called for the harshest possible punishment, then the name together with the newspaper's statement would have been the factors influencing public opinion. So the name would not have been the ONLY factor influencing public opinion.

3 – Wrong
If this statement were true, then the newspaper's wording also would have influenced public opinion. So the name would not have been the ONLY factor.

Since only statement 1 is correct, A is the answer.

---

29) C
Add up all of the weights of the apples:
173 + 182 + 188 + 197 + 207 + 219 + 224 = 1390 g
The sum of weight of two packs ideally needs to be = 600 x 2 = 1200 g

Difference = 1390 – 1200 = 190 g
This is closest to 188 g so C is the answer.

---

30) B

A – Wrong

The text says that "candidates with lower qualifications would have to be recruited" suggests that those with lower qualifications are not ideal candidates and that they would not be good teachers. So A is an assumption that the text makes.

B – Correct

The text states that the idea of reducing the sizes of classes is not justified for other reasons. (Little improvement in children's education. The expense is just an additional reason why reducing class sizes is not justified.

C – Wrong

This is assumed in the sentence "California had only risen to 48th"

D – Wrong

This is assumed in the sentence "children who do well at school are those that recruit their teachers from the brightest graduates".

---

31) D

This can only be solved by visualisation. However, we can easily eliminate E and B. If you know that visualisation questions are hard and take time, skip them! And move on to the other simpler, workable questions. You can always come back and do it after when you have time. Also, ask your exams officer if you can take scissors into the exam. (Rules don't say you can't bring scissors). Take permission though!

---

32) C

We can use approximate values for the earnings.
Top 20% earn = $162,000 + $51,000 = $213,000
Bottom 20% earn = $16,000 + $17,000 = $33,000
Ratio = 213000: 3,000 = 6.5:1
Since we rounded down the bottom 20% and rounded up the top 20%, we need to decrease the overall ratio. So, C (6 : 1) is the answer.

---

33) C

In the table, the overall average is $40,000. This is the average of the 10 categories.
So total income = $40,000 x 10 = $40,000
Top 10% earn = $160,000 (approximate value)
Percentage earned by the top 10% = $(^{160,000}/_{400,000})$ x 100 = 40%

---

34) C

Total money earned by top 20% = 160,000 + 50,000 = $210,000
20% x 210,000 = $42,000
$42,000 is spread amongst the bottom 80%.
Money given to each category = 42,000 ÷ 8 = $5250

Total earnings of bottom 10% = $16,203 + $5250 = $21,453
This is closest to C ($21,500)

35) B
1 – Wrong
The graphs do not provide data for people within a country. It only provides data for between countries.

2 – Correct
Graph 1 shows that the lower the level of income inequality, the more healthy the people are.

Since only statement 2 is correct, B is the answer.

2010 Section 2

1) E
Homeostasis (temperature, the water level in body etc.) is related to the hypothalamus. This rules out A, B and C.

When our temperature rises, the hair muscles relax, meaning our hair (on hands) lay flat. We can rule out option F.

Our arterioles dilate (become wider or larger) to create a larger surface area. This allows more heat to be radiated out of our body. This rules out option D.

Hence E is correct.

2) E
We need to use the formula: $n = {}^m/_{Mr}$ to find out the moles of each of the elements in the compound.

mass of iodine = 63.6g
Mr of Iodine = 127
moles = $^{63.5}/_{127}$ = 0.5 moles

mass of oxygen = 20g
Mr of oxygen = 16
moles of oxygen = $^{20}/_{16}$ = 1.25

Molar ratio = $^{1.25}/_{0.5}$ = 2.5
So for every 1 mole of iodine, there will be 2.5 moles of oxygen. This can only be seen in option E.

I_2O_5. Molar ratio = $^5/_2$ = 2.5
So E is correct.

3) A
This may seem slightly confusing.

To start with, we need to know the starting mass of protactinium-234.

We know that all of protactinium-234 undergoes decay. So all of starting mass of protactinium-234 must have undergone decay to make uranium-234.

We know the total mass of uranium-234 formed was 16 g. This means that the starting mass of protactinium-234 also must have been 16g. The time it took to decay into half (8g) was 1.2 minutes. Hence A is the answer.

Another way of doing this is to see the difference between the production of uranium-234. Within the first 1.2 minutes, 8 g was formed. After the second 1.2 minutes, 4g was formed. After the third 1.2 minutes, 2g was formed. From this, we can see that after every 1.2 minutes, the production of uranium-234 becomes half until the maximum amount of uranium-234 is formed.

4) C

Since the big container is full of water, it represents 1 (whole). The water from the big container is emptied into the smaller container in such a way that both contain the same amount. This is only possible when half of the water in the big container is emptied into the smaller container. So, the big container has 0.5 times its capacity. Hence, p=0.5. This rules out A, D and E.

Now, the smaller container has an equal amount of water as the big container i.e. 0.5. However, q is the volume of water times its OWN capacity. Try visualising the situation. Half of the water from a big container is emptied into a smaller container.

Let's say that the big container had 10 units of water, which is its full capacity. Let us say the smaller container had a capacity of 7 units of water. Half of the volume of water from the big container, i.e. 5 units are emptied into the smaller one. Therefore, q would be 5/7 full. This is more than 0.5 times its capacity as 0.5 times is capacity would be 3.5 units. Hence, q > 0.5.

---

5) C

1 - Wrong

Insulin decreases the blood glucose levels

2 - Correct

Oestrogen increases the thickness of the inner lining of the uterus

3 - Correct

Adrenaline increase heart rate.

Statements 2 and 3 are correct. So C is the answer.

---

6) D

Be careful! The question states that 12g of CARBON (i.e. not carbon dioxide) is used in stage 2.

In the 2nd equation:
Mass of carbon = 12g
Mr of carbon = 12
Moles of carbon used = $^{12}/_{12}$ = 1 mol
Molar ratio of C and 2CO = 1:2
Hence mole of CO produced = mole of carbon (i.e. 1 mol) x 2 = 2 mol

In the 3rd equation:
It is stated that all of the CO formed in the second equation is used in the third equation.
Moles of CO used = 2 mol
Molar ratio of CO used and CO_2 formed = 3:3 = 1:1
Moles of CO_2 formed = 2 mol
n of CO_2 = 2
Mr of CO_2 = 12 + 16 + 16 = 44
mass = n x Mr = 2 x 44 = 88g

7) A

The amplitude is the maximum displacement of a wave from its CENTRE.

The amplitude of this wave is $^{16-10}/_2 = 3m$

We know that $f = 1/T$

Time period (T) is the total time taken for one oscillation, i.e. time between 2 consecutive troughs or peaks. On the x-axis, the time is given. Let us take the peaks at 6 hours and 18 hours. This gives us a

value for $T = 12$ hours $= 12 \times 3600s$

Hence, $f = {}^1/_{(12 \times 3600)}$

$A = 3m$, $f = {}^1/_{(12 \times 3600)}$. This corresponds to option A.

8) C

In order to return to the same position, a player has to land on the opposite direction but the same distance.

e.g. A player lands on Right and distance 2. In order to return to the original position, the player has to land on Left direction with distance 2.

Probability of landing on Left $= {}^1/_4$

Probability of landing on 2 $= {}^1/_4$

Probability of returning on the same position $= {}^1/_4 \times {}^1/_4 = {}^1/_{16}$

9) B

A - Wrong

A gene pool consists of all of the alleles within an individual. Natural selection refers to the survival of individuals with and advantageous gene (or alleles within a gene) but not a gene pool.

B - Correct

This is correct. Individuals with advantageous allele will be favoured by natural selection.

C - Wrong

A high reproductive capacity does not necessarily mean that it will have the advantageous allele needed to survive in its environment.

D - Wrong

Geographic distribution is not relevant in natural selection.

E - Wrong

Geographic distribution is not relevant in natural selection.

10) D

Be careful! It specifies "**complete combustion** of fuels". This makes the whole difference as we will discuss now.

1 - CH_4 is not produced in combustion.

2 - CO is produced in INCOMPLETE combustion

3 - CO_2 is produced in combustion as all carbon reacts with the oxygen combustion

4 - H_2O is produced as the hydrogen in the hydrocarbons reacts with oxygen during combustion

5 - He is never produced in combustion

6 - NH_3 is not produced

---

11) C

It is important to know what α-particles are and what ß-particles are.

An α-particle is basically a Helium atom which contains 2 protons and 2 neutrons (i.e. mass number of 4 and atomic number of 2). Emission of an α-particle means that the atom's mass number decreases by 4 and atomic number decreases by 2. Since 3 α-particles are emitted, mass number decreases by (3 x 4 =12) 12 and atomic number decrease by (2 x 3 = 6) 6.

So far, the current mass number of the atom is 207 and the atomic number is 80.

A ß-particle is an electron. So when a ß-particle is emitted, the atom loses an electron and the atomic number increases by 1.

Since 2 ß-particles are emitted, atomic number increases by 2 i.e. 80 + 2 = 82.

So, we have an atom, which has a mass number of 207 and atomic number of 82. This corresponds to option C.

---

12) C

Total time taken by first group = 54 x 20 = 1080s

We know number of people in second group = 'P'

Mean time of second group = 'T'

Total number of people = 20 + P

Total time taken by second group = T x P

Total time taken by both groups = 1080 + (T x P)

In order to get total mean time (56), we need to divide total amount of time by total number of people.

56 = (1080 + TP) ÷ (20 + P)

56 (20 + P) = 1080 + TP

1120 + 56P = 1080 + TP

1120 - 1080 = TP - 56P

40 = P (T - 56)

$P = \dfrac{40}{T - 56}$

Hence, the answer is C.

---

13) F

1 - Wrong

Transmitter molecules diffuse to the receptors to be recognised. They are not formed in the receptors.

2 - Wrong

The signal is transmitted across the synapse by diffusion

3 - Wrong
This statement does not even make sense. Transmitter molecules are released before the signal is transmitted across the synapse.

4 - Correct
It is an impulse, which causes the transmitter molecules to be released.

5 - Correct
The signal is transmitted across the synapse by diffusion.

Hence, 4 and 5 are correct.

---

14) A

1 - If a positively charged ion gains a negatively charged electron, the total charge on the atom would be 0. Hence, this is correct.

2 - If a negatively charged ion loses a negatively charged electron, the total charge on the atom would be 0. Hence, this is correct.

3 - If an ion has charge (2-) and it gains two negatively charged electrons, the total charge would be (4-) and not 0. Hence, this is wrong.

4 - If an ion has charge (2-) and it loses one negatively charged electron, the total charge would be (1-) and not 0. Hence, this is wrong.

5 - If two ions, which have charge (1-) lose two electrons, the products should be two atoms with charge (0). In this equation, the products should be 2I and not I.

6 - If an ion with charge (2+) gains two negatively charged electrons, the product would be an atom without any charge. Hence, this is correct.

The answer is A.

---

15) B

When switch Q is closed, the current has three pathways to go:
1 - the path which has bulbs X and Y
2 - the second path which has 2 bulbs
3 - the third path with switch Q.

When switch Q is opened, current only has 2 pathways. Therefore, current through bulb X will increase causing it to become brighter.
When switch P is closed, the series circuit becomes a parallel circuit. This causes current to travel through two pathways: the first one through switch P and second though the bulb. Current received by bulb Y would decrease causing it to go dimmer.

---

16) C
This involves the use of the rule of similarity.
Triangles ABC and ADE are similar.

$$^{AB}/_{BC} = {}^{DA}/_{DE}$$

$$^4/_x = {}^x/_{x} + 3$$
$$4x + 12 = x^2$$
$$x^2 - 4x - 12 = 0$$

Factorising,
$$x^2 - 6x + 2x - 12$$
$$x (x - 6) + 2 (x - 6)$$
$$(x - 6) (x + 2)$$

So x = 6 or x = -2
Since the length cannot be negative, x = 6.
Since DE = x + 3, DE = 6 + 3 = 9 cm

---

17) E
Let the recessive allele be 't'
We know P and Q have the recessive allele. Since the condition is caused by a recessive allele, the person must have been homozygous recessive. Therefore, the person with the condition must have the genotype 'tt'
However, we are told that only persons R and X have the condition, meaning that P and Q must not be homozygous recessive. Hence, P and Q must be heterozygous. Their genotype must be 'Tt'

	T	t
T	TT(25%)	Tt (50%)
t	Tt (50%)	tt (25%)

We are asked to find out the percentage probability of S, T and U being carriers of the recessive allele. They cannot have the genotype 'tt' as we know that they do not have the condition themselves.
Ideally, we would think that all three of them have a 50% probability of being a carrier. However, the probability of U being a carrier has to be 100%. Since X has the condition, U must definitely have the recessive allele.
Probability of S and T carrying the recessive allele is 50%.
P(S) = 50%
P(T) = 50%
P(U) = 100%
Hence, the answer is E.

18) B
To solve this question, we need to balance the charges to 0.

A - Wrong
Mg = 2+
2H = 2+
$2PO_4$ = 6-
2 + 2 - 6 = -2

B - Correct
Mg = 2+
4H = 4+
$2PO_4$ = 6-
2 + 4 - 6 = 0

C - Wrong
Mg = 2+
3H = 3+
PO_4 = 3-
2 + 3 - 3 = +2

D - Wrong
Mg = 2+
6H = 6+
$2PO_4$ = 6-
2 + 6 - 6 = +2

E- Wrong
2Mg = 4+
H = 1+
PO_4 = 3-
1 + 4 - 3 = +2

F - Wrong
2Mg = 4+
2H = 2+
PO_4 = 3-
4 + 2 - 3 = +3

19) B
A straight line on the distance-time graphs shows us constant velocity (no change in velocity).
Since there is no change in velocity, acceleration must be zero.
So R and S are definitely wrong.
A straight line on velocity-time graphs shows us constant acceleration.
Equation for acceleration = (final velocity - initial velocity) ÷ time

Acceleration in P = $^{10 - 0}/_{24}$ = 0.4
Acceleration in Q = $^{60 - 10}/_{20}$ = 2.5 (almost 2.4). Hence, the answer is B (Q only).

20) A
Total surface area of a cylinder = $2\pi rh + 2\pi r^2$
Volume of a cylinder = $\pi r^2 h$
Since they are numerically the same,
$2\pi rh + 2\pi r^2 = \pi r^2 h$
$2\pi r (h + r) = \pi r^2 h$
$2 (h + r) = rh$
$2h + 2r = rh$
$2r = rh - 2h$
$2r = h (r - 2)$
$h = {}^{2r}/_{r-2}$

21) B
1 - Correct
Gametes are the only cells in animals produced by meiosis.

2 - Correct
Mitosis is basically replication of cells.

3 - Wrong
Meiosis results in 4 haploid nuclei.

4 - Wrong
Mitosis results in 2 identical diploid nuclei.

5 - Correct
Mitosis occurs during asexual reproduction. An identical individual (clone) is formed during asexual reproduction.

1, 2 and 5 are correct statements. So, B is correct.

22) C
Mr of benzene = (12 x 6) + (1 x 6) = 78
Mass of benzene given = 3.9 g
Moles of benzene = $^{mass}/_{Mr}$ = $^{3.9}/_{78}$ = $^{1}/_{20}$ moles = 0.05 mol

Molar ratio of benzene and nitrobenzene = 1:1
Moles of nitrobenzene = 0.05 moles
Mr of nitrobenzene = (12 x 6) + (1 x 5) + (14 x 1) + (16 x 2) = 72 + 5 + 14 + 32 = 123 ≈ 120
Mass of nitrobenzene = moles x Mr = 0.05 x 120 = 6g
Percentage yield = $^{3.69}/_{6}$ x 100 = $^{369}/_{6}$ = 61.5% ≈ 60%
Hence, C is correct.

23) G

It is important to remember that power = energy per second.

Potential energy (PE) of water when it reaches a height of 5m = m x g x h

PE = 5 x 10 x 5 = 250J

This is the energy of 5kg of water which is released per second.

Hence, power = 250 J/s or 250 W

We know that all kinetic energy is converted to potential energy when it reaches a height.

Therefore PE = KE = 250 J

$KE = \frac{1}{2}mv^2$

$250 = 0.5 \times 5 \times v^2$

$100 = v^2$

v = 10 m/s

Hence the answer is G.

---

24) C

Let side of first square = A = 1
Let side of second square = B
Let side of third square = C
Let side of fourth square = D

Using Pythagoras theorem,

Second Square

$B^2 = (\frac{1}{3})^2 + (\frac{2}{3})^2 = \frac{1}{9} + \frac{4}{9} = \frac{5}{9}$

$B = \sqrt{(\frac{5}{9})} = \frac{\sqrt{5}}{3}$

Third square

$C^2 = (\frac{1}{3} \times \frac{\sqrt{5}}{3})^2 + (\frac{2}{3} \times \frac{\sqrt{5}}{3})^2 = (\frac{\sqrt{5}}{9})^2 + (\frac{2\sqrt{5}}{9})^2 = \frac{5}{81} + \frac{20}{81} = \frac{25}{81}$

$C = \sqrt{(\frac{25}{81})} = \frac{5}{9}$

Fourth square

$D^2 = (\frac{1}{3} \times \frac{5}{9})^2 + (\frac{2}{3} \times \frac{5}{9})^2 = (\frac{5}{27})^2 + (\frac{10}{27})^2 = \frac{25}{729} + \frac{100}{729} = \frac{125}{729}$

$D = \sqrt{(\frac{125}{729})}$

Area of fourth square = D x D = $D^2 = \frac{125}{729}$

---

25) E

1 - Wrong
The nervous system does not only rely on electrical impulses to work. It also relies on transmitter chemicals and molecules, nerve cells, spinal cord and the brain.

2 - Correct
e.g. the nervous system sends signals to contract or relax an effector muscle.
The pituitary gland releases ADH to reabsorb water from the kidneys.

3 - Correct
The central nervous system produces reflex actions (fastest responses in the body).

4 - Wrong
The nervous system also relies on chemicals such as noradrenaline or acetylcholine to work.

5 - Correct
Parts of the nervous system such as the hypothalamus control the pituitary gland (which is part of the hormonal system).

2, 3 and 5 are correct.

---

26) B
The first ring has 6.
The second has 4 **extra**. (Total 6 but 2 are from the first ring).
The third has 4 **extra**. (Total 6 but 2 are from the second ring).
The fourth has 3 **extra**. (Total 5 but 2 are from the third ring).

Total so far = 6 + 4 + 4 + 3 = 17
2 carbons are present in the CH_3 groups and 1 is present in CO_2H group.
Total = 17 + 2 + 1 = 20

---

27) D
Height of car after 50m = $^{50}/_{20}$ = 2.5

PE = mgh
PE = 800 x 10 x 2.5
PE = 8000 x 2.5 = 20,000J

Force of engine against friction = 500N
Work done against friction = Force x distance = 500 x 50 = 25,000J

Total work done = 20,000 + 25,000 = 45,000J = 45 kJ

2010 Section 3

1) A prime minister or president is a person who holds a lot of responsibility. They work tirelessly to ensure efficient functioning of their country. If the country faces any kind of problem, then the prime minister or president is usually the person who is held accountable.

The statement's wording conveys the message that it is wrong to have a 'serious ambition' to be prime minister or president. There have been many leaders in the past and even now who forsook their values and morals in order to gain political power. An ideal leader is one that cares for their public and their country. A person with an ambition to become a leader, on the other hand, only wants personal gain.

In a democracy, the public elects a prime minister or president. The citizens of the country have the right to choose their leader and hence, the only way to become a leader is to do good things rather than solely place your focus on becoming a leader. A person that assumes power in non-democratic countries without any elections is most likely to be ambitious since they do not want anyone opposing them. They are more likely to lie, deceive the public and use unethical methods to obtain political power. Their corruption may also lead to economic instability within the country. An individual who gains power through ambition may also have narrow-minded views, which may cause certain sections of the society to suffer.

Some may argue that having an ambition to become a leader may not be a wrong thing. Their intention, however, must be to do good things for the society and not exploit their power. An ambitious mind is required for a person who represents thousands or millions of people. They are the inspiration for many and in order to live up to the expectations of the citizens, they need an ambitious mind in order to succeed in their endeavours.

To conclude, an individual who has an ambition to be a leader, should have good intentions in order to be successful. An ambitious person with bad intentions will be a liability for the country.

---

2) According to the statement, the people who partake in activities that may cause serious injuries or even death should not be treated by publicly funded health service.

This argument is logical, as the people who do extreme sports know that they may potentially get injured. They are fully aware of the consequences and yet, they do it for the thrill. Some may argue that injuries caused by extreme sports should be deemed self-inflicted and that NHS resources should only be used to treat patients who did not purposefully put themselves in danger. It should be the duty of every person to keep themselves healthy. Usage of NHS resources to treat people who regularly do extreme sports reduces the resources available for illnesses, which were not self-inflicted.

On the contrary, some may argue that extreme sports participants who pay taxes should have full access to the public health service. They regularly pay money to fund the NHS and hence, denying them treatments will be unethical. "Never discriminate unfairly against patients" is a statement in the Good Medical Practice booklet. If extreme sports injuries are considered self-inflicted, then conditions caused by smoking, drug abuse, overeating and alcohol consumption should also be considered self-inflicted. This statement could be used as a deterrent to discourage people from taking risks that could change their life and health completely. If treatments were denied for self-inflicted injuries, then many people would discontinue any activities that could potentially place themselves in danger.

To conclude, patient autonomy is very important in any healthcare system and should be respected. It should not matter how an injury was inflicted as every citizen has a right to healthcare.

3) According to the statement, a pet is a person's property. Therefore, an owner should have the right to decide their pet's fate.

Pets can have certain conditions in which they have to endure a lot of pain and hence causes their quality of life to become poor. Pets can often be more aggressive and lose their appetite when they have an illness.
In such circumstances, an owner might choose to get their pet painlessly euthanized since they are unable to bear the sight of their pet's agony. A vet must first inform the owner about all the treatments available for the condition. If there is no treatment available, then letting the pet suffer in pain may be considered as unethical.

On the other hand, a vet should never agree to such a demand if an owner wants a healthy pet to be euthanized for any reason. If an owner cannot afford to keep a pet, then the pet can easily be adopted by another home or animal shelter. This can help to avoid unnecessary deaths. It would be unethical and immoral to kill a healthy animal.

Animals have a right to live just like humans. It would be ridiculous to think about euthanizing a healthy human. Therefore, the same should apply to animals and pets.

Owners are the people who take care of pets and they do this with love and affection. Owners can influence a vet's decision only if their request is reasonable. If the pet can be treated and numerous treatments are available, then the owner can choose which treatment would be best for their pet.
However, owners do not have the right to do whatever they wish with their pets especially if it affects the pet's health.

4) Science provides us with explanations for all events happening right now. It is the basis of everything and gives us an idea of how different things work around us.

It helped to explain how our body systems work together to keep us alive, how evolution allowed some species to survive and others to become extinct and how plants are able to make their own food. Through science, we were able to progress in the field of technology. Technology assists us in providing safer and faster treatments. The use of CT scans and X-ray machines allows us to diagnose different medical conditions so we can provide the most appropriate treatment. According to the statement, science is only capable of telling us what events are possible and how they occur. It, however, does not tell us what events are right. For example, through science, we were able to formulate theories of how the universe came to existence. However, these are just possible theories and we are still not sure which explanation is correct.

Similarly, the Theory of Relativity and the Theory of Evolution are still just possible explanations, which are open to criticism.

Together with this, science is objective, which means that it is only rational and logical. It does not involve any emotions or morals. For example, science allowed us to create treatments using embryonic stem cells. However, the use of embryonic stem cells is still controversial as it involves the destruction of an embryo, a potential human life. Science does not tell us whether these things are right or not. Science cannot help us to make moral and sensitive decisions such as whether euthanasia should be allowed or not.

Science cannot explain many abstract ideas such as love. We only know that hormones play a role in this but the existence of emotions is still a mystery.

However, without science, we would not be able to explain phenomena that occur around us. This is why science is just as important as morals and ethics.

1) D
Match each row to the bar charts given. You will see that D does not match any of the rows.

2) E
A – Wrong
This option just outlines a cause and effect. The noise of modern human life will be a cause of the extinction of whales.

B – Wrong
The text provided does not mention sea-based wind farms so this is not correct.

C – Wrong
This option is too strong. The phrase "will be able to adapt" suggests that something will definitely happen. This cannot be concluded from the passage.

D – Wrong
The passage just points out the fact that due to loud noise, whales have to adapt their voices. This option is slightly off-putting but it is not clearly stated that whale numbers are decreasing due to loud human noise.

3) C
Cost of deluxe room with meals = $80
Cost of deluxe room without meals = $65
Cost of 6 nights = 65 x 6 = $390
Cost of hiring a car = $5 + ($5 × 6) = $35
Total cost = $390 + $35 = $425

4) E
A – Wrong
The passage is only focused on the negative aspect of internet. Even though this option may seem correct, it is wrong to shift the focus of the text. We must find out the flaw of the negative aspect of the passage; not the flaw of its focus.

B – Wrong
Again, we must not shift the focus to pointing out some positive aspects. Identify the flaw of the negative aspect!

C – Wrong
This is irrelevant. It may seem relevant because it mention children growing up and going to work. However, the focus of the text is mainly children.

D – Wrong
This may be the most tempting option out of the previous three. However, the passage is

making a link between children playing computer games and social interaction. This option does not find a flaw in this link.

E – Correct
This option is correct because the passage does not provide evidence of children playing video games and reduced social interaction.

5) F
The only way to get this correct is by visualisation. You will notice that if 3 is rotated clockwise 2 times and placed on X, it is correct. If you rotate 4 clockwise once, then it will also be correct.

6) C

A – Wrong
The text does not assume that people who have poor memory cannot become taxi drivers.

B – Wrong
This is clearly wrong, as the text does not mention anything about people believing it is easy to become a taxi driver.

C – Correct
The line "so all that learning…also increases their memory power" suggests that memory power increases after they have learnt the road network of London. IF the same group of prop were to undergo brain scans before they learnt, then the same results would not have been observed.

D – Wrong
Nothing mentioned in the text about why people choose to become taxi drivers.

7) A
Firstly, we must see the planes that are able to travel 5600 miles. C, E and F can be ruled out since their capacity is less than 5600 miles.
This is not a trick question and there is no need for calculations. The fuel consumption column is divided into two columns: fuel consumption on empty plane and additional per passenger. The easiest way to get to the answer is to select the option, which has the lowest value for each of the two columns. 3 is lowest in empty plane column and 0.01 for additional per passenger column. Therefore, 'A' is the answer.

8) D

A – Wrong
The graph only provides information about the relative pay of men and women rather than the actual pay.

B – Wrong
We do not have any information about the willingness of employers to employ women based on their age.

C – Wrong
We do not know the actual difference between the pay gap at the ages of 22 and 30. We are only given information for the ranges (22-29) and (30-29)

D – Correct
From the graph, you can see that the women who are in their 40s and 50s earn more than 20% less than what men earn.
If a man earns £1, then a woman in their 40s would earn = (100 – 22.8)% x 1 = 77.2% x 1 = £0.772
If a man earns £1, then a woman in their 50s would earn = (100 – 20.6)% x 1 = 79.4% x 1 = £0.794

Both these values are less than £0.80 so D is the answer.

---

9) C
Let pay of males be = 'p'
We know that males were paid 22.8%.
According to the formula given in the question,
$100 \times \left(\frac{male\ pay\ -\ female\ pay}{male\ pay}\right)$ = gender gap percentage

Substituting, we get
$100 \times \left(\frac{p\ -\ 16000}{p}\right) = 22.8$
$\frac{p\ -\ 16000}{p} = \frac{22.8}{100} = 0.228$
$p - 16000 = 0.228p$
Rearranging, we get,
$p - 0.228p = 16,000$
$0.772p = 16000$
$p = \frac{16000}{0.772} \approx £20,700$

---

10) C
Long hours and intensity of work deter mothers, in particular, from taking up senior positions. The assumption is that women would be ready to take these positions if they were in a different scenario.

A – Wrong
Gender of the employer is totally irrelevant.

B – Wrong
The text clearly says the "senior positions deterred mother form seeking promotions for which they were qualified".

C – Correct
This paraphrases the assumption that I have mentioned above.

D – Wrong
Nothing is mentioned about the pay that women receive in the third paragraph.

---

11) D

This question only deals with paragraph 4, as said in the question.

A – Wrong
There is no information about part-time jobs of people in their 60s and hence this is irrelevant.

B – Wrong
The statement given in this option is assumed and cannot be definitely proven. The wages are not given so we cannot work it out.

C – Wrong
Again, the same assumption is made in this option as in B.

D – Correct
This is the only option left. If we work out the maths, then we get the same answer. We can use the formula given in the question. Let us round up the £8.82 value to £9

$$^{15-9}/_{15} \times 100$$

$$^{6}/_{15} \times 100 = 40\%$$

This percentage is roughly the same as the 41.2% given in paragraph 4. So this is the correct answer.

12) D

This may seem tricky but remember there are 81 tiles of the SAME SIZE. This means that there are no smaller or larger tiles.

1st tile:

2nd tile:

3rd tile:

4th tile:

5th tile:

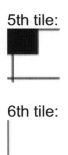

6th tile:

---

13) B

The evidence so far collected by researchers is that chimps, who are unable to understand language, share 99% of their DNA with humans, who are able to understand language. The HAR1 is what makes chimps and humans dramatically different. Putting 2 and 2 together, HAR1 is associated with language.

A – Wrong

This would weaken the hypothesis as A suggests that chimps also have a gene which is 98% identical to HAR1. This would mean that HAR1 is not related to language.

B – Correct

A mutation in HAR1 causes language impairment. This means that HAR1 is directly associated with language and damage to HAR1 causes problems in language.

C – Wrong

C does not specify what type of communication. Hoover, even if we assume that communication is related to language and that HAR1 is found in parts of the brain, **which are not** related to communication, then this would weaken the argument.

D – Wrong

This is irrelevant to the questioning as all genes are expressed in the brain before birth.

E – Wrong

Asian, we cannot correlate communication with language. Even if we assume that communication and language are the same things, then D actually weakens the hypothesis. If chimps were taught symbol language, then this means that they also possess a gene associated with language. Since chimps do not have HAR1, then this would mean that HAR1 is not associated with language.

---

14) C

The best way to solve this question is to draw a table of wins, draws and losses.
We know that each team plays the others only once. So each team plays a total of 4 matches.
Central has 2 points = Only possibility is 0 wins, 2 draws and 2 losses
Northern = 8 points, only possibility is 2 wins, 2 draws, 0 losses
Southern = 5 points, only possibility is 1 win, 2 draws, 1 loss
Western = 1 point = 0 wins, 1 draw, 3 losses

	Wins	Draws	Losses
Central	0	2	2
Eastern			
Northern	2	2	0
Southern	1	2	1
Western	0	1	3
Total	**3**	**7**	**6**

There were 6 losses in total whilst only 3 wins. Therefore, Eastern must have won 3 times. Eastern must not have lost a single match, as that would disrupt the win-loss ratio, meaning that it must have drawn once.

3 wins and 1 draw = (3 × 3) + (1 × 1) = 10 points

Hence, the answer is C.

---

15) B

1 – Wrong

The passage does not contain any information about who makes or defines human rights. Hence this is incorrect.

2 – Correct

This is correct. The text assumes that a right is either constitutional or human. It does not take into consideration that a right can be both.

3 – Wrong

This is irrelevant as the prisoners choice does not matter. The text only focuses on whether they should be allowed to vote or not.

---

16) D

Volume = Area x Depth

Depth = Volume / Area

Firstly, use approximate values. Using the exact values given in the table will waste time during calculations.

A – Wrong

$\frac{80000}{400000} = \frac{1}{5} = 0.2$ km

B – Wrong

$\frac{28000}{70000} = \frac{4}{10} = 0.4$ km

C – Wrong

$\frac{19000}{32000} = 0.59$ km

D – Correct

$^{24000}/_{32000} = {}^3/_4 = 0.75$ km

E – Wrong

$^{300}/_{24000} = {}^1/_{80} = 0.0125$ km

Baikal clearly has the greatest average depth.

---

17) C

1 – Wrong

The text does not focus on the number of people that have consumed the infected beef. It's the last sentence "so there will be two further outbreaks of vCJD, as those who consumed infected beef grow older" It's main focus is on the future outbreaks that will occur. So this is irrelevant.

2 – Wrong

This is clearly false as those with the M-V combination do develop vCJD as they grow older.

3 – Correct

The passage assumes that inheritance of the combination of genes is more important for susceptibility rather than the M variant only. There can be two combinations with the M variant: M-V and M-M. Both these combinations allow vCJD to develop. M-M develops vCJD now and M-V in the future.

---

18) B

Wage of Jasper = £240 + [5x(43 - 21)] + (20 × 6) = £470
Wage of Ruby = £470 + £40 = £510
Age of Ruby = 43 – 8 = 35 years
Using the formula given in the question:
Let number of working years for Ruby be 'N'
240 + [5 x (35 - 21)] + (20 x N) = 510
20N = 510 – (240 + 70)
20N = 200
N =10 years
So, Ruby has been working in the company for a total of 10 years. However, the question asks for the difference ("how much longer than Jasper has Ruby been employed").
We know Jasper has been working for 6 years.
So Ruby has been working for (10 – 6 = 4) 4 more years than Jasper.

---

19) A

To solve this question, we need to use the following method:

Drilling:
Small strike (probability = 0.1) will lead to a loss of (-800,000 + 80,000 = -720,000)
Medium strike (probability = 0.8) will lead to a profit of (1,200,000 – 800,000 = 400,000)
Big strike (probability = 0.1) will lead to a profit of = (4,600,000 – 800,000 = 3,800,000)
Sum of possibilities = (-720,000 x 0.1) + (400,000 x 0.8) + (3,800,000 x 0.1) = $628,000

Not drilling:
No sale (probability = 0.2) will lead to no profit or no loss
small sale (probability = 0.6) will lead to a profit of (500,000 – 0 = 500,000)
Big sale (probability = 0.2) will lead to a profit of = (1,000,000 – 0 = 1,000,000)
Sum of possibilities = (0 x 0.2) + (500,000 x 0.6) + (1,000,000 x 0.2) = $500,000

Hence the probability of making a profit is larger when drilling is done.

20) D

A – Wrong
Drilling a medium strike will also make profit.

B – Wrong
A medium strike would result in $400,000 profit. If a sale was made, the minimum profit would be $500,000, which is more than a medium strike profit.

C – Wrong
Probability of making a loss (10% = 0.1) is less than the probability of making a profit (90% = 0.9)

D – Correct
Probability of making a medium strike = 80% (0.8).
Probability of selling the right = 60% + 20% = 80% (0.8)

Hence D is correct.

21) F

Statement 1:
Y-Oil bought right for = $500,000
Cost of drilling = $800,000
Total cost = $800,000 + $500,000 = $1,300,000
Money made from medium strike = $1,200,000
Hence, Y-Oil would make a loss of $100,000. Therefore statement 1 is true.

Statement 2:
The only way to make a profit is by landing a big strike, which has a probability of 10% (0.1). This probability is less than 80% so statement 2 is true.

Statement 3:
If drilling costs are reduced, new cost would be = 0.75 x $800,000 = $600,000
Purchase price of rights = $500,000
Total cost = $600,000 + $500,000 = $1,100,000
Medium strike income = $1,200,000
Hence, Y-Oil would make a profit if they reduced the drilling price by 25%. Statement 3 is true.

All statements are true. Therefore, F is the correct answer.

22) E
The question is basically asking us to find out which statement would be more profitable.

1 –
We know that the sum of possible outcomes of drilling = $628,000
If the company pays the insurance premium, then the profit would be = 628000 -200000 = $428,000

2 –
Probability of oil spill = 0.03
0.03 x 10,000,000 = $300,000
If company does not pay insurance and gets an oil spill, expected outcome:
628000 -300000 = $328,000

3 –
If the company decides against drilling, minimum profit = $500,000

So order of favourable option: 3, 1, 2

23) D
Let us look at the left hand side first.
So far, the left hand side adds up to 18. It needs 13 more to make 21. The 13 can only be made up of 6 and 7. We do not know which order though.

On the right side, we have a total of 11. It needs 10 more to become 21. The 10 cannot be made from 6 and 4 since 6 is needed on the left hand side.

If we put 6 at the top left, we get a total of 15 on the top row. 6 more is needed. Since 6 is needed, 8 cannot be on the top right. Hence, 2 will be at the top right.
So far, we have 6 + 9 + 2 = 17 on the top row. If we put 4 on the third house on the top row, we can get 21.

If we put 7 above the 3 on the left hand side, we get:
6 + 5 + 7 + 3 = 21

If we put 8 on the bottom left, below the 1, we get:
2 + 10 + 1 + 8 = 21

Hence, between 3 and 5, number 7 is present.

24) A
The manager's quote means that Petermass will not play if Fredericks is fit, and may or may not play if Fredericks is not fit. There is no guarantee that Petermass will play if Fredericks is not fit.
Jed: This is correct. The only chance Petermass has of playing is if Fredericks is not fit. If Fredericks is fit, then Petermass will definitely not play.

Ned: If Fredericks is not fit, then there is only a possibility that Petermass will play. It is not definite that Petermass will play.

Ted: This is not necessarily true. There can be a possibility in which Petermass and Fredericks can both be unfit and not play.

---

25) C
The one which has equal proportions (vinaigrette A) 90 ml oil and 90 ml vinegar
90 ml of A would contain 45 ml oil and 45 ml vinegar
90 ml of A is added to the second vinaigrette (B)
180 ml of B has: 120 ml oil ($^2/_3$) and 60 ml vinegar ($^1/_3$)
When 90 ml of A is added to 180 ml of B, total volume of new mixture = 180 + 90 = 270 ml
270 ml of the mixture has (120 + 45) oil and (60 + 45) vinegar = 165 ml oil and 105 ml vinegar
Ratio of oil and vinegar = 33 : 21
90 ml of this mixture has: ($^{165}/_3$) oil and ($^{105}/_3$) vinegar = 55 ml oil and 35 ml vinegar
[We divided by 3 because the large mixture had 270 ml and we took out 90 ml. $^{270}/_{90}$ = 3]
A now has: (45 + 55) oil and (45 + 35) = 100 ml oil and 80 ml vinegar
B now has: (165 – 55) oil and (105 – 35) = 110 ml oil and 80 ml vinegar

---

26) C
A – Wrong
Having a gravity similar to Earth is not a sufficient enough condition for supporting life.

B – Wrong
Liquid water being able to form oceans, lakes and rivers is not a sufficient enough condition for supporting life.

C – Correct
This is correct because of the line "planets like this **must** be really common".

D – Wrong
"is probably **in the order of** 10 or 20 per cent" is different from "10 or 20 per cent of systems **have**".
This statement is too strong.

E – Wrong
The text says that "there could be" and not "there are". One word makes the whole difference.
This statement is too strong.

---

27) A
There is no definite way to solve this. You can try and draw or visualise different combinations of the pieces and try to make either a 4 x 3 or a 6 x 2 rectangle.
However, you will soon realise that none of the combinations can make either of the two rectangles.

---

28) C
1 – Correct
In order to make a fair comparison between the two types of buses, we need to know the distance that can be covered using one tonne of hydrogen and one tonne of traditional fuel. Using this data, we can then decide how much pollution each type of bus will produce.

2 – Wrong
We do not really need to know the distance covered by each bus on a weekly basis. Also, the new buses travel on the same routes as the old ones. So they will be covering roughly the same distance as the traditional buses.

3 – Correct
We also need to know the amount of carbon dioxide produced by one tonne of traditional fuel. Then we can compare this with the amount of carbon dioxide emitted by hydrogen and make an informed decision about which fuel is better.

4 – Correct
The text does say that transportation of fuel to the depot also needs to be considered. To make a fair comparison, we need to know how much carbon dioxide is emitted when each type of fuel is transported.

Statements 1, 3 and 4 are correct. So, C is the answer.

---

29) D
Claire's speed = 6 km/hr
Distance that can be covered in 20 minutes (one-third hour) = $\frac{1}{3}$ x 6 = 2 km

So if Claire had left 20 minutes she would have covered 2 km more. Since she was 3 km away from the library, she would have been 1 km away if she had left on time.

Since Claire and Charles usually meet at the library, Charles has to cover 3 km whilst Claire would have to cover 1 km. So Charles' speed is three times that of Claire.

Charles' speed = 3 x 6 = 18 km/hr

---

30) B
The existence of a sterile neutrino is a possible explanation for the pulsars whizzing through the universe at high speeds.

A – Wrong
This statement is too strong as it says, "Sterile neutrinos **must** be the cause of the phenomenon".
The word 'must' is too strong.

B – Correct
This uses the appropriate words "**could be** caused by the existence of sterile neutrinos".

C – Wrong
Again "best explanation" is too strong to use, as we have not heard any other hypotheses.

D – Wrong
Again, this statement is too strong. D is effectively stating that sterile neutrinos are definitely the cause of pulsars.

---

31) C

The 4 stacks that are at the sides (not in the middle 6) have 6 cylinders. Since there are 20 cylinders on day 11, then there must be 14 cylinders in the middle 6 stacks.

We know that all 6 stacks must have at least one cylinder on each of them. The view from X shows 6 cylinders in the middle. There are 6 on the view from X and each of the stacks must have at least one cylinder. This means that a maximum of 4 cylinders can be missing.

A, B, E and F are too full. They definitely cannot be the answers.

D is still possible if the middle 2 stacks only have one cylinder each. The middle six stacks would therefore have 14 cylinders.

C is not possible because the top middle two sacks would have to be 2 cylinders tall and middle two stacks would have to be 1 cylinder tall.

32) C

Average doctor sees 1500 patients a year.
Consultation rate per patient per year in 2006 = 5.26 ≈ 5.00
Total number of consultations in a year = 1500 x 5 = 7500
Number of consultations per doctor per day = $7500/250$ = 30
This is closest to C (32).

33) D

Consultation rate for nurses in 1995 = 0.8
Proportion of patients seen by nurses = $0.8/3.9$ ≈ 0.2

Consultation rate in 2006 = 1.8
Proportion of patients seen by nurses = $1.8/5.26$ ≈ 0.34
Increase in consultation rate = 0.34 − 0.2 = 0.14

Percentage increase = $(0.14/0.2)$ x 100 = 70%

This is closest to D (67%).

34) C

It would be best to look at the age group which has the largest discrepancy on the graph provided in the question. Let us take age group 30-34.

Female consultation rate in 2006 = 6
Male consultation rate in 2006 = 2

Ratio = 6 ÷ 2 = 3

The ratio is definitely above 2 so C is the answer.

35) C

A – Wrong
Increased health issues can cause people to see the doctor more often for regular health-check-ups. So this is relevant.

B – Wrong
Since people of all ages have become equally less health, there would be an increase in consultations for treatments.

C – Correct
People getting older does not change the fact that there is still the same age group in the age demographics. Ageing cannot be or is the least satisfactory as a potential explanation for the increase in consultations.

D – Wrong
GPs increasing the amount of preventative medicine they do is relevant to as to why there has been an increase in the consultations between 1995 and 2006.

213

2011 Section 2

1) F
A - insulin can fit in the pancreas row.
B - Adrenaline increases heartbeat rate, so this option can fit in the first row
C - Pituitary gland is the gland, which secretes ADH, so it fits.
D - Testes secrete testosterone so it fits in the fourth row
E - Ovary secretes oestrogen so it fits in the second row
F - Carbohydrase is an enzyme. It is neither a gland, hormone nor a function. So it does not fit anywhere, hence is the correct answer.
G - ADH (hormone in third row) regulates water level in blood. So this fits.

---

2) B
This question deals with valencies.
X, being in group 3, has a valency of +3. It has 3 electrons in its outer shell. It needs to donate its 3 electrons to be stable.
Y is in group 6, meaning it needs 2 electrons to be stable. Its valency is -2.
To find the formula we can use the following technique:

The two arrows represent a criss cross, meaning -2 goes to X and +3 goes to Y.
So the formula is X_2Y_3.

---

3) C
Formula for kinetic energy = $\frac{1}{2}mv^2$
Let mass of P and Q be 'm'
KE of P = $\frac{1}{2}m(10)^2$ = 50m J
KE of Q = $\frac{1}{2}m(20)^2$ = 200m J
So, KE of Q is four times P
The squared in the KE formula makes it four times.
Then the height of Q will be twice of P.
So GPE of Q would be twice as much as P.
This corresponds to option C.

---

4) C
$3x(3x^{-1/3})^3$
$3x(3^3x^{-3/3})$
$3x(27x^{-1})$
$3x(\frac{27}{x})$
$3(27) = 81$

214

5) F

1 - Mitosis produces genetically identical cells. So it cannot introduce variation. This is wrong.
2 - Meiosis introduces variation in species. It cannot produce genetically identical cells. This is wrong.
3 - In mitosis, the 2 daughter cells produced are diploid. So this is correct
4 - In meiosis, the 4 daughter cells produced are haploid. So this is correct.
5 - Mitosis only produces 2 daughter cells. This is correct.

6) D

1 - When temperature increases, molecules gain more kinetic energy, therefore they move around a lot. This increases the probability of more collisions with surrounding molecules per unit time. So statement 1 is correct.

2 - Since the molecules gain more kinetic energy, the probability of collisions with more activation energy will also increase. So statement 2 is correct.

3 - An increase in kinetic energy does not alter the orientation of molecules. So, statement 3 is wrong.

7) E

A - Wrong
The definition of nuclear fission is splitting of a nucleus into two smaller nuclei. The definition given in this statement is wrong.

B - Wrong
The definition of half-life is wrong. Half-life is the time taken for half of the substance to decay.

C - Wrong
Number of neutrons = Mass number - Atomic number. (Not Atomic number - Mass number)

D - Wrong
Fission is used in nuclear power stations.

E - Correct
When a nucleus emits a ß-particle, the number of particles in the nucleus itself remains the same (since mass number does no change).

F - Wrong
When a nucleus emits an α-particle, it loses two neutrons and two protons.

8) D

Number of degrees in a clock (circle) = 360°
Number of divisions in a clock = 12
Angle between each division = $360/12$ = 30°

This clock shows 9:45. The hour hand is 3/4 of the way between 9 and 10, whilst the minute hand is on 9.
We know angle between each division = 30°
So angle between 9 and 10 = 30°
Angle between hour hand and minute hand = $\frac{3}{4}$ x 30° = 22.5°

---

9) C

1 - All individuals within a species show variation. e.g. All humans have some sort of variation in our genes such, as different eye colour or faces. So 1 is correct.

2 - Competition between individuals within a species is called intraspecific competition (intra=within). e.g. Lions have to compete with other lions for food.

3 - This is true. Let us explain this with an example. Let us take the cubs of a lion. The cubs, which are more tolerant of higher temperatures, will more likely be able to survive for a longer period of time. On the other hand, if a cub, born with genes which are not tolerant of high temperatures will be more likely to die earlier than the other cubs.

4 - This is not necessarily true. Individuals who have disadvantageous adaptations will also be able to breed. 4 is wrong.

5 - This is true.

---

10) D

In the hydrocarbon shown, there are 10 carbon atoms and 18 hydrogen atoms. We cannot double count the corners in the middle (since there is an overlap).

(12 x 10) + (18 x 1) = 138

---

11) B

The current flows from positive to negative, meaning it flows from the bigger line on the battery to the smaller line on the other side of the battery. It flows clockwise.

The diode breaks the circuit. If the switch on the branch is open, then it means that no current is flowing to the circuit. So the ammeter would show 0.

If the switch is closed, it means that current flows through the branch but not on the side in which the diode is placed. Current would equal to voltage divided by resistance. We know resistance equals 3.
Current = $\frac{6}{3}$ = 2A
So B is correct.

12) D
The easiest way to solve this is to assign values to the integers given in options A, B, C, D and E. However, the inequalities in the question should still be true)

A - This cannot be 100% proven as true.
Let us say $x = 10$ and $w = 20$, this cannot be true.
However, $w(20) < x^2$ ($10^2 = 100$) is true.

B - This cannot be 100% proven as true.
We are only told that $w < x^2$ and $x > y^2$. We cannot determine the inequality between w and y.

C - Again, we cannot determine the inequality between w and z.

D - This can be proven as correct.
Since $x > y^2$, and y^2 will always be equal to (if $y = 1$) or greater than y, we can get the inequalities:
$x > y^2$ and $y^2 \geq y$, we can determine the inequality $x > y$.

E - This cannot be proven correct.

13) E
Read the question carefully! It says, "when blood **first** enters that muscle"
When blood first enters the muscle, it's oxygen concentration would be higher than the muscle and the carbon dioxide concentration would be lower than in muscle to allow diffusion of both gases.
The first column should have low and the second column should have high. We can rule out A, B and C.
We know that the process involved is diffusion. Hence, we can rule out F since it says osmosis.
We know oxygen concentration in muscle would be low since it uses oxygen for respiration.
So, D is incorrect, leaving us with E.

14) C
We know that when a metal bonds with a non-metal, an ionic bond is formed. This means that NaCl and Na_2O do not form covalent bonds whilst all others form covalent bonds. So C is correct.

15) B
Equation for Force is: Force = mass x acceleration
We know the mass is 50g which is equal to 0.05kg
To find the acceleration we need to use the XUVAT or SUVAT equations:
$v^2 - u^2 = 2as$
$v = u + at$
$s = ut + 1/2 \, at^2$
$s = 1/2 \, (u + v) \, t$

We have
v = 300m/s,
u = 0 m/s,
s = 60cm = 0.6m, t = not known (cannot use eq 2, 3 and 4)
a = value we want to find out.

Therefore, we will have to use the first equation, $v^2 - u^2 = 2as$.
$300^2 - 0^2 = 2 \times a \times 0.6$
$9000/_{1.2} = a$
a = 7500 m/s
Force = 0.05 x 7500 = 3750 N = 3.75×10^3 N

---

16) E
Let x = 1.
Equation 1: y = 3x - 2. y = 3(1) - 2. y = 1
Equation 2: $y = x^2$. $y = 1^2$. y = 1 (equations 1 and 2 will intersect)
Equation 3: $y = 1 - x^2$. y = 1 - 1. y = 0 (this is pretty close to 1 and 2)

Equation 4: y = x + 6. y = 1 + 6. y = 7 (very far away from all graphs but it is farthest away from equation 3)

The furthest graphs are 3 and 4. You can also notice that since equation 4 has a plus sign, the points will always be much higher than equation 3 since equation 3 has $1 - x^2$.
Alternatively, you can draw a quick graph to see which equations will intersect. Whatever suits you best!

---

17) D
1 - If the condition is dominant, then P, Q, R and S must be recessive. Since T has the condition, it must have at least one dominant allele. Therefore, the reason why U has the condition is because it obtained the allele from T.

2- We know that statement 2 could definitely be a reason. If the sperm carried the allele and one allele is enough to cause the condition, then 2 could be reason. We can eliminate B and E.

3 - If the egg from S had a mutation, then it certainly could have caused the condition.

All statements could be reasons why U has the condition. Hence, D is correct.

---

18) E
Set up algebraic equations for any of the elements present.
e.g. Cu on the left side appears 'a' times. Cu appears 'x' number of times on the right side.

a = x
However, all of the options have a = x. (Option A has a = 2, x = 2)

Let us try N
b = 2x + 2
Try substituting the values of 'b' and 'x' from the options given.
Option A cannot be correct.
Option B cannot be correct.
Option C can be correct.
Option D can be correct.
Option E can be correct

Let us make an equation for O
3b = 6x + y + 2
Try substituting the values of b, x and y from the options given.
Option A cannot be correct.
Option B cannot be correct.
Option C cannot be correct.
Option D cannot be correct.
Option E can be correct

So E is the correct answer.

---

19) A
V (voltage) is directly proportional to I (current). If voltage increases, then current
also increases since there is a constant temperature.
We know the equation: V = IR
Voltage increases and Current increases. Since they both increase proportionally,
resistance would have to remain the same.

---

20) B
Let hypotenuse of smaller triangle = H
Let hypotenuse of larger triangle = A
Let hypotenuse of largest triangle = B

Using Pythagoras theorem,
$H^2 = 1^2 + 3^2$
$H^2 = 1 + 9 = 10$
$H = \sqrt{10}$

Since the triangles are similar,
$\frac{3}{\sqrt{10}} = \frac{\sqrt{10}}{A}$
$A = \frac{10}{3}$
Since larger triangle and largest triangle are similar,
Small edge of the largest triangle = $\frac{1}{3} \times (\frac{10}{6}) = (\frac{10}{9})$
Area of a right angled triangle = ½ x base x height = ½ x $(\frac{10}{9})$ x $(\frac{10}{3})$ = $(\frac{100}{54})$ = $(\frac{50}{27})$ cm²

21) D

All body cells such as red blood cells and skin cells have double the amount of DNA as gametes.

Zygotes also have double the DNA as gametes.

The easiest one to spot is from the '0' column. Only an enucleated egg cell has '0' DNA.

Since egg cell is a gamete, it will have '1' DNA. Since nerve cell is a body cell, it will have '2' DNA.

So, D is the answer.

22) D

Mass of PbS in 478kg of ore = 70% of 478 = 0.7 x 478 = 334.6kg ≈ 335 kg

Mr of PbS = 207 + 32 = 239

$n = \frac{335}{239} \approx \frac{336}{240} = 1.4$ moles

Moles of Pb = 1.4 moles

$n = \frac{m}{Mr}$

$m = n \times Mr$

$m = 1.4 \times 207 = 289.8$

Hence D is the answer.

23) C

When a wave travels from a less dense medium to a denser medium (such as from air to glass), its speed decreases and it refracts. So, we can eliminate options E, F, G and H.

Speed = wavelength x frequency

FREQUENCY NEVER CHANGES DURING REFRACTION.

Since frequency does not change but speed decreases, therefore, its wavelength must also decrease.

Since the wavelength in air was 600nm, its new wavelength must be lower than 600nm.

Hence, we can eliminate options B and D.

Frequency remains unchanged.

Frequency of light in air = speed/wavelength = $(3 \times 10^8) \div (600 \times 10^{-9}) = 5.0 \times 10^{14}$ Hz

24) B

The only way to get a total of 12 is to get 6 on both dices.

Since the first die is fair, probability of getting a 6 = $\frac{1}{6}$

We know probability of getting a total of 12 is $\frac{1}{18}$.

We get 1/18 when we multiply probability of 6 on first die with probability of 6 on the second die.

Therefore, probability of getting a 12 on second die = $\frac{1}{18} \div \frac{1}{6} = \frac{6}{18} = \frac{1}{3}$

Probability of getting other numbers = $1 - \frac{1}{3} = \frac{2}{3}$

Only way to get a total of 2 is if we get 1 on first die and 1 on the second die.

Since 1 to 5 have the same probability, probability of getting a 1 on the second die = $2/3 \div 5 = 2/15$

Probability of getting a 1 on first die = $1/6$

Probability of getting a total of 2 = $1/6 \times 2/15 = 2/90 = 1/45$
Hence, B is the answer.

25) D
This is slightly tricky. It is important to realise which number indicates what.

1 on the graph indicates the change in the internal environment.
2 indicates the point at which the response to the change is initiated.
3 indicates the time taken to bring the level back to normal.

Since someone has a condition, which makes their homeostatic system less responsive, it would take longer for their system to start the response.
Hence, D is correct. 2 would be higher as the person's homeostatic response would take longer to respond.

26) E
Reacting with air essentially means that it is reacting with oxygen.
Different elements present in CH_3SCH_3: C, H and S
Carbon will form its oxide, Hydrogen will form its oxide (water) and sulphur will form its oxide.
There would be three products: CO_2, H_2O AND SO_2
Therefore, the answer could only be E.

27) B
50 beats per minute means after every $60/50$ seconds (1.2 seconds), there is one beat.
When soldiers at the front put down their right foot, the soldiers at the back put down their left foot.
Therefore, the beat is adjusted to 1 every $30/50$ seconds (0.6 seconds).
Minimum distance = $(30/50) \times 330 = 198$ m

2011 Section 3

1) Democratic freedom basically means that people have the power to choose who represents them in the government. In a democracy, an individual exercises many rights. These include freedom of expression, right to life, right to a fair trial and many others. The statement suggests that a person, living in a democratic country, should be allowed to say whatever they want in public without any restrictions or limitations.

Being allowed to say anything in public can have some serious consequences as people can take advantage of this to run their own propaganda. They can use freedom of speech as an excuse to make unreasonable, prejudiced and extreme statements, which can cause confusion within the public. Such individuals can lie blatantly and mislead other people into thinking that whatever they are proclaiming is true. This is dangerous for young minds that cannot differentiate between right and wrong.

Legislations should be put in place to ensure that freedom of speech is used in a constructive manner. It can be used to oppose anything that is wrong and unjust. Laws should be made to deter people from using their freedom of speech to spread hatred and discrimination. Any declarations that are made in public should first be censored to prevent children from being exposed to any obscene or abusive language.

Limitations allow harmony to be maintained between two sections of society. Hence, the statement is wrong up to a certain extent.

---

2) The statement says that people are amused by a doctor's competence to heal a patient. However, it is nature that is responsible for curing the disease and not the doctor. According to Voltaire, doctors should have qualities that prevent patients from worrying.

Science has allowed humans to progress rapidly in the field of medicine. The use of vaccines, machines and targeted drugs enables doctors to prevent, diagnose and treat diseases quickly and safely. Many treatments require intensive research to guarantee whether or not that treatment is useful. Guidelines are created to make sure that treatments are provided safely and in the correct manner. Pharmacists are given their own set of instructions to ensure that they provide patients with the correct dosage. An artist is a person who uses paint to make a painting. Without an artist, the paint cannot make a painting itself. Similarly, a doctor is a person who uses scientific knowledge to allow nature to cure a disease effectively. Without a doctor, nature cannot cure a serious illness or disease itself.

Doctors also need to consider the importance of ethics. They must be sociable, empathetic and compassionate with their patients. In order for a treatment to be effective, the patient must know that they are feeling better. Another aspect of medicine is placebo. It is better than no treatment. Patients often feel better just by knowing that they are in the care of someone who has good scientific knowledge and skills to cure a disease.

In addition to this, qualities such as teamwork, open-mindedness, and leadership are also important for the smooth functioning of medical staff.

---

3) Scientific objectivity expresses the idea that perspectives, bias or personal beliefs should not influence the methods and results of science. Science should be based only on research, logic and evidence.

"A scientific man", in this statement, refers to a person who uses science on a daily basis, such as doctors, engineers, pharmacists and scientists. According to Darwin, such an individual cannot allow emotions or wishes to affect their scientific work.

A "heart of stone", according to Darwin, refers to objectivity. The case of Andrew Wakefield proves the importance of objectivity in science. Wakefield was bribed by a law firm to prove that MMR vaccines caused autism in children. He manipulated his results and put his subjects through unethical procedures to prove the link between MMR vaccines and autism. Many people believed this to be true and did not vaccinate their children. This, unfortunately, resulted in the deaths of many children from measles, mumps and rubella. Scientists must ensure that their experiments are strictly controlled. Proclamations should be made only after peer review and strong evidence.

On the other hand, scientists make hypotheses based on personal beliefs and findings. Without any personal interest, Sir Isaac Newton would not have been intrigued by gravity and motion. Similarly, Thomas Edison's wish to invent the light bulb caused him to fail 1000 times before he could succeed. Edward Jenner discovered the smallpox vaccine because he believed that exposure to cowpox rendered the body immune from smallpox. It was their passion and determination, which led to scientific discoveries that revolutionised the world.

A person's imagination is the basis of progress. It was imagination that allowed the Wright brother to invent the aeroplane and Ernst Ruska to construct the electron microscope. Therefore, without any wishes and affections, our desire to understand the world and universe would diminish.

---

4) According to the statement, healthcare for pets should be free just like it is for humans. Animals also experience pain and illness like us. They are a very important part of our lives and hence, their healthcare should also be the responsibility of the government.

Pet owners treat their pets like a family member and shower them with love and affection. Many pet owners who are not able to afford veterinary care often have to abandon their pets. By providing free veterinary care, the number of abandoned and neglected pets would decrease considerably. Some may argue that if the government can pay for self-inflicted injuries, then pet healthcare should also become free.

The contrary argument is that people should only adopt pets if they are capable of providing them with their basic necessities for the rest of the animal's lifespan. If they cannot afford veterinary care, then they should either get pet insurance or not adopt a pet. If veterinary care becomes free, it would be unfair for the people who do not own pets to pay taxes to fund free pet healthcare. If veterinary care becomes government funded, the likelihood is that owners may start to pay less attention to their pet's health. This is definitely undesirable.

A solution would be to provide free pet health care if pet owners pay extra tax to fund this service. This is fair and potential pet owners would have to consider the extra costs before adopting a pet.

It is difficult to come to a definite conclusion with regards to this matter. Humans seem to treat themselves as being superior to other animals. Some may even think that human life is more important than animal life. Therefore, NHS resources should be used to save a human's life rather than an animal's life. Others may think that all animals share the same planet and hence, all life is equally important.

1) D

Population of Republic of Bondia = Total population of six islands

Total population of six islands = 8,628,709

10% of 8,628,709 = 862,870

Islands which have less than 10% of population of Bondia = Brosnan and Dalton

Out of Brosnan and Dalton, we need to know which island's area is more than 20% of the area of Bondia.

Total area of Bondia = 26315

20% of 26315 = (10% of 26315) x 2 = 2631.5 x 2 ≈ 5200 km^2

Island with area more than 5200 = Dalton

Brosnan has an area of 5079 which is less than 5200 so that cannot be the answer.

Answer = Dalton

---

2) C

A – Wrong

The word 'need' indicates that this statement is a bit too strong and hence should not be the answer.

B – Wrong

The text clearly suggests that some groups of people are unable to produce vitamin D efficiently. Therefore, sunlight definitely is not the best way to obtain vitamin D.

C – Correct

Even though this statement may seem too specific as the text also mentions other groups of people, but in fact, this is the best statement out of all the options given. Also, the hint lies in the first line of the second paragraph. "Based on these finding…pale-skinned people…vitamin D supplements" suggest that this is the conclusion of the text.

D – Wrong

No mention of skin cancer in the text

E – Wrong

We cannot determine who needs the vitamin D supplements more.

---

3) F

It is essential that you realise that the tile is in the shape of a plus. The individual squares are not the tiles.

The person only wants to use 5 tiles.

Out of the options, there are 5 tiles, which will give an equal number of tiles and an equal area of each pattern. There is one tile which will disrupt the equilibrium

The best way to solve this is by removing one tile and seeing whether the number of tiles with a particular patter is the same or not.

If we remove A, we have 4 white tiles, 6 black tiles. Hence this is wrong.

If we remove B, we have 6 white tiles, 5 black tiles. Hence this is wrong.

If we remove C, we have 5 white tiles, 3 black tiles. Hence this is wrong.
If we remove D, we have 5 white tiles, 6 black tiles. Hence this is wrong.
If we remove E, we have 5 white tiles, 5 black tiles, 6 checked tiles. This is wrong.
If we remove F, we have 5 white tiles, 5 black tiles, 5 checked tiles and 5 spotted tiles. Hence F is correct.

---

4) B

The main conclusion of the paragraph is "If you make extra demand…only fossil fuels…can provide the extra capacity".

A – Wrong
We can infer this but it is not the main conclusion of the passage as the UK grid is not the main focus of the text.

B – Correct
This statement correctly paraphrases the conclusion of the text.

C – Wrong
Wind power is not the main focus, so it cannot be the conclusion of the text.

D – Wrong
We cannot infer this from the information given to us.

---

5) E

The most efficient way to solve this question is by calculating the area for the shrubs, pond, veg areas and lawn. Then, if we subtract this value from the total area, we can get the area for which we have to use the slabs for.

Length of 2 shrubs areas = $18 - (1+1+0.5+1+3) = 11.5$ m
Total area of 2 shrubs area = $11.5 \times 4 = 46$ m²

Length of total veg area = $18 - (1+3+1+0.5+0.5+1) = 11$ m
Width of all veg areas = 3 m
Total area of the 3 veg area = $11 \times 3 = 33$ m²

Width of pond area = width of the Veg area as seen from the diagram
Total area of the pond area = $3 \times 3 = 9$ m^2

Length of lawn area = $12 - (1+3+1+1) = 6$ m
Width of lawn area = 3 m
Total area of the lawn area = $6 \times 3 = 18$ m²

Total area of back garden = $18 \times 12 = 18 \times (10+2) = 180 + 36 = 216$ m²
Area to be covered by slabs = $216 - (46+33+9+18) = 110$ m²

Area of 1 slab = 0.5×0.5 (squares have equal dimensions) = 0.25 m²
Number of square slabs = $110 \div 0.25 = 440$ slabs
Hence the answer is E.

6) E
The argument made in the text is the last line "Discussing news and serious issues…will help their children read well." We must find a flaw in this argument.

A – Wrong
The comparison of the influence of discussion with parents with the influence of discussion with friends is irrelevant and does not find a flaw in the argument stated above.

B – Wrong
Again, eating meals together cannot find a flaw in the argument made above.

C – Wrong
The location of teenagers is irrelevant.

D – Wrong
We do not need to find a flaw in the advantage of good reading ability in a teenager's development. We need to find a flaw in the link made between discussion of news and good reading ability.

E – Correct
The flaw in the argument is that the text just casually makes a link between discussion and reading. There is not evidence or proof to back up the argument.

7) A
In the diagram, there are more squares than triangles. Therefore, we can easily eliminate B, C and D. B states that there are more triangles than squares, which is incorrect. C and D state that there are equal numbers of squares and triangles. Hence, this is wrong.
Option E just counts all the squares, triangles and hexagons and then makes the ratio. This cannot be correct. This only leaves us with option A.

8) C
Sum of patient days over both years = 11549 + 30432 = 41,981 ≈ 42000
Expressing 42000 per 100,000 = 0.42
Number of cases over both years = 0 + 3 = 3 cases
Rate is calculated as number of cases per 100,000 patient days = 3/0.42 = 300/42 ≈ 7.15
Hence C is the answer.

9) D
The highest number of cases comes from organisation 3. The number of cases = 26
Total no. of cases = 1 + 26 + 4 + 3 + 2 + 3 + 1 + 12 + 5 + 12 = 69 cases ≈ 70 cases
Percentage = $(26/70)$ x 100 = $(13/35)$ x 100 = $(13/7)$ x 20 ≈ $(14/7)$ x 20 = 40%
We rounded 13 up to 14. Since we rounded up, we need to round 40% down to 38%.
Hence the answer is D.

10) B
Patient days for organisation 2 in 2010 = 16,163 ≈ 16,000
Number of months = 11 (data is till November only)
Rate = $16,000/11$ ≈ 1500 patient days per month

Since rate is constant, there must have been 1500 patient days in December too.
Total no. of patient days = 16,000 + 1500 = 17,500
Patient days per 100,000 = 17500/100,000 = 0.175 ≈ 0.18
Number of cases = 1
Rate = $\frac{1}{0.18}$ = $\frac{100}{18}$ = 5.5555…
This is closest to option B. Hence B is the answer.

11) E

A – Wrong
Although this may seem like it is true but we only have one organisation that only has a small hospital. Therefore, it is difficult to come to a conclusion.

B – Wrong
This is definitely not true.

C – Wrong
The data does not specify which type of hospital the cases were found in. So we cannot conclude this.

D – Wrong
We know Cdl occurs in large hospitals. We know Cdl can occur in small hospitals by looking at organisation 2. We cannot definitely determine whether Cdl can be found in DC or TC hospitals. So this is not true.

E – Correct
This is correct. None of the above options can be definitely determined.

12) B
First bus on Thursday is at: 09:15
Time taken to travel from Airport to Pafaka centre = 50 minutes
So Nicola will reach Pafaka centre at: 10:05

She needs to reach back to the airport at 17:00
She will need to take a bus, which is early enough so that she can arrive back after the 50 minutes of travel. We need to look at the second table.

22:40 is not an option
21:25 is not an option
20:20 is not an option
19:45 is not an option
16:30 is not an option. 16:30 + 50 minutes = 17:20. This is too late
15:20 is the option as she will reach back to the airport at: 15:20 + 50 minutes = 16:10

She will be at the Pafaka centre from 10:05 to 15:20
This means that she will be there for 5 hours and 15 minutes.
Option B is the answer.

13) D

The phrase "is what one would expect" indicates that the melting of the Arctic Ice is a possible explanation for the unusual weather experienced by the UK.

A – Wrong
It is not the **only** explanation. It is a possible explanation. The word "only" is too strong.

B – Wrong
We cannot infer that if the ice were not melting the unusual weather would not have been present.

C – Wrong
'Must' is too strong and hence this is wrong.

D – Correct
The word "could" suggests that the melting of Arctic ice is a possible explanation and hence this is the correct answer.

14) D

This can only be solved by visualisation or by making the net and folding it into a cube. Only try and solve this question when you have finished the remaining 34 questions.

15) C

The argument made in the text is the last line of the text "So parents of children with autism…using the sprays". We must find a flaw in this

A – Wrong
If oxytocin causes feelings of envy, then this would mean that parents would be damaging their children's health. This, instead, strengthens the argument.

B – Wrong
This statement actually strengthens the argument as since there have been no scientific studies made, parents could potentially be damaging their children's health.

C – Correct
This is definitely correct. If levels of oxytocin are low in the sprays and it does not have any effect on children, then parents would not be damaging their children's health.

D – Wrong
The type of culture an individual lives in is not directly relevant to the question.

E – Wrong
This strengthens the statement as such effects could cause damage to a child's health.

16) C

Let us calculate the number of tiles on the floor = 15 x 10 = 150 tiles
Let us divide the floor into 6 sections. Each section looks like this:

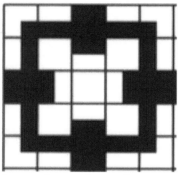

In each section, there are 25 tiles.
5 completely white tiles = 0% black
4 completely black tiles = 100% black x 4 = 4
4 one-quarter black tiles = 25% black x 4 = 1
12 half-black tiles = 50% black x 12 = 6
4+1+6 = 11
Percentage black = (11/25) x 100 = 44%
Since this section represents the whole diagram, we can say that the entire floor is 44% black.

---

17) G
1 – Wrong
The word "would" suggests that improving staff levels will definitely reduce death rates. Also, this statement makes a casual link between staff levels and death rates.

2 – Wrong
If patients are unable to be saved in hospitals, then enhancing the weekend provision of community and primary care services would be ineffective as well.

3 – Wrong
Patients should be admitted when they are seriously ill or injured. It does not matter whether the staff levels are low or high.

Since all statements are wrong, G is the answer.

---

18) A
Let the sample size be 100
Between 75 and 85 households own a dishwasher
Between 35 and 40 households own a tumble dryer
Less than 5 households own nothing.
Let us say B number of people own both.
100 = (75 to 85) + (35 to 40) + (0 to 5) + B

Maximum value = 85 + 40 + 5 – 100 = 130 – 100 = 30%
Minimum value = 75 + 35 + 0 – 100 = 110 – 100 = 10%
Hence the answer is A (10% – 30%).

---

19) B

The answer is in the Category A section of the Definitions.

It states that 75% of the cases received a response in 8 minutes. This means that 25% of the cases received a response after 8 minutes.

In the third bullet point of the executive summary, it is stated that 2.23 million Category A cases were reported in 2011.

25% of 2.23 million ($\approx$ 2.24 million) = 0.56 million

20) D

Percentage of Category A cases = 33.7% $\approx$ 34%
Percentage of Category B cases = 39.8% $\approx$ 40%
Percentage of Category C cases = 100% $-$ (34 + 40) = 26%

It is better to divide each of the pie charts into 4 quarters to give you an idea of there 25%, 50%, 75% and 100% are. You can easily do this using a ruler or a pencil.

Category C is the lowest. Therefore, we can easily eliminate options A and B.
C is a little bit confusing but we can see that the portion of Category A and C are roughly the same. Hence, C is wrong as the difference between Categories A and C is 8%
D is correct by process of elimination.

21) B

A – Wrong
1.47 million calls did not result in transportation to the scene. A response within 8 or 19 minutes is irrelevant as there was no transportation whatsoever.

B – Correct
This is correct. Since there was no emergency, 1.47 million calls did not require a transport to the scene

C – Wrong
This option correlates a 'genuine' emergency with transportation. Even if a call was not a 'genuine' emergency, people can still be transported to a scene.

D – Wrong
Category C does not mean that a treatment or transportation is not required. D is completely wrong.

22) A

2011
75% of Category A cases were responded within 8 minutes
Number of Category A cases in 2011 = 2.23 million $\approx$ 2.24 million
Number of Category A cases receiving a response within 8 minutes = 75% x 2.24 = 1.68 million

2010
74.3% $\approx$ 74% of Category A cases were responded within 8 minutes
Number of Category A cases in 2010 = 2.08 million $\approx$ 2.10 million

Number of Category A cases receiving a response within 8 minutes = 74% x 2.24 = 1.55 million

Difference = 1.68 – 1.55 = 0.13 million
The closest to this is 0.12 million
The answer is option A.

23) B
Let the order of the squares be like this:

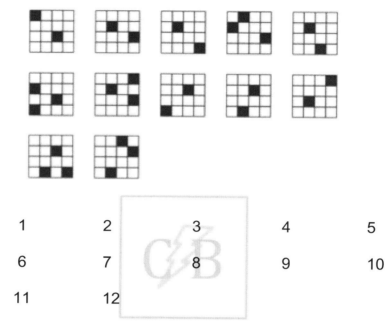

1	2	3	4	5
6	7	8	9	10
11	12			

Pattern 1 – The 1st diagram has the same pattern as the 3rd, 8th and 10th
Pattern 2 – The 2nd diagram has the same pattern as the 9th
Pattern 3 – The 4th diagram has the same pattern as the 12th
Pattern 4 – The 6th diagram has the same pattern as the 7th and 11th
Pattern 5 – The 5th diagram has its own pattern. Diagram 2 and 9 look similar but diagram 5's pattern cannot be obtained by rotating diagram 2 and 9.
Therefore, there are different 5 patterns. The answer is option B.

24) E
The argument made in the text is the last line of the text.

A – Wrong
This would, in contrast, weaken the argument. Since the argument made is that water cannons should be used when appropriate, this statement contradicts the argument.

B – Wrong
This is irrelevant and does not strengthen the argument.

C – Wrong
This weakens the argument made in the text. If tear gas or rubber bullets are equally as effective as water cannons, then these methods should be adopted instead of water cannons.

D – Wrong
This mentions how expensive water cannons can be. So option D weakens the argument.

E – Correct
If the public supports the use of water cannons, then this strengthens the argument.

---

25) C

Let us first find the maximum number of points 1 can score in a single round. To get the maximum score, all three darts need to land on 6.

Max score possible = 18

We know the minimum score can be 0 but the question asks for scores other than 0.

Next minimum score has to be 2. It cannot be 1 because if two darts land outside, the score becomes 0.

Our range of scores = 2 to 18

To easily solve this question, we need to find the scores that we cannot score.

Remember: If a dart lands outside all of the circles, the player's score for the turn SO FAR is halved.

So let us say the order of dart thrown was: 4, miss, 6. The total score would be 8.

After the dart lands on 4, total score so far = 4

After the dart misses, total score so far = 4/2 = 2

After the dart lands on 6, total score = 2+6 = 8

Scoring 2 = 2, 2, miss

Scoring 3 = 2, miss, 2

Scoring 4 = 4, 4, miss

Scoring 5 = 2, miss, 4

Scoring 6 = 6, 6, miss

Scoring 7 = 2, miss, 6

Scoring 8 = 4, miss, 6

Scoring 9 = 6, miss, 6

Scoring 10 = 4, 4, 2

Scoring 11 = Not possible

Scoring 12 = 4, 4, 4

Scoring 13 = Not possible

Scoring 14 = 6, 4, 4

Scoring 15 = Not possible

Scoring 16 = 6, 4, 6

Scoring 17 = Not possible

Scoring 18 = 6, 6, 6

No. of scores possible = 13

Hence the answer is option C.

---

26) D
The reasoning made in the text:
All art is copying, then forgery is art.

A – Wrong
Water (art) is liquid (copying) and liquid (copying) is fluid (forgery), then water (art) is fluid (forgery).
This is not the reasoning made in the text. It would have been correct if the reasoning was that fluid (forgery) is water (art).

B – Wrong
Petrol (art) is flammable (copying) and volatile (forgery), so everything volatile (forgery) is flammable (copying).
This is not the reasoning made in the text.

C – Wrong
Being overweight (art) is unhealthy (copying) so maintaining the right weight (not art) is healthy (not copying).
This is not the reasoning made in the text.

D -Correct
The French (art) are European (copying) and Spaniards (forgery) are European (copying), so the French (art) are Spaniards (forgery).
This is correct.

---

27) C
Let us start with the $2000 that came in June. We know that the shop was closed in May. This means that the $2000 came from the month of April.

One quarter of the money is paid two months later. June is two months after April. Since $2000 were obtained in June from April, total sales made in April must have been = 2000 x 4 = $8000

Of these sales, 0.5 is paid immediately. Out of $8000, $4000 was kept in April. One quarter of sales, i.e. $2000 is paid next month (May). In May, no sales were made since the shop was closed. So $3000 was obtained from March and April. From April, $2000 is paid in May. So, money made in May from March = $3000 - $2000 = $1000. One quarter of sales from March must have been paid in May. Total sales made in March = 4 x $1000 = $4000. Out of this half is paid immediately, i.e. $2000.
From the table we can see that total money obtained in March = $4000. We know $2000 out of this $4000 was made from the sales in March. The remaining $2000 must have been made from sales from Jan and Feb.

One quarter of sales from March (i.e. $1000) is paid next month (i.e. April). From the table, we know total money obtained in April was $5000. $4000 of the $5000 was made from sales in April. We also now know that the remaining $1000 is obtained from sales made in March. So no money is obtained from sales made in February.

Total sales made in Feb = $0
We now know that all $3000 made in Feb must have been from Jan and before Jan.

From the table, total money obtained in March = $4000. We know $2000 out of this $4000 was made from sales from Feb and Jan. Since no sales were made in Feb, all $2000 of this must have been obtained from Jan. Total sales made in Jan = $2000 x 4 = $<u>8000</u>.

Now add all the figures, which represent the sales made in the months Jan – Feb (underlined figures).

$8000 + $4000 + $8000 = $20,000. So the answer is C.

---

28) G
1 – Correct
Even skiing involves travel. Since all travel damages the environment, it does not prove that ski holiday, which also involves travel does not damage the environment.
2 – Correct
The argument made in the text is that ski resorts use less energy as compared to other resorts. If the information given in sentence 2 is correct, then this conflicts the information given in the text.
3 – Correct
The author fails to consider the damage that is caused by ski industries by factors other than energy consumption.

Since all statements find a weakness in the text, G is the answer.

---

29) C
Let the money refunded be 'R'
Let total money before refunds = 'M'
Money after refunds = £12240
M – R = £12240
40% paid £15 and 60% paid £20
Let the number of people who attended the concert = 'P'
(0.6P x 20) + (0.4P x 15) = £12240
12P + 6P = £12240
18P = 12240
P = 12240 ÷ 18 = 680 people

If 680 people paid £20 in advance, M = 680 x 20 = £13600
Refund = 13600 – 12240 = £1360
Hence, C is the answer.

---

30) C
1 – Wrong
Authors "give a one-sided view" is too bold of a statement and hence is wrong.
2 – Wrong
Nothing is mentioned about whether companies "aim to influence the content of the articles".

3 – Correct

This statement uses the appropriate words and paraphrases the first two sentences of paragraph.

Only statement 3 can be inferred. So C is the answer.

---

31) C

Since Jill is so sure that she will finish third, she must be at lest 7 points ahead of the player who is last. She must also be 7 points behind 2nd place.

Karen and Gemma must have equal number of points as no matter what positions they finish in after the 10th round, there would be no ties.

We need to take into consideration the highest number of points that the person in 4th could possibly have. Therefore, we need to assume that they win the 10th round and get 6 points. Also, total number of points gained in each round = 6 + 3 + 1 = 10 points.

After the 10th round, total number of points should add up to 100. After 9th round, 90 etc.

A – Wrong

If 4th place had ended the competition with a total score of 13, they would have 7 points at the end of the 9th round. Jill would have 14 points (7 points ahead of 4th place) and Karen and Gemma would both have a score of 21 each (7 ahead of Jill). This adds up to 63. This is much smaller than 90.

B – Wrong

If 4th place had ended the competition with a total score of 15, they would have 9 points at the end of the 9th round. Jill would have 16 points (7 points ahead of 4th place) and Karen and Gemma would both have a score of 23 each (7 ahead of Jill). This adds up to 71. This is smaller than 90.

C – Correct

If 4th place had ended the competition with a total score of 19, they would have 13 points at the end of the 9th round. Jill would have 20 points (7 points ahead of 4th place) and Karen and Gemma would both have a score of 27 each (7 ahead of Jill). This adds up to 87. This is rather close to 90

D – Wrong

If 4th place had ended the competition with a total score of 21, they would have 15 points at the end of the 9th round. Jill would have 22 points (7 points ahead of 4th place) and Karen and Gemma would both have a score of 29 each (7 ahead of Jill). This adds up to 95. Even though this is close to 90, you must remember that the score cannot be higher than 90.

E – Wrong

If 4th place had ended the competition with a total score of 23, they would have 17 points at the end of the 9th round. Jill would have 24 points (7 points ahead of 4th place) and Karen and Gemma would both have a score of 31 each (7 ahead of Jill). This adds up to 103. This is much higher than 90.

---

32) A

Number of annual deaths per vehicle in 1930 = 7000
Number of vehicles on the road in 1930 = 2.3 million
Number of annual deaths per vehicle now= 3180
Number of vehicles on the road now = 27 million

$$\frac{3180 \times 100}{7000} = \text{approximately } 40\% = 0.4$$

Since there is approximately 10 times the number of vehicles now, we need to divide 0.4 by 10 = 0.04

33) D
We need to identify the statement that can prove or say that roads are getting safer.

A – Wrong
This does not prove that roads are safer.

B – Wrong
Mentioned in the article already.

C – Wrong
This does not prove that roads are safer.

D – Correct
This allows us to trust the statistics provided in the text. This proves that roads are becoming safer.

E – Wrong
Mentioned in the article already.

34) C
Simple calculation: 40% of 319,928
Since the question asks for the nearest 1000, we can treat 319, 928 as 320,000
40% of 320,000 = 40 x 3200 = 128,000

35) A
A – Correct
This option is correct by process of elimination. If DfT underestimates the number of deaths and serious injuries, then this explains why their statistics are so much lower than the hospital statistics.

B – Wrong
Roads becoming safer is not relevant to discrepancies.

C – Wrong
Hospital admissions remained unchanged. If fewer people were being admitted to the hospital for minor injuries, then there would have been a decrease in hospital admissions.

D – Wrong
This would mean that there would be more serious injuries and hence, the DfT statistics would be higher than the ones given in the text.

E – Wrong
This would make DfT statistics higher than the hospital statistics.

2012 Section 2

1) F

Be careful of what the question is saying. Which of the situations could RESULT in a homeostatic response?

1 - A rise in internal condition. An example could be increase in blood glucose level in the body.

2 - A reduction in internal condition. An example of this could be decrease in water level in body.

3 - An example could be increase in environmental temperature.

4 - An example could be decrease in environmental temperature.

2) D

Mr of 1-bromobutane = (12 x 4) + (1 x 9) + 80 = 137

Moles of 1-bromobutane = $^{mass}/_{Mr}$ = $^{2.74}/_{137}$ = 0.02 mol

Molar ratio of 1-bromobutane and butan-1-ol = 1:1

Moles of butan-1-ol = 0.02 mol

Mr of butanol = (12 x 4) + (1 x 9) + (16) + (1) = 74

Mass of butanol = moles x Mr = 0.02 x 74 = 1.48 g

Mass of butan-1-ol obtained = 1.11g

Percentage yield = ($^{1.11}/_{1.48}$) x 100 = 75%

Hence, the answer is D

3) B

When an atom decays and its atomic number decreases by 2, we can conclude that it must have emitted α-particles, which are helium atoms. If it emits a helium atom, its mass number must also decrease by 4.

Therefore, P must equal to N-4.

We can eliminate options D, E and F.

Now, we know that atom Y decays further and its mass number P remains the same but its has a new atomic number Q. If an atom decays and its mass number remains the same but the atomic number changes, we can conclude that it must have emitted a ß-particle, which are just high-energy electrons. When an electron is emitted, the atomic number increases by 1.

After the first decay, R was reduced by 2 and after the second decay, R gained 1.

R-2+1 = R-1

P = N - 4

Q = R -1

This corresponds to option B.

4) A

Radius of largest circle = 4d ÷ 2 = 2d Area of largest circle = $\pi (2d)^2 = \pi 4d^2$

Radius of third largest circle = 3d ÷ 2 = 1½d

Area of third largest circle = $\pi (1\frac{1}{2} d)^2 = \pi 2\frac{1}{4}d^2$

Radius of second largest circle = 2d ÷ 2 = 1d = d

Area of second largest circle = $\pi (d)^2 = \pi d^2$

Radius of smallest circle = d ÷ 2 = ½d

Area of smallest circle = $\pi (\frac{1}{2}d)^2 = \pi \frac{1}{4}d^2$

Area of the larger shaded area = $\pi 4d^2 - \pi 2\frac{1}{4}d^2 = \pi d^2 (4 - 2\frac{1}{4}) = \pi 1\frac{3}{4} d^2$

Area of the smaller shaded area = $\pi d^2 - \pi \frac{1}{4}d^2 = \pi d^2 (1 - \frac{1}{4}) = \pi \frac{3}{4} d^2$

Total shaded area = $\pi 1\frac{3}{4} d^2 + \pi \frac{3}{4} d^2 = \pi d^2 (1\frac{3}{4} + \frac{3}{4}) = \pi d^2 2\frac{1}{2} = \frac{5}{2}\pi d^2$ (Since $2\frac{1}{2} = \frac{5}{2}$)

5) B

Let us first name the areas first.

Area 1 is the brain

Area 2 is the bronchi

Area 3 is alveoli

Area 4 is the blood vessel

We know bronchitis will occur in the bronchi. Therefore area 2 will be affected by bronchitis. We can eliminate option C, D, E and F.

We know that nicotine, which is present in cigarettes, affects the brain, which is area 1. Therefore, we can eliminate option A.

Carbon monoxide affects the red blood cells in blood, which travels in the blood vessels (area 4). Carbon monoxide inhibits the uptake of oxygen in haemoglobin.

Emphysema is a disease, which damages the alveoli, so emphysema would affect the alveoli (area 3).

Hence, the correct answer is option B.

6) C

This is rather a simple question. You must have seen a similar diagram in AS biology in the cell membrane topic.

The tail is always hydrophobic (hydro-water and phobic-fear; so hydrophobic means it does not like water), meaning it does not like to get in contact with water. Hydrophilic means it can react with water.

The head of the molecule shown is always hydrophilic and the tail is always hydrophobic.

So, the answer is C.

7) F

None of the radiation was stopped by paper, meaning no α radiation was present.

Some of the radiation was stopped by aluminium, which means that ß radiation was present. However, some radiation was still detected even after aluminium was placed which suggests that γ radiation was also present.

So the answer is ß and γ, which is option F.

8) E

$G = 5 + \sqrt{[7\,(9 - R)^2 + 9]}$

$G - 5 = \sqrt{[7\,(9 - R)^2 + 9]}$

Squaring both sides,

$(G - 5)^2 = 7\,(9 - R)^2 + 9$

$(G - 5)^2 - 9 = 7\,(9 - R)^2$

$\dfrac{(G - 5)^2 - 9}{7} = (9 - R)^2$

Square Rooting on both sides,

$\sqrt{\dfrac{(G - 5)^2 - 9}{7}} = 9 - R$

$\left\{\dfrac{\sqrt{(G - 5)^2 - 9}}{7}\right\} - 9 = -R$

To change the sign of R from negative to positive, we need to multiply both sides by -1

$(-1) \times \left\{\dfrac{\sqrt{(G - 5)^2 - 9}}{7}\right\} - 9 = -R\,(-1)$

$R = 9 - \left\{\dfrac{\sqrt{(G - 5)^2 - 9}}{7}\right\}$

So the answer is E.

---

9) A

We need to know that neurones that detect a certain stimulus are called sensory neurones.

1 - Sensory neurones are the neurones that detect stimulus first in a reflex action. If sensory neurones are unable to detect a certain stimulus, then there will be no reflex action to the stimulus. So 1 is correct.
2 - If the patient can see that the stimulus is taking place and they know it will cause harm to the body, they can then take appropriate action to stop the application of the stimulus.
3 - The patient would not be able to sense pain as the neurones are unable to sense the pain.
4 - Again, they will not be able to sense the pain.

Only statements 1 and 2 are correct, meaning that option A is correct.

---

10) D

The easiest way to solve this is to try all the options and see which option is correct.

---

11) D

Work is only done when a force is applied and a body moves for a distance in the direction of the force.

Diagram 1
The person is sitting on a chair. There is a force (weight) but there is NO movement in any body (person nor chair). So the force is not doing any work. Therefore, diagram 1 would not be in any column.

Diagram 2
The wheelbarrow is being lifted upwards in the direction of the force. So the force 'F' is doing work. However, the distance (d) labeled on the diagram is not the distance moved by the force. The distance labelled is perpendicular to the direction of the force. Hence, work done = F x d, does not apply to this diagram.
Diagram 2 will be in the first column but not in the second column.

Diagram 3
The pulley is pulling the weight upwards by applying force 'F'. The weight moves by the distance 'd' as the distance labeled is in the direction of the force. Hence, the formula work done = F x d, is applicable in this case.
Diagram 3 would be in the first and second column.

The correct answer is D.

---

12) E
Let us break up the problem into smaller pieces and solve them individually.

(2×10^5)

$(5 \times 10^3)^2 = (25 \times 10^6)$

So,
$$\frac{2 \times 10^5}{25 \times 10^6} = 0.08 \times 10^{11} = 8 \times 10^9$$

$\sqrt[3]{(8 \times 10^9)} = 2000$

$(4 \times 10^3) - (4 \times 10^2) = 4000 - 400 = 3600$
$\sqrt{3600} = 60$

So 2000 - 60 = 1940

---

13) E
1 - The fact that the outer circle produced by the antibiotics Q and R are very similar in size means that they could be equally as effective.

2 - Bacterial resistance is not mentioned in the question and is thus irrelevant. The fact of the matter is that the antibiotics are doing their job, which means that there is hardly any resistance.

3 - S represents the distance up to which the bacteria are killed. This means that is statement could be correct.

---

14) F

By looking at all the options, we can see that all of the formulae given have 3 copper atoms. This means that 1 of the molecules; either $CuCO_3$ or $Cu(OH)_2$ have 2 moles and the other has 1 mole.

1st possibility - $2CuCO_3 + Cu(OH)_2 -> Cu_3C_2H_2O_8$
2nd possibility – $CuCO_3 + 2Cu(OH)_2 -> Cu_3CH_4O_7$

The first possibility is correct as the option is given but the second possibility is not correct as the option is not given.

---

15) B

We have been given the speed and wavelength of the microwave in air.
When the microwaves enter a plastic food container, the speed reduces.

By using the formula, $c = f \times \lambda$, we know speed is directly proportional to wavelength. If the speed decreases, the wavelength will also decrease. The only options, which have a lower wavelength than 12 cm, are A, B and C. Therefore the wavelength would be 8cm.

By using the formula, $f = c/\lambda$, we can calculate the new frequency. We need to convert 8 cm to meters. 8 cm = 0.08 m
$f = c/\lambda$
$f = 2.0 \times 10^8 \div 0.08 = 2.5 \times 10^9$

---

16) C

First, draw a line perpendicular to AB from C. Label the line be CP.

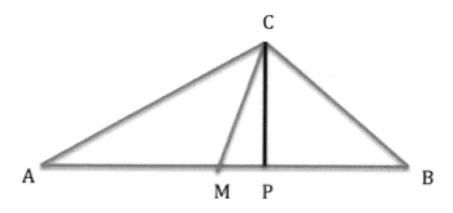

We have $\tan A = {}^{CP}/_{AP} = {}^1/_6$

So, CP = 1, AP = 6

We have $\tan B = {}^{CP}/_{BP} = {}^2/_3$

Since CP = 1, BP = ${}^3/_2$ = 1.5

Since BP = 1.5, then AP = 6
AB = AP + BP = 1.5 + 6 = 7.5

Since M is the mid point, BM = ${}^{7.5}/_2$ = 3.75
PM = BM - BP = 3.75 - 1.5 = 2.25

$\tan\theta° = {}^{CP}/_{PM}$

$${}^{CP}/_{PM} = {}^1/_{2.25}$$

$${}^1/_{2.25} = {}^4/_9$$

---

17) C

1 - Since ADH is a hormone, it has to travel in the bloodstream. So this is correct.

2 - ADH causes water to be reabsorbed into the bloodstream from the kidney. Hence, urine produced would be concentrated and not dilute.

3 - Same concept. Increased ADH will cause an increase in concentrated urine and not dilute urine.

4 - This is correct. ADH is released by the pituitary gland to reabsorb water from the kidney to prevent dehydration. If ADH is reduced, dehydration can occur.

The answer is C.

---

18) D

A - Wrong
Chlorine is above zinc and vanadium in the reactivity series. So there is no displacement.

B - Wrong
Sodium is above zinc and vanadium in the reactivity series. So there is no displacement.

C - Wrong
Aluminium is above zinc and vanadium in the reactivity series. So there is no displacement.

D - Correct
Vanadium is above iron in the reactivity series so the iron cannot displace it.

E - Wrong
Magnesium is above zinc and vanadium in the reactivity series. So there is no displacement.

---

19) D
Since the filament breaks, there is no pathway for current along the wire connected to lamp X.
Current can only flow through the branch (which is now converted from parallel to series).
We know that resistance in series is always greater than resistance in parallel.
Therefore, overall resistance would increase.
Since overall resistance increases and voltage remains the same, reading in ammeter 1 must decrease.
$R = V/I$ shows that resistance is inversely proportional to current. So provided that voltage is the same, if overall resistance increases, the overall current must decrease.
When lamp X was working, the current had 2 paths, 1 through lamp X and the second, through the branch. Now that lamp X has blown, all current must be flowing through ammeter 2.
Therefore, the current in ammeter 2 increases.

Reading on ammeter 1 = decreases
Reading on ammeter 2 = increases
Total resistance of the circuit = increases
Hence, the answer is D.

---

20) B
Since the balls are arranged in a way to give the smallest possibility for a player to win, the first bag must have 2 red balls and 1 yellow ball and 1 blue ball. The second bag must have 2 red balls and 2 yellow balls.

Probability of choosing either bag = $^1/_2$

Let us say a player picked bag 1.
The only way to win is to pick 2 red balls.
Probability of picking a red ball = $^2/_4 = ^1/_2$
In order to win, the player must pick a second red ball.
Probability of picking a second red ball = $^1/_3$
Probability of picking two same-coloured balls from Bag 1 = $^1/_2$ x $^1/_2$ x $^1/_3$ = $^1/12$

Let us say a player picked bag 2.
Only way to win is to either pick 2 red balls or 2 yellow balls.

1st ball
Probability of picking a first red ball = $^2/_4 = ^1/_2$
Probability of picking a first yellow ball = $^2/_4 = ^1/_{12}$

2nd ball
If the player picked a red ball first, they must pick a red ball again if they want to win.
Probability of picking a second red ball = $^1/_3$

If the player picked a yellow ball first, they must pick a yellow ball again if they want to win. Probability of picking a second yellow ball = $^1/_3$

Probability of picking two same coloured balls from Bag 2 = 2($^1/_2$ x $^1/_2$ x $^1/_3$) = $^1/_{12}$ x 2 = $^2/_{12}$

There are three possibilities to win:
2 red balls from bag 1 = Probability of $^1/_{12}$
2 red balls from bag 2 = Probability of $^1/_{12}$
2 yellow balls from bag 2 = Probability of $^1/_{12}$

Probability of winning = ($^1/_{12}$ x 3) = $^3/_{12}$ = $^1/_4$

---

21) D

1 - Since 1 of the phenotypes was not seen, it means that the offspring with both RECESSIVE alleles did not survive.

2 - For any scientific research, a large sample size is very important as it reduces the effect of chance. Therefore, this statement is correct. A small sample size could be the reason why a different ratio was seen.

3 - Chance could also be a reason.

Hence, D is the answer.

---

22) B

When an atom decays by ß decay, its mass number remains the same.
Tritium undergoes beta decay into Helium-3 (isotope of Helium which has a mass number 3). You may have figured it out already as all three options have He as a product.

It may seem that HTO will form HeOH as both are single molecules. However, He is a noble gas and does not react with or form molecules with other elements. Therefore, HeOH cannot be a product.

Tritium will form a He atom on its own.

Let us look at equations 2 and 3 and try to balance them. We can substitute He with T as we know T will form He.

$4HTO \rightarrow 2H_2O + O_2 + 4T$
$HTO \rightarrow H_2O + H_2 + T$ (not possible to balance)

If we try to balance both equations, you will realize that it is not possible to balance the second equation.

Hence only equation 2 is possible. B is the answer.

---

23) D

Let us find the GPE when the cyclist is 100m in vertical height. Also, this is the amount of GPE that will be lost when the cyclist descends 100m.
GPE = mgh = 100 x 10 x 100 = 100,000 J

To find the resistive force, we need to use the formula: Work done = Force x Distance
Rearranging to get Force, we get Force = Work done/Distance

In order to find the distance, we need to use the 1 in 10 information that is given to us.
We know that the cyclist descends 100m in vertical height.
Using the ratio of 1 : 10, we get 100 : 1000
So the distance travelled by the cyclist = 1000m

Work done is equal to the GPE lost by the cyclist.

Force = $\frac{100,000}{1000}$ = 100N

---

24) A

The explanation to this question is a bit complicated (or confusing). If you have any question, feel free to comment down in the comments section.

It is important to use variables (such as 'x' or 'y' or 'z') when we are not given any values in the question.
Let cost of wood be = W
We know cost of metal is three times cost of wood.
Hence, cost of metal = 3W

Let amount of wood used = r
Therefore, total cost of wood = (W x t)
Let amount of metal used = u
Therefore, total cost of metal = (3W x u)
Total cost of sign = Wr + 3Wu

Let the diameter of sign = D
Wood is proportional to size of diameter: **r = D²**
Metal is proportional to the square of diameter: **u = D**

Since the diameter is doubled (2D), we get the following equations:
r = (2D)² = 4D² = **4r (Since D² = r)**
u = 2D = **2u (Since D = u)**
New total cost = (W x 4r) + (3W x 2u) = 4Wr + 6Wu
Since the diameter is doubled, the total cost will be tripled.
Therefore the new cost is three times the old cost.

246

4Wr + 6Wu = 3[Wr + 3Wu]
4Wr + 6Wu = 3Wr + 9Wu
Wr = 3Wu
r = 3u

Percentage of metal = Amount of metal ÷ Total amount of material
Total amount of material = amount of wood (r) + amount of metal (u)
Amount of metal = u

Percentage of metal = $u/_{r + u}$
Since r = 3u, we get:
Percentage of metal = $u/_{3u + u} = u/_{4u} = 1/4 = 25\%$

---

25) E
Let the dominant allele be: **T**
Let the recessive allele be: **t**

If only U has a recessive condition, their genotype must be **tt**. This means that S and T must be heterozygous.
Since we want the minimum number of heterozygous people, we must assume that R has to be **TT**.
In order for S to be **Tt** and R to be **TT**, only one of P and Q needs to heterozygous.
This means that if only U has the recessive people, 3 people must be heterozygous.

If R and U both have the recessive condition, P and Q must both be heterozygous.
This means that if R and U have the recessive condition, 4 people (P, Q, S and T) must be heterozygous. Hence, E is the answer.

---

26) E
Since temperature is proportional to pressure, pressure will initially increase to allow both gases to react.
Now let us write out the reaction equation.

$C_2H_4 + H_2 \rightarrow C_2H_6$
Using the equilibrium rules, we can see that moles of products are ½ of moles of reactants.
This means that as the reaction progresses, pressure will decrease.
Hence, E is the answer.

---

27) G
P - Wrong. We can immediately eliminate P since speed of sound in air = 330m/s

Q - Wrong. Amplitude is the distance between 0 and maximum displacement. Here the amplitude would be half of the distance travelled by the wave, i.e. ½ x 5 = 2.5mm

R - Wrong. We first need to know the frequency of the sound wave to find the wavelength.

Frequency = $1/_T$ = $1/_{(0.2 \div 1000)}$ = 5000 Hz
Speed = Frequency x Wavelength
Wavelength = Speed ÷ Frequency = 330 ÷ 5000 = 0.066m = 66mm (hence 5.5mm is wrong)

S - Frequency = $1/_T$ = $1/_{(0.2 \div 1000)}$ = 5000 Hz = 5 kHz

Since only statement S is correct, G is the correct answer.

2012 Section 3

1) According to Voltaire, being doubtful about something is not pleasing but being certain about something is preposterous.

By being uncertain about something, a person is able to ensure its validity and reliability. For example, if a pupil is not able to understand something in class, they can clear their doubts by receiving help from a teacher. However, if the student misunderstands something a concept and is certain that they have understood it correctly, they may risk failing an exam.

Similarly, scientists cannot be certain about anything unless they have done extensive research and their findings have been reliable and reproducible by other scientists. Even though they have used the right apparatus and carried out valid experiments, human error is always possible. Therefore, it is important to be open minded and think about all possible errors that may have occurred during the experiment. The experiment is therefore repeated by those scientists and others to check reliability and reproducibility.

However, certainty is not absurd in many cases. For example, if we throw something towards the sky, it is certain that it will fall back down due to gravity. There is a boundary between being certain and being unreasonable. Certainty allows us to be confident in our actions. Edwards Jenner was certain that exposure to cowpox helps to build immunity against smallpox which led to discovery of vaccines.

It is good to have doubts first in order to be certain about something later. However, stating that "certainty is absurd" is too strong of a phrase. Scientists must be sure about their finding before proclaiming something in public.

2) According to Chancellor, those who are non-egocentric and selfless seem to be more attractive than those who care more about themselves. He is trying to convey the message that one should care less about their own health and longevity, as there are more important things in the world.

Some may think otherwise. If a person does not take care of their own health, they become prone to dangerous medical conditions and may cause them to be unable to help those around them such as their family and friends. Some may say that "in order to be selfless in the future, it is important to be selfish in the present." By allowing yourself to take care about your health and wellbeing, you can worry about others health and wellbeing for a longer time. Another aspect of this is that, if everyone takes responsibility to look after their own health, there may be less patients in the world, resulting for a healthier population all together. This may help to take the pressure off the NHS so they may focus on treating diseases which are genetically caused.

Others may argue that it is important to consider providing people whose health is in much worse condition with extra health and support. E.g. giving up seats on public transport for elderly and pregnant women. This can help prevent causing their health to worsen especially if the person has pain in standing up.

It is indeed true that as humans, we should value each other lives and wellbeing. However, in the process, we should not disregard our own health. If we are healthy, we can help to keep other healthy as well.

---

3. According to the statement, a scientist is not a person that answers questions correctly. A scientist is a person that is curious and asks the right questions in order to obtain more knowledge. Their ability to ask the right questions allows them to make important discoveries and inventions.

Scientists first formulate a hypothesis and predict results. They then carry out experiments to prove their hypothesis. If their method is valid and results are reliable, they can then formulate theories. Hence, we increase our knowledge about how nature works.
For example, if Edwards Jenner had not asked why milkmaids who had cowpox did not later get smallpox, our knowledge about immunology might still have been missing.

Of course, there is no point in asking the right questions if they are not answered. Without, any answers, our scientific knowledge would not grow. Therefore, some can argue that obtaining the right answers is more important than asking the right questions.

Scientists must ensure that they can carry out studies and researches which can assist future scientists to answer questions which are not answerable yet today. An example would be "How did the Universe come into existence?" Most scientists believe that the Big Bang is the answer to that question because the evidence supports it. However, it is only a theory yet. There have been cases in the past where the theories have been falsified many decades after their formulation.

Without the right questions, we cannot obtain answers and without the right answers, we cannot obtain more scientific knowledge. Therefore, it is important ask the right questions and answer them to learn and improve our knowledge of our surroundings.

---

4) Dolphins are extraordinary animals. They show highly developed forms of communication and have known to be compassionate. There are also accounts of dolphins helping humnans and other creatures. The statements argues that since dolphins are very intelligent, they should be given a special status in the animal kingdom just like humans. Without the right questions, we cannot obtain answers and without the right answers, we cannot obtain more scientific knowledge. Therefore, it is important ask the right questions and answer them to learn and improve our knowledge of our surroundings.

Some may argue that since dolphins are animals, they should be treated like other animals. Giving them a special status just because of their intelligence would be unfair. Every organism plays an important role in the environment and on this planet. For example, decomposers provide nutrients to plants and plants remove carbon dioxide from the atmosphere and give oxygen for animals. Providing different statuses to different animals and organisms would cause people to think some organisms are more important than others. Some may say that this way of thinking is unethical and could prove to be harmful in the future.

The question then arises: should more intelligent humans be given more importance than less intelligent humans? The answer is obviously no. Therefore, dolphins should not be treated differently than other animals. Some believe that all animals, including humans, are equal and should be treated in the same manner.

However, the counter-argument could be that there should be more focus on protection of such intelligent animals. In many places around the world, dolphins are endangered. Therefore, they should be given more protection so that they do not become extinct. This could be one way of saying that they should be given a special status.

Protection of all animals is absolutely crucial for the ecosystem to be in balance. However, using intelligence as a measure to proclaim special status to different animals is unnecessary as every animal and organism is intelligent in their own right. Einstein's quote, "Dot judge a fish by its ability to climb a tree" is relevant in this case.

2013 Section 1

1) A

Since Carla cannot work on a Monday and 2 operators have to be on duty, Bob and Amy must work on Monday.

We can eliminate option E since it says that none of the operators work for four consecutive days in a week.

We know that Bob works for a maximum of three days and we know he has to work on Monday, Tuesday and Friday. This means that his days are complete and he will not work on Wednesday and Thursday.

Since 2 operators have to work on a day, Amy and Carla will work on Wednesday and Thursday.

We know Carla must work on Wednesday and Thursday. We can eliminate options B and C, leaving us with options A and D.

We know that Amy cannot work for 4 consecutive days as that is the rule. We know she has to work on Monday, Wednesday and Thursday so far. If she works on Tuesday, she would be working for 4 consecutive days, which is wrong.

Since Amy cannot work on a Tuesday and 2 operators must work on a single day, Bob and Carla must work on a Tuesday.

Therefore, Carla works on Tuesday, Wednesday and Friday.

So the answer is A.

---

2) C

A – Wrong
The text specifies that the new criteria make planets look too hot for liquid water to form. The new criteria also make Earth look too hot which is not true as Earth does contain water.
Therefore, there is a possibility that life could exist on Kepler-22b

B – Wrong
This is actually the opposite of what is given in the text. According to the new criteria, lesser and lesser planets are habitable than previously thought.

C – Correct
The last line suggests that there is some inaccuracy in the new criteria. This statement clearly summarises the content of the text and hence is the correct answer.

D – Wrong
There is no evidence given in the text that can prove this statement correct. Also, the main focus of the text is the new criteria that cosmologists now use and it is not entirely focused on Kepler-22b. This statement is too specific.

---

3) C

We first need to take the difference between each of their birthdays and see which difference is divisible by 7.

$182 - 128 = 54$

$218 - 128 = 90$

281 − 128 = 153
218 − 182 = 36
281 − 182 = 99
281 − 218 = 63

The only difference, which is divisible by 7, is 63. This equals to exactly 9 weeks. Adam is born on the 218th day whilst Tara is born on 281st day. This means that Tara was born exactly (exactly means on the same day of the week) 9 weeks after Adam on the same day. Hence, Adam and Tara is the answer. Option C is the answer.

---

4) C
The last line of the text is the conclusion.

A – Wrong
The line in the text "our bodies are like vehicle" is just a simile. This statement is out of context and hence is insufficient to be called a conclusion.

B – Wrong
Although this statement is true and is given in the text, it is unable to summarise the entire paragraph. The focus of the text is that in order to burn calories and lose weight, it is important to exercise. This statement is hence, not the conclusion.

C – Correct
This statement correctly paraphrases the last line of the text.

D – Wrong
Even though this is correct, it does not mention anything about how people can lose weight. The conclusion of the text is that in order to lose weight, people must either do more and/or eat less.

E – Wrong
The last line says that we can also lose weight by eating less. Hence, this is wrong.

---

5) D
Cost of a spruggle on the second day: 75% of 12 = £9
Let no. of spruggles sold on day 1 = 'S'
So no. of spruggles sold on day 2 = 2S
Money obtained on day 1 = S x 12 = 12S
Money obtained on day 2 = 2S x 9 = 18S
We know he obtained £342 more on second day.
12S + 342 = 18S
342 = 6S
S = 57
On the first day, he sold 57 spruggles and on the second day he sold 2S = 57 x 2 = 114 spruggles
In total, he sold 114 + 57 = 171 Spruggles

---

6) C

A – Wrong

The discovery of other tools does not necessarily challenge the theory. These other tools could have been made by the Clovis after they came to America.

B – Wrong

Even if the Ice Age had lasted longer, it does not necessarily mean that people from Asia could not have entered the Americas.

C – Correct

If it was found that there were human settlements dating to 12,000 BC, this would mean that there were humans in America 14,000 years ago. This means that there were humans in America before the Clovis moved there 13,500 years ago. Hence, the Clovis would not have been the first inhabitants of the Americas.

D – Wrong

Extinction of the big mammals has very little correlation with the Clovis moving into the Americas. This does not seriously challenge the theory.

E – Wrong

If this were true, it would have been easier for the Clovis to reach America from Asia.

---

7) A

We cannot directly identify Ian's surname since all of the surnames provided can be Ian's surname. All of the surnames given have more than three letters and do not contain the letters 'i', 'a' and 'n'

So the only way to solve this question is by process of elimination.

Let us start with first names that have 5 letters:

Simon's and Dylan's surnames cannot be Doyle, Floyd or Shore since the first name and the second name cannot contain the same number of letters. The only remaining surnames are Hyde and Rush.

Dylan's surname cannot be Hyde as the letter 'y' is repeated. So Dylan's surname would be Rush.

Hence, Simon's surname is Hyde.

Boys with first names that have 4 letters:

Liam's surname cannot be Doyle or Floyd as they contain the letter 'L'. So Liam's surname must be Shore.

Eric's surname cannot be Doyle as it contains the letter 'e'. So Eric's surname must be Floyd.

The only remaining surname is Doyle. The answer is A.

---

8) D

A – Wrong

The truth is that children are less carefree today than they were in the past. Statement A is the opposite.

Clearly wrong. The text focuses on children and not chocolate.

C – Wrong
This option is clearly wrong. The text focuses on children and not blondes having more fun.

D – Correct
This option is clearly the correct answer. The text entirely focuses on the importance of relationships when it comes to children. Today, children are less carefree than before.

9) A
A is basically paraphrasing the sentence given in the question. We now have more money and more misery. This means that even though we are getting richer, we are not getting any happier.
Even though B should be hypothetically correct, the evidence shows that it is in fact wrong.
C and D are irrelevant as these two statements are neither suggested by the text nor can they be inferred from the text.

10) D
1 – Wrong
People who work shorter hours may not necessarily spend their extra time with their children.

2 – Wrong
The text, in no way, suggests that failing to gain wealth and success will not cause stress.
Since both statements are wrong, D is the answer.

11) B
The evidence given later on in paragraph 4 is a story of a two-year old who just wanted to be with someone she loved and trusted every day. Since the evidence is given as a story, it is anecdotal.

12) B

MOON	♂	TIN	SILVER
⊙	MERCURY	SATURN	♀
COPPER	LEAD	⊙	SUN

JUPITER	IRON	MARS	♂
♄	♀	MERCURY	VENUS
GOLD	SATURN	♃	SUN

The easiest way to do this is by using the symbols and matching it with the other cards.
The only pair that can be formed is the third card (third in the top row) and the fifth card (first in the second row).
The third card has Tin written at the top, Saturn in the middle and the symbol for Gold and Sun at the bottom.
The fifth card has Jupiter (which is equivalent to Tin) written at the top, the symbol for Saturn and Lead in the middle and Gold written in the bottom.

---

13) D
The answer to this question is the last line of the sentence "In the interests of providing the most desirable outcome.."
A – Wrong

Although this is a true statement, it does not support the argument.
B – Wrong
Although this is a true statement, it does not support the argument.
C – Wrong
Although this is a true statement, it does not support the argument. This may seem to be the correct answer but if placebos do help patients to feel better, then they should be used.
D – Correct
If a treatment (even placebos) provides a beneficial outcome for a patient, then that treatment should be given.
E – Wrong
This may also seem to be the answer but D is more correct as the outcome for the patient is more important and relevant.

---

14) B
Since four is the first digit, the second or third digits cannot be eight as 'e' comes before 'f' and the digits are in alphabetical order. It can also not be five as 'fo' in four comes after 'fi' in five. They can neither be four nor zero, as all four digits must be different.
We can form an equation to match the information provided to us.
We know 4 has four letters
We know 0 has four letters
Let the 2nd digit be S
Le the 3rd digit be T
$4 + 0 + S + T = 8 +$ Number of letters in S + Number of letters in T
$S + T = 4 +$ Number of letters in S + Number of letters in T

By placing in different digits, we get the answer to be 9 and 2.
Total number of letters in 9 and 2 = 4 + 3 = 7
So the answer is B

---

15) B
A – Wrong
The text actually states that improved performance in extreme sports causes greater exposure to danger. The statement given in A actually strengthens the argument.

B – Correct

If this statement is true, then people would not mind taking risks in order to escape the safety. Also, it would contradict the sentence "…do to counter the stress and pressure of work..".

C – Wrong

This sentence actually strengthens the argument as it points out that designers encourage risk-taking. The last sentence "..equipment that are designed to make the sports safer…greater exposure to danger".

D – Wrong

This statement just states the opposite of what the paragraph says. It does not 'weaken' it.

---

16) C

Months starting with J = January, June and July
Months starting with A = April, August
Months starting with M = March, May
Jenny's and Alice's birthdays are two months apart
2 months from January = March. This cannot be correct
2 months from June = August. This can be correct
2 months from July = September. This cannot be correct
Hence, the only possibility is for Jenny to be born in June and Alice to be born in August.
Alice's and Michael's birthdays are five months apart
5 months after August = January
5 months before August = March
Hence Michael's birthday is in March.
Difference between March and June = 3 months
This corresponds to C.

---

17) D

The argument made in the text is that the ability to sleep well deteriorates with age. We must find a weakness in this argument.

1 – Correct

This statement identifies a weakness. This statement provides a new reason why old people sleep less than young people. The reason behind old people sleeping less is not because of their age but because of their impairment in memory.

2 – Wrong

Although this may be a factual statement, it does not provide a weakness in the argument made by the paragraph.

3 – Correct

This statement says that ageing is not the only reason why old people are unable to sleep well. It identifies a weakness and states that changes in the brain due to ageing causes deterioration in memory and sleep patterns.

Statements 1 and 3 are correct. So, D is the answer.

18) B

This question is only asking about September.
Possible square numbers in the hours place: 01, 04, 09 and 16
Possible square numbers in the minutes place: 01, 04, 09, 16, 25, 36, and 49
Possible square numbers in the day place: 01, 04, 09, 16, and 25
Possible square numbers in the months place: 09
We need to find out how many different digits there are in the numbers above.
There are: 01, 04, 09, 16, 25, 36 and 49.
So there are 6 different numbers. We just need to square 6 to find the answer. $6^2 = 36$. Hence, B is the answer.
Alternatively, you can find the different possibilities but it will take too much time.

---

19) B

The region just below X cannot be red, blue or yellow as it shares borders with red, blue and yellow. Hence, it has to be green.
The region to the top right of X can either be red or yellow. When it is yellow, X can either be red or blue. When it is red, X can either be yellow or blue.
Hence, X can either be red, blue or yellow.

---

20) C

Remember that a chessboard already has two colours: black and white.
If the circle is contained within a square, it could be the opposite colour of the square and no rules will be broken.
However, if the circle was larger than a square and not contained within a square, it would have to be a different colour to black and white as no same colour can be both sides of the border. Hence, either none or one extra colour would always be needed.

---

21) A

Try drawing maps with different variations of three straight lines. You will realise that each segment can only share borders with two other segments and both these neighbouring segments can be of a different colour to the first segment.
Hence only 2 colours would be required.

---

22) B

Again, check if two colours will suffice. You will notice that this is not possible. Since there is an odd number of triangular faces on each pyramid, the fifth face cannot be of the same colour as the first or the fourth.
Check if three colours suffice. You will realise that this is correct.

---

23) D

The top-left tile has 1 quarter of the area separated. That is one type of tile.

259

The tile, which is just to the right, is divided into half. This is the second type of tile.

Three types of tiles form the big black square in the middle.
The middle tile is completely black. This is the third type of tile.

The tile at the top left of the square has one-quarter of its area shaded black. This is the fourth type of tile.

The tile to the right of this tile has one-half of its area black and the other half white. This is the fifth type of tile.

There are also 4 smaller squares surrounding the big black square.
These squares have a sixth type of tile, which has one-quarter of the tile marked out and another quarter of the tile, which is black.

The other four shapes that have 6 sides have two more types of tiles.
One tile is three-quarters black and one quarter white.

The last type of tile is similar to the sixth type of tile but flipped vertically.

---

24) B
The argument made in the text is that governments should make alcohol more expensive and make it less appealing by banning advertising.

A – Wrong
This statement would not strengthen the argument made by the text but would instead; strengthen the argument made by alcohol companies. The statistics provided in this statement does not provide a reason why governments should make alcohol more expensive.

B – Correct

This statement helps to explain why the government should increase the prices. The case seen in Scotland shows that alcohol consumption increased due to a decrease in prices. If the prices go up, the alcohol consumption would decrease.

C – Wrong

Even though this statement could be true, the focus of the text is alcohol consumption in general. Its focus is not on the wealth of the people who drink it.

D – Wrong

This statement does not explain why the government should increase prices and ban advertising. We need some evidence as to why the government should do so. This evidence is only explained by statement B.

---

25) B

Since all eight digits have to different, one clock must show 19 in the hours place and the second clock must show 20 in the hours place.

When the correct time is 20:00, the first clock must show 19:44 and the second clock must show 20:25

The successive minutes must be within the range of 19:44 and 19:59 for the first clock and within the range of 20:25 and 20:41 for the second clock.

Since all eight digits have to different, the clocks cannot show 1, 9, 2 or 0 in the minutes as these numbers are in the hours of the first and the second clock. Since the second clock cannot show 2 in the minutes, the second clock must show minutes that are after 20:31.

When it is 20:31 in the second clock it is 19:50 in the first clock. This cannot be correct, as there is 0 in both clocks.

20:34 = 19:53. This is wrong as 3 in both clocks

20:35 = 19:54. This is wrong as 5 in both clocks

20:36 = 19:55. This is wrong as 5 is repeated in clock 1

20:37 = 19:56. This could be correct

20:38 = 19:57. This could be correct

20:39 = 19:58. This is wrong as 9 repeated in both clocks

20:40 = 19:59. This is wrong as 0 repeated in clock 2

20:41 = 20:00. This is wrong as 2 and 0 repeated in both clocks

The consecutive minutes are 20:37-19:56 and 20:38-19:57.

The options given to us are 3, 4, 5, 6, 7 and 8. Out of these options, 3, 5, 6, 7 and 8 appear on the clocks during the consecutive minutes. This means that the answer is 4.

---

26) A

This question is actually easier than it seems. It is important to understand the question first. The die is rolled and the die rolls in the direction in which the letters P, Q, R and S are labelled. The die on the board is the starting position. It is important that you understand the orientation of the die on the board as compared to the orientation of the die to the left.

The number that will land on P is the number directly underneath 1. This is 6.

The number that will land on Q is the number adjacent to 6, facing towards Q. This is 7.

The number that will land on R is the number adjacent to 7, facing towards R. This is 4.
The number that will land on S is the number adjacent to 4, facing towards S. This is 1.

27) C

This is easy once you look at all of the options.
The correct answer is yes.
If Al (married) was looking at Beth (if unmarried), then a married person was looking at an unmarried person.
If Beth (married) was looking at Charles (who is definitely unmarried), then a married person was looking at an unmarried person.

It does not matter whether Beth was married or unmarried; a married person would be looking at an unmarried person.

28) D

The last line "seems that many children are simply not ready to face this reality at such a young age without damaging consequences" suggest that children should not be exposed to such harsh realities at a young age.
Only statement D supports this argument whilst all the others state the opposite.

29) E

This question requires great spatial awareness skills and it is certainly a question that can prevent you from the answering other ones, as it requires some time to do it if you are trying to solve it in your mind.
It is advisable to bring scissors to the exam in case such questions come up. (No rules against scissors but please check with your exams officer). Cut the net out and fold the cube in a way so that each side has 4 squares.

Also, do such questions at the end when you have successfully completed all of the other ones and have some time left.

30) D

The argument made in the paragraph is the last sentence of the paragraph.

1 – Correct
The last line of the paragraph assumes that gripping objects underwater could be advantageous to us.

2 – Wrong
Although this may be true, it is irrelevant to the argument made in the paragraph.

3 – Correct
This is one of the fundamental principles of evolution. Advantageous characteristics must have evolved because they were advantageous. Hence, this must have been assumed in the paragraph.

Statements 1 and 3 are assumptions and hence, D is the answer.

31) A
Sum of upper row so far = 9 + 5 = 14
Value needed = 29 – 14 = 15
15 can only be made by (7 + 8) or (11 + 4). 12, 10 and 9 are already used in other rows.

Sum of lower row so far = 10 + 12 = 22
Value needed = 29 – 22 = 7
7 can only be made by (4 + 3). 5 and 6 are already used in other rows.

Since 4 definitely needs to be in the lower row, it cannot be in the upper row. So 7 and 8 definitely sit in the upper row.
If 8 sits in the top right corner and 4 sits in the bottom right corner,
Value of vertical row = 8 + 6 + 4 = 18
Value needed = 29 – 18 = 11
So 11 will sit above 6.
The seating plan would be like this:

5	9	7	8
1			11
2			6
10	3	12	4

The person sitting in front of 9 would be 3. So A is the answer.

---

32) B
The text gives us the information that cannabis users are 41% more likely to have any psychosis.
If 1% of non-cannabis users develop psychosis, 1.41% of cannabis users in the sample will have psychosis.
In the second paragraph of the text, it is mentioned that about 20% of young people use cannabis.
20% of 10,000 = 2000 people
1.41% ≈ 1.40%
1.4% of 2000 = (1.40 ÷ 100) x 2000 = 1.4 x 20 = 28

---

33) A
Probability of getting psychosis by reasons others than cannabis = y.
Since 80% of the population do not use cannabis, probability of getting psychosis by reasons other than cannabis = 80% x y = 0.8y

20% of the population use cannabis. However, they have the same probability 'y' of getting psychosis plus the 41%.

This gives us the equation:
$$(0.41 \times 0.2y) \div [(1.41 \times 0.2y) + 0.8y] = 0.082 \div 1.08 \approx 0.08/1.1$$

Percentage = $(0.08 / 1.1) \times 100 = 8\%$

---

34) B

A – Wrong
Age is irrelevant.

B – Correct
The text states that an increase in use of cannabis can lead to psychotic illness. This statement provides an alternate link that those with psychotic illness can lead to them using cannabis.

C – Wrong
This statement suggests that the link made between the use of cannabis and the development of psychotic illness may not be valid. This is irrelevant to the question.

D – Wrong
This suggests that there may be more cannabis users than we think which is irrelevant to the question.

---

35) C

A – Wrong
The cause of psychotic illness could have been something else rather than the increase in cannabis use. (Age, memory etc.)

B – Wrong
This provides other factors that could cause psychosis which is the opposite of what we need to answer the question.

C – Correct
This clearly suggests that an increase in the strength of cannabis causes an increase in psychosis among users.

D – Wrong Age
is irrelevant

E – Wrong
This does not strengthen the link made in the text.

2013 Section 2

1) H

1 - both the nervous system and the endocrine system can be involved in homeostasis. e.g. hypothalamus in the brain detects a decrease in water level in the body. Pituitary gland secretes ADH to reabsorb more water to prevent dehydration

2 - chemicals in the nervous system could include noradrenaline. Endocrine system secretes hormones, which are chemicals.

3 - pituitary gland is in the brain and receives information from the hypothalamus. Brain is part of the nervous system.

Statements 1, 2 and 3 are correct.

2) D
You must try and remember the reactivity series. This question is totally dependent on that.
If the element in the salt is lower down in the reactivity series compared to element it is being reacted with, a displacement reaction will occur.

1 - Al is more reactive than Pb and so will displace Pb.
2 - K is more reactive than F- and hence no displacement reaction will occur
3 - Al is more reactive than Fe so no displacement reaction will occur
4 - Zn is more reactive than Cu so a displacement reaction will occur

1 and 4 are the correct answers so option D is correct

3) D
1 - Microwaves are absorbed by water molecules. An example of this when water molecules in food absorb microwaves from the microwave oven and heat up the food.

2 - The ionising properties of X rays means that they can damage the DNA in the cells of the human body.

3 - Infra red waves do not penetrate matter

Only statements 1 and 2 are correct so D is correct

4) A
Substitute the values given in the problem

$$\frac{4.6 \times 10^7 + 7\,(2 \times 10^6)}{4.6 \times 10^7 - 2\,(2 \times 10^6)}$$

$$\frac{(4.6 \times 10^7) + (14 \times 10^6)}{(4.6 \times 10^7) - (4 \times 10^6)}$$

$$\frac{(4.6 \times 10^7) + (1.4 \times 10^7)}{(4.6 \times 10^7) - (0.4 \times 10^7)}$$

$$\frac{6 \times 10^7}{4.2 \times 10^7}$$

The two (10^7) will cancel out

$$\frac{6}{4.2} = \frac{1}{0.7} = \frac{10}{7}$$

---

5) F

A logical way of solving this question is to identify the products which will be formed when these three enzymes are added to the mixture.

Carbohydrase enzyme will break carbohydrates into sugars which are non-acidic.

Protease will break protein into amino **acids.** Amino acids are slightly acidic which means they would lower the pH

Lipase will break fats into fatty **acids** and glycerol

So the action of enzymes protease and lipase will lower the pH of the mixture

---

6) B

In order to produce more T, we need the forward reaction to occur.

The forward reaction is exothermic since ΔH is negative. This means that the forward reaction releases energy. If we lower the temperature, the forward reaction will be favoured. Therefore, more T will be formed if temperature is low.

High pressure causes the equilibrium shifts to the side with the lower number of moles. There are 5 moles on the left side and 2 moles on the left side. Therefore a high pressure will favour a higher production of T.

If we add more of the reactants, more products will be formed. If we add R and S, more T will be formed.

So we need the following conditions:

Low temperature, high pressure, add R and S. This corresponds to B.

---

7) H

With the switch open, the circuit was in series. With the switch closed, the circuit became parallel.

Parallel circuits have a lower overall resistance than a series circuit.

With the equation, V=IR, we know that current is inversely proportional to resistance. The overall voltage cannot change.

Since voltage doesn't change and resistance decreases, current must increase.

Since the switch is now closed, there are two pathways for current to pass through: 1st one being through the resistor and second being through the switch.

This means that Q has the full voltage. Therefore, Q increases and R decreases. The answer is H.

---

8) F

Break the problem into smaller parts

1st step:

$x^2 (1 - 16x^2) = x^2 - 16x^4$

2nd step:

$2x^3 (4x - 1) = 8x^4 - 2x^3$

3rd step:

$\dfrac{x^2 - 16x^4}{8x^4 - 2x^3}$

4th step:

$4 - \dfrac{x^2 - 16x^4}{8x^4 - 2x^3}$

$\dfrac{4 (8x^4 - 2x^3) - (x^2 - 16x^4)}{8x^4 - 2x^3}$

$\dfrac{32x^4 - 8x^3 - x^2 + 16x^4}{8x^4 - 2x^3}$

$\dfrac{48x^4 - 8x^3 - x^2}{8x^4 - 2x^3}$

$\dfrac{x^2 (48x^2 - 8x - 1)}{x^2 (8x^2 - 2x)}$

$\dfrac{48x^2 - 8x - 1}{8x^2 - 2x}$

5th step: Factorising the numerator $48x^2$
$- 8x - 1$
$48x^2 - 12x + 4x - 1$
$12x (4x - 1) + 1 (4x - 1)$
$(12x + 1) (4x - 1)$

6th step: Factorising the denominator $8x^2 -$
$2x$
$2x (4x - 1)$

267

7th step:

$$\frac{(12x + 1)(4x - 1)}{2x(4x - 1)}$$

$$\frac{(12x + 1)}{2x}$$

$$\frac{12x}{2x} + \frac{1}{2x}$$

$$6 + \frac{1}{2x}$$

---

9) F

Sensory neurones are the longest since they have to cover the length from the point of stimulus to the spinal cord.
Motor neurones are shorter than sensory neurones but longer than relay neurones since they have to travel from the spinal cord to the muscle erector.
Relay neurones are the shortest as they are only in the spinal cord.

---

10) B

We must first write down the full equation for the reaction.

$2Na + 2H_2O \rightarrow 2NaOH + H_2$

Moles of Na = m/Mr = $(1.15 \div 23) \approx (1.2 \div 24) = 0.05$ mol
Molar ratio $(NaOH:H_2) = 2:1$
Moles of $H_2 = (0.05 \div 2) = 0.025$ mol

We know 1 mol gives $22.4 dm^3$ of gas
0.025 mol = 22.4 x 0.025 = 0.56 dm^3
$1 dm^3 = 1000 cm^3$
0.56 dm^3 = 560 cm^3
The answer is B

---

11) C

-When the angle of incidence is lower than the critical angle, refraction occurs. and light leaves the medium.
-When the angle of incidence is equal to the critical angle, the light travels along the boundary of the two mediums.
-When the angle of incidence is greater than the critical angle, total internal reflection occurs.
Angle of incidence is equal to angle of reflection.

Diagram 1:
The angle of incidence (40°) is less than the critical angle given in the question (42°). Since it is lower than the critical angle, the light will refract out of the glass block. Therefore the passage would be P. Since it refracts, there is no Total Internal Reflection (TIR).

Diagram 2:
Now, you may be confused that why TIR does not occur in this case. A condition for TIR is that light must travel from a dense medium to a less dense medium (glass to air and not air to glass).
TIR does not occur when light travels from air to glass. Instead, light refracts, meaning that it follows the S path.

Direction in diagram 1: P
TIR in diagram 1: No
Direction in Diagram 2: S
TIR in diagram 2: No
Hence, the answer is C.

---

12) B

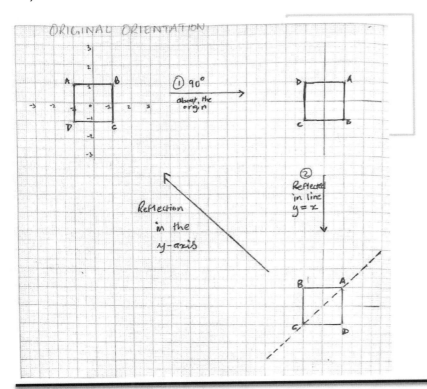

---

13) C
This might be a tricky question but actually, the answer is in the question itself.
The question asks what is not needed to produce a fluorescent protein. This is why the answer is C. We do not need a fluorescent protein in order to produce another a fluorescent protein.

---

14) A
A - Correct
Mg has 2 electrons in its outer shell. Each of these electrons will go to each of the Cl atoms. These chloride atoms will have the same electronic structure as an Ar atom. However, the Mg atom would have the electronic structure of a Ne atom.
Hence, this is the answer.

B - Wrong
Carbon has 4 electrons in its outer shell. It forms a triple bond with O. Both C and O would have eight electrons in their outer shells.
These N atoms form a triple bond between each other. Both atoms would have eight electrons in their outer shell.
Hence, this is not the answer.

C - Wrong
C covalently bonds with 4 H atoms. C would have eight electrons in its outer shell and each of the H atoms would have 2 electrons in their outer shell.
The N covalently bonds with 3 H atoms and forms a co-ordinate bond with a fourth H+ ion. The Nitrogen will have eight electrons in its outer shell and each of the H atoms would have 2 electrons in their outer shell.

D - Wrong
N covalently bonds with 3 O atoms. It forms a single bond with 2 O atoms and a double bond with the third O atom. All atoms would have eight electrons in their outer shells.
C covalently bonds with 3 O atoms. It forms a single bond with 2 O atoms and a double bond with the third O atom. All atoms would have eight electrons in their outer shells.

E - Wrong
Na has 1 electron in its outer shell. This electron will go to the F atom. Both Na and F atoms will have the same electronic structure as a Ne atom.

---

15) D
Half-life of X = 4.8 hours
Number of half lives of X in 24 hours = $24 \div 4.8 = 5$
Count rate of X after 5 half lives = $320 \div 2^5 = 10$

Half-life of Y = 8 hours
Number of half lives of X in 24 hours = $24 \div 8 = 3$
Count rate of Y after 3 half lives = $480 \div 2^3 = 60$

Total count rate = $10 + 60 = 70$

---

16) D

Let us write down the information given into proportions first.

$x \propto z^2$

$y \propto \frac{1}{z^3}$

Making powers equal,

$x^3 \propto z^6$ **(equation 1)**

$y^2 \propto \frac{1}{z^6}$

$z^6 \propto \frac{1}{y^2}$ **(equation 2)**

Using eq 1 and 2,

$z \propto x^3 \propto \frac{1}{y^2}$

So the cube of x is inversely proportional to the square of y.

---

17) A

1 - Correct

If the egg does not divide then the organism cannot form.

2 - Wrong

There is no use of sperm cells

3 - Correct

If the implantation fails, then the cloning will obviously fail

4 - Wrong

The egg must divide and not differentiate

5 - Correct

If the enucleated egg and the transferred nucleus are not compatible, then the cloning will not take place

Statements 1, 3 and 5 are correct so A is the answer.

---

18) E

Reaction equation:

$NaOH + HCl \rightarrow NaCl + H_2O$

Volume of HCl = 50 cm³ = 0.05 dm³
Concentration of HCl = 0.5
Moles of HCl = 0.05 x 0.5 = 0.025 mol

Molar ratio of NaOH : HCl = 1 : 1
Moles of NaOH = 0.025 mol
Mr of NaOH = 23 + 16 + 1 = 40

Moles = Mass ÷ Mr
Mass = Moles x Mr
Mass = 0.025 x 40 = 1 g

Mass of sample = 1.20 g
Percentage purity = (1 ÷ 1.2) x 100 = 83.3%

19) D
Total resistance of the circuit = $R_1 + R_2$
Voltage = V

We know current remains the same across both resistors.
Current of circuit (I) = V ÷ ($R_1 + R_2$)

We know V = IR
Voltage across R_1 (V_1) = I x R_1
V_1 = [V ÷ ($R_1 + R_2$)] x R_1 = VR_1 ÷ ($R_1 + R_2$)

We know P = VI
Power across R_1 = V_1 x I
P_1 = [VR_1 ÷ ($R_1 + R_2$)] x [V ÷ ($R_1 + R_2$)]
$P_1 = V^2R ÷ (R_1 + R_2)^2$
Hence the answer is D.

20) D
It is advisable to skip such long and tricky questions and finish the other simpler ones first.

We need to use a lot of Pythagoras in this question.
Side of smaller cube = 1cm
Side of 2nd cube = A
Side of 3rd cube = B

5 faces of the smallest cube can be seen.
Surface area of the smallest cube = 1 x 1 x 5 = 5 cm²

The vertices of the smallest cube are at the midpoints of A.
You can see that multiple right-angled triangles are formed.

$1^2 = (½A)^2 + (½A)^2$
$1 = ¼A^2 + ¼a^2$
$1 = ½a^2$
$2 = A^2$
$A = √2$
4 faces of the 2nd cube can be seen and the top face is partially covered by the smallest cube.

Surface area = 5 x √2 x √2 = 10cm²
Area covered by one of the faces of the smaller cube = 1 x 1 = 1cm²
So total surface area of the 2nd cube = 10 - 1 = 9cm²

Again the vertices of the second cube are at the midpoints of B.
You can see that multiple right-angled triangles are formed.

$(√2)^2 = (½B)^2 + (½B)^2$
$2 = ¼B^2 + ¼B^2$
$2 = ½B^2$
$4 = B^2$
$B = √4 = 2cm$
5 faces of the largest cube are uncovered and 1 is partially covered.
Surface area = 6 x 2 x 2 = 24cm²
Again the top face is partially covered by the 2nd cube.
Surface area of one of the faces of the 2nd cube = √2 x √2 = 2cm²
Total surface area of largest cube = 24 - 2 = 22cm²

Total surface area of solid = 22 + 9 + 5 = 36 cm²

---

21) E
The complete set of genes of an organism is found in a cell meaning the liver cell would have the gene for amylase as well as sex chromosomes.
However, starch is broken down before it reaches the liver. Hence starch is not found in the liver cell.

1 and 2 are found in an adult liver cell. So, E is the answer.

---

22) C
Number of Cr on LHS = 2
Number of Cr on RHS = d
So d = 2 (there are no other Cr on the left and right hand sides)

Total charge on left side so far = -2 + 1 = -1
Total charge on right side = 2 x (+3) = +6
To balance charges, b = +6 - (-2) = + 6 + 2 = +8
b = 8

Let us form an equation for the total number of H

$4a + b = 4c + 2e$
$4a + b - 4c = 2e$
$e = \dfrac{4a + b - 4c}{2}$

Let us form an equation for the total number of O
a + 7 = 2c + e
e = a + 7 - 2c

Putting the two equations together,

$$\frac{4a + b - 4c}{2} = a + 7 - 2c$$

4a + b - 4c = 2 (a + 7 - 2c)
4a + b - 4c = 2a + 14 - 4c
4a + b = 2a + 14
2a + b = 14
Substituting value of b,
2a + 8 = 14
2a = 6
a = 3
Number of carbons on LHS = 2 x a = 2 x 3 = 6
Number of carbons on RHS = 2c
2c must equal to 6
c = 3

Using the equation (e = a + 7 - 2c),
e = 3 + 7 - 2(3)
e = 10 - 6
e = 4

23) D
A - Wrong
With the equation F = ma, we know that F $\propto$ a and hence this can be a graph of Force against acceleration.

B - Wrong
With the equation V = IR, we know that V $\propto$ I and hence this can be a graph of voltage against current.

C - Wrong
With the equation KE = ½mv², we know that KE $\propto v^2$.

D - Correct
With the equation c = λ x f, we know that λ $\propto 1/f$ and hence this cannot be a graph of wavelength against frequency.

E - Wrong
With the equation W = F x d, we know that W $\propto$ d and hence this can be a graph of work against distance.

24) C

We need to find out the probability of either 2 blue balls or 2 red balls.
Each of the scenarios has 3 possibilities.
That is, 2 red balls can be obtained by RRB, RBR, BRR
2 blue balls can be obtained by BBR, BRB, RBB

Probability of 2 red balls = $\frac{2}{10} \times \frac{1}{9} \times \frac{8}{8} \times 3 = \frac{42}{720}$
Probability of 2 red balls = $\frac{8}{10} \times \frac{7}{9} \times \frac{2}{8} \times 3 = \frac{336}{720}$
Probability of 2 balls being the same colour = $\frac{42}{720} + \frac{336}{720} = \frac{384}{720} = \frac{8}{15}$

25) C

Manx cat with a tail   x   Manx cat without a tail

	t	t
T	Tt	Tt
t	tt	tt

Manx cat without tail = 50%

Manx cat without a tail   x   Manx cat without a tail

	T	t
T	TT (dead)	Tt (67%)
t	Tt (67%)	tt (33%)

Manx cat without tail = 67%
Hence, C is the answer.

26) B

We know that a catalyst always remains unchanged at the end of a reaction. This means that at the end of the reaction, NO must be recovered. Hence, reaction 6 will definitely be one of the reactions.
Since 6 is only mentioned in option B, B is the answer.

27) E

KE = $\frac{1}{2}mv^2$ = 1800 J
v = 30 m/s

F = ma
a = F/m = 20/4 = 5 m/s^2

v = u + at
v = ?
u = 30
a = 5
t = 2

v = 30 + (5 x 2) = 40 m/s

KE = $\frac{1}{2}$mv^2 = $\frac{1}{2}$ x 4 x 40^2 = 2 x 40 x 40 = 3200 J
EXTRA energy = 3200 - 1800 = 1400 J

2013 Section 3

1) According to Gibson, a system or an occurrence can be studied efficiently when they fail to function properly. For example, if an owner tries to fix a car himself or herself, they can identify the different components of the car and study their functions. The owner can work out which component caused the car to break down. On the other hand, it is difficult to examine something if it is in perfect working order. Similarly, fMRIs are used to identify different parts of the brain. If a sighted person opens their eyes, their occipital lobe lights up in an fMRI. However, the occipital lobe does not light up in the fMRI of a blind person.

On the contrary, studying something, which is completely "coming apart", can lead to misunderstanding. Let us use the example of the car again. If a car were completely stripped of its parts, the owner would not be able to identify the importance and function of each part. Similarly, if the fMRI of a dead person was studied, no parts of the brain would light up. Therefore, the doctors would not be able to study what each part does.

In order to examine something efficiently, some parts of it must work and other parts must not. Without any background knowledge of the functions of different parts of a system, it would be near impossible to work out what each part does.

2) According to the statement, a surgeon should be presented with more difficult cases. Tough cases challenge surgeons, as they involve more risks and increased probability of mortality. The risk of patient death might cause a surgeon to be reluctant to do surgery. If a surgeon's high patient mortality rate was made public, patients would not want that surgeon to operate on them.

Publicising mortality rates of a surgeon can create unnecessary stress on the doctor. The pressure of having a high mortality rate can cause the surgeon to make unnecessary mistakes during surgery. It can also lead to demotivation and loss in confidence. In addition to this, public mortality rate records can be misleading as they do not provide important information such as the cause of death and duration of hospital stay.

On the other hand, some may argue that league tables should not affect a doctor's confidence. It does not matter what their mortality rates are. They should always treat patients to the best of their ability and should always act in a patient's best interest. A patient should have some knowledge about their doctor as they are putting their lives into a surgeon's hands.

The performances of surgeons should not be available online for everyone to see as they can have negative outcomes. However, it should be compulsory for a surgeon to first inform their patient about their mortality rates. This can help the patient to make an informed decision and also keep the records private.

3) According to Darwin, people who know little about science are more confident about the limits of science than those who know a lot. For example, those who know little about science

may be certain that science will never be able to solve mysteries such as why humans feel emotions and how life became existent.

A common problem in the modern world is the use of the internet for self-diagnosis. Patients read online articles on the possible conditions that they may be suffering from and gain incorrect knowledge. Some patients remain adamant that they are suffering from a certain illness when in reality, they may have a completely different condition.

On the contrary, a person who has extended knowledge about a subject may become certain that progress in that particular subject is not possible. In such a case, it is important for someone else, who is less knowledgeable, to study that subject and ensure whether progress is possible or not. In 1934, Albert Einstein said that it is not possible to obtain nuclear energy. In 1954, the USSR managed to supply electricity using nuclear power.
Different opinions are always necessary for science as they can often provide weaknesses and flaws in researches.

There is some truth to the statement made by Darwin. However, it is not applicable to all situations and hence should not be generalised.

---

4) According to the statement, owning a pet is unnecessary and the expenses used to keep a pet can instead be used to provide resources for the ever-growing human populations.

It is indeed a fact that the population of the world is increasing at a rapid rate and resources are limited. We need more food, clean water, clothes and shelter to support this growing population. Efforts should be made to ensure that less money is wasted on unnecessary things. Some may argue that owning pets could be an unnecessary luxury. The money spent on a pet's food, water and health could be used for a better purpose.

On the contrary, pets are considered to be family members to pet owners. They are cared for with love and affection because they are an integral part of the owner's family. When a pet passes away, some owners hold a funeral in their memory, just like a human being.
Other than this, it is a person's wish to adopt a pet. If they want to spend their money on a pet, then they should be allowed to do so. Prohibiting a person from spending money on whatever they wish is a breach of their rights. There is no guarantee that money will be spent on something better such helping those in need.

Also, there are a lot of things in this world which cannot be justified. If owning a pet is unjustified, then consumption of alcohol, drugs and smoking should be treated in the same manner. People spend thousands of pounds on alcohol and cigarettes throughout their lifetime. These substances also lead to many fatal diseases such as diabetes and lung cancer. Treating these diseases can count as a waste of resources.

More effective measures, such as lessening wastage of food and clean water, should be adopted. Owning a pet and lesser resources for the growing population are not necessarily correlated. There are a lot of emotions attached to owning a pet. Therefore, it would be unethical to think about separating a pet from its owner.

2014 Worked Solutions

2014 Section 1, 2 and 3 Worked solutions are available for free on the following websites:

Section 1: https://www.admissionstesting.org/Images/258226-specimen-bmat-2014-section-1-explained-answers.pdf

Section 2: https://www.admissionstesting.org/Images/258232-specimen-bmat-2014-section-2-explained-answers.pdf

Section 3: https://www.admissionstesting.org/Images/258236-past-paper-2014-section-3-responses-with-examiner-comments.pdf

Please note that the author of this book does not own 2014 Section 1, 2 and 3 worked solutions and does not claim to own them. These worked solutions are provided by admissionstesting.org
The author of this book is not affiliated to these worked solutions in any way, shape or form.

1) D

Stuart > Ruth > Margaret

Ruth >Tim

Tim > Adrian

From these inequalities, we can conclude the following:

Stuart > Ruth > Margaret and Tim

We cannot conclude who is taller between Margaret and Tim. The only information given to us is that both of them are shorter than Ruth.

We know Tim is taller than Adrian. However, since we cannot determine who is taller between Tim and Margaret, we also cannot determine who is taller between Margaret and Adrian.

A – this is incorrect. We do not know who is taller between Margaret and Adrian.

B – We know Ruth is taller than Tim and Tim is taller than Adrian. So Ruth must definitely be taller than Adrian. So, this is incorrect.

C – We know that Stuart and Ruth are definitely taller than Adrian. So this is incorrect.

D – Ruth and Stuart are definitely taller than Adrian. We do not know who is taller between Margaret and Adrian. Hence, this option is correct.

E – Stuart is definitely taller than Adrian

2) E

A – Wrong

The passage mainly focuses on TB and not weak immune systems. The conclusion must be something to do with TB. The statement may be true but it does not conclude the content of the passage. So this is wrong.

B – Wrong

Again, this statement only focuses on poor diet rather than the disease TB. This can be a reason for the increase in TB but not a conclusion of the passage.

C – Wrong

Seriousness and being unfamiliar with TB are two different things.

D – Wrong

It could be true but this is not a conclusion. It is important to stick with the content of the passage and the conclusion must contain a summary of what is in the passage. There is nothing written about overestimation in the passage.

E – Correct

The line "three quarters of those diagnosed in the UK every year were born outside the UK" helps us to identify the conclusion of the passage. Hence this is correct.

3) A

The value for 1st September would be the value for August since the reading at last day of August would be the reading for 1st September. Therefore, the greatest distance would be the reading for November – value for August.

I suggest you round off all the values to the nearest 100 as this would make it much easier

Red van = 78900 – 68200 = 10, 700
Orange = 73700 – 64400 = 9300
Yellow = 81200 – 71300 = 9900
Green = 75100 – 64800 = 10, 300
Blue = 83400 – 74000 = 9400
Indigo = 78200 – 68600 = 9600
Violet = 72800 – 63100 = 9700

The highest is the red van, so the answer is A.

---

4) A

We need to find a flaw in the last line of the text (which is the conclusion) "attractive male film start and models are likely to make successful cyclists." This line makes a correlation between attractiveness and successful cyclists. The flaw would be something to do with this correlation.

A – Correct
This is correct. The study did not suggest that being attractive would make you successful in sport.

B – Wrong
This is an incorrect statement as a non-subjective measurement has been taken using cycling performance

C – Wrong
This statement could be true but it does not have anything to do with the last line of the passage and so, is irrelevant. Also, the passage does not intend to extend this correlation with other sports.

D – Wrong
No other sports or sportspersons are mentioned. This statement is completely irrelevant.

E – Wrong
This could be true but it does not identify a weakness or flaw in the passage given itself.

---

5) D

The better of the two scores is used to identify the qualifiers. We must first make a list of scores which were the highest from 1 to 15

1 – 6.12
2 – 6.88
3 – 7.08
4 – 7.34
5 – 6.71
6 – 5.90

7 – 7.06
8 – 6.58
9 – 6.14
10 – 7.17
11 – 6.52
12 – 5.70
13 – 7.29
14 – 6.97
15 – 6.53
The top 3 scores were: 7.34, 7.29, 7.17
The scorers who came within 50cm of third place must be within the limit of 6.67-7.17
Number of scores within that limit: 6.88, 7.08, 6.71, 7.06, 6.97 (5 scores)
Number of qualifiers = 3 + 5 = 8
So, D is the answer.

---

6) C
The passage mostly talks about how seed banks can help to reduce the effects of climate change on crops in the future. The conclusion should also mention seed banks and how they can help avert the disaster.

A – Wrong
Even though this is true, it does not conclude the whole passage. The passage mainly focuses on seed banks.

B – Wrong
"Will avert" gives the impression that seed banks are the ultimate solution to the problem and that no other solutions are required to tackle the situation. "Will avert" is too strong. The last sentence also says "seed banks are not the only answer"

C – Correct
This is correct. The text does say that "seed banks with catalogues showing traits…Farmers can then begin to trial"

D – Wrong
Whilst this is a true statement, it only focuses on Africa and Southeast Asia. It is mentioned that Africa and Southeast Asia will be worst affected, however, this does not mean that farmers in other areas should not begin trialling. The passage also states "we need to develop worldwide seed banks"

E – Wrong
"will not be unable to grow" is again, a strong suggestion. Indeed, it is mentioned that their yield will decline, but it does not say that it "will be unable to grow" in the future. Also, this statement is a reason why seed banks should be created. It is not the conclusion to the whole passage.

7) C

We first need to calculate what the prices are on Wednesday relative to the prices on other days.

Helen

Helen bought £1000 worth of this share on Monday.
Price on Tuesday = 120% x 1000 = 1.2 x 1000 = £1200
Let price on Wednesday = 1200P
Price on Thursday = 125% (1200P) = 1.25 x 1200P = 1500P
We know Helen made a total profit of £350
So Helen must have sold the shares for £1350.
1500P = 1350
P = 1350 / 1500 = 0.9
So on Wednesday, the price was 90% of the price on Tuesday, i.e. a 10% decrease

Paul

The price of shares on Wednesday bought by Paul would be 90% of £3000
0.9 x 3000 = £2700
Loss = 3000 – 2700 = £300

8) B

A – Wrong
There is no data given to us about offenders who only served half of their sentence.

B – Correct
From the second table, we can see that 22% of offenders who served non-custodial sentences have reoffended whilst the figure for short-custodial sentences is 55%.

C – Wrong
Even though 70% of the young offenders reoffended, that does not mean that they are not punished again. Hence, this statement does not fully support the evidence given.

D – Wrong
"Inevitable" is too strong of a word. It is not certain that an offender released from serving a sentence will reoffend in the future.

E – Wrong
We cannot conclude this from the text given to us.

9) D

Number of prisoners who reoffended within 1 year = 44% of 50,000 = 22,000
Number of prisoners who reoffended within 5 year = 66% of 50,000 = 33,000
Difference = 33,000 – 22,000 = 11,000

10) A

A – Correct

In the sentence "giving offenders a community service order instead of a prison sentence", the words "instead of" suggests that the offenders could either have been given community service or a prison sentence.

On the other hand, in study 2, it may be that the prisoners who were given a custodial sentence were not eligible for a non-custodial sentence.
Therefore, the comparison between the passage and study 2 is invalid.

B – Wrong

It does not matter whether the offenders are first-time. There is no relevance between this statement and the question.

C – Wrong

Again, it does not matter whether offenders have already served a sentence before or not.

D – Wrong

This is a distracting statement and could confuse you. However, according to the passage, suspended sentences reduce the rate of reoffends by 9%. They are not related to the comparison made in the question.

---

11) E

A – Wrong

It does not provide any proof of the effects that restorative justice has on offenders that have already received a prison sentence.

B – Wrong

This statement, in contrast, weakens the argument. The question states that offenders should be subjected to restorative justice instead of prison whilst this statement states that offenders should be subjected to natural justice.

C – Wrong

The question states that offender should meet victims whilst the statement states that victims do not want to meet their offenders. The statement is contradicting the question and hence cannot strengthen it.

D – Wrong

Completely irrelevant to the question and the passage. There is no mention of tax-payers or their money in the passage or the question.

E – Correct

This statement provides proof that issuing community service has reduced reoffending rates by 20%. Hence, this is correct instead of A.

12) D
We need to use the numbers 9, 5 3 and -2 to make the scores given to us for each team

Crosswords: 22
9 + 5 + 5 + 3 = 22

Jigsaws: 21
9 + 9 + 5 + (-2) = 21

Rubiks: 24
9 + 5 + 5 + 5 = 24

Solitaires: 23
It is not possible to make 23 out of 9, 5, 3 and (-2)

Tangrams: 25
9 + 9 + 9 + (-2) = 25

Hence, D is the answer.

13) D
The main focus of the passage is that people employed **high profile jobs such as** footballers should not be allowed back in employment if they have served prison sentence for serious crimes.

A – Wrong
The focus is on high profile employees and not just footballers and football fans. Football is just an example used in the text.

B – Wrong
Whilst this statement could be true, it depends on the nature of the crime that they have committed.

C – Wrong
Football is only an example used. The focus is on high profile jobs.

D – Correct
This is the best option out of all five. The passage assumes that the individual rights of a person are less important than the risk posed to other people in society.

E – Wrong
This is not an assumption.

14) B
The key to answering this question is remembering that making a new colour requires equal amounts of other colours.
Brown requires equal quantities of red, yellow and green. Since the mural contains 30% brown, it must have 10% red, 10% yellow and 10% green. (equal amounts of all three colours make brown)

Green requires equal amounts of blue and yellow. So there is 5% blue and 5% yellow extra. So far there is: 10% red, 15% yellow and 5% blue.

The mural also contains 20% red. Adding the initial 10% red in brown, there is a total of 30% red so far.

10% of blue
10% of yellow
10% of orange = 5% red and 5% yellow
10% of purple = 5% blue and 5% red
10% off green = 5% yellow and 5% blue

In total the mural contains:
Red = 10 + 20 + 5 + 5 = 40%
Yellow = 15 + 10 + 5 + 5 = 35%
Blue = 5 + 10 + 5 + 5 = 25%

Since 20ml of red is left, 80ml was used (there was initially 100ml of each colour).
40% = 80ml
1% = (80÷40) = 2ml
100% = 2 x 100 = 200ml
The mural contains 200ml of total colours.
Since the mural has 25% blue, amount of blue = 0.25 x 200 = 50ml

---

15) A
A – Correct
The text clearly states that "if we accept that it is ethical to test on primates…such research could be done using primates". This statement paraphrases the conclusion correctly.

B – Wrong
Although this may be correct, the text says that even though we have computer modelling, we are still unable to cure neurological conditions.

C – Wrong
Nothing is mentioned about creating lesions directly to patients' brains.

D – Wrong
The text supports experimentation on primates. This statement contradicts the text.

E – Wrong
The text does **not** say that experimentation on primates '**will**' enable us to cure neurological conditions.

---

16) D
The question states that there are 15 other girls apart from Maisy.
Therefore, there are a total of 16 girls in the school together with 10 boys.
Total number of children in school = 16 + 10 = 26

Since a family cannot have more than 2 children in the school, a child cannot have more than 1 sibling.

Three girls each have one younger sister. (6 girls)
Two girls each have one younger brother. (2 girls and 2 boys)
Two boys each have two brothers. (4 boys)

The last sentence states that two other boys have sisters in school. That is the vice-versa of the two girls with brothers.
Number of girls that have a sibling = 6 + 2 = 8
Number of boys that have a sibling = 4 + 2 = 6
Total number of children that have a sibling = 8 + 6 = 14
Number of children that do not have a sibling = 26 – 14 = 12
Hence, D is the answer.

---

17) A
The argument is the first line of the paragraph. "The rate of recorded heart attacks among women…soon start to fall because a new blood test…has been developed…provides a more accurate diagnosis…". We must find a flaw in this statement.
Firstly, the text does not mention anything about heart attacks in men. So we can eliminate options B and E.
The flaw is that with a more accurate diagnosis, the recorded rate of heart attacks in women is likely to increase rather than decrease. This is stated by option A.

C – Wrong
The text does not suggest, in any way, that a blood test is the only way of diagnosing when a heart attack has taken place. There could be other methods as well.

D – Wrong
Nothing is mentioned about the effectiveness of the treatment given for heart attacks.

---

18) E
Points scored by spans = 42 x 8 = 336
Points scored by beats = 36 x 5 = 180
Points scored by tips = 720 – (252 + 180) = 204

Most points were scored by spans. Hence, spans would have more area than the other two types of goals.

We can eliminate options B, D and F.

We know the proportion of points scored by spans would be less than 50% since 50% of 720 is 360.
A and C show that proportions of points scored by spans are more than 50%.

Hence, E is the answer.

---

19) C
330ml contains 9 lumps of sugar.
Multiples of 330 = 330, 660, 990, 1320, 1650, 1980, 2310

2 litres = 2000 ml ≈ 1980 ml
1980 ÷ 330 = 6 sets of 9 lumps of sugar
Lumps of sugar in 2 litre bottles = 6 x 9 = 54
Hence the answer is C.

---

20) C
Currently, teenagers are taking 50% more than the recommended level. This means that their consumption is 150%. Of this 150%, 30% of the sugar is consumed from soft drinks.
Let the recommended consumption = 100g
Current intake = 150% fo 100 = 150g
Consumption by sugary drinks = 30% of 150 = 45 g

If their consumption from soft drinks is reduced to one-third, the new consumption = 1/3 x 45 = 15g
Reduction = 45 – 15 = 30g
So the new overall consumption = 150-30 = 120g
This is 120% of the recommended level. So it is 20% above the recommended level.

---

21) C
Sales in 2011 = 5727 million litres
Reduction = 10% of 5727 = 572.7
New sale = 5727 – 572.7 = 5154.3 million litres ≈ 5100

Tax = 20p per litre
Tax = £0.20 x 5100 = £1020 million

This is closest to £1031 million, so C is the answer

---

22) A
Read the definitions of the taxes first to get an idea of what they are first.

A – Correct
Sales tax is according to the price of the drink. If the prices decrease, the tax will also decrease which means that retailers will be able to remain competitive. This is why statement A weakens the argument given in the question.

B – Wrong
It does not matter whether other foods are taxed by volume tax or sales tax.

C – Wrong
There is no comparison made between sales tax and volume tax in this statement. So this is wrong.

D – Wrong
There is no comparison made between sales tax and volume tax in this statement. So this is wrong.

E – Wrong
There is no comparison made between sales tax and volume tax in this statement. So this is wrong.

---

23) E
Since the question says that the tourist visited 5 attractions by taking the shortest route, it makes sense to add the shortest routes possible from the hotel.
So they definitely went to the Courts, which is 60m.
They then took the shortest route to the Fountain, which is 80m.
Then the Arch, which is 80m from the Fountain.
Then, the Castle, which is 90m from the Arch.
Then the Tower, which is 110m from the Castle.
Then back to the Hotel, which is 110m from the Tower.
Adding this up: 60 + 80 + 80 + 90 + 110 + 110 = 530m
So the tourist did not go to the Palace.

---

24) B
The argument made in the text is that drinks with caffeine (which have been banned) can boost the effectiveness of short-term memory, which could help students to recall key information. We need to identify the statements which can counteract this argument. However, these statements must be linked to each other.

A – 1 and 2
This is wrong. These two statements are not linked to each other and neither of these statements weakens the argument above. They discuss nothing about memory.

B – 1 and 3
Correct. Both these statements are connected by sleep and statement 3 links the lack of sleep with poor memory.

C – 2 and 4
This is wrong. These two statements are not linked to each other and neither of these statements weakens the argument above. They discuss nothing about memory.

D – 3 and 5
This is wrong. These two statements are linked to each other by sleep. However, neither of these statements mention that caffeine causes sleep deprivation.

---

25) F
Let the first digit be **F**
Let the third digit be **T**
Let the fourth digit be **M**
Let the fifth digit be **N**

Let the sixth digit be **S**
We know the second digit is 8.

```
      F8
  +   TM
      NS
      80

     F8T
 +   MNS
     800
```

REMEMBER: All digits are less than 10, meaning that the sum of two digits cannot be higher than 17. (19 = 9 + 10), (18 = 9 + 9 but no two digits can be same)

By looking at the second addition, we can see that T + S = 10
Ways to make 10 = (7+3), (6+4). It cannot be 8+2 as 8 is already a digit and it cannot be 5+5 as no two digits can be the same. The 1 from the 10 will be carried over in the sum 8 + N.
Since 8 + 1 + N = 10, N = 1

The 1 will be carried over to F + M.
F + M + 1 = 8
F + M = 7
This can only be either 4 + 3, 5 + 2. It cannot be 6 + 1 as N = 1.

Going to the first sum, 8 + M + S = 20 (it cannot be 10 or 30 or more).
M + S = 12
This can only be 7 + 5

The 2 from 20 will be carried over
F + T + N + 2 = 8 (N=1)
F + T = 5

Possibilities of T = 7, 3, 6, 5.
Since F + T = 5, then T < 5
So T is either 4 or 3.
If T = 4, then F = 1 (which cannot be true as N = 1)
So T = 3.
F = 5 – 3 = 2

F + M = 7
M = 5

M + S = 12
S = 7

The passcode is 2 – 8 – 3 – 5 – 1 – 7
The last digit of passcode = S = 7

26) C

The main argument made by the text is that "...studies in the 1980s...dangers of eating too much of these fats were based on a misleading data set". However, the text does not take into consideration the studies, which had reliable and valid data set. It comes to a conclusion just by only taking into account the studies, which had a misleading data set.

A – Wrong
The focus is not about enjoying saturated fat in a balanced diet.

B – Wrong
The main focus of the text is not on coronary heart disease, so this cannot be the answer.

C – Correct
This correctly describes the flaw in the text. The paragraph does not take into account other reliable studies. Hence the assumption is that other studies have not suggested risk to health from saturated fat.

D – Wrong
The text does not assume that people limit saturated fat intake. This is clearly wrong.

E – Wrong
This option does not discuss anything about the main focus of the text which is risk to health by saturated fats.

---

27) C

5% own neither phones nor laptops.
So the overlap would be somewhere in the remaining 95%.

The best method to do it:

The minimum
The total percentage is 100%.
Start from 5% and add 55%(minimum of laptop) to it. This gives us 60%. Let the remaining 40% be mobile owners.
Since minimum of mobile = 70% and we have got 40%, the overlap must = 60 – (100 – 70) = 60 – 30 = 30%.
However, the percentage of people that own neither is actually fewer than 5%, which means that the percentage of people that own both would be a bit smaller. So 25% is correct.

The maximum
The total percentage is 100%.
Start from 5% and add 65%(maximum of laptop) to it. This gives us 70%. Let the remaining 30% be mobile owners.
Since maximum of mobile = 80% and we have got 30%,
The overlap must = 70 – (100 – 80) = 70 – 20 = 50%.

So the range is 25% – 50%

---

28) A

Argument: People are different in whether they are more alert in the morning or at night due to different levels of melatonin. Therefore, employers should allow flexible working hours to accommodate people's sleep patterns.

A – Correct

If statement A is true, then the causation is reversed (i.e. sleeping patterns affect the level of melatonin). The text suggests melatonin decides whether a person is a night owl or a morning lark. However, if it were true that sleeping patterns affect the level of melatonin, then this would weaken the argument.

B – Wrong

This supports the argument that melatonin tablets can affect a person's sleeping pattern.

C – Wrong

No mention of health.

D – Wrong

The text does not focus on the amount we sleep. It focuses on when we sleep during the day.

E – Wrong

Again, nothing relevant to owl and lark behaviour. So this is wrong.

29) A

Total Area of 1 narrow wall = 4 x 2.5 = 10m²
Area of narrow wall with door = 10 – (1 x 2) = 8m²
Area of narrow wall with window = 10 – (2 x 1.5) = 7m²
Total Area of narrow walls = 8 + 7 = 15m²

1 tin paints 15m²
If person paints with high quality paint, two coats are needed = 15 x 2 = 30m²
Cost for 1 coat which is 15m² = £15
Cost for 2 coats of 15m² each = 15 x 2 = £30

If person paints with budget paint, three coats are needed = 15 x 3 = 45m²
Cost of three coats = 11 x 3 = £33
So the person should use quality paint for these walls.

Area of a wide wall = 5 x 2.5 = 12.5 m²
Total area of wide walls = 12.5 x 2 = 25m²

If person paints with high quality paint, two coats are needed = 25 x 2 = 50m²
Since 25m² is larger than 15m², the person would have to buy 2 tins (30m²) for 1st coat.
Cost of 2 tins = 15 x 2 = £30
5m² of paint would be left over. The person still needs to paint 25m². Using the 5m², which is left over, there would be 20m² left. The person would still need to buy 2 more tins.
Cost for 2 more tins = 15 x 2 = 30
Total cost = 30 + 30 = £60

If person paints with budget quality paint, three coats are needed = 25 x 3 = 75m²
Since 25m² is larger than 15m², the person would have to buy 2 tins (30m²) for 1st coat.
Cost of 2 tins = 11 x 2 = £22
5m² of paint would be left over. The person still needs to paint 50m². Using the 5m²,which is left over, there would be 45m² left. The person would still need to buy 3 more tins.
Cost for 3 more tins = 11 x 3 = 33
Total cost = 22 + 33 = £55

To paint the wider walls, the person should opt for the budget paint.
Total cost = 30 + 55 = £85

---

30) D
Argument: A&E is not attractive to doctors, which is why doctors choose other specialities. One solution is to pay higher wages to permanent A&E doctors.

If it were true that doctors are motivated by money and choose to work for agencies in A&E to supplement their salary, then higher wages will surely attract doctors to choose to work in A&E permanently. This is why D is correct.

---

31) B
Remember: all **six pairs** add up to give a different total.
On the die given, we know that 5 will be opposite 6. This gives a total of 11.
The other opposite pairs can either be: (4, 2) & (3, 1) OR (4, 1) & (3, 2)
If the other two pairs are (4, 2) and (3, 1), we get the sums to be 6 and 4 respectively.
It cannot be (4, 1) & (3, 2) as this would give the same sum of 5.
So we have the sums: 11, 6 and 4.

Let us first eliminate the options, which have the sums 11, 6 or 4.
These are options E, F and G. E, F and G have pairs which give a sum of 6 which we cannot have as the first die already has a pair with sum 6.

A – Wrong
(2, 1) (3, 6) (4, 5)
(3, 6) & (4, 5) give a total of 9 which cannot be correct.

B – Correct
(2, 1) (4, 6) (3, 5)
This gives sums of 3, 10 and 8. The other die gives us sums of 11, 6 and 4. Since none of the pairs gives us the same sums, B is correct.

C – Wrong
(4, 1) (2, 6) (3, 5)
(3, 5) & (2, 6) give a total of 8 which cannot be correct.

D – Wrong
(4, 1) (3, 6) (2, 5)
The pair (2, 5) gives us a sum of 7. However, it is clearly mentioned in the question that none of the opposite pairs of either die has a total of 7.

32) G

1 – Correct
Total number of defendants convicted = 1371 + 1552 + 1342 = 4265
Each year, the success rate is 98%. Over the three years, this will become 6%.
6% of 4265 = 255.9 ≈ 256
Total number of people tried = 4265 + 256 = 4521
This is more than 4300 so statement 1 is correct.

2 – Correct
In 2012, 97.9% (≈ 98%) were prosecuted successfully. 2% were acquitted.
This 98% = 1552
100% = (1552 ÷ 98) x 100 = 1584
Number acquitted = 1584 – 1552 = 32
This is over 30 so statement 2 is correct.

3 – Correct
Total number of prison sentence would be the sum of the sum of the prison sentences imposed on individuals + sum of the suspended prison sentences.
220 + 88 + 178 + 86 + 140 + 74 = 786
Number of suspended prison sentences = 538
⅔ x 786 = 524
Since 538 is more than 524, statement 3 is also correct.

All statements are correct. So G is the answer.

---

33) B
If the figure for animal cruelty had not risen by 6.6% to 566 and had stayed the same as the year before, then number of people convicted = 531 (Given in the passage).
If the trend for animal cruelty conviction was the same as that of the rest of England and Wales and the figure had decreased by 11.7% (≈12%), number of conviction in North England in 2013 = 88% of 531 = 467
This is a decrease of = 566 – 467 = 99
Number of total convictions that would have been if North England had followed the same trend as the rest of England and Wales in 2013 = 1371 – 99 = 1272
This is closest to 1274. So B is the answer.

---

34) C
1 – Wrong
No statistics are given for West Yorkshire for 2012. Also, the text does not say whether the increase between 2012 and 2013 was the greatest or not.

2 – Wrong
The 6.6% increase was for the whole of North England. From this, we cannot infer what the increase was only in West Yorkshire.

3 – Correct
⅔ x 1371 = 548

Number of convictions in North England in 2013 = 566
Since 566 is more than 548, statement 3 is correct.

C is the answer because only statement 3 is correct.

35) B
Argument presented in the Reader's comment:
More convictions were present in North England because more complaints were made in North England. More complaints were made in North England because more people care about animals in the North as compared to the South.
We must find a statement, which, if true, can weaken this argument.

A – Wrong
It does not matter about the number of complaints made per person in the North and in the rest of the country. We need to look at the total number of complaints made and not the number of complaints per person.

B – Correct
This statement suggests that the number of complaints made in all parts of the country is approximately equal. However, the proportion of complaints that result in convictions is higher in the North than any other part, which means that there is more animal cruelty in the North as compared to other parts. This weakens the argument.

C – Wrong
This does not address the argument made in the reader's comment.

D – Wrong
It does not matter which animal is re-home more in which part of the country.

E – Wrong
Again, this statement does not address the argument.

2015 Section 2

1) E

The brain is not involved in the REFLEX to a stimulus. Hence, E is the correct answer.

A - Sensory neurone senses a stimulus and then transmits an electrical impulse to the central nervous system.

B - Muscle cells need to contract in order to produce a movement

C - The motor neurone is the neurone that signals the muscle cells in the erector muscle to take action

D - Relay neurones are like bridges, which connect sensory neurones and motor neurones. They pass on the electrical impulses from the sensory neurones to the motor neurones.

E - Brain is not part of the reflex arc. Since the reflexes need to be rapid, automatic and protective (RAP), it will take too long for the electrical impulses to travel to the brain and back. The reflex arc involves the central nervous system for RAP reflexes.

2) C

Only alkenes are the organic compounds, which turn orange-brown bromine water to colourless.

Alkenes have double bonds and have a formula in which there is double the number of other atoms as there are carbon atoms.

e.g. C_2H_4, C_3H_6, C_4H_8

1 – C_2H_4 is an alkene so it will decolourise bromine water

2 – propene is an alkene but polypropene is not as it does not have a double bond.

3 – $CH_2C(CH_3)_2$ can be simplified to C_4H_8. This is an alkene and hence it will decolourise bromine water.

4 – CH_3CH_2I is a halogenoalkane and so, it will not decolourise bromine water.

Only 1 and 3 are alkenes. Hence C is the answer.

3) B

Black surfaces are better absorbers and emitters of infrared than white surfaces.

In winter, people need to keep themselves warm. The white, shiny surfaces will reflect infrared back into the person to keep them warm inside their clothes.

Better absorbers - Black
Better emitters - Black
Better colour of clones in winter - White (good reflectors of radiation)

4) B

Number of beads = 8
Number of black beads = 3

Probability of picking a black bead first time = $\frac{3}{8}$

Since the bead is not replaced, the bag now contains 7 beads in total.

Since a black bead would have been taken out, there would be 2 black beads left in the bag out of the total 7 beads.

Probability of picking a second black bead = $\frac{2}{7}$

Probability of both beads being black = $\frac{3}{8} \times \frac{2}{7} = \frac{6}{56} = \frac{3}{28}$

---

5) A
The respiration is ANAEROBIC, meaning no oxygen is used.

Carbon dioxide is only formed in aerobic respiration. In anaerobic respiration, no carbon dioxide is formed.

Water is never formed in both types of respiration.

So, there would be 'no' in all three columns. The answer is hence, A.

---

6) A
'a' is the energy change.

'b' is the energy of reactants

'c' is the activation energy

'e' is the energy of products

Here, the energy of products is more than energy of reactants.

Therefore, (products - reactants) would give a positive value. Here it is labelled 'a'

In the reverse reaction, the energy of reactants would be more than the energy of products.

Therefore, (products-reactants) would give a negative but equal value. Therefore, it would be '-a'

---

7) D
Step down transformer decreases the voltage and increases the current.

Power = voltage x current

If voltage decreases but current increases, then there is no change in the power transferred.

---

8) E
Divide the isosceles triangle into two right-angled triangles by joining the midpoint of the largest side with the top vertex. Label the midpoint of QR as M.

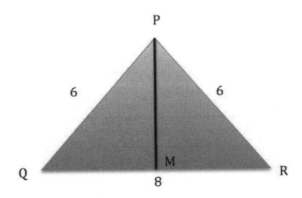

QM = 8 ÷ 2 = 4 (since M is the midpoint of QR)
We first need to find the value of PM.
Using Pythagoras,
$PQ^2 = QM^2 + PM^2$
$6^2 = 4^2 + PM^2$
$36 - 16 = PM^2$
$PM^2 = 20$
$PM = \sqrt{20} = \sqrt{(2 \times 2 \times 5)} = 2\sqrt{5}$

Tanθ = Opposite ÷ Adjacent = PM ÷ QM

$\tan\theta = \dfrac{2\sqrt{5}}{4} = \dfrac{\sqrt{5}}{2}$

---

9) D

We first need to know the genotype of mouse 2. We know mouse 1 is homozygous dominant, meaning it is CC. The white mouse must then be homozygous recessive, cc.

	C	C
c	Cc	Cc
c	Cc	Cc

There is a 100% chance that mouse 2's genotype is Cc.
If mouse 1 and mouse 2 breed, these could be the following genotypes of the offsprings:

	C	C
C	CC	CC
c	Cc	Cc

The offsprings could either be homozygous or heterozygous.
Percentage heterozygous = 50%
Since 'C' is the dominant allele and all genotypes contain the C allele. Therefore, all phenotypes would be black only.
So we have 50% heterozygous, black only phenotype and homozygous and heterozygous genotypes. this only corresponds to row D in the question table.

---

10) D

Firstly, alkali metals are the elements in group 1 of the periodic table.

A - Rubidium is more reactive than the hydrogen present in the water. Therefore, hydrogen would be formed and not rubidium
B - Melting points and boiling points decrease as you move down group 1. Therefore, sodium

would have a higher melting and boiling point than rubidium.

C - Reactivity increases down group 1. Therefore, rubidium would react more vigorously than sodium in water.

D - All elements of group 1 are stored in oil so they do not react with air. Therefore, rubidium is also stored in oil.

E - Rubidium has a valency of +1 and SO4 has a valency of -2. The formula would be Rb_2SO_4 and not $RbSO_4$.

---

11) A

1 - This statement is correct as neutrons emitted in nuclear fission can cause further fission

2 - The definition of half-life is wrong. Half-life is the time taken for the radioactivity of a specified isotope to fall to half its original value.

3 - Nuclear FUSION creates heat and light in the Sun.

Only statement 1 is correct. So A is correct.

---

12) B

Since 6 out of the 7 options mention 'all values of X' we can use X = 1 to make everything simpler.

$$a = \frac{3}{5 + X}$$

$$b = \frac{3 + X}{5}$$

$$c = \frac{3 + X}{5 + X}$$

Substituting X = 1,

$$a = \frac{3}{5 + 1} = 3/6 = 1/2$$

$$b = \frac{3 + 1}{5} = 4/5$$

$$c = \frac{3 + 1}{5 + 1} = 4/6 = 2/3$$

The order of inequalities: a < c < b

However, option G states that the order of fractions depends on the value of X. In order to prove this wrong, we need to use a different value for X. Let us say X = 2.

$$a = \frac{3}{5 + 2} = 3/7$$

299

$b = \dfrac{3 + 2}{5} = 5/5 = 1$

$c = \dfrac{3 + 2}{5 + 2} = 5/7$

Still, the order remains the same: a < c < b

---

13) B

On a hot day, more sweating occurs, which results in a decline in water level in the body. So compared to a cold day, the water level in the body on a hot day would be less.
Temperature does not affect the mass of urea produced in a day. So the mass of urea would remain the same. Hence the answer is B.

---

14) C

A - They clearly do not have the formula C_nH_{2n+2}. They have the formula C_nH_{2n}
e.g. Cyclohexane has 6 carbons and 12 hydrogen
B - They do not react with bromine water. ALKENES react with bromine water.
C - They are saturated compounds. As you can see, all carbon atoms have the maximum number of hydrogen atoms attached to them. Also, all alkanes also have single bonds, meaning they are fully saturated.
D - They burn in excess oxygen to produce CO_2 and H_2O.

E - This is incorrect as they have similar properties to each other and have the same general formula, C_nH_{2n}
F - They are not giant covalent bonds

---

15) A

$\sum F$ (horizontal direction) = 50-40 = 10 N to the right
We know the mass = 2kg
Force = mass x acceleration

Acceleration = force/mass = 10/2 = $5.0 m/s^2$ to the right
$\sum F$ (vertical direction) = 25N-20N = 5N upwards
Acceleration = force/mass = 5/2 = $2.5 m/s^2$ upwards
Hence, the answer is A

---

16) E

Ratio = 1: $^2/_3$: $^4/_5$
In order to find 1, we need to use Charity C's value

$^4/_5$ = 3000
(We can make the equation so we have 1 on the left hand side)
$^4/_5$ x 1 = 3000

1 = $^{(3000 \times 5)}/_4$ = £3750
So charity A earned £3750

Charity B earned = $\frac{2}{3}$ x 3750 = £2500
Total earned = 3750 + 3000 + 2500 = £9250

---

17) H
In order to convert carbon in plants into carbon in animals, animals need to use digestive enzymes. So process 2 would use digestive enzymes.

Same principle applies to process 3. Decomposers digest carbon in animals. So process 3 uses digestive enzymes.
During respiration, carbon in decomposers is converted to carbon dioxide in air. So 4 uses respiratory enzymes.

In order to convert carbon dioxide in the air to carbon in plants, plants use photosynthesis. This neither involves digestive enzymes nor respiratory enzymes. So 1 should not be in either of those columns.

Column 1 (digestive enzymes) = 2 and 3
Column 2 (respiratory enzymes) = 4 only
The answer is H.

---

18) C
A - a catalyst would increase the rate of reaction rather than decrease it. A is wrong
B - This is not true as gases have a larger surface area than solids and we know that the higher the surface area, the higher the rate of reaction. B is wrong
C - this is true because activation energy is the energy required to start a reaction. If the activation energy is high, there will be lesser successful collisions. This means that there would be a slower rate of reaction. C is correct
D - Increasing the temperature means that the particles would have more energy and there would more successful collision. This would result in a higher rate of reaction. D is wrong.
E - This is not necessarily true as all products and reactants are gas, meaning that there may not be a change in volume

---

19) G
When a ß-particle is emitted, an electron is emitted. This means that the proton number (atomic number) increases by 1. The mass number DOES NOT change when a ß-particle is emitted.
Therefore, X = W+1
When an α-particle is emitted, a Helium atom is emitted. This means that the mass number decreases by 4 and the atomic number decreases by 2.
So, Y = V-4
So the answer is G.

---

20) D
Number of pupils in first group = n
Mean of first group = m

Total sum of scores for the first group = nm

A new score of another pupil is added.
Total number of pupils now = n + 1
Mean score now = m - 2
Total score now = (n + 1) x (m - 2)

n (m - 2) + 1 (m - 2)
nm - 2n + m - 2   **(equation 1)**

However, it is mentioned that the student's score = n
Therefore, total score now = nm + n   **(equation 2)**

equation 1 = equation 2

nm - 2n + m - 2 = nm + n m
- 2 = nm + n - nm + 2n m -
2 = n + 2n
m - 2 = 3n

n = $\dfrac{m - 2}{3}$

---

21) A
1 - All DNA has a double helix structure meaning mitochondria and human white blood cells contain double-helix DNA. So 1 is correct.
2 - Human cells do not contain a cell wall. Therefore, we can conclude that 2 is wrong.
3 - Mitochondria do not have a nucleus since the passage states that mitochondria may once have been aerobic bacteria. We know bacteria do not have a nucleus. 3 is wrong
4 - Both must have a cell membrane since all cells have a cell membrane.

Statements 1 and 4 are correct.
So A is the answer.

---

22) C
In order to answer the question, we only need to find out how many electrons each of the species have in their atom.

$_{17}Cl^-$ has 17 protons. Since it has a charge of (-1), it must have one more electron than proton. Therefore it has 18 electrons.

$_{17}Cl^+$ has 17 protons. Since it has a charge of (+1), it must have one more proton than electron. Therefore it has 16 electrons.

$_{18}Ar$ has 18 protons. Since it has no charge, it must have equal number of electron and proton. Therefore it has 18 electrons.

$_{19}K^+$ has 19 protons. Since it has a charge of (+1), it must have one more proton than electron. Therefore it has 18 electrons.

$_{20}Ca^+$ has 20 protons. Since it has a charge of (+1), it must have one more proton than electron.
Therefore it has 19 electrons.

$_{19}K^-$ has 19 protons. Since it has a charge of (-1), it must have one more electron than proton. Therefore it has 20 electrons.

The only species which have the same electronic arrangement are $_{17}Cl^-$, $_{18}Ar$ and $_{19}K^+$ [all having 18 electrons]

Hence C is the answer.

---

23) D
We know the initial velocity (u) = 20m/s
Final velocity (v) = 0 m/s (driver comes to a rest)
It is important to note that the driver applies the brake AFTER his reaction time is complete.
Reaction time = 0.7 x 2 (driver is tired) = 1.4s
So 1.4 s after the child is seen, the driver applies the brake.
We first need to find the distance travelled in the initial 1.4s
Distance = speed x time = 20 x 1.4 = 28m
To find the distance travelled in the latter 3.3s, we need to use a SUVAT equation.
The SUVAT equations are:
$s = ut + \frac{1}{2}at^2$
$s = \frac{1}{2}(u + v)t$
$v^2 = u^2 + 2as$
$s = vt - \frac{1}{2}at^2$

The best SUVAT equation to use is the second one.
$s = \frac{1}{2}(u + v)t$
$s = \frac{1}{2}(20 + 0)\,3.3$
$s = \frac{1}{2}(20)\,3.3$
$s = 10 \times 3.3$
$s = 33m$
Total distance covered = 33 + 28 = 61m

---

24) D
Let us first solve the first part of the problem

$$\frac{2x + 3}{2x - 3} + \frac{2x - 3}{2x + 3}$$

303

$$\frac{(2x + 3)^2 + (2x - 3)^2}{(2x - 3)(2x + 3)}$$

$$\frac{(4x^2 + 6x + 9) + (4x^2 - 6x + 9)}{4x^2 - 9}$$

$$\frac{8x^2 + 18}{4x^2 - 9}$$

Let us now solve the second part of the problem

$$\frac{8x^2 + 18}{4x^2 - 9} - \frac{2}{1}$$

$$\frac{8x^2 + 18}{4x^2 - 9} - \frac{8x^2 - 18}{4x^2 - 9}$$

$$\frac{8x^2 + 18 - (8x^2 - 18)}{4x^2 - 9}$$

$$\frac{8x^2 + 18 - 8x^2 + 18}{4x^2 - 9}$$

$$\frac{18 + 18}{4x^2 - 9}$$

$$\frac{36}{4x^2 - 9}$$

Remember that we solved $(2x - 3)(2x + 3) = 4x^2 - 9$
So the answer is:

$$\frac{36}{(2x - 3)(2x + 3)}$$

---

25) G
For this question, it is important to ignore the mention of Y chromosome. The only way to determine the sex of a fruit fly is by the ratio of X and A chromosomes.
XAA:
The ratio (X:A) = 1 : 2 = 0.5 : 1
So the fruit fly will be male
XYAA:
Ratio = 1 : 2 = 0.5 : 1
So the fruit fly will be a male

XXAA:
Ratio = 2 : 2 = 1 : 1
So the fruit fly will be a female
XXYAA:
Ratio = 2 : 2 = 1 : 1
So the fruit fly will be a female
XXYYAA:
Ratio = 2 : 2 = 1 : 1
So the fruit fly will be a female

Hence the answer will be G.

---

26) B
The main formula that needs to be used is: moles = mass ÷ Mr
Mr of CH_4 = 12 + (1 x 4) = 16
Mr of CO_2 = 12 + (16 x 2) = 44
Mr of O_2 = 16 x 2 = 32
Moles of CH_4 = (1.6 ÷ 16) = 0.1 mol
Moles of CO_2 = (4.4 ÷ 44) = 0.1 mol
Moles of O_2 = (8 ÷ 32) = 0.25 mol However,
the molar ratio O_2 and CO_2 = 2 : 1 Mole of
CO_2 is = 0.1 mol
Therefore, Moles of O_2 used = 0.1 x 2 = 0.2 mol Moles
of unreacted O_2 = 0.25 - 0.20 = 0.05 mol
Mass = Moles x Mr = 0.05 x 32 = 1.6g

---

27) D
1 - Force = mass x acceleration (F = ma)
Force required = 4kg x 1.25 = 5N.
Hence statement 1 is correct.

2 - Speed = frequency x wavelength (c = f x λ)
f = c ÷ λ
4 = 5 ÷ 1.25
Hence statement 2 is correct.

3 - Voltage = Current x Resistance (V = IR)
However, 4 ≠ 5 x 1.25
5 x 1.25 = 6.25
So statement 3 is wrong.

Only statements 1 and 2 are correct. So the answer is D.

305

2015 Section 3

1) Picasso tries to say that computers are only capable of answering questions. They are only able to help remove someone's curiosity but they cannot make someone curious. Therefore, they are useless. Computers were initially made to solve large and complex mathematical problems quickly. They were calculators. They required an input of questions to fulfil their function.

To argue against the statement, one can say that during Picasso's time, computers were not advanced and their purpose was very limited. There was no Internet or artificial intelligence. Picasso was not exposed to the technology available today. They are an integral part of our life. Without computers, it is almost impossible to live in the 21st century. Many industries, ranging from medicine to tourism, depend on computers to provide safer and faster services. Hospitals require computers to store and access patient files, images, X-rays and MRI scans. This database prevents hospitals from misplacing files and records. Together with this, every bit of information on this planet is available online. Anyone can access details about any topic within seconds. Therefore, computers are now able to carry out more sophisticated functions rather than only give answers. People can contact each other hundreds of miles away, using a computer, in a very short space of time.

The limits of technology are still indeterminable. Our technology has allowed us to send machines to Mars successfully. Soon, we may be sending humans to other planets as well. Artificial intelligence enables humans to speak to virtual assistants and obtain more knowledge about different topics around the world.
With regards to medicine, technology has not been able to replace human medical staff yet. However, nothing is impossible and hence such a possibility should not be ruled out.

Picasso's statement should be read in the context of his era. Indeed, this statement would hold some truth then. However, the case is completely different today and the abilities of computers are more advanced now.

---

2) According to the Hitchens, anything that is said to be true without any evidence can be disregarded without any proof. This statement is true in most situations. If there is no evidence to back a belief, then that belief does not need any proof to be dismissed.

In this case, Hitchens is probably referring to different cultures and folklore. There is no evidence, which can prove the existence of different religious faith. In the scientific world, evidence is required to prove a hypothesis or belief. Scientists first need to formulate a hypothesis and predict the outcomes of an experiment. They then carry out the experiment using a valid method and get reliable results. If these results are repeatable and reproducible, scientists then make a theory.

The question then arises: what type of evidence is required to prove something's existence? In science, qualitative and quantitative data is needed. There have been multiple cases in the past in which scientific studies 'with evidence' were falsified later. The most famous example is the case of Andrew Wakefield who tried to prove that MMR vaccines caused autism in children.

In addition to this, if the testimony of a person is trusted in court, then the religious beliefs of millions of people should also be regarded. Together with this, the Deep Brain Stimulation technique is used for Parkinson's disease. However, we do not know how it works as we have not been able to study its mechanism. According to Hitchens, we should discard this technique but that would be wrong as it helps many patients.

Everything depends upon the results produced by something. In order to fully trust something, we need proof in most of the cases. It is difficult to believe something, which cannot be backed by evidence. However, the case of Andrew Wakefield teaches us to make sure whether the evidence provided is reliable or not. It is important to ensure the origin of the proof. On the other hand, the Deep Brain Stimulation technique shows us that if something without evidence is providing positive results with minimal to no harm, we should not disregard it.

3) The statement tries to convey the message that a doctor must not focus on treating only individual patients but also consider other people of society. On average, a doctor sees 15-20 patients every day. This figure obviously varies depending on the location and time of the year. The doctor cannot afford to care for only one patient per day. They have the responsibility to care for many others and hence, need to consider time management. This statement can also refer to the resources available for patients. For example, a limited number of organs can cause confusion amongst the medical staff as to which patient needs the organ more.

On the contrary, some may say that a doctor should only focus on the patient they are caring for at that particular time. They need to work in the best interests of the patient. It would be unethical to deny treatment to a patient because of the needs of other members of society. An example of this is treating criminals who have committed serious crimes such as murders. Society would not want such people to receive treatment as those resources could be used to treat innocent people. On the other hand, a doctor needs to consider the principles of beneficence and non-maleficence. They cannot let a patient suffer in pain if treatments are available.
Another ethical situation is treating a patient who is bound to die soon. Should such patients be given life support and medications when a patient who has a higher chance of surviving can be treated using that life support system and those medications? There are many ethical questions such as these, which a doctor must consider. Some may argue that even though a patient has a high chance of not surviving, they have the right to treatment and medications until their death. On the other hand, some may argue that the patient who has a much higher chance of surviving needs to be treated quickly to ensure that they survive.

To conclude, a physician must consider many legal and ethical aspects of treatments before providing them to patients. They must take into account the desires and wishes of the patient to provide effective treatments with minimal wastage of resources.

4) This statement is trying to say that domesticated animals and wild animals of the same species should behave differently. Indeed, behaviours of wild animals can cause trouble for

domesticated animals as well as humans. For example, wild dogs tend to hunt with their sharp teeth and claws. They are aggressive towards anything they see moving. However, such behaviour in domesticated dogs cannot be allowed, as this would cause harm to other animals and humans.

Every organism needs basic necessities such as food and water. They need to obtain these necessities in any way possible to survive. Neglected domesticated animals may tend to attack other animals such as birds or hamsters. Domesticated herbivores such as sheep or cows may attack other members of the herd to assert their status and dominion. According to some people, taming animals is unethical. They may argue that we alter animals' innate behaviour to accommodate our wishes. Forcing animals to suppress their natural instincts is immoral. Together with this, people may debate that our love and affection for pets is the reason why their instincts have dulled.

On the contrary, it can be argued that the behaviour of domesticated animals must have changed over time. Humans also protect many animals from dying out. Our breeding programmes and laws have saved many species of animals from extinction. Therefore, human interference is necessary to protect animals to an extent.

Ultimately, domesticated animals are necessary for humans. Farm animals such as cows are needed to provide milk. Sheep are needed for wool in the textile industry. Dogs and cats are considered to be integral parts of families. Therefore, it is necessary for them to exist as they are valued by society.

2016 Section 1

1) D
Number of pupils in year 4 = $120 - (24 + 40 + 16 + 24) = 16$
Total number of girls = 48
Total number of boys = $120 - 48 = 72$

There is a 1 in 12 chance that a boy selected at random is in Year 4.
Let the number of boys in year 4 = 'N'

$^1/_{12} = {}^N/_{12}$
$N = {}^{72}/_{12} = 6$
So, there are 6 boys in Year 4.

We know the total number of pupils in Year 4 is 16.

Probability of that year 4 pupil selected at random is a boys = $^6/_{16} = {}^3/_8$
Probability = 3 in 8
So, the answer is D

2) B
A – Wrong
The world must emit less than 1000 gigatonnes of CO_2 every year whilst Indonesia only emits 1.6 gigatonnes.

B – Correct
Since the peat is also on fire together with the forests, some CO_2 will remain in the atmosphere.

C – Wrong
There is no guarantee that next year will emit more or less CO_2 compared to this year. Hence this cannot be concluded.

D – Wrong
There are other ways in which global warming can occur (e.g. burning of fossil fuels). Therefore, only controlling forest fires cannot prevent global warming.

3) B
Let us break down the cost for 1st stay and then the 2nd stay

1st Stay:
Total nights stayed = 5
Cost of first two nights = $100
Cost of the 3rd, 4th and 5th night = $40 x 3 = $120
Cost of 5 days of car park = $5 x 5 = $25
Total cost for 1st stay = $100 + $120 + $25 = $245

2nd stay:
Since John is staying for 7 or more consecutive nights; he will be charged $40 per night.
Cost of 8 nights = $40 x 8 = $320
Cost of 7 night car park with permit = $25
Cost of car park for 1 extra night = $5
Total cost for car park = $25 + $5 = $30
Total cost for 2nd stay = $320 + $30 = $350

Difference = $350 – $245 = $105

---

4) B

A – Wrong
The passage does not suggest this in any way. Therefore, this cannot be a flaw.

B – Correct
Since musicians undertake music training, their brains may develop the tendency to synchronise to different types of music. Hence, they are more able to synchronise to slow music than non-musicians.

C – Wrong
This is the easiest option to eliminate. The passage does not suggest that non-musicians may undertake musical training in the future. This is not a flaw.

D – Wrong
Although this statement may be true by itself, the passage only focuses on synchronisation to slow music. It does not discuss any different ability of a musician. Therefore, this statement is irrelevant to the question.

---

5) A
Firstly, we must determine which test is on the x-axis and which is on the y-axis

If the written test was on the x-axis, the point 68 (which is the highest on the written test) would be the one which is furthest to the right. The next highest score is 66, so it will be the point which is just left of 68. The third highest is 64, meaning that it will be to the left of 66. However, if this were true, the distance between the points 64, 66 and 68 would be the same. Since this is not shown on the graph, x-axis cannot be the written test.
X-axis = practical test
Y-axis = written test

Since we know which axes is which test, we can also conclude that the scores on the y-axis go up in 10s and the x-axis goes up in 5.
If we move from left to right, the order of students would be:
Ina, Liz, Els, Joe, Fio, Gho, Amy, Kai, Ben, Den, Haz
Obviously, looking at the scores, we can see that there should be two points on 10 score in the same vertical line as Fio.

---

6) D

A – Wrong

The government's plan is only to increase fees of claims which are worth more than £200,000. This plan is not for everyone.

B – Wrong

Although this may seem to be correct, the government is not actually trying to do this. Even before this increase in fees, there were still costs to make a claim. The passage is suggesting that this increase in fees is wrong not the fees itself.

C – Wrong

Again, only claims of more than £200,000 or more will be affected. If individuals or businesses have claims of less than this amount, then they will not face a problem.

D – Correct

This statement only says that the government should reconsider and justice will be inaccessible to most people (not all people). Other statements generalised the increase in fees to all people but this is not true.

E – Wrong

The passage mainly focuses on the increase in fees whilst this statement focuses more on only the last sentence of the paragraph. Therefore, this statement does not conclude the whole passage.

7) D

We can conclude that Paul turned 50 in 2015 as even though his income increased, his tax decreased.

Let Paul's income in 2014 be: 'I'

No tax on the first $9000 of income in 2014.

Tax on the next $25000 = 20% of $25000 = $5000

Tax on the further income = 30% of [T-(9000+25000)]

Total tax = 0.3 x [T-(9000+25000)] + $5000

We know he paid $5600 in 2014. Therefore,

0.3 x [T-(9000+25000)] + $5000 = $5600

0.3 x [T-(9000+25000)] = $600

$[T-(9000+25000)] = {}^{600}/_{0.3} = £2000$

T – 34000 = 2000

T = 36000

His income in 2014 = 36000

His income in 2015 = 36000 + 2000 = $38000

Hence, D is the answer.

8) C

The only products sold form April to June are Products 1, 2 and 3.

Units of Product 1 sold = 800

Units of product 2 sold = 800

Units of product 3 sold= 800

We must multiply these units with the respective prices per 100 units of each product:
($^{800}/_{100}$ x 1500) + ($^{800}/_{100}$ x 2000) + ($^{800}/_{100}$ x 1500) = $12000 + $16000 + $12,000 = $40000
The answer is C

---

9) D

Product 2 was released at the start of March.
Three months after release would be: March, April and May
We can see from the graph that there is a bar for the months Jan-Mar for product 2. However, since product 2 was only released at the start of March, all units sold in that bar would be for the month of March.
Units sold in March = 900
Sales = ($^{900}/_{100}$) x 2000 = £18000
Let sales in the first three months = 'S'
Two-thirds of the sales were in March.
$^{2}/_{3}$ x S = £18000
S = £27,000
Sales in April and May = 27000 – 18000 = £9000
The bar for Apr-Jun gives us the sales from April to June (obviously).
Units of product sold from Apr-Jun = 800
Sales = ($^{800}/_{100}$) x 2000 = £16000
We know that sales in April and May were £9000
Therefore, sales in June = 16000 - 9000 = £7000
Therefore, the answer is D.

---

10) D

Product 6 was launched at the start of November. Therefore, the bars for sales of product 6 are for November and December.
Units sold in November and December = 600
Sales made = (600/100) x 4000 = £24,000
Since the cost of 100 units is £4000
Cost of 1 unit must be £40
From the second graph, we can see that sales of product 6 are £6000 in December.
Units sold in November = 6000 ÷ 40 = 150 units
We know that a total of 600 units were sold in November and December.
Units sold in December = 600 -150 = 450 units

---

11) E

Total units of Product 1 sold = 1000 + 800 + 700 + 500 = 3000 units
Months = Jan-Dec = 12 months
Average monthly sale = 3000 ÷ 12 months = 250 units

Total units of Product 2 sold = 900 + 800 + 800 + 700 = 3200 units
Months = March, April-June, Jul-Sep, Oct-Dec = 10 months
Average monthly sale = 3200 ÷ 10 = 320 units

Total units of Product 3 sold = 800 + 1100 + 700 = 2600 units
Months = May, June, Jul-Sep, Oct-Dec = 8 months
Average monthly sale = 2600 ÷ 8 = 325 units

Total units of Product 4 sold = 700 + 500 = 1200 units
Months = Jul-Sep, Oct-Dec = 6 months
Average monthly sale = 1200 ÷ 6 = 200 units

Total units of Product 5 sold = 700 + 700 = 1400 units
Months = Sep, Oct-Dec = 4 months
Average monthly sale = 1400 ÷ 4 = 350 units

Total units of Product 6 sold = 600 = 600 units
Months = November and December = 2 months
Average monthly sale = 600 ÷ 2 = 300 units

Hence, the answer is E (350 units)

---

12) D
In Bolandia,
21:23 means 21 minutes to 11 pm
23:04 means 23 minutes to 4 am in the morning.
In real time, Helen went to sleep at 22:39 and woke up at 03:37
22:39 + 5 hours = 03:39
Since she woke up at 03:37, we need to subtract 2 minutes from 5 hours, giving us 4 hours 58 minutes.

---

13) A
A – Correct
The passage just assumes that high earners in sport and entertainment are not generally intelligent.

B – Wrong
The passage does not make a correlation between IQ and education. Therefore, this is wrong.

C – Wrong
The passage only states that the professions of parents were not considered.

D – Wrong
This is not necessarily true. The word 'guarantees' is too strong and besides, the passage focuses on the correlation between parental income and IQ whilst this statement only focuses on the level of intelligence.

---

14) D
We need to identify after how many months did Sam have MORE than $1300 in her bank account.

After Jan: 1000 + 300 = $1300
After Feb: 1300 – 200 = $1100
After Mar: 1100 + 200 = $1300
After Apr: 1300 + 0 = $1300
<u>After May: 1300 + 400 = $1700</u>
<u>After June: 1700 – 200 = $1500</u>
After Jul: 1500 – 400 = $1100
After Aug: 1100 + 200 = $1300
<u>After Sept: 1300 + 200 = $1500</u>
After Oct: 1500 – 100 = $1400
<u>After Nov: 1400 + 300 = $1700</u>
<u>After Dec: 1700 – 100 = $1600</u>

Sam had more than $1300 after the months of May, June, September, November and December.
So the answer is 5 months (option D)

---

15) B

A – Wrong
The passage only states that a brain-friendly lifestyle can help to retain more synapses but it does not state that a poor lifestyle causes loss of synapses.

B – Correct
The passage clearly states that in sentence 5. "…a brain-friendly lifestyle…extra synapses" suggests that elderly people who have lived a 'brain-friendly' lifestyle are expected to have higher number of synapses.

C – Wrong
This irrelevant to the text. The passage mainly focuses on the correlation of a 'brain-friendly' lifestyle in young age and number of synapses in old age. It does not mainly focus on the little understanding of deteriorating cognitive performance.

D – Wrong
The word 'ensure' is too strong. Yes, the passage links reading, socialising and staying healthy with a good life in old age but it does not 'ensure' it.

E – Wrong
This is just completely wrong and irrelevant.

---

16) A
We have the information that the players are sitting in a circle and we have been given the order of the players in a clockwise direction. Let us draw the order then.

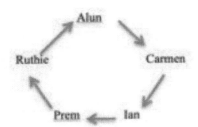

We can also draw a quick table to show which people are to the left and right of a certain person.

	Left	Right
Alun	Carmen	Ruthie
Carmen	Ian	Alun
Ian	Prem	Carmen
Prem	Ruthie	Ian
Ruthie	Alun	Prem

It is important to remember that each player starts off with 5 coins.
1. After Alun's throw, Ruthie has 7 coins and Carmen has 7 coins
2. After Carmen's throw, Alun has 1 coin and Ian has 7 coins. Carmen remains with 2 coins.
3. After Ian's throw, Carmen has 4 coins and Prem has 6 coins. Ian himself has 2 coins.
4. After Prem's throw, Ian has 3 coins and Ruthie has 9 coins. Prem remains with 1 coin.
5. After Ruthie's throw, Prem has 3 coins and Alun has 2 coins.

At the end of the round, these are the results:
Alun – 2
Carmen – 4
Ian – 3
Prem – 3
Ruthie – 4
Therefore, Alun remains with the least coins.

17) A
A – Correct
This is the only sensible option out of the 4 given. If sales of a new antibiotic are controlled, then there are fewer chances of developing drug-resistant bacteria.

B – Wrong
This would, in contrast, weaken the argument. Since some countries allow antibiotics to be bought without a prescription, people can argue that the local government can also do the same.

C – Wrong
No viruses mentioned in the text.

D – Wrong

The text says nothing about livestock, so we can eliminate this straight away.

---

18) D

Since the person already has £25000, they need: £150000 – £25000 = £125000

Percentage = ($^{125000}/_{150000}$) x 100 = 83.3%

We can then eliminate options A and B since we need a loan of more than 83%. Option A (mortgage 1) and option B (mortgage 2) offer only 75% and 80% respectively.

Mortgage 3 cost of 1 year = (500) + (5% x 125000) = 500 + 6250 = £6750
Mortgage 4 cost of 1 year = (2000) + (3% x 125000) = 2000 + 3750 = £5750
Mortgage 5 cost of 1 year = (1000) + (4% x 125000) = 1000 + 5000 = £6000
Hence the cheapest is Mortgage 4 which is option D

---

19) C

Number of wells drilled in Texas from 2005-2011 = 33,753 ≈ 34000

Number of wells drilled in Texas in 2012 = 13,540 ≈ 14,000

Percentage of wells drilled in 2012 compared 2005-2011 = ($^{14,000}/_{34000}$) x 100 = 41% ≈ 40%

Number of wells drilled in Oklahoma in 2005-2011 =2694 ≈ 2700

40% of 2700 = 1080

This is roughly equal to 1081, which is option C

---

20) C

Louisiana

Number of wells drilled = 2327 ≈ 2400

Amount of water used = 12000

Amount of water per well = $^{12000}/_{2400}$ = 5

Utah

Number of wells drilled = 1336 ≈ 1400

Amount of water used = 590 ≈ 600

Amount of water per well = $^{600}/_{1300}$ = 0.46

Difference = 5 - 0.46 = 4.54×10^6 = 4,540,000 gallons per well

This figure is close to 4,500,000. So the answer is C

---

21) E

1 : Correct

The answer lies in the last sentence of the 'Chemicals Used' paragraph. Fracking fluids consist of 99.2% water and 0.8% chemicals.

From the table, volume water used in Texas from 2005-12 = 110,000 million gallons

Let volume of fracking fluid used = F

99.2% (≈ 99%) of F = 110,000

0.99 x F = 110,000

$F = 110,000 \div 0.99$

0.8% of $(110,000 \div 0.99) \approx 880$

The figure is in fact 880 million (we did not use million in our calculation). So Statement 1 is correct.

2 : Wrong
The text mentions that the volume of pollution produced by completion of fracking wells = volume of pollution produced by 28 coal stations.

Volume of pollution produced by the completion of fracking wells = 100, 551, 000
So, volume of pollution produced by 28 ($\approx$ 30) coal stations = 100, 551, 000

Volume of pollution produced by 1 coal station = $(100,551,000 \div 30) \approx 3,351,700$
This is not equal to 36,000,000 of CO_2

3 : Correct
In the paragraph 'Water used', it is stated that the water was enough to meet the demands of 200,000 households.
According to the table, volume of water used in Colorado = 26,000million

Volume used per household = $(26,000,000,000 \div 200,000) = 130,000$ gallons

Statements 1 and 3 are correct. So E is the answer.

22) H
1 – Wrong
Amount of water available cannot be correlated with the amount of water consumed. The evidence is shown in the case of Texas in the paragraph 'Water used'. Even though the state was going through a drought, its consumption level was the greatest.

2 – Wrong
Even if the technology needed to extract shale gas has developed, it does not provide evidence for the variability seen in water consumption across the states.

3 – Wrong
The questions asks for the explanation for the wide variation in water consumption **per well**. It does not matter how many wells each of the states have dug.

All of the statements are wrong. Hence H is the answer.

23) D
The best way to solve this question is to draw around the given figures to see if all of the three pieces of the card can be put together.

A – This figure does not include the square as one of the vertices is missing.
B – A vertex of the isosceles- looking triangle and some vertices of the square are missing.
C – A vertex of the triangle is missing.
D – This is correct as the square, isosceles-looking triangle and the right-angled triangle can

all be outlined.
E – The square cannot be outlined.

---

24) C
The main focus of the text is that more calories are burnt more efficiently whilst walking rather than other forms of activity.

A – Wrong
The age of the people that prefer waking is irrelevant to the focus of the text.

B – Wrong
This statement shifts the focus of the text to one sport: Tennis. We cannot generalize Tennis with other sports. This statement is too specific.

C – Correct
Bear in mind, the question does mention 'if true'. This means that those who play sports drink beer afterwards (beer has a lot of calories). This provides an explanation as to why people who play sports decrease their BMI by a short margin.

D – Wrong
This statement shifts the focus away from the effect of walking on BMI to why people play sport.

---

25) D
Let us calculate the difference between the beginning of the first film and ending of the last film.
Beginning of first film = 10:15
Ending of last film = 22:45
Difference = 12 hours 30 minutes.

Number of films = 3+3 = 6 films
Time taken to finish one set = 12 hours 30 minutes
Total time for 6 movies = 2 x (117+109+119) = 690 minutes = 11 hours 30 minutes.
Total interval between first three films = 12hours30mins – 11hours30mins = 60 minutes
Now, this is where this gets a bit tricky. 6 films do not mean that there will be 6 breaks.

Here is what will happen:
Movie – **Break** – Movie – **Break** – Movie – **Break** – Movie – **Break**–Movie – **Break** – Movie
In total, there will be 5 breaks. 60 minutes distributed in 5 breaks = 12 minutes per break.

---

26) B
The conclusion of the paragraph is that self-help books make readers more anxious and depressed and hence, they have the opposite effect on a person.

A – Wrong
The focus of the paragraph is the effectiveness of self-help books. This statement does not provide a flaw in the conclusion.

B – Correct.

Self-help books are made for anxious and depressed people. Hence, these are the people that would be most benefited from such books.

C – Wrong

This statement is already considered in the text. The last sentence says that those who read such books are more likely to become anxious and depressed when compared to people who have never read them. This means there could be some people who are depressed and anxious even though they have never read self-hep books.

D – Wrong

Although this statement may be true, it is not a flaw in this case. The text discusses the connection between anxiety and self-help books but does not mention anything about a lack of this connection.

---

27) F

Firstly, make an extra column next to the pulse column.
The best way to solve this question is to find the difference between systole and diastole for each of the readings and write the differences in the extra column.
A lot of the candidates would often think that it should be the highest systole pressure – diastole pressure. This is often risky as the number of results given in the table is very high and you can never be sure whether the formula of (highest systole pressure – diastole pressure) would work.
The answer is F. A pulse of 86 was taken when the systole was 149 and diastole was 81.

---

28) D

A – Wrong

The text clearly says 'If this study is to be believed'. This shows that the text is unsure whether the new study is more accurate than the old study.

B – Wrong

The text does not suggest this at all. The new study suggests that cancer can be caused by extrinsic factors but the text is unsure whether the new study is accurate or not.

C – Wrong

The text does not suggest any cancer prevention methods. So this is irrelevant.

D – Correct

The last sentence '…to a significant extent within your control' suggests that the text is assuming people have control over extrinsic factors.

---

29) B
Draw out a string after every step of the question.

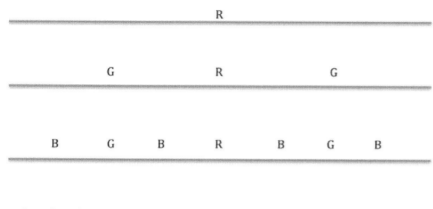

Another way to do this is:

We know the red mark would be at the half of the string = $^1/_2$

The green marks would be at the half points of the half marks = $^1/_4$ and $^3/_4$

The blue marks would be at the half of the half of the half points = $^1/_2 \times ^1/_4 = ^1/_8$. i.e. at every $^1/_8$ point. Blue marks would be at: $^1/_8$, $^3/_8$, $^5/_8$, $^7/_8$

Purple marks would be at $^1/_{16}$, $^3/_{16}$, $^5/_{16}$, $^7/_{16}$, $^9/_{16}$, $^{11}/_{16}$, $^{13}/_{16}$, $^{15}/_{16}$

We know the green marks are present at $^1/_4$ and $^3/_4$. We need to find the number of points that are larger than $^1/_4$ but smaller than $^3/_4$.

$^1/_4 = ^2/_8 = ^4/_{16}$

$^3/_4 = ^6/_8 = ^{12}/_{16}$

The points are: $^5/_{16}$, $^3/_8$, $^5/_8$, $^7/_{16}$, $^9/_{16}$, $^{11}/_{16}$, and $^1/_2$

Number of points between green marks = 7. Option B is the answer.

---

30) D

A – Wrong

This statement is just blatantly denying the content of the text. We must find a flaw in the argument and not just deny it without evidence.

B – Wrong

The text focuses on whether machines will gain consciousness or not. We have to find a flaw in the argument of machines gaining consciousness. We do not need to find a flaw in how long it will take.

C – Wrong

The text does not correlate science fiction with technological progress. It tries to put a valid explanation of why such an event can occur.

D – Correct

The text makes claims that are slightly unrealistic and does so with lack of evidence. The concept of consciousness is still unclear in living organisms so the text cannot provide evidence of consciousness of the machines.

---

31) D

Let total score of Sables be = S
Therefore, total score of Argents = S+1

Fess = 7 points
Pale = 2 points

SABLES
Number of fesses = number of pales
Let this number be N
Number of points scored by fesses = N x 7 = 7N
Number of points scored by pales = N x 2 = 2N
S = 7N + 2N = 9N ———equation 1

ARGENTS
Argents scored one less fess than Sables.
Number of fesses for Argents = N-1
We know Argents score twice as many pales than fesses.
Number of pales = 2(N-1)
Number of points scored by fesses = (N-1) x 7 = 7N – 7
Number of points scored by pales = 2(N-1) x 2 = (2N-2) x 2 = 4N-4
S+1 = 7N – 7 + 4N – 4 = 11N – 11
S = 11N – 11 – 1 = 11N – 12—— equation 2

From equation 1 and equation 2, we get:
9N = 11N – 12
12 = 11N – 9N
12 = 2N
N = 6

Argents score 2(N-1) pales and N = 6
Number of pales scored by Argents = 2(6-1) = 2(5) = 10

---

32) A

Polyunsaturate content of Olive oil = 10g
Polyunsaturate content of Sunflower oil = 65.7g
Total polyunsaturate content = 75.7g ≈ 76
Total mass of mixture = 100g + 100g = 200g
Percentage = (76 / 200) x 100 = 38%
This is close to 37.9%. Option A is the answer.

---

33) A
A – Correct
In the second paragraph, it is mentioned that the ratio of omega 6: omega 3 in hunter-gatherer diets was 1:2. Their diets are more appropriate than the modern ones.

B – Wrong
The text only mentions the diets of hunter-gatherer. It does not mention anything about variability in hunter-gatherer diets around the world.

C – Wrong
The third paragraph clearly mentions that the fall in heart disease was related to consumption of polyunsaturated fats.

D – Wrong
The text contradicts this statement. In the third paragraph, it says that polyunsaturated fats have cardio protective nature.

E – Wrong
A higher ratio increases the cardio protective effect.

---

34) B
Mass of fat taken in one day = 143g ≈ 140
Mass of fat that comes from vegetable oils = 30%
30% of 140 = 42 grams

Mass of Erucic acid in 100g canola oil = 0.6g
Mass of Erucic acid in 42g canola oil = $(^{42}/_{100})$ x 0.6 = 0.252g
PTDI value = 500mg = 0.5g
Percentage = $(^{0.252}/_{0.5})$ x 100 = 50.4%
This is roughly 52% so the answer is B.

---

35) D
Sunflower oil does not contain any omega-3. It can only contribute to the omega 6 ratio.
Ratio of omega-6:omega 3 in flaxseed oil = 0.2:1
Let us say we use 100g of flaxseed oil. It would contain 12.7 g of omega 6 and 53.3 g of omega 3.
However, we need 2 times as much omega 6 than omega 3. Since we have 53.36g of omega-3, we would need 106.6g of omega 6. We already have 12.7g of omega 6 from the flaxseed oil.
Mass of omega 6 need from sunflower oil = 106.6g – 12.7g = 93.9g

100g of sunflower oil contains 65.7g of omega 6.
100g = 65.7g
x = 93.9g
x = $(^{100}/_{66})$ x 94 = 142g
Mass of sunflower oil in the mixture = 142g
Total mass of mixture = 100g + 142g = 242g
Percentage of flaxseed oil = $(^{100}/_{242})$ x 100 = 41%
The answer is D.

2016 Section 2

1) D
This is rather a simple question.

The two large blood vessels are the vena cava and the aorta. We can distinguish between 1 and 2 by their lumen size. The blood vessel with the larger lumen is the vena cava and the one with the smaller lumen is the aorta.
Therefore, 1 is the vena cava and 2 is the aorta.

The blood vessel coming out of the aorta (4) is the renal artery and the one coming out of the vena cava (3) is the renal vein.

Since most of the urea is deposited in the kidney, the blood coming out of the kidney would have little to no urea. Hence, the renal vein would have the least concentration of urea.

All of the urea, which is deposited into the kidneys, then travels to the ureter (5), which connects the kidneys to the bladder. Therefore, the highest concentration of urea would be in the ureter (5).

2) F
1 – there is no element in group 12 and period 3
2 – X has 3 electrons in its outermost shell and so has a valency of +3. Oxygen has 6 electrons in its outermost shell. It can accept 2 electrons and so, it has a valency of -2. If X reacts with Oxygen, the formula would be X2O3.
3 – Valency of X = +3. Valency of Br = -1. Formula would be XBr3
4 – The atomic number is the number of protons in an atom. The number of electrons in an atom is equal to the number of protons. No. of electrons = 2+8+3 = 13. Hence, number of protons = 13
5 – Alkali metals are only in group 1. X has 3 electrons in its outermost shell. Hence, X is in group 3.

The number of outermost electrons helps to determine which group the atom is in.

3) D
Mass of cylinder with 250cm³ = 170g
Then, the mass is increased to 470g when the object is submerged.
Mass of object = 470-170 = 300g.

When two objects are placed in the measuring cylinder, volume increases from 250 to 350.
Volume of two objects = 350-250 = 100cm³
Volume of 1 object = 100/2 = 50cm³
Density = Mass/Volume = (300/50) g/cm³

4) A

The only thing that can determine whether two lines are parallel is if they have the same gradient.

The line that crosses the two points will have the gradient:

$m = (y2 - y1) / (x2 - x1) = (9 - 3) / [6 - (-3)] = 6 / 9 = 2 / 3$

Using $y = mx + c$, the only equation in the options which has the gradient (2/3) is A. (m in option A is 2/3)

---

5) B

It is easy to identify W as a chromosome. This rules out options D, E and F.

X and Y are substances, which cut out a length of DNA. Therefore, they must be restriction enzymes.

Z is a substance, which fuses DNA strands. Only ligase enzyme is capable of doing so. Even if you did not know the theory, the answer could have been obtained by the process of elimination.

We know the function of X and Y is the same so they must also be the same substance. However, Z has a different function from X and Y, so it must be a different substance. So, X and Y are the same whilst Z is different. This only corresponds to B.

---

6) E

A – calcium carbonate is the solute whilst water is the solvent. Water can evaporate, leaving the solute behind in the container.

B – pentane and octane have different numbers of carbon atoms, and hence different chain lengths. Octane has 8 carbon atoms whilst pentane has 5. Therefore, the boiling point of octane would be higher than pentane. Hence, pentane would evaporate first and then condense and separated from octane.

C – Silicon dioxide is not a good soluble solid and can easily be separated by filtration.

D – Sodium chloride and water have different boiling temperatures.

E – ethanol can dissolve in water and hence ethanol is not immiscible. A separating funnel can separate only immiscible substances.

---

7) D

1 – chemical properties rely mainly on the number of electrons. Mass numbers are the sum of protons and neutron within an atom's nucleus. Hence, changing the mass numbers would not change the chemical properties. Therefore, 1 is correct.

2 – An atom's atomic number is the number of protons in the atom. Since the atomic number is 28, the atom will contain 28 protons. Therefore, 2 is correct.

3 – Mass number is equal to the number of protons + number of neutrons. An atom cannot have a mass number of 62 and have 62 neutrons. This would mean that it contains no protons which is incorrect.

---

8) B

Average mass of first group = 75 kg

Total mass if group of N people = 75 x N = 75N

Three people join the group. Total number of people now = N + 3
Average mass now = 78
Total mass now = 78 (N + 3) = 78N + 234

Average mass of the three people = 90 kg
Total mass of three new people = 90 x 3 = 270 kg
Total mass of new group = Total mass of initial group + Total mass of three new people

78N + 234 = 75N + 270
78N − 75N = 270 − 234
3N = 36
N = 12

---

9) F
Sentence 2 helps us to identify the type of enzyme.

- Amylase breaks starch into glucose
- Lipase breaks lipids into fatty acids and glycerol
- Protease breaks proteins into amino acids

Hence, the enzyme is a protease. This rules out options A, B, C and D.

Sentence 1 helps us to know that pH is acidic. We know that the stomach secrets hydrochloric acid. Therefore, the answer is F 'protease from the stomach'

---

10) F
This is a simple addition question.

No. of N = 2
Mass number of N = 14
Total mass of N = (14 x 2) = 28

No. of H = 20
Mass number of H = 1
Total mass of H = (20 x 1) = 20

No. of Fe = 1
Mass number of Fe = 56
Total mass of Fe = (56 x 1) = 56

No. of S = 2
Mass number of S = 32
Total mass of nitrogen = (32 x 2) = 64

No. of O = 14
Mass number of O = 16
Total mass of nitrogen = (16 x 14) = 224

Now, we add all of these values together = 28 + 20 + 56 + 64 + 224 = 392

The answer is F.

---

11) B

By increasing the rotating speed, amplitude will get larger and frequency will increase (more rotations per second).

Let us say initial amplitude is 1 (1 box up from midpoint to crest) and frequency is 3 (3 waves shown).

A – frequency increases but amplitude remains the same. This is wrong.

B – frequency increases and amplitude increases. This is correct.

C – Amplitude remains the same. Frequency decreases. This is wrong.

D – Amplitude increases. Frequency decreases. Wrong.

E – Amplitude increases but the frequency remains the same. Wrong.

---

12) D

There are two circles in this diagram: The grey circle and the outer circle.

In order to get the diameter of the grey circle, we need to subtract 2mm (2 x 1mm) from 1.6 cm.
Diameter of grey circle = 1.6 – 0.2mm = 1.4cm
Radius = 0.7cm = 7mm
Area of a circle = πr^2
Area of internal cross-sectional area (grey circle) = $\pi(7)^2 = 49\pi$ mm²

---

13) B

1 – carbon dioxide is produced as a waste product of aerobic respiration but is not involved in anaerobic respiration. So this is incorrect.

2 – glucose is produced in both types of respiration.

3 – lactic acid is produced as a waste product in anaerobic respiration but is not involved in aerobic respiration.

Hence, only 2 is correct which corresponds to option B.

---

14) C

An important aspect you have to take into consideration before answering this question is the terms being used in the electrolytes: 'aqueous' and 'molten'
Aqueous means that it is in solution water, meaning it will react with water.
Molten means the pure compound is being electrolysed.

A – The compound is aqueous. Calcium is more reactive than hydrogen, meaning hydrogen would be the product at the cathode

B – Oxygen would be the product at the anode

C – This is correct. Potassium is more reactive than hydrogen, meaning hydrogen would form at the cathode whilst oxygen would be formed at the anode

D – Aluminium would be the product at the cathode whilst oxygen would be the product at the anode. The two are at the wrong positions

E – there is no hydrogen in molten sodium chloride. So hydrogen should not be the product at the cathode.

15) D
Let us start by calculating the time delay first.
Total distance = 45000 + 45000 = 90000 Km
Speed = 3.0×10^8 m/s = 3.0×10^5 km/s
Time = (90000) ÷ (3.0×10^5 km/s) = 0.3 s
We can rule out options A, B, C, E, F and G. We are left with options D and H.
We know the formula: $c = f \times \lambda$
$\lambda = c/f = [(3.0 \times 10^8) \div (1.5 \times 10^{10}$ Hz$)] = 0.02$ m
Since the number obtained for wavelength is larger than the wavelength of visible light, the waves must be microwaves.
Hence the answer is: D

---

16) C
Split the trapezium into a triangle and a square. Draw a perpendicular line from PS to the point Q.
Let the point on PS be A. So AQ is perpendicular to PS.

Since QR will be equal to AS, AS = 5cm
PA + AS = PS
PA = PS − AS
PA = 11 − 5 = 6cm

$\tan\theta = 4/3$ and $\tan\theta = ^{AQ}/_{PA} = ^{AQ}/_6$

$\tan\theta = 4/3 = ^{AQ}/_6$
$^{24}/_3 = AQ$
AQ = 8cm

AQ = RS = 8cm

Area of triangle PQA = $^1/_2$ x PA x AQ = $^1/_2$ x 6 x 8 = 24 cm²
Area of rectangle QRSA = QR x RS = 5 x 8 = 40 cm²

Total area = 24 + 40 = 64 cm²

OR you can use the formula for trapezium
$[^1/_2(QR + PS) \times RS] = [^1/_2 \times (5 + 11) 8] = [16 \times 4] = 64$cm²

---

17) G
Statements 1 and 4 are termed gain of function mutation. This is a type of mutation in which the altered gene possesses a new molecular function. So these statements are correct.

Statement 2 and 3 are termed loss of function mutation. These mutations result in the product having less or no function. So these statements are correct.

---

18) E
Firstly, we need to know what a diprotic acid is. A diprotic acid is an acid that can donate two protons per molecule to an aqueous solution.
We know the acid can donate 2 protons. We know NaOH is only able to accept 1 proton.

So we need twice the volume of NaOH to neutralise the acid.

We know that the concentration of NaOH is half that of the acid. In order to match the concentration and the volume, we need 4 times the amount of NaOH to neutralise 30cm³ of the acid.
Volume needed = (30 x 4) = 120cm³

---

19) D
Power = Energy/time
Time = 10 milliseconds = 0.01 seconds
Energy = 125J

Power = 125/0.01 = 12500 Watts

We know the voltage = 500V and that Power = Current x voltage
Current = Power ÷ Voltage
Current = 12500 ÷ 500 = 25 A

---

20) C

$$\frac{a}{b} = \frac{c}{d} + \frac{e}{f}$$

Let us first solve the right hand side (RHS).

$$\frac{c}{d} + \frac{e}{f}$$

$$\frac{cf + ed}{df}$$

$$\frac{a}{b} = \frac{cf + ed}{df}$$

adf = b (cf + ed)

adf = bcf + bed

adf − bcf = bed
f (ad − bc) = bed

$$f = \frac{bde}{ad - bc}$$

---

21) A

1 – mitosis does not involve a mate. So 1 is correct
2 – mitosis involves replication of cells and not growth of cells. 2 is wrong
3 – mitosis only involves replication of cells not repair of cells. 3 is wrong
4 – all cells except gametes undergo mitosis, meaning that stem cells also undergo mitosis. 4 is correct.

Only statement 1 and 4 are correct. So A is the correct answer.

22) B

A higher concentration of acid indicates that the rate of reaction would be faster than the original experiment.

Only B and A fit this condition so we can eliminate C, D and E.

Since the amount of acid present is the same ($100cm^3$ x 1 mol/dm^3 = $50cm^3$ x 2 mol/dm^3), the overall amount of carbon dioxide produced would be the same as the initial experiment. Therefore, B is the answer.

23) E

No matter which planet you take the object to, the MASS will remain the same as it is on Earth.
Mass of object on Earth = 15N/10 = 1.5 kg

Kinetic energy = Potential energy
Potential energy = mass (1.5kg) x gravitational acceleration (?) x height (10m)

Gravity is 5 times (15N/3N) weaker on the planet. Therefore the acceleration must also be 5 times weaker. Gravitational acceleration = 10/5 = 2 N/kg

Potential energy = 1.5 x 2 x 10 = 30J
Kinetic energy = 30J

The answer is, therefore, row E.

24) D

This is simpler than it looks like (trust me!). There are only 4 different blood groups: A, B, AB and O.
The possibility of the criminal having blood group AB is: 25% (one out of the four possible blood groups).

25) H

In family P, a grey mouse was mated with a white mouse. Since all 4 offsprings were grey, we can conclude that the white coat must be recessive.
Therefore, all of the grey mice can be heterozygous. Since there are 12 mice in the diagram, all of them could potentially be heterozygous.
Hence the answer is H.

26) D

From the equation given, amount of gas X used will be equal to the amount of Z produced. Since the reaction occurred in a tightly sealed syringe under exclusion of air and to completion, 100cm³ of gas Z will be produced (since 100cm³ of gas X was used).

27) C

REMEMBER: From the equation $c = f \times \lambda$, we know speed is directly proportional to wavelength.

Speed of light in glass is $^2/_3$ that of the speed of light in air.
Hence, the wavelength of light in the glass will also be $^2/_3$ that of the wavelength of light in air.

Similarly, speed of light in water is $^3/_4$ times that of the speed of light in air.
Hence, the wavelength of light in water will also be $^3/_4$ times that of wavelength of light in air.

The wavelength of the ray of light in water = 360 nm (Given)
To calculate the wavelength of light in air, we need to divide 360 by $^3/_4$.
Wavelength of the ray of light in air = $360 \div (^3/_4) = 360 \times (^4/_3) = 480nm$

The wavelength of light in glass is $^2/_3$ that of the wavelength of light in air.
Wavelength of light in glass = $^2/_3 \times 480 = 320nm$

Hence, C is the answer.

2016 Section 3

1) Hugo conveys the message that it is easier to resist a physical confrontation than a spreading mindset. Battles and wars can be won using weapons and soldiers. However, if an idea spreads throughout the population of a country, it is difficult to counter it. An example of this is the French Revolution. The idea of liberty, equality and fraternity spread like wildfire in the minds of the French citizens, which caused the revolution to begin. Similarly, there have been many incidences where a single idea was the reason for a change in the entire system of a country or civilisation. Ideologies of different people varied in the history of change. Gandhi used the idea of non-violence to lead the protests for independence in India. However, the dictator of Libya was overthrown using extremely violent methods.

On the contrary, an idea or mindset can be dismissed using physical force on a large scale. Dictatorships such as North Korea, Cuba (Fidel Castro) and Libya (Gaddafi) are great examples which describe how mindsets can be overpowered by physical force. Extreme punishments can act as deterrents to prevent the development of revolutionary ideas. In some countries, protests against the leader or leading party are illegal and severe sentences cause people to refrain from any form of defiance. If fear is implanted in the hearts of the citizens, it is possible to dissolve any possible form of resistance.

An idea requires determination and willpower to be successful. If all the people think and act in the same way with the same persistence, an idea can become extremely powerful. In most countries, the army is always smaller compared to the population, quantitatively. If the entire population demanded reform, the army would not be able to stop any protests or demonstrations. However, such protests often take the shape of violence causing many people to sacrifice their lives for a better future.

---

2) According to the statement, fashion does not influence science in any way. These two terms are not correlated and hence, science is independent of any external matters.

(Note: it is important to highlight the differences between science and fashion)

Scientific theories/laws are permanent and are applicable in every place on Earth and outer space. Science allows us to obtain knowledge about the natural phenomena that occur around us. Science requires decades of intense research and studies before discoveries can be made. It is based on facts, evidence and truth.

On the other hand, fashion is temporary. Fashion or trends in 20th century differ substantially from those in the 21st century. Trends that are acceptable now were probably considered impermissible one hundred years ago. Together with this, fashion varies from individual to individual, culture to culture and location to location. It is based on opinion and not facts.

On the contrary, some may argue that trends do play a role in influencing scientific progress. In order to gain a superior global status, the USSR and USA competed against each other to be the first country to carry out a manned mission to the moon in the 1960s. At that time, scientific progress intensified towards space exploration. Similarly, mobile phone companies are still competing with each other to provide better technological devices which can multi-task to a greater degree. It can be argued that fashion does have an impact on the direction of scientific progress.

To conclude, science itself is free from trends or fashion. Scientific principles stay the same forever whilst fashion changes from time to time. However, trends can change the direction of scientific research to make discoveries relevant to the events happening at present.

---

3) Doctors play a very important role in society. People depend on doctors for healthcare and treatments. Strike actions by doctors can have a serious impact on patients' health. It is not an easy decision. If on-duty doctors choose to carry out strikes instead of work, then they may be violating the pillars of non-maleficence and beneficence. If the patient is in a life or death situation, strict legal actions can be taken against the doctor who was supposed to look after them.

On the contrary, some may argue that doctors are humans just like other workers. The government should attend to their wishes and needs. Doctors usually go on strike due to long working hours and the shortage of workforce. Such unhealthy conditions can cause the staff members to fatigue both physically and mentally. This will deteriorate their health and cause them to develop stress and high blood pressure. Such working conditions are neither suitable for doctors nor for patients. It is important for doctors to remain healthy so they can treat patients more effectively.

Strikes in the United Kingdom are much more difficult to carry out compared to other countries. Most of the patients in the UK depend on public healthcare rather than private healthcare. However, the populations of countries such as India and China depend mainly on private healthcare than public healthcare. Since doctors in private hospitals and clinics are paid well and have shorter working hours, they do not need to partake in strikes. In the UK, most of the patients rely on NHS for treatments. Therefore, it is difficult for doctors in the NHS to go on strikes.

Doctors should be given the right to strike because they are humans and their needs should be fulfilled just like other workers. However, strikes should be carried out in an organised and professional manner. Steps should be taken to ensure that there is a minimal compromise with patient care. On-duty doctors should not be allowed to strike as this would cause harm to patients. Emergency care should not be stopped, as there are many life or death situations in the A&E department. The junior doctors' strike was organised so that there was little to no harm was done to the patients' health. Emergency cover was not withdrawn except on the last day of the strike (26th April 2016). There was no significant effect on the number of recorded deaths.

A doctor's duty of care to patients can be quite hectic. Doctors need to face the fact that a patient's life is in their hands. A single mistake can cause the patient much suffering and pain. Doctors even need to face the deaths of patients on many occasions. Such experiences, together with long working hours, can cause doctors to feel overworked and stressed.

Therefore, it is important for their employers to give them sufficient time off from work to allow them to remain healthy enough to treat their patients efficiently.

---

4) Animal welfare refers to well being of nonhuman animals. According to the statement, animals should be given a number of political and constitutional rights if we truly care about their welfare. Since they share the same planet as us and need basic necessities such as food and water, they should be considered as members of society just like humans. Since humans have different rights such as the right to vote and freedom of speech, animals should also be given some rights.

However, this statement is vague and does not say which political rights should be given to animals. Nonhuman animals do not have the intellectual capacity to understand what elections are and what a democracy is. It is not possible for us to make them understand the systems created by humans. Even if we somehow manage to help them understand the concept of politics, we cannot be certain whether they have the ability to make decisions.

If we provide animals with the right to freedom, it would not be possible for us to take 'ownership' of them. Hence, the milk, textile, pharmaceutical and food industries will fail to function.
Some may, therefore, argue that it is not necessary for animals to be given rights for their welfare. We provide high-quality medical care for animals and protect them from exploitation. Many organisations such as the RSPCA provide protection and care for animals around the world. In addition to that, laws and legislations protect endangered animals from being poached.

Since this issue involves many ethical and moral considerations, it is difficult to come to a specific conclusion. Of course, animals should be treated with respect and care, as they are a vital part of our community. However, giving them political rights may seem unnecessary, as they are not able to comprehend the concept of rights. Therefore, it is only necessary that we provide them with basic necessities such as food, water, shelter and protection.

2017 Section 1

1) C
Amount of yellow paint used = 1500 − 900 = 600 ml
Yellow is only used in making orange paint. Equal amounts of red and yellow paint are used to make orange.

So amount of red used in making orange = 600 ml
Total amount of orange paint made = 600 + 600 = 1200 ml

Since he made exactly the amount of paint that he needed, he used 1200 ml of orange paint.
40% = 1200
1% = $^{1200}/_{40}$ = 30 ml
Hugh painted the room 60% pink
60% = 30 x 60 = 1800 ml

Ratio of red and white paint = 1: 3
Total parts = 1 + 3 = 4
Amount of red paint used to make pink paint = $^{1800}/_4$ = 450 ml
Total red paint used = 600 + 450 = 1050 ml
Total red paint left = 1500 − 1050 = 450 ml

2) D
A –Wrong
This statement makes a correlation between long-term use of antidepressant drugs and worse outcome for patients. However, this correlation is false, as the text does not suggest that the patient's condition becomes worse.

B –Wrong
Although this may be a correct statement, we cannot infer from the text that doctors are being advised to do so.

C –Wrong
There can be other reasons for the increase in the number of patients (e.g. increase in population). So we cannot conclude that antidepressant drugs are not effective in the long term.
Also the word 'clearly' is too strong.

D –Correct
This statement uses the appropriate words and summarises the text completely. 'Provides no evidence' suggests that the statement neither concludes that long-term health is improving nor does it say that long-term health is not improving.

3) D
We can eliminate option C because Chestnuts' cost is $900,000, which is more than the family's budget.

Bellavista and Everglade only satisfy 3 out of the 5 wishes. So B is wrong.

Acorns fulfil 4 wishes.
Cost per bedroom = $\frac{\$825,000}{5}$ = $165,00

Dayview fulfils 4 wishes.
Cost per bedroom = $\frac{\$640,000}{5}$ = $160,000

Since Dayview fulfils 4 wishes and has the cheapest cost per bedroom, option D is the answer.

---

4) A
The argument made in the text is that "nuclear power stations…would create tens of thousands of tons of lethal, high-level radioactive waste" and that "the expansion of all nuclear power production shout therefore be stopped and existing plants shut down."

We need to find a weakness in the argument.

A – Correct
A is the answer as it suggests that there are solutions to the nuclear waste problem and that safety is taken into consideration.

B – Wrong
This actually strengthens the argument as it suggests that the significance of nuclear power will decrease in the future.

C – Wrong
C is wrong because it makes an unnecessary comparison between wind power and nuclear power. So C is irrelevant to the question.

D – Wrong
We do not know whether 2.5 billion tonnes of carbon dioxide is a lot or a small amount. So we cannot determine whether this weakens or strengthens the argument.

---

5) D
There is no definite way to solve this problem except visualisation. It is advisable that you skip this question and not waste too much time. Solve the other questions first and then come back to this one at the end.

---

6) C
The argument: "..can prevent the development of prostate cancer by eating healthy diet and taking regular exercise".

The flaw is that the text assumes that a healthy diet can prevent the development of cancer.

There is no mention of other types of cancer so options A and D are wrong.

The text does not necessarily assume that all men can achieve major changes to diet and exercise. It just advises all men to try and achieve proper diet and exercise.

7) B
Since no boys chose rounders, all children who chose rounders must be girls.
Number of girls that chose rounders = 10 + 6 + 14 + 10 = 40
Number of children that chose running = 10 + 6 + 6 + 6 = 28
Since equal number of boys and girls chose running, number of girls that chose running = 14
Number of boys that chose running = 14
Since no girls chose swimming, all children who chose swimming must be boys.
Number of boys that chose swimming = 4 + 6 + 8 + 10 = 28

Let total number of boys = B
Let total number of girls = G

Equal number of boys and girls took part in the survey.
B = G

Let total number of boys that chose football = P
Let total number of girls that chose football = Q

B = G
14 + 28 + P = 14 + 40 + Q
P = Q + 12

Total number of children that chose football = 11 + 11 + 14 + 12 = 48
We know that P + Q = 48
Since P = Q + 12
Q + 12 + Q = 48
2Q = 36
Q = 18

8) C
We can safely use estimate values for this question.
Total number of offenders at the beginning fo the period = 42, 721 ≈ 43,000
Number of reoffenders at the end of the 9 year follow-up period = 74% of 43,000 = 31, 820
Number of reconvictions at the end of the period ≈ 1100 per 100 offenders
Number of reconvictions per offender = (43,000 ÷ 100) x 1100 = 473,000
Number of reconvictions per reoffender = (473,000 ÷ 31820) = 14.86
Since we have overestimated the values for offenders and number of reconvictions, we must round down now. This approximately gives us 14.3. So C is the answer.

9) E
1 – Correct
Number of offenders reconvicted after 2 years = 55% of 43,000 = 23650 ≈ 24,000
Number of offenders reconvicted after 1 year = 43% of 43,000 = 18490 ≈ 19,000
Percentage = (19000 ÷ 24000) x 100 ≈ 79%
So the percentage is over 77%.

2 – Wrong

Total number of reconvictions (from previous question's calculation) = 473,000
Reconvictions in year 2 = (43000 ÷ 100) x (348 − 185) = 430 x 163 = 70,090 ≈ 70,100
Reconvictions in year 3 = (43000 ÷ 100) x (499 − 348) = 430 x 151 = 64,930 ≈ 65,000
Total number of reconvictions in years 2 and 3 = 70100 + 65000 = 135,000
Fraction = (135,000 ÷ 473,000) ≠ ⅓

3 – Correct

Number of reconvictions in first year = (43,000 ÷ 100) x 185 = 79, 550
So this is more than 77,000 reconvictions.
Since statements 1 and 3 are correct, E is the answer.

---

10) C

The last sentence of the text states "offenders who received shorter sentences (less than 12 months) formed 24.2% of the cohort, but **committed 39% of all offences** that led to a conviction in the first year of the follow-up".
Number of offences in the first year = (43000 ÷ 100) x 185 = 79, 550
39% of 79,550 ≈ 31,000

---

11) G

1 – Correct
If a lot of re-offenders are being sent to prison, this would definitely cause a decline to occur.

2 – Correct
If a lot of the original offenders die, this would cause the decline to occur.

3 – Correct
Harsher sentencing would prevent some of the original offenders from doing any more offences, causing the decline to occur.

Since all statements are correct, G is the answer.

---

12) D

A – Wrong
A is wrong because the text clearly says that the performer who plays the role of Gracie cannot play any other characters.

B – Wrong
B is wrong as the performer who plays Rose also plays Guard 1. This performer cannot play the third role of Teddy, as Teddy and Guard 1 are both in scene 1.

C – Wrong
C is also wrong as the performer who plays Rose also plays Guard 1. This performer cannot play the third role of Sarah, as Sarah and Rose are both in scene 10.

D – Correct
D is correct. Graham and Carl are not together in any of the scenes.

E – Wrong
Sarah is to be played by a female performer and Graham is to be played by a male performer.

F – Wrong
F is also wrong as the performer who plays Rose also plays Guard 1. This performer cannot play the third role of Guard 2 as Guard 1 and Guard 2 are both in scene 1.

---

13) B
In this question, it is important to remember that we have not been given any information about drops in trace elements other than selenium. So we cannot say that selenium is definitely the cause of the extinctions.

A – Wrong
We are not given any information about why marine life developed on Earth. We just know that without trace elements, we die but we do no know whether they helped to develop marine life.

B – Correct
This is correct as it does not use any strong words such as 'must' which is used in A. Also since, selenium is one of the trace elements, we can assume that a drop in its levels could contribute to the extinction.

C – Wrong
We cannot determine whether selenium is more crucial than other trace elements.

D – Wrong
'Must' is a very strong word to use, as we are not given any information about the other trace elements.

---

14) B
Citrons
Total number of seats for Citrons before elections = 80
Number of seats gained from Jonquils = 47
Number of seats gained from Saffrons= 10
Number of seats lost to Jonquils = 11
Number of seats lost to Saffrons = 18
Total number of seats for Citrons now = 80 + 47 + 10 − 11 − 18 = 108

Jonquils
Total number of seats for Jonquils before elections = 126
Number of seats gained from Citrons = 11
Number of seats gained from Saffrons= 15
Number of seats lost to Citrons = 47
Number of seats lost to Saffrons = 33
Total number of seats for Jonquils now = 126 + 11 + 15 − 47 − 33 = 72

Saffrons
Total number of seats for Saffrons before elections = 34
Number of seats gained from Jonquils = 33

Number of seats gained from Citrons = 18
Number of seats lost to Jonquils = 15
Number of seats lost to Citrons = 10
Total number of seats for Saffrons now = 34 + 33 + 18 – 15 – 10 = 60

None of the parties has more than 50% of the seats. So options A, C and D are wrong.
Saffrons have exactly 25% of the total number of seats (60 out of 240). So on the pie chart,
there should be a portion, which represents exactly 25%. So E is wrong.
B is the answer.

15) A
The reasoning made in the argument:
Earth got water from dust cloud or meteorites. Since less deuterium is found in water on Earth
than in meteorites, Earth got its water from the dust cloud.

A – Correct
Compare soil to earth, dust cloud or meteorites to acidity and alkalinity and camellias to
deuterium. Since there are camellias growing here, which cannot tolerate alkalinity (less
deuterium on Earth than in meteorites), the soil must be acidic (Earth must have gotten its
water from the dust cloud).

B – Wrong
This statement is not of the same reasoning because there is an obvious answer to 'Were the
dinosaurs warm-blooded or cold-blooded?'. There was not an obvious answer as to where the
Earth got its water. Research had to be done before any conclusion could be made

C – Wrong
There is no evidence that life exists on them. This reasoning is wrong as it is just assuming
that since a Goldilocks planet is neither too hot nor too cold and there are many of them in the
Universe, there must be life on them.

D – Wrong
This option states "Most people travel by bus". This suggests that there are some people that
travel by taxi. So people do reach the airport by both taxi and bus. However, Earth can only get
its water by either dust cloud or meteorites and not both.

16) D
Possible digits that could make up the codes: 1, 2, 3, 4, 5, 6, 7, 8, 9
The best way to solve this is by trying out the digits given in the options given.

Is there a way to obtain 19 by not using 1 as any of the eight digits? No. Try using any of the
possibilities and you will realise that 1 is needed in order to get 19.

Is there a way to obtain 19 by not using 3 as any of the eight digits? No. Try using any of the
possibilities and you will realise that 3 is needed in order to get 19.

Is there a way to obtain 19 by not using 5 as any of the eight digits? No. Try using any of the
possibilities and you will realise that 5 is needed in order to get 19.

Is there a way to obtain 19 by not using 7 as any of the eight digits? Yes.

The combination could be:
9 + 6 + 3 + 1 = 19
8 + 5 + 4 + 2 = 19

Is there a way to obtain 19 by not using 9 as any of the eight digits? No. Try using any of the possibilities and you will realise that 9 is needed in order to get 19.

---

17) D
The argument is that "it should be illegal to let your child work in show business".

1 – Wrong
Break-ups and mental breakdowns are not related to the main argument of the text. Therefore, this is wrong. 1 does not give a flaw in the argument that it should be illegal to let your child work in show business.

2 – Wrong
Again, addictions and broken relationships is not the main theme of the text. Statement 2 does not find a flaw in the argument.

Since both statements are wrong, D is the answer.

---

18) B
After baking the cake and making 60 biscuits:

- Amount of flour left = 1000 – 225 – 400 = 375 g
- Number of eggs left = 12 – 2 = 10
- Amount of milk left = 2500 – 250 = 2250 ml
- Amount of butter = 600 – 150 – 400 = 50 g
- Amount of sugar = 600 – 330 – 200 = 70 g
- Number of lemons left = 5

The recipe given is for 8 pancakes. So, we need to divide each of the values by 8.

- Amount of flour = $^{100}/_8$ = 12.5 g
- Number of eggs = $^2/_8$ = 0.25
- Amount of milk = $^{200}/_8$ = 25 ml
- Amount of butter = $^{50}/_8$ = 6.25 g
- Amount of sugar = $^{20}/_8$ = 2.5 g
- Number of lemons = $^1/_8$ = 0.125

In order to quickly calculate the number of pancakes that can be made, we need to identify which ingredient has the least amount left compared to the amount needed.
In this case, it is the butter. 50 g is left and 6.25 g is needed for 1.

The ratio of 'amount left : amount needed' is higher for other ingredients compared to butter.
Number of pancakes that can be made with 50 g of butter = $^{50}/_{6.25}$ = 8

---

19) B
A – Wrong
We are not concerned about scientific fields other than genomics. So A is definitely wrong.

B – Correct
If empty cells were counted as spreadsheet errors, then definitely, the support given by data is weakened.

C – Wrong
The word 'majority' in option C suggests that some of the papers observed have not been successfully replicated.

D – Wrong
We are not concerned with the new version of Microsoft Excel. So D is wrong.

---

20) B
1 – Wrong
Looking at the graph of supplementary files, number of supplementary files in 2015 = 170
Number of journals = 18
Statement 1 is basically saying: At least half of the journals observed (0.5 x 18 = 9) published a paper whose supplementary files contained spreadsheet errors.
By looking at the data, this statement is clearly false.

2 – Correct
Number of files with genome errors in 2011 > 100
Number of files with genome errors in 2009 = 50
Therefore, statement 2 is correct.

3 – Wrong
Number of papers in Nature with errors = 23
Number of papers in BMC Bioinformatics with errors = 21. So this is clearly false.

Since only statement 2 is correct, B is the answer.

---

21) D
Look at graph 1 and look for the 'OVERALL AVERAGE' bar.

Journals with errors more than average:

1. BMC Genomics
2. Nucleic acid Res
3. Nature Genet
4. Genome Biol
5. Genome Res

6. Genes Dev
7. Nature

Number of Papers affected in each of the above journals

- Number of papers affected in BMC Genomics = 158
- Number of papers affected in Nucleic acid Res = 67
- Number of papers affected in Nature Genet = 9
- Number of papers affected in Genome Biol = 63
- Number of papers affected in Genome Res = 68
- Number of papers affected in Genes Dev = 55
- Number of papers affected in Nature = 23

Sum of number of papers affected by these journals:
158 + 67 + 9 + 63 + 68 + 55 + 23 = 443

Total number of papers affected = 704
Percentage = $\frac{443}{704}$ x 100 = 62.9261 ≈ 63%

So D is the answer.

---

22) C
80% = 704 papers
1% = 8.8
100% = 880
So total number of papers published were = 880
Out of these 880, 80% (704) were affected.

In 2016
Increase in number of papers = 10% of 880 = 88
Total number of papers published = 880 + 88 = 968
Increase in number of pages with errors = 20% of 704 = 140.8
Total number of pages with errors = 704 + 140.8 = 844.8

In 2017

Increase in number of papers = 10% of 968 = 96.8
Total number of papers published = 968 + 96.8 = 1064.8
Increase in number of pages with errors = 20% of 844.8 = 168.96 ≈ 169
Total number of pages with errors = 844.8 + 169 = 1013.8

In 2018
Increase in number of papers = 10% of 1064.8 = 106.48
Total number of papers published = 1064.8 + 106.48 = 1171.28
Increase in number of pages with errors = 20% of 1013.8 = 202.76
Total number of pages with errors = 1013.8 + 202.76 = 1216.56

The number of pages with errors exceeds the total number of pages published in 2018. So C is the answer.

---

23) E

We know that the first missing piece (left of the two missing ones) has at least 2 outward curves (OC) and at least 1 inward curve (IC)

The second piece has at least 2 OC and 1 IC.

A is wrong because the first piece has no IC.

If you cannot solve the question by imagination, try cutting out the different pairs (don't cut A of course as you already know it is wrong) and try using them to fit the black area.

E is the answer.

---

24) E

The text's argument is that the toll of childbirth <u>causes</u> women to age faster and die early. We must find a flaw in this argument.

A – Wrong
Assuming that women were ignorant of the toll is not related to the argument made. It does not find a flaw in the causal link made by the text.

B – Wrong
Even though this may seem to be correct, the passage only focuses on women in rich nations. Therefore, we cannot just say that the flaw is that: it can only make conclusions about women in a rich nation. We still need to find a flaw in the causal link.

C – Wrong
Infant mortality rate is irrelevant to the text. Infant mortality rate is the number of deaths per 1000 live births of children aged one year or less. The text does not mention anything about it.

D – Wrong
Not necessarily true. Average birth rate in 1920 was 4.2 which still counts as multiple pregnancies. These women lived up to the age of seventy which is actually much later than the age of fifty-five. So the text doesn't imply that all women who have multiple pregnancies will die early.

E – Correct
This is correct because it directly finds a flaw in the causal link made in the text. It states that since women in 1920 had fewer children than women 200 years ago and they lived longer, the lesser toll of childbirth caused them to live longer. However, it does not take into consideration that other factors could have caused an improved life expectancy.

---

25) E

Old speed = 30 kph

New speed = 30 – 3 = 27 kph

Let distance travelled on old route = D

Therefore, distance travelled by new route = D + 4

Let time taken on old route = T
Time taken on new route = 1.25T

Old distance
D = 30 x T = 30T —— (1)

New distance
D + 4 = 27 x 1.25T = 33.75T
D = 33.75T – 4 —— (2)

Using (1) and (2),
33.75T – 4 = 30T
33.75T – 30T = 4
3.75T = 4
T = 1.07 hours

D = 30T = 30 x 1.07 = 32.1 km
New distance = 32.1 + 4 = 36.1 km
This is close to 36 km so E is the answer.

---

26) C
The text states, "this level of detection of such risk factors could equate to the prevention of over 2,000 heart attacks and strokes". However, it further goes on to say that the researchers did not go on to monitor the health of those identified as having such risks.

We, therefore, cannot be sure whether 2,000 heart attacks or strokes were prevented or not.

A – Wrong
This does not fully justify the spending of resources as we do not know whether the health checks were effective or not as we do not know whether 2,000 heart attacks were prevented.

B – Wrong
We cannot conclude this as the researchers did not monitor the people's progress and hence we cannot say whether the screening helped to influence people's health-related behaviours.

C – Correct
Since the researchers did not go on to monitor the health of those identified as having such risks, we cannot be sure whether 2,000 heart attacks or strokes were prevented or not.

D – Wrong
Since we do not know whether the screening was effective or not, we cannot justify the expenditure of resources on long-term outcomes of individuals.

E – Wrong
Other age groups are not mentioned in the text, so we cannot infer this information.

---

27) B

- Number of plates of prawns that can be prepared in a 400 g pack = 400 ÷ 50 = 8
- Number of plates of cockles that can be prepared in 200 g packs = 200 ÷ 50 = 4
- Number of plates of whelks that can be prepared in 200 g packs = 200 ÷ 50 = 4
- Number of plates of salmon that can be prepared in 200 g packs = 200 ÷ 50 = 4
- Number of plates of squid that can be prepared in 200 g packs = 300 ÷ 50 = 6

We must find the lowest common multiple of 8, 4 and 6. This is 24.
So we must prepare 24 plates. This will allow no seafood to be left over.

- Number of prawn packs needed to make 24 plates = 24 ÷ 8 = 3 packs. If Charlie buys 2 packs, she gets third free. So total cost of prawns = €4.08 x 2 = €8.16

- Number of cockles packs needed to make 24 plates = 24 ÷ 4 = 6 packs. If Charlie buys 4 packs, she gets two packs free. So total cost of cockles = €4.08 x 4 = €16.32

- Number of whelks packs needed to make 24 plates = 24 ÷ 4 = 6 packs. If Charlie buys 4 packs, she gets two packs free. So total cost of whelks = €4.08 x 4 = €16.32

- Number of salmon packs needed to make 24 plates = 24 ÷ 4 = 6 packs. If Charlie buys 4 packs, she gets two packs free. So total cost of salmon = €4.08 x 4 = €16.32

- Number of squid packs needed to make 24 plates = 24 ÷ 6 = 4 packs. When Charlie buys the first two packs, she gets the third free. However, she will have to pay for the fourth pack. In total, she will have to pay for 3 packs. So total cost of squid = €4.08 x 3 = €12.24

Total amount spent = 8.16 + 16.32 + 16.32 + 16.32 + 12.24 = €69.36

Cost of each plate = 69.36 ÷ 24 = €2.89

28) E
1 – Correct
The sentence "…can lower levels of violence…encourages police officers to better regulate their own behaviour". This suggests that the text assumes that the level of force used by police sometimes exceeds that which is required by the situation.

2 – Wrong
Nothing is mentioned about police departments in different countries so there can be no assumptions made about police departments in different countries.

3 – Correct
The text suggests that the chief reason for body-worn video cameras is that it ensures that the officers issue a clear warning that their interaction is being filmed. Therefore, the text must

assume that in cases where bystanders have filmed public-police interactions, the individuals involved may not know that they are being filmed.

Since statements 1 and 3 are correct, E is the answer.

---

29) E
One spot from three faces of the die is lost.
The first view of the die shows that a spot from 4 and a spot from 6 is missing.
The second view shows that a spot from 3 is missing.
Opposite faces must always add up to 7.

1 is opposite 6
2 is opposite 5
3 is opposite 4

This can only be done through visualisation and a LOT OF remembering. Since there are so many options, it is actually very hard to solve this less than 2 minutes. Since time is of the essence, I must advise that you skip this question and do the other easier ones first.

---

30) C
The argument made in the text is the last two sentences of the text:

"A beneficial use of fMRI...to conduct brain training for those with weaker connectivity" and "If exercises were developed to help people...their brain connectivity was improved, they too could benefit from more 'positive' lifestyle attributes".
The flaw here is that just because strong brain connectivity is <u>associated</u> with 'positive' lifestyle traits, the text assumes that strong brain connectivity <u>causes</u> the 'positive' lifestyle traits.
Hence, C is the answer as it paraphrases the flaw correctly.

A – Wrong
High educational attainment is just one of the 'positive' lifestyle traits mentioned in the text. It is not the main focus of the text so this flaw is incorrect.

B – Wrong
Ignoring and not mentioning are two different things. This text was made for the purpose of giving information about strong brain connectivity. We cannot just say that it ignores the other healthcare needs that could be addressed through the use of fMRI technology. Therefore, B is irrelevant.

D – Wrong
Injury to the brain is irrelevant to the text.

---

31) D
Number of pairs of interests mentioned in the table:

- Cricket and Hockey
- Golf and Rugby
- Hockey and Snooker
- Football and Snooker
- Cricket and Rugby
- Football and Golf

There are 6 different combinations for 6 different friends.
Each of the friends sitting either side of Jess shares one common interest with her.
Possible interests that Jess could have:
Rugby and Golf
Cricket and Golf
Football and Cricket
Football and Golf

There are no combinations of (Football and Cricket) or (Cricket and Golf).
So Jess must like either **(Football and Golf)** or **(Rugby and Golf)**.
The only individuals, who have friends with interests Football and Golf or Golf and Rugby opposite them, are David and George.
If the person sitting opposite Jess was David,
The person sitting on the left of David likes football and snooker. However, the person sitting to the right of Jess likes football and snooker. This means that David must be to the right of the person who likes football and snooker. This means that David cannot be opposite to Jess. Since David is not opposite Jess, Jess must like Golf and Rugby. Therefore, George is sitting opposite Jess.

So D is the answer. Here is the circle:

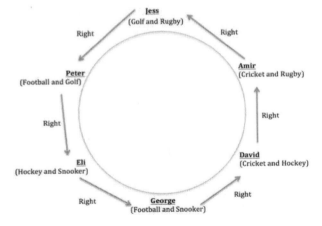

32) C

1 – Correct

If public transport is prioritised and interventions are made in roads by public transport, then this could result in an increase in London's road congestion.

2 – Correct

If road works are increased, then automatically, some roads would have to be blocked in order to carry out the road works. This would cause traffic congestion.

Since both statements are correct, C is the answer.

---

33) E

Cost of congestion to London's GVA = £5.5 billion
Cost of strikes in **six** undergrounds = £10 million **each**
Total cost of strikes = 10 million x 6 = £60 million
Ratio = 5.5 billion ÷ 60 million = 91.666 ≈ 92

---

34) C

1 – Wrong

We know that car ownership is falling and that the congestion problem is getting worse. However, we cannot say that car ownership has not reduced the congestions. We do not know what the congestion problem would have been like if car ownership had not declined. It could have been worse than the present situation. So we cannot infer statement 1.

2 – Wrong

We know that the number of journey stages and trips on bicycles increased from 1% in 2000 to 2% in 2014. However, we also know that the congestion problem is getting worse. Therefore, we cannot say that increasing cycle tracks would make London's congestion problem better. So 2 is wrong.

3 – Correct

The sentences "getting out of taxi before reaching their destinations because his cab was stuck in traffic" and "the bus service has started to decline after years of increase because of slower speeds and worse reliability" suggests that due to the rise in traffic, people are being deterred from using certain forms of public transport.

Since only statement 3 is correct, C is the answer.

---

35) B

The proposal for restoring original boundaries is made to decrease loss in London's GVA. The answer is B because if the wider boundaries of the congestion charge zone were restored, the profitable retail areas will suffer due to a decrease in customers.

People will be deterred from going to such retail areas, hence, decreasing the profit made.

Since the aim was to increase London's GVA, the GVA may actually suffer if people do not come to the profitable retail areas.

1) A
P is the gall bladder, which secretes only bile.

Q is the stomach. In the stomach, proteins are broken down. So proteases must be secreted. Also, hydrochloric acid is also secreted. This means that it has a high hydrogen ion (H^+) concentration.

R is the pancreas, which secretes all of the three enzymes: protease, lipase and amylase. Also, the pancreas secretes insulin to control blood glucose concentrations.

So A is the answer.

2) E
You must first know what anodes and cathodes are.

The anode, which is made out of copper, will form positive copper ions. So the reaction at the anode would be:
$Cu \rightarrow Cu^{2+} + 2e^-$

These positive copper ions will then travel to the cathode and form copper atoms. The reaction would be:
$Cu^{2+} + 2e^- \rightarrow Cu$

3) D
1 – Microwaves have larger wavelengths than visible light.
2 – All waves (visible or any other electromagnetic waves) travel at the same speed in vacuum.
3 –Gamma has the smallest wavelength of any electromagnetic wave.
4 – X-rays are used to look for broken bones and not radio waves.

Since all statements are wrong, A is the answer.

4) F
$(\sqrt{5} - 2)^2$
Using the $(a - b)^2 = (a^2 + b^2 - 2ab)$ rule,

$(\sqrt{5})^2 + (2)^2 - (2 \times \sqrt{5} \times 2)$

$5 + 4 - 4\sqrt{5} = \underline{\mathbf{9 - 4\sqrt{5}}}$

5) G
<u>**1**</u> **– Correct**
Change in the alleles of the gene coding could have caused the change in DNA.

2 – Correct
The order of amino acids in the enzyme could have changed the protein structure of the enzyme and hence, caused the condition SCID.

3 – Correct
The order of bases in the gene coding could have changed the DNA structure.

4 – Correct
If the shape of the active site is different, then this would have prevented the production of healthy white blood cells.

Since all are correct, G is the answer.

---

6) D
Remember mass number = no. of protons + neutrons

1 – Wrong
This ion contains 16 protons.
No. of neutrons = 34 – 16 = 18. We need 20 neutrons.

2 – Correct
This ion contains 17 protons.
No. of neutrons = 37 – 17 = 20.
Number of electrons in a Cl atom = 17
Since this ion has a charge of (-1), number of electrons = 17 + 1 = 18

3 – Wrong
This atom contains 18 protons.
No. of neutrons = 40 – 18 = 22. We need 20 neutrons.

4 – Correct
This ion contains 19 protons.
No. of neutrons = 39 – 19 = 20.
Number of electrons in a K atom = 19
Since this ion has a charge of (+1), number of electrons = 19 – 1 = 18

5 – Wrong
This atom contains 20 protons.
No. of neutrons = 40 – 20 = 20.
However, number of electrons in a Ca atom = 20. We need 18 electrons

Since only 2 and 4 are correct, D is the answer.

---

7) F
1 – Correct
At higher temperatures, there will be more heat energy. Since there will be more heat energy, the rate of evaporation will be greater.

2 – Wrong
Rate of evaporation is greater when there is wind (movement of air).

3 – Correct
Greater the surface area, the greater the number of water molecules in contact with air. Hence, there is a greater rate of evaporation.

F is the answer.

---

8) A
Out of 20 patients, 5 have a migraine.
Probability of the first patient having migraine = $5/20$ = ¼

Since 1 patient with migraine is already picked, number of patients left with migraine = 5 – 1 = 4
Total number of patient remaining = 20 – 1 = 19
Probability of the second patient having migraine= $4/19$
Probability of both patients having migraine = $4/19$ x ¼ = $4/76$ = $1/19$

---

9) E
Experiment 1 – Movement of water but no movement of glucose
There is distilled water in both the tubing and in the test tube. Even though there is no concentration gradient, water molecules will still move across the membrane. Since there is no glucose, there will be no movement of glucose.

In experiments 2, 3 and 4, there are glucose and water molecules present. Hence, water and glucose molecules will move across the membrane.

---

10) C
If it helps, you can write down the reaction equation. This will show you that hydrogen gas will be produced.

$Mg + 2HCl \rightarrow MgCl_2 + H_2$

1 – Wrong
A decrease in energy does not decrease the amount of gas produced.

2 – Correct
Since the concentration of one of the **reactants** decreases, the magnesium would have less hydrochloric acid to react with. This would produce less hydrogen gas bubbles.

3– Wrong
The activation energy cannot increase all of a sudden mid-reaction.

Since only statement 2 is correct, C is the answer.

---

11) C

The resistors are in series.

1 – Wrong
Voltage is different in each component of the circuit.

2 – Correct
Resistance of R_1 is twice that of R_2.
Since $V \propto R$, voltage in R_1 will also be twice that of R_2.

3 – Wrong
Voltage of R_2 is half of R_1

4 – Correct
The current across all components in a series circuit will be the same.

5 – Wrong
Current is the same in both resistors.

6 – Wrong
Current is the same in both resistors.

Since statements 2 and 4 are correct, C is the answer.

12) F

You need to identify that triangles PQT and PRS are similar.

$$\frac{QT}{PT} = \frac{RS}{PT + TS}$$

$$\frac{0.3}{PT} = \frac{1.5}{PT + 1.8}$$

0.3 (PT + 1.8) = 1.5PT
0.3PT + 0.54 = 1.5PT
0.54 = 1.2PT
PT = 0.54 ÷ 1.2 = 0.45
PS = PT + TS
PS = 0.45 + 1.80 = 2.25 cm

13) E

1 – Correct
The gamete is always haploid meaning it would contain half the number of chromosomes as other body cells. Since body cells of sheep have 54 chromosomes, the gametes would contain 27 chromosomes.

2 – Correct
Stem cells are the cells, which make the embryo. So stage 4 would have the same properties as stem cells.

3 – Wrong
The gamete used is produced by meiosis.

Since statements 1 and 2 are correct, E is the answer.

---

14) E
In order for a species to disproportionate, the species must occur twice in the products.
In reactions 1 and 4, all species occur only once in the products.

In reaction 2,
Cu appears twice in the products.
Oxidation state of Cu in Cu_2O in the reactants = +1
Oxidation state of Cu in Cu_2 in the products = 0 (so reduced)
Oxidation state of Cu in CuO in the products = +2 (so oxidised)

In reaction 3,
Cl appears twice in the products.
Oxidation state of Cl in Cl_2 in the reactants = 0
Oxidation state of Cl in HCl in the products = -1 (so reduced)
Oxidation state of Cl in HClO in the products = +1 (so oxidised)

In reaction 5,
Hg appears twice in the products.
Oxidation state of Hg in Hg_2Cl_2 in the reactants = +1
Oxidation state of Hg in Hg in the products = 0 (so reduced)
Oxidation state of Hg in $HgCl_2$ in the products = +2 (so oxidised)

In reactions 2, 3 and 5, simultaneous oxidation and reduction of the same species have occurred.

---

15) F
The question clearly says that Uranium-238 is bombarded by neutrons. So the 1st stage would involve absorption of a neutron.

This would cause the mass number to increase from 238 to 239, forming Plutonium-239.

The following stages must involve ß-decay as the atomic number increases from 92 and 94. In each ß-decay, the atomic number increases by 1. So 2 ß-decays would allow the atomic number to increase from 92 to 94.

---

16) A

$$g = \frac{GM}{R^2}$$

$$gR^2 = GM$$

$$M = \frac{gR^2}{G}$$

Substituting the values,

$$M = \frac{10 \times (6 \times 10^6)^2}{7 \times 10^{-11}}$$

$$M = \frac{10 \times 36 \times 10^1}{7 \times 10^{-11}}$$

$$M = \frac{36 \times 10^{13}}{7 \times 10^{-11}}$$

$$M = \frac{36 \times 10^{13-(-11)}}{7}$$

$$M = \frac{36 \times 10^{24}}{7}$$

$$M = 5.15 \times 10^{24} \approx 5 \times 10^{24}$$

---

17) G

You will need to identify that the artery is a coronary artery. The coronary artery supplies the muscles of the blood with oxygen and nutrients.

1 – Wrong
The coronary artery supplies the muscles of the blood with oxygen and nutrients. HOWEVER, the site of diffusion of glucose and oxygen will be the capillaries and not the artery.

2 – Correct
Arteries carry blood at high pressure.

3 – Correct
Arteries have muscles cells.

G is the answer.

---

18) C

A monoprotic acid is an acid, which gives a single proton or hydrogen ion in aqueous solution. Since magnesium is in group 2, its valency would be 2.

Therefore, the product of magnesium and propanoic acid would be $Mg(C_3H_5O_2)_2$.
So, we can eliminate options B, D and E.

Since the other reactant is $MgCO_3$ and not just Mg, carbon dioxide will also be produced as one of the products. Therefore, A is wrong.

---

19) E

It is important to understand the situation.
The last line states that the reflected sound from the 8m wall reflects from the 2m wall and is then detected by the microphone.

So the waves cover the entire width of 10m and the extra 2m.
So total distance covered by sound waves = 10 + 2 = 12m
Time = 0.010s
Speed = Distance ÷ Time = 12 ÷ 0.01 = 1200 m/s

20) E

$$\frac{1}{2x} + \frac{1}{x-1} - \frac{1}{x}$$

Let us do the first part of the problem.

$$\frac{1}{2x} + \frac{1}{x-1} = \frac{x-1+2x}{2x(x-1)} = \frac{3x-1}{2x(x-1)}$$

$$\frac{3x-1}{2x(x-1)} - \frac{1}{x} = \frac{x(3x-1) - [2x(x-1)]}{x(2x)(x-1)}$$

$$\frac{3x^2 - x - 2x^2 + 2x}{x(2x)(x-1)} = \frac{x^2 + x}{x(2x)(x-1)} = \frac{x(x+1)}{x(2x)(x-1)}$$

$$\frac{(x+1)}{(2x)(x-1)}$$

21) D

We first need to figure out whether the freckles are caused by a recessive allele (let us say 'f') or a dominant allele (let us say 'F').

Let us start with individuals 5 and 6. Assuming that the condition is caused by a recessive allele, then both 5 and 6 <u>must</u> be ff. If they are both ff, then their offsprings <u>must</u> also be ff since there is 100% chance of being ff.

	f	f
f	ff	ff
f	ff	ff

Since their offspring 7 and 8 do not have the freckles, this means that freckles must be caused by a dominant allele.

This means that since freckles can only be caused by the presence of a dominant allele, individuals 2, 4, 7 and 8 who do not have freckles must be homozygous recessive (i.e. ff).

Let us now look at individuals 1 and 2.

355

Since 1 has freckles, he can either be FF or Ff. If 1 is FF and 2 is ff, then there is a 100% chance of their offspring having freckles.

	F	F
f	Ff	Ff
f	Ff	Ff

However, one of their offspring, 4 does not have freckles. So 1 <u>must</u> be heterozygous.

Since 1 is heterozygous and 2 is homozygous recessive,

	F	f
f	Ff	ff
f	Ff	ff

There is a 50% chance (0.5) that a child produced by 1 and 2 will have freckles.

We know now that any offspring of 1 and 2 who has freckles can only be heterozygous (Ff). So 5 must definitely be heterozygous. 6 cannot be FF, as this means that all of their offspring would have freckles. Therefore, 6 must be heterozygous as well.

	F	f
F	Ff	Ff
f	Ff	ff

There is a 75% chance (0.75) that a child produced by 5 and 6 will have freckles.

---

22) B
Mr of hydrated copper (II) sulfate = (64) + (32) + (16 x 4) + (10 x 1) + (16 x 5) = 250
Mass of hydrated copper (II) sulfate = 10 g

Moles = Mass / Mr = 10 / 250 = 0.04 mol
We know moles = concentration x volume
We have the volume as 100 cm³. This is equal to 0.1 dm³

Moles = concentration x volume
Concentration = Moles / volume
Concentration = (0.04 ÷ 0.1) = 0.4 mol/dm³

---

23) F
Newton's Third Law:
If a body A exerts a force on body B, then B will exert an equal and opposite force on A.

The information given to us says that the floor (body A) exerts a force on the table (B). So the table must also exert an equal and opposite force on the floor.

---

24) C
Area of the quarter of circle = 0.25 π r²
0.25 π (6)²
0.25 π 36
9π

In order to find the area of the triangle, we first need to find the base (B). We need to use Pythagoras for this.
(9)² = (6)² + (B)²
81 = 36 + B²
45 = B²
B = √45 = √(3 x 3 x 5) = 3√5

Area of triangle = 0.5 x 6 x 3√5 = 3 x 3√5 = 9√5
Total area of shape = 9π + 9√5

---

25) G
1 – Wrong
The enzyme is produced by the activation of the gene and not the internal temperature.

2 – Correct
The last line of the paragraph says that IF the cat had grown in a warmer temperature, the ears, front of the face, paws and tail would have been paler. 2 suggests that the temperature of those parts of the body were cooler than the rest of the body and hence, they are darker. So 2 is correct.

3 – Correct
Activation of the gene produces the enzyme, which makes the coat colour pale. The environment causes the colour change in the ears, front of the face, paws and the tail.

---

26) B
Let us first write down the reaction equation.
$2Na + 2H_2O \rightarrow 2NaOH + H_2$
We have the Mr of Sodium = 23 and its mass = 0.23g
Moles = Mass / Mr = (0.23 / 23) = 0.01 mol
Molar ratio (Na : H) = 2 : 1
So moles of hydrogen gas produced = 0.01 ÷ 2 = 0.005 mol
Volume of 1 mole of gas at room temperature = 24 dm³
So volume of 0.005 mol of gas = (24 x 0.005) = 0.12 dm³

---

27) C
We know that KE = 0.5mv²

We first need to find out whether the graph will go through zero or not.
Using the equation above, we can see that if $v^2 = 0$, then K.E. will also be equal to 0.
So the graph does go through 0,0.

y = mx + c
Since c (y-intercept) = 0, we get the equation,

y = mx
K.E. = 0.5 mv²

We know the K.E. is on the y-axis and the square of speed is on the x-axis.
Therefore, m (gradient) in the equation (y = mx) would be 0.5 m (0.5 mass).
We know that the mass = 2.5 kg
So gradient = 0.5 x 2.5 = 1.25

2017 Section 3

1) Obedience is a behaviour, which allows a person to be respectful and considerate of rules and laws. Being obedient should not be confused with compliance. It is a choice, which humbles a person in front of superiors. It teaches a person discipline, honesty and punctuality. These qualities are essential for a leader who aims to guide people in the right direction.

According to Aristotle, a person who has never learnt obedience can never learn to be a good leader. For example, a footballer can never be a good captain if they continuously disobey the decisions of the coach. A captain is someone who leads a team to victory. This requires the other team members to be submissive towards the captain. If the captain does not follow the coach, the other team members, naturally, would not obey the captain. An undisciplined and disobedient captain would lead the team towards failure.

Together with this, an obedient person knows the feeling of following. If they become a leader in the future, they will know how to treat their followers with respect and integrity. This mutual respect between leaders and followers is essential for success.

In the medical industry, junior doctors need to follow the instructions of senior doctors to learn and widen their knowledge of medicine and treatments. If junior doctors disobey their seniors and show signs of disrespect in the process, it is likely that they will not be good senior doctors in the future due to their attitude.

On the contrary, some may argue that a commander can naturally have leadership qualities. They do not need to be obedient to lead their army or team to success. An example of this is nepotism in kingdoms in the past in different parts of the world. It was essential for the sons or daughters of kings or queens to rule the kingdom in the future. In the past, princes and princesses did not really need to be obedient to the rules and laws. They were privileged and hence did not need to follow the rules that were put in place for other people. However, there have been many instances where princes or princesses had proven to be excellent leaders. They showed exceptional leadership qualities to command their army and people. Therefore, it may not be necessary to be obedient to be a good commander.

To conclude, being obedient teaches a person to be polite and humble. These qualities are essential for leaders to manage those under them. Every system in this world requires order and to maintain order, obedience is key. A good leader is a person who has worked their way up in this system by respecting and following the instruction of seniors. Even those who have natural leadership skills need to obey teachers and parents. It is vital for them to learn respect for others.

---

2) The statement can be interpreted, as "the only duty a scientist has is to reveal the truth." This means that a scientist should not have any other moral concerns or interests. A scientist's primary duty is to uncover the truth behind natural events that occur around and within us. To do this, they need to carry out various experiments and researches, which may involve some unethical procedures.

For example, animal experimentation could be considered immoral. Many pharmaceutical companies require animal experimentation to check the effects and side effects of drugs. Many people oppose animal testing as animals are exposed to cruel procedures and drugs, which cause suffering and even death. However, without animal testing, we would not have discovered the medicines and treatments that we have today. For example, insulin was discovered when pancreases of dogs were extracted and studied. This discovery was critical to saving the lives of diabetics.

On the contrary, some may argue that scientists who work for the military often overlook the social impacts of their inventions. A prime example of this is Fritz Haber. He was a scientist in the German army. He proposed the use of toxic gas against enemy soldiers. Many chemicals were tested and then gaseous chlorine was used to cruelly kill the opposition. Soon, toxic warfare became famous around the world and different chemicals were introduced to aid the military. If Haber had thought about the consequences of his research, this would not have happened.

To conclude, it is important for scientists to reveal the truth. However, it is the humane duty of every scientist to consider the consequences of their researches. Science should be used for the betterment of humans and nature.

---

3) Ageing is the natural process of growing old. It happens to everyone and is neither preventable nor reversible. It happens because our cells stop working and break down, causing conditions such as cancer and heart disease. Scientists are trying to find 'cures' for ageing so we can make it preventable and treatable. They are trying to look at ageing as if it is a disease. The statement is, therefore, trying to say that we should not look at ageing as a disease.

All organisms grow old and have a certain lifespan. It is inevitable that every organism on this planet is going to die at some point in time. As straightforward as it may sound, ageing is just a stage in an individual's life, which indicates that they are getting close to their death. Curing ageing and prevent individuals from living their normal lifespan can lead to some serious consequences in the future. Firstly, the birth rate would exceed the death rate substantially. The problem of overpopulation can cause problems for all people. Lesser food and clean water availability will lead to poor quality of life for everyone.

Secondly, curing ageing would probably involve changing genetic codes in our DNA. Since every organism has a different genetic code, it would be difficult to determine which genetic code to change. A single mistake could lead to serious problems for the individual. Therefore, we need to ensure whether the risk outweighs the advantages.

There have been many cases in the past, which prove that interfering with nature can lead to more problems for the whole planet.

On the contrary, if cures for ageing are found, people will be able to live a more fulfilling life. They will be able to accomplish more things and explore the planet more. Hypothetically, diseases that come with ageing such as heart diseases and cancer will affect lesser people. If this is true, fewer resources will be used to treat such diseases. These resources can instead be used to treat other conditions such as genetic disorders.

To conclude, ageing is a natural degenerative process, which every organism goes through. It is crucial to prevent overpopulation and cures for ageing will only worsen this situation. However, quality of life should also be taken into consideration. If ageing is prevented, diseases caused can also be prevented. More research is required to provide treatments for such diseases. If curing ageing can allow us to treat such conditions, it would be right to treat ageing as if it were a disease.

1) B

Length of path = 3.2 km = 3200 m

Every 400m, there is a seat. Total number of seats = 3200 ÷ 400 = 8

We must add 1 to this value because we must count the one at the start. So total number of seats along the path = 9

There are 2 bins beside each seat. This gives use 9 x 2 = 18 bins.

Every 100 m, between each seat there is a bin. If we start from the first seat, there will be 3 bins between first seat and second seat. Therefore, between 9 seats, there will be 3 x 8 = 24 bins.

Total no. of bins = 24 + 18 = 42

Alternatively, you can draw a diagram to help you. The circles are the benches and the red lines are the bins.

2) B

A – Wrong

11% (100 – 38 – 51) of the people have the VV combination. However, we are not given information about whether people with VV combination can get the disease or not. We cannot assume that those with VV combination will not be susceptible to the disease.

B – Correct

The second to last statement, which states that someone with the MV combination recently died of the disease. This means that having one V variant of the gene does not guarantee resistance to vCJD.

C – Wrong

Eating infected beef does cause vCJD in everyone with the MM combination. This can be inferred from the third to last line.

D – Wrong

51% have the MV combination. However, it is not entirely certain that all 51% of the people will develop vCJD in the future. There is no statement in the passage, which guarantees that all people with MV combination will develop vCJD.

3) D

The manager observed in the time period 10:00 to 12:00. We only need to focus on times, which are within this 2-hour period.

Phil:
Entered 9:27 and left 11:03. (Time manager observed = 11:03 – 10:00 = 1 hour 3 minutes)
Entered 11:42. (Time manager observed = 12:00 – 11:42 = 18 minutes)
Total time observed = 1 hour 21 minutes

Quentin:
Entered 11:23 and left 11:46. (Time manager observed =23 minutes)
Entered 11:42 and left 11:55. (Time manager observed = 13 minutes)
Total time observed = 36 minutes

Rob:
Entered 8:20 and left 10:17. (Time manager observed = 10:17 – 10:00 = 17 minutes)
Entered 10:26 and left 11:00. (Time manager observed = 34 minutes)
Entered 11:38. (Time manager observed = 12:00 – 11:38 = 22 minutes)
Total time observed = 1 hour 13 minutes

Sanna:
Entered 9:35 and left 10:10. (Time manager observed = 10:10 – 10:00 = 10 minutes)
Entered 10:16 and left 11:50. (Time manager observed = 11:50 – 10:16 = 1 hour 34 minutes)
Total time observed = 1 hour 44 minutes

Theresa:
Entered 8:44 and left 10:02. (Time manager observed = 10:02 – 10:00 = 2 minutes)
Entered 10:42 and left 12:25. (Time manager observed = 12:00 – 10:42 = 1 hour 18 minutes)
Total time observed = 1 hour 20 minutes

Sanna was in the office for the largest amount of time during the two-hour period. So D is the answer.

---

4) C
The argument implied by the text is that state nurseries should not be affected by financial restrictions. The person based this argument on his or her own experience (that their child blossomed at the state nursery).
Therefore, C is the answer.

---

5) D
We are looking for a person who uses 2 functions for the same time and 2 other functions for the same amount of time.
(The white section is equal to the black section. The light grey and semi-dark grey are equal in proportions too)

The darkest grey section is in lesser proportion than the light grey and semi-dark grey. So it cannot be Amos. She uses browser and social media for 30 mins but uses apps for 40 mins, which is more than browser and social media.

The darkest grey section is in a higher proportion than the white and black sections. It cannot be Bryn as calls are in lower proportion (10 mins) than email and apps.
It cannot be Clive, as he does not use any two functions for the same amount of time.

Dolly: Email and social media can represent the black and white (two smallest equal sections), calls and apps can represent the light grey and semi-light grey (two largest equal sections) and browser can represent the darkest grey section.
It can be Dolly.
Eshan uses three functions for equal amounts of time. So the pie chart cannot represent Eshan.
So the answer is Dolly.

---

6) C
The main conclusion is the last line of the passage.

A - mainly focuses on the regulation of social media whereas the conclusion deals with the relationship between social media and democracy. So A is wrong.
B - the last line uses the term 'social media' whereas option B uses the term 'technological developments'.
C – Option C is correct because the last line states that social media has "undermined democracy". Undermined means 'lessen the effectiveness of'. So social media has basically made democracy weaker. C states this.
D - mainly focuses on the availability of truthful information whereas the conclusion deals with the relationship between social media and democracy. So D is wrong.
E - mainly focuses on organised protests and direct action whereas the conclusion deals with the relationship between social media and democracy. So E is wrong.

---

7) D
From floor 11, the nearest floor is 15. This is a difference of 4 (15 – 11) floors. It takes 3 seconds to move from one floor to the consecutive floor.
So total so far is 3 x 4 = 12 seconds

From floor 15, 6 and 24 are equally close to each other. However, previously, the lift moved from 11 to 15, so it is travelling upwards. Therefore, floor 24 is the preferred floor for the lift. It takes 9 x 3 = 27 seconds to do this.
So total so far is 39 seconds.

From floor 24, the lift will go to floor 6. This will take 18 x 3 = 54 seconds.
Total = 54 + 39 = 93 seconds

From floor 6, it will go to floor 4. This will take 6 seconds.
Total = 99 seconds.

However, the lift has stopped on 3 floors before opening at floor 4. These are floors 6, 15 and 24. We must 9 seconds for each floor. This is 27 seconds.

Total = 99 + 27 = 126 seconds
So D is the answer.

---

8) B
To solve this, we need to use the 2nd table and find the ratio of unpaid work of men and work for each age category. (Use approximate figures)
25 and under: 12/8 = 4/3 = 1.33
26 to 35 = 34/17 = 2
36 to 45 = 33/20 = 1.65
46 to 55 = 26/18 ≈ less than 1

(Of course you can calculate the actual figure but that would be a waste of time as we know that the highest figure so far is 2. If the fraction is definitely less than 2, there is no point calculating the actual ratio).
56 and over = 25/17 ≈ less than 1
So the answer is B (26 to 35).

---

9) B
1 – We cannot infer the exact amount of housework done by men and women as we are only given information about unpaid work.

2 – This is correct. If you work out the ratios of all the types of work, you will find that laundry is the type of unpaid work that men spend the least time on relative to women.

So only statement 2 is correct. B is the answer.

---

10) C
People with high income spend more time on non-leisure travel than people with low income. (Please note that the word '**cannot**' changes the meaning of the question entirely)

Option A is a plausible explanation. If people on lower incomes are less likely to have a car, they are more likely to spend less time on non-leisure travel.

Option B is a plausible explanation. If people on lower incomes do not commute to work so often, they are more likely to spend less time on non-leisure travel.

Option C is not a plausible explanation. If people on lower incomes use public transport, they would still be spending time on non-leisure travel. It does not matter whether they are driving or using public transport.

Option D is a plausible explanation. If the lower income group includes students who spend little time on transport, they are more likely to spend less time on non-leisure travel.

So option C is the correct answer.

---

11) C

Women carried out an overall average of 60% more unpaid work than men.
Value of total unpaid work = £1000 billion
We can make up an equation to state this. Let 'Y' be value of unpaid work carried out by men.
Value of unpaid work by women = 160% x Y= 1.6Y

Y + 1.6Y = £1000 billion
2.6Y = £1000 billion
(Taking 2.6 ≈ 2.5),
Y = 400 billion
Women did = 1000 − 400 = £600 billion worth of unpaid work.

The actual value would be higher as we rounded 2.6 to 2.5 so C (£615 billion) is the answer.

12) C

Customer 1 was not refunded any money because the train arrived only 1 minute late.
Customer 2 was not refunded any money.
Customer 3 would have been refunded $6 since their train was more than 20 minutes late.
Customer 4 would have been refunded $4 since their train was more than 10 minutes late but less than 20 minutes late.
Customer 5 would not have been refunded any money.
Customer 6 would not have been refunded any money.
Customer 7 would not have been refunded any money.

Customer 8 would not have been refunded any money.
Customer 9 would have been refunded $6 since their train was more than 20 minutes late.
Customer 10 would have been refunded $6 since their train was more than 20 minutes late.

Total money refunded by company = 6 + 4 + 6 + 6 = $22
So the answer is C.

13) D

The argument of the passage is the last line. According to the argument, it is better for young people to show aggression through rugby than by violent behaviour. (Hence rugby should not be banned).

1 – Correct

Since it is important for young people to channel their aggression in a controlled manner, activities such as rugby are important. However, if it is unfeasible for the school to replace rugby with other activities, rugby is the only activity by which young people can channel their aggression in a controlled manner. Therefore, this strengthens the argument as it suggests that it is important for rugby to be present in school.

2 – Correct

If aggression is a natural and unavoidable behaviour, it should be channelled in a controlled manner rather than channelling it through violent behaviour. Therefore, rugby is important for young people to channel their natural and unavoidable aggression. So this strengthens the argument.

3 – Wrong
This suggests that only rugby and no other sport can cause head or spinal injury. This weakens the argument as it suggests that rugby is the most dangerous sport and hence should be banned.

So D is the answer.

---

14) F
In such types of questions, look for the most mentioned name first. In this case, it is Roger. This is will be a start to the puzzle. Let us assume for now Roger belongs to a football team.

If Roger and Qayla belonged to a football team, Phillip mentioned both names correctly. So this cannot be the case.

If Roger and Phillip belonged to a football team, Qayla mentioned both names correctly. So this cannot be the case.

No one mentions Roger and Sam so this cannot be the case.

If Roger and Trista belonged to a football team, Sam mentioned both names correctly. So this cannot be the case.

If Roger and Ursula belonged to a football team,
Phillip, Qayla, Sam and Trista mentioned one name correctly and lied about the other name. This matches the conditions described.
So F is the answer.

---

15) A
1 – Correct
The Right promotes freedom and prosperity of the business which means that businesses should not be regulated and should be allowed to do things, which help them prosper. This is what newspaper owners do. Newspaper owners use their power and influence, which can be favourable for their businesses.

2 – Wrong
We cannot infer what political opinion is presented in the British press. So the 2nd statement cannot be concluded from the above passage.

So A is the answer.

---

16) A

The faster pump has exactly double the flow rate of the slower pump.
Let us say he uses the fast pump to fill the larger container first and the slow pump to fill the smaller container.

Let us say it takes 10 minutes (you can use any time as volume of containers is not specified) to fill the smaller container with half its volume. In 10 minutes smaller container will be filled with 60 litres (6 litres per minute) whilst the larger container will be filled with 120 litres (12 litres per minute). Using this assumption, smaller container must have a volume of 120 litres in total.

Now the containers are swapped with each other. The fast pump fills the smaller container and the slow pump fills the larger container. Both of them are filled at the same time. We have assumed that smaller container has a volume of 120 litres. Now that the faster pump is being used to fill the remaining 60 litres of the small container, it takes 5 minutes to fill the remaining 60 litres. Total time taken to fill smaller container = 15 minutes.

Slower pump is being used to fill the remaining volume of larger container. It already has 120 litres and it takes 15 minutes in total to fill the larger container.
In the remaining 5 minutes, the larger container will be filled with 6 x 5 = 30 litres.
Total volume of larger container = 120 + 30 = 150 litres.

Extra volume of larger container = 150 – 120 = 30 litres
Percentage larger = (30 ÷ 120) x 100 = 25%

17) A

The passage describes a cause and effect situation. For this question, you have to associate the cause described in the passage with the cause described in the options and the effect described in the passage with the effect described in the options.

Cause in passage = Whereabouts being kept secret or not
Cause in options = Tide being out or not out

Effect in passage = Risk management possible or not possible
Effect in options = Island can be reached or not

The passage states that if whereabouts were secret, risk management was possible. Replace this statement with 'if tide is out, island can be reached'

The passage states that since whereabouts were not secret, risk management was not possible. Replace this statement with 'since tide is not out, island cannot be reached'

So the answer should be:
'If tide is out, island can be reached. Since tide is not out, island cannot be reached.'
This is given by option A only.
The other options confuse the cause and effect.

18) E

This requires just listing all the possible arrangements.

When 4 yellow and 2 red skittles are used,
There are 15 possible arrangements.

When 4 red and 2 yellow skittles are used,
There are 15 possible arrangements.

When 3 yellow and 3 red skittles are used,
There are 20 possible arrangements.

In total, there are 50 possible arrangements.

19) A

For this, you need to find the ratio of fatalities per crash.
8% of fatal crashes occurred during cruise but 16% of the fatalities occurred when the crash occurred during cruise.
Ratio = 16/8 = 2
Cruise is the phase of flight, which has the highest ratio of fatalities per crash. So A is the answer.

20) C

We must look at phases of flight from descent to landing. So the order is descent, then initial approach, then final approach and then landing.

Descent takes 11% of the time out of a 1.5-hour flight.
1.5 hours = 90 minutes
11% of 90 = 9.9 minutes

Initial approach takes 12% of the time out of a 1.5-hour flight.
12% of 90 = 10.8 minutes

Final approach takes 3% of the time out of a 1.5-hour flight.
3% of 90 = 2.7 minutes

Landing takes 1% of the time out of a 1.5-hour flight.
1% of 90 = 0.9 minutes

Total time = 9.9 + 10.8 + 2.7 + 0.9 = 24.3 ≈ 24 minutes

So the answer is C.

21) D

Out of all the options, D is the correct one.

A – Wrong

In 1990s, total number of crashes = 235
Crashes due to pilot error = 140.
Proportion = $^{140}/_{235} \approx 0.6$
You can see that in any decade, proportion of crashes due to pilot error is approximately 0.6
So proportion of crashes due to pilot error was **not** unusually high in the 1990s.

B – Wrong

In 2010s, total number of crashes = 66
Crashes due to mechanical error = 11.
Proportion = $^{11}/_{66} \approx 0.17$
You can see that in any decade, proportion of crashes due to pilot error is approximately 0.17
So proportion of crashes due to mechanical error was **not** unusually low in the 2010s.

C – Wrong

Proportion of crashes due to bad weather in 1960s = 14/248 ≈ 0.06
Proportion of crashes due to bad weather in 1970s = 13/238 ≈ 0.06
Proportion of crashes due to bad weather in 1980s = 11/205 ≈ 0.05
Proportion of crashes due to bad weather in 1990s = 13/235 ≈ 0.06
Proportion of crashes due to bad weather in 2000s = 7/112 ≈ 0.06
Proportion of crashes due to bad weather in 2010s = 5/66 ≈ 0.08
So proportion of crashes due to bad weather did not steadily decrease over the period.

D – Correct

Proportion of crashes due to sabotage in 1960s = 12/248 ≈ 0.05
Proportion of crashes due to sabotage in 1970s = 25/238 ≈ 0.10
Proportion of crashes due to sabotage in 1980s = 23/203 ≈ 0.11
Proportion of crashes due to sabotage in 1990s = 19/235 ≈ 0.08
Proportion of crashes due to sabotage in 2000s = 10/112 ≈ 0.09
Proportion of crashes due to sabotage in 2010s = 6/66 ≈ 0.09
So proportion of crashes due to sabotage was unusually low in the 1960s.

E – Wrong

If you work out the estimate proportions, you will realise that the proportions of crashes due to other causes increased steadily over the period.

22) C

The reasoning in the last paragraph is that 2015 was actually the safest year on record if one discounts sabotage.
In order to discount sabotage (which caused the majority of the fatalities that year), one has to assume that sabotage does not make air travel less safe. So C is the answer.

23) B
Let the first digit be A
Let the second digit be B
Let the third digit be C
Let the fourth digit be D

B – A = 1
D – C = 1

A + D = BC

We know, B – A = D – C = 1
B + C = A + D

We also know A + D = BC

So,
A + D = B + C = BC
BC = B + C

There is only one possibility which satisfies BC = B + C. That is if both numbers are 2.
2 + 2 = 4
2 x 2 = 4

So B and C are 2.
A must be 1.
D must be 3.

So the code is 1223. The fourth digit is 3.

---

24) C
A is wrong because the passage does not say or assume that the only purpose of keeping domestic cats is to have a positive effect on native wildlife.

B is wrong because the passage says, "domestic cats caught and killed so-called invasive species". So it is certain that numbers of invasive species decreased because of the presence of domestic cats.

C is correct because the passage only gives the example of Canberra. The passage assumes that Canberra is representative of the general environmental effects of keeping domestic cats.

D discusses the purpose of keeping domestic cats. However, there is nothing assumed about the purpose of keeping domestic cats in the passage.

---

25) B
The key to answering this question is realising that no charity will receive more than $100.

STARS will receive the second highest amount of money. We have no information about what the other charities will receive. We are given 5 options for what STARS's least amount would be.

There will be three charities that will receive less money than STARS. We must use the options provided to work out the answer. By using each option, we must use the maximum amount that the remaining 3 charities will get.

If STARS obtained $25, we must assume that the 3 charities will get $24, $23 and $22.
This gives us a total of $94 (25 + 24 + 23 + 22). This means that the remaining 5th charity will get:
$200 - $94 = $104

However, this does not satisfy the condition that no charity can receive more than $100. So A is wrong.
If START obtained $27, the 3 charities will get $26, $25, $24.
Total = $102
5th charity will get = 200 – 102 = $98
So $27 is the least amount that can be given to STARS. So B is the answer.

26) D
The argument made by the passage is the sentence "More action is urgently needed…health and mortality."

A neither strengthens nor weakens the argument, as it does not make a statement for or against breastfeeding.

B weakens that argument as it states that women in developing countries rely on bottle-feeding so it must be more beneficial than breastfeeding.

Although C states that commercial promotion of bottle-feeding is being limited by campaigns, it does not give a reason why breastfeeding is beneficial. So it does not directly strengthen the argument.

D states that breastfeeding is good for the mother and the child. Therefore, it strengthens the argument because it gives an additional reason why breastfeeding is beneficial. (It is good for the mother as well).
So D is the answer.

27) A
To get the least possible cost, the discounts must be applied to the most expensive pizzas on the order.

India's pizza costs $5,
James' cost $8. ($6 + $2 for one topping)
Keira's cost $6.
Lance's cost $8.
Maddie's cost $12. ($8 + $4 for two toppings)
Nellie's cost $9. ($5 + $4 for two toppings)
Nellie's cost $10. ($8 + $2 for one topping)

The two most expensive pizzas are $12 and $10. Naturally, the buy 4 get 1 free will apply to $12 pizza.
Buy 1 get 1 half price applies to $10 pizza.

So total = 5 + 8 + 6 + 8 + 9 + 5 = $41.00
So the answer is A.

---

28) D
The passage tries to convey the message that routine health screening is not always the best option and targeted screening programmes are more beneficial.

Option A only discusses about better off people leading healthier lifestyles. However, the passage does not only focus on better off people.

Option B is wrong. The value of universal screening programmes has not been underestimated at all and this is not suggested by the passage.

Option C only focuses on breast cancer screening whilst the passage only used breast cancer screening as an example. So C is wrong.

Option D is correct because the last line of the paragraph clearly implies that instead of universal screening programmes, targeted screening programmes are more beneficial.

---

29) C
Let die with 0 to 5 spots be die X.
Let die with 2 to 7 spots be die Y.

In the diagram of the two dice shown together, the left die is die Y. We can come to this conclusion because 3 and 2 are adjacent to each other, which cannot happen in the die, which has 0 to 5 spots. So the right die is X.

A cannot be the answer. One of the faces of die in option A has 6 spots so it cannot be die X. It cannot be die Y because opposite faces must add up to 9 which means 6 must be opposite 3. In option A, however, 6 and 3 are adjacent.

B cannot be the answer. It cannot be X because 3 is adjacent to 2. It cannot be Y because if you try and align faces of die in option B exactly as it is in the picture of Y, you will realise that face with 3 spots swaps with the face with 2 spots.

D cannot be the answer. It cannot be X as one of its faces has 6 spots. It also cannot be Y. This requires good spatial visualisation skills. Let me try and explain. In the picture of Y (left die), one spot of 3, one spot of 2 and one spot of 5 all meet at one vertex (point of cube). If you try and align die in option D as it is in pic of Y, you will realise this does not happen. The following picture is a picture of what die in option D would look like. If you compare the following picture with the picture of Y, you will realise that D is not correct.

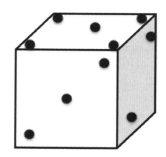

E cannot be the answer. It cannot be Y because 5 and 4 are adjacent to each other. It cannot be X because if you aligned die in option E as it is in pic of X (with 4 as top face), you will realise that in option E, 3 is in place of 2. So E is wrong.

Therefore, the answer is C.

---

30) D
The argument is that a transition from fossil fuels to biofuels is necessary. We must look for statements that weaken this argument, i.e. statements which say that transition from fossil fuels is not necessary.

1 – Wrong
If longer growing seasons and other impacts of climate change will lead to increased food harvests, it is will be feasible for the transition from fossil fuels to biofuels to occur. So this does not weaken the argument (instead it strengthens it).

2 – Wrong
Again, this statement shows how biofuels can be easily produced and hence, does not weaken the argument.

So D is the answer.

---

31) A
Let marks awarded for research = R
Let marks awarded for design = D
Let marks awarded for construction = C
Let marks awarded for evaluation = E

According to the information provided,
1) D – C = 2   (Rearrange to get C = D - 2)
2) D – E = 11   (Rearrange to get E = D - 11)

We know he got a total of 48 marks.
R + D + C + E = 48
R + D + D – 2 + D – 11 = 48
R + 3D = 61
3D = 61 – R
$D = {}^{61-R}/_3$

Now substitute the values of R given in the options.

Option A
R = 10
$D = {}^{61-R}/_3$
$D = {}^{61-10}/_3$
D = 17

When D = 17,
C = 15, E = 6
Total = 17 + 15 + 10 + 6 = 48

So option A is correct. If you try all other options, you will either get decimals (which is incorrect as one of the conditions is that all marks are expressed in whole numbers) or incorrect totals.

Exception: Option D
When R = 13,
D = 16, C = 14 and E = 5
This also gives us a total of 48.
However, one of the conditions is that the smallest difference between the marks awarded to any two of Bruno's sections was 2. If R = 13, C = 14. Therefore, the smallest difference would be 1 and not 2. So option D is also incorrect.

___

32) D
We cannot obtain the answer to this question from the tables. We know that 'conditionally indispensable' amino acids are those, which can be formed in our body under some circumstances.

The second paragraph gives information about how some amino acids can be converted into others (phenylalanine to tyrosine and methionine to cysteine). We can, therefore, infer that tyrosine and cysteine must be conditionally indispensable as they are formed in our body under some conditions.

33) B
According to table 2, for a person aged 19+, 5 mg/kg of bodyweight of tryptophan is needed.
Weight of man = 70 kg
Mass of tryptophan needed = 70 x 5 = 350 mg

According to table 1, mass of protein intake = 0.8 x 70 = 56 g
Per gram of protein, 4 mg of tryptophan is consumed.
Since 56 g of protein is consumed, mass of tryptophan consumed = 56 x 4 = 224 mg
Difference = 350 − 224 = 126 mg

34) A
Newborn baby
Mass of breast milk consumed = 560 g
Mass of protein consumed = 2.5% of 560 = 14 g (info from 3rd paragraph 1st line)
For each gram of protein, 55 mg of isoleucine is consumed.
Mass of isoleucine consumed = 55 x 14 = 770 mg

8-week old baby
Mass of breast milk consumed = 700 g
Mass of protein consumed = 1% of 700 = 7 g
For each gram of protein, 55 mg of isoleucine is consumed.
Mass of isoleucine consumed = 55 x 7 = 385 mg

Ratio = 770 : 385 = 2 : 1

35) B
We need to use the 1st table for this.
Ratio of threonine between infants and adults = 44 : 19 = $^{44}/_{19}$
Using this ratio, we can find an estimate for histidine.
$21 \div {}^{44}/_{19} = 21 \times {}^{19}/_{44} \approx 9$ mg

2018 Section 2

1) H
Pancreatic juices contain amylases, lipases and proteases. Since cystic fibrosis prevents the secretion of pancreatic juices, the medication must contain amylases, lipases and proteases.

2) C
Q has electronic configuration of 2, 8, 2
Z has electronic configuration of 2, 7

Q needs to lose 2 electrons to have full outer shell and Z needs 1 electron to have full outer shell.
Q has a valency of 2 and Z has a valency of 1. (two Z atoms are needed for each Q atom)
So the Empirical formula would be QZ_2

The bonding would be ionic because Q loses two electrons and each Z atom gains one electron.

3) E
1 – False. All light travel at the same speed in vacuum.
2 – True. Red light always has a larger wavelength than green light.
3 – False. All light travel faster in vacuum than in water.
4 – True. Frequency of blue light is always greater than frequency of red light.

So the answer is E (2 and 4).

4) B
$^{48}/_{40}$ is $^6/_5$
$m^5 \div m^2 = m^3$
$p \div p^3 = p^{-2}$

The simplification is $^6/_5 \, m^3 \, p^{-2}$
So the answer is B

5) A
In Denitrification, nitrate ions are reduced to produce nitrogen gas (N_2). This is only shown by process 1. So the answer is A.

6) C
1 – Wrong. Covalent bonds in position 1 are between one liquid and the other liquid. However, in position 3, only one of the liquids is obtained so the **same** covalent bonds are **not** formed.

2 – Correct. In position 3, the particles are in liquid form but in position 2, particles are in gas form. Particles are closer in liquid form than gas form.

3 – Wrong. In position 1, heat is being supplied to the mixture. So it is an endothermic process. Also, breaking bonds requires energy so it must be an endothermic change.

Since only statement 2 is correct, C is the answer.

---

7) E
Using $c = f \lambda$,
Speed of wave in material = 50 x 0.4 = 20 m/s
Time = Distance ÷ Speed = 100 ÷ 20 = 5 s

---

8) C
We need exactly 70p worth of coins. So that is one 50p coin and one 20p coin. Best way to do this is to draw a tree diagram.

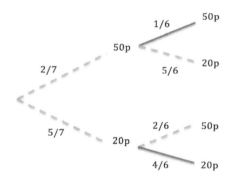

We can only take the dashed paths shown above.
1st dashed path gives us = 2/7 x 5/6 = 10/42 = 5/21
2nd dashed path gives us = 5/7 x 2/6 = 10/42 = 5/21

Total = 5/21 + 5/21 = 10/21
So the answer is C.

---

9) B
We must first identify the type of cell division that occurred. 4 cells divided 5 times to form 128 cells. Mitosis produces 2 daughter cells after each division whilst meiosis produces 4 after each division.

If it was Mitosis,
4 - 8 - 16 - 32 - 64 - 128

If it was Meiosis,
4 - 16 - 64 - 256 - 1024 - 4096

So the type of cell division was mitosis.

1 - Correct. All cells would have the same number of chromosomes.
2 - Wrong. If the cells were gametes, they would have divided by meiosis instead of mitosis.
3 - Correct. Mitosis produces clones of the original cells.
4 - Wrong. It is mitosis, not meiosis.

So the answer is B (1 and 3).

---

10) C
In iron (III) oxide, iron has an oxidation state of +3. In iron (in products), iron has an oxidation state of 0. So iron is reduced, which means it has gained electrons. So A is wrong.

The oxide ions in iron (III) oxide each have a charge of -2. So B is wrong.

Iron (III) oxide oxidises carbon in CO. In CO, carbon has an oxidation state of +2 but in carbon monoxide, it has an oxidation state of +4. So Iron (III) oxide oxidises carbon from +2 to +4. So, Iron (III) oxide is an oxidising agent. C is the answer.

The value of ΔH is negative which indicates that this process is exothermic. D is wrong.

Electric current is not used in this reaction so this is not an example of electrolysis. So E is wrong.

---

11) E
Speed does not necessarily change when a vehicle changes direction, as speed is a scalar quantity. So A, B and C are wrong.

Velocity is a vector quantity so when a vehicle changes direction, its velocity changes.

Momentum is a vector quantity as its equation is p = mv, it depends on velocity. If a vehicle changes direction, its velocity changes so its momentum also changes.

Kinetic energy does not change, as it is a scalar quantity. Energy does not depend on direction and is always positive. So when a vehicle changes direction, it is not necessary that its kinetic energy will also change.

Only momentum and velocity change. So E is that answer.

---

12) F
It is important for you to realise that the diameter of the circle is the diagonal of the rectangle.

Let width of rectangle be W. So length is 3W
2(3W + W) = 24 cm
8W = 24 cm

W = 3 cm
Length = 3 x 3 = 9 cm

Diagonal = hypotenuse of one right-angled triangle.
Diagonal^2 = $3^2 + 9^2$
Diagonal^2 = 9 + 81
Diagonal^2 = 90
Diagonal = $3\sqrt{10}$
Radius = $(3\sqrt{10} \div 2)$ cm

Area of circle = $\pi (3\sqrt{10} \div 2)^2 = \frac{90}{4}$ cm^2
Area of rectangle = 9 x 3 = 27 cm^2
Area of shaded area = $(\frac{90}{4}) \pi - 27$ cm^2

Obviously, this is not one of the options. However F is the same as the answer. So F is correct.

---

13) H
All cells shown in the question form tissues. Epithelial cells together form epithelial tissue. Mature red blood cells form blood, which is a connective tissue. Muscle cells form muscle tissue.

---

14) B
The two spikes at 35 and 37 indicate two isotopes of element X.
The spike at 70 is due to two isotopes of mass 35 existing as a diatomic molecule. (35 + 35 = 70)

The spike at 72 is due to two isotopes of mass 35 and 37 existing as a diatomic molecule. (35 + 37 = 72)

The spike at 74 is due to two isotopes of mass 37 existing as a diatomic molecule. (37 + 37 = 74)

So B is the answer.

---

15) E
PE at the top of the lift = 200 x 10 x 1.8 = 3600 J
All PE is converted to KE just before contact with ground.
$\frac{1}{2} mv^2$ = 3600
(200) v^2 = 7200
v^2 = 36
v = 6 m/s

---

16) B
Let difference between r and r + 1 = M
Let difference between r + 1 and r + 2 = N
Let difference between r + 2 and r + 3 = O

The sum of the difference = 126
M + N + O = 126

By understanding the example given in the question, we can infer that:
N = M + 1
O = N + 1

Since N = M + 1,
O = M + 1 + 1 = M + 2
M + N + O = 126
M + M + 1 + M + 2 = 126
3M + 3 = 126
3M = 123
M = 41

M is the difference between r^{th} and $(r + 1)^{th}$ triangular number.
From the example described in the question, we know that:
Difference = initial triangular number + 1.

E.g. Between 2nd triangular number and 3rd triangular number, difference = 3
Initial triangular number is the 2nd triangular number.

Therefore,
M = (r^{th} triangular number) + 1
41 - 1 = r^{th} triangular number
r^{th} triangular number = 40

So the answer is B.

17) F
When diaphragm flattens, it contracts. So statement 2 is correct.
Volume of thorax increases. So statement 3 is correct.
Pressure decreases so statement 6 is correct.
F is the answer.

18) E
The double bond between 2nd and 3rd carbon atom becomes a single bond. The carbon atoms that were part of the double bond will each have a methyl group attached (CH_3). This is only shown by option E.

In A, there are no methyl groups.
In B, there are methyl groups on every alternate carbon atom. So this is wrong.
In C, not all carbon atoms part of the polymer chain have a methyl group.
In D, not all carbon atoms part of the polymer chain have a methyl group.

19) B
Maximum current is when there is minimum resistance. The lowest value of resistance = 10 + 2 = 12 Ω
I = V/R = 6/12 = 0.5 A

Minimum current is when there is maximum resistance. The highest value of resistance = 10 + 20 = 30 Ω
I = V/R = 6/30 = 0.2 A

Difference = 0.5 - 0.2 = 0.30 A

20) A
We can find the total mass of the first 16 sweets.
Total mass of 16 sweets = 16 x 9.5 = 152 g

Then 4 more sweets, each of mass 'x' were added.
Mass of the 4 sweets = 4x
Total mass of 20 sweets = 152 + 4x
Average mass = (152 + 4x) ÷ 20

Now substitute values given in the option into the equation.

Option A:
If x = 12,
Average mass = 10g
If x = 14.5,
Average mass = 10.5 g

So x must be greater than 12 but less than or equal to 14.5
So A is correct.

Option B is wrong because it does says (x < 14.5). 'x' can be lesser than OR equal to 14.5, which is why option A is correct.

Option C is wrong because it does says (12 ≤ x). 'x' cannot be equal to 12 as mean mass of a sweet MUST be greater than 10 g.

Options D, E and F are just completely wrong.

21) A
The chemical inhibits respiration, which means that glucose in the cell is not converted to energy. Therefore, there is glucose present in the cell.
Therefore, glucose does not move into the cell.
Water moves into the cell because there is a higher water concentration outside the cell than inside the cell.
So A is the answer.

22) C

Mass of oxygen = 105 – 57 = 48

To find the empirical formula, we divide the masses of the elements with their Ar.

For fluorine, $^{57}/_{19}$ = 3

For oxygen, $^{48}/_{16}$ = 3

Then, we divide all obtained values by the lowest value. In this case, we only receive one value, 3.

So the empirical formula is OF

Since it is relative molecular mass is double of empirical formula mass, the molecular formula would be O_2F_2.

---

23) B

Mass number only decreases by alpha decay. After each alpha decay, the mass number decreases by 4.

Decrease in mass number = 244 – 220 = 24

Number of alpha decays = 24 ÷ 4 = 6

After 6 alpha decays, the atomic number will decrease by 12.

So atomic number would decrease to 82 (94 – 12 = 82)

After each beta decay, the atomic number increases by 1. We know the atomic number of radon is 86. So there must be 4 beta decays to increase the atomic number from 82 to 86.

After 6 alpha decays and 4 beta decays, plutonium-244 becomes radon-220.

So the answer is B.

---

24) B

$$\frac{x \quad 1}{x - 1} \quad - \quad \frac{x^2 + 3}{x^2 + 2x - 3}$$

First we need to factorise $x^2 + 2x - 3$ by splitting the middle term

$x^2 + 2x - 3$

$x^2 + 3x - x - 3$

$x(x + 3) - 1(x + 3)$

$(x - 1)(x + 3)$

$$\frac{x \quad 1}{x - 1} \quad - \quad \frac{x^2 + 3}{(x - 1)(x + 3)}$$

The common denominator is $(x - 1)$

We get,

$$\dfrac{x - \dfrac{(x^2 + 3)}{(x + 3)}}{x - 1}$$

Solve the numerator first,

$$x - \dfrac{(x^2 + 3)}{(x + 3)}$$

$$\dfrac{x(x + 3) - x^2 - 3}{(x + 3)}$$

$$\dfrac{x^2 + 3x - x^2 - 3}{(x + 3)}$$

$$\dfrac{3x - 3}{(x + 3)}$$

$$\dfrac{3(x - 1)}{(x + 3)}$$

The whole fraction is:

$$\dfrac{3(x - 1)}{(x + 3)} \div (x - 1)$$

$$\dfrac{3(x - 1)}{(x + 3)} \times \dfrac{1}{(x - 1)}$$

$(x - 1)$s cancel out

We are left with:

$$\dfrac{3}{(x + 3)}$$

So B is the answer.

25) C
Let dominant allele be **B**
Let recessive allele be **b**

Genotype of male fly = Bb
Genotype of female fly = Bb
Simple monohybrid cross produces 3 genotypes: BB, Bb and bb (You should know how to do the cross).
Number of phenotypes is only 2. BB and Bb produce brown flies whilst bb produces black flies.
Max number of genotypes : Max number of phenotypes = 3 : 2
So C is the answer.

---

26) C
Xenon hexafluoride has 1 xenon atom and 6 fluorine atoms. (The prefix hexa- means six)
Fluorine is diatomic gas. In order to receive 6 fluorine atoms, we need to use three fluorine gas molecules ($3F_2$)
Xenon is a noble gas so it is present as an atom only.

We can write down the equation too.
$Xe + 3F_2 \rightarrow XeF_6 \quad \Delta H = -330$ kJ/mol

Number of F – F bonds broken = 3
Energy = 158 x 3 = 474 kJ/mol

There are 6 Xe – F bonds.
Let energy of 1 Xe – F bond = M (any letter)
474 + 330 = 6M
6M = 804
M = 134 kJ/mol

---

27) E
When the material is living the ratio is $1000 : 10^{15}$
When the material died, the ration became $100 : 10^{15}$
This means that the ratio decreased by a factor of 10.
1 half-life = 6000 years
Let number of half-lives be M
$^{1000}/_{100} = 2^M$
$10 = 2^M$
We know $2^3 = 8$ and $2^4 = 16$
So number of half-lives is a decimal between 3 and 4. (Let us take it as 3.5)

Number of half-lives = 3.5
Number of years = 6000 x 3.5 = 21,000 years
This is close to 20,000 so E is the answer.

385

2018 Section 3

1) According to Mill, a person should be allowed to do what he/she desires as long as the liberties of others are not infringed. There should be little intervention from other parties (e.g. the government). A person should be lawfully allowed to literally anything they think is correct as long as it does not affect anyone else negatively. With this statement, Mill directly argues against law paternalism and tries to protect individual rights.

To the contrary, this does not apply to children of course. They lack the cognitive capabilities to make informed and sensible decisions. In this case, other parties such as parents or relatives need to step in and take decisions for children. Another exception is mentally handicapped people. Other people need to make rational decisions for these people in order to help and support them to the best of their ability. In other cases, those who are fully capable of making informed decisions may sometimes make decisions, which can cause harm to themselves and others. An example is when someone tries to commit suicide. The police may need to intervene and help that person.

Freedom means lawfully doing whatever you want. However, in the situations described above, other parties do need to limit a person's autonomy when needed. The government needs to establish laws, which prevent people from doing activities that can put their own lives and other people's lives in danger and protect other people from crimes. As long as a person does what they want within the limits of the law, Mill's statement holds true.

2) According to Franklin, scientific explanations and discoveries cannot fully explain certain aspects of life. Her statement conveys the message that there are some mysteries in life, which cannot be solved by science alone. Even after numerous scientific discoveries and breakthroughs (e.g. structure of the atom and DNA), Franklin believes that science is unable to provide answers for many remaining questions.

By life, Franklin could be referring to the origin of everything in the universe. It is true that the most probable answer to the origin of the universe is the Big Bang Theory. However, it is still a theory and there is very little evidence to prove this theory. Another mystery of life could be the origin of all living beings on Earth. How can inorganic molecules come together and produce an organic living being? Such questions, according to Franklin, cannot be answered by science.

On the contrary, science has provided explanations for many things, which were at first, considered to be non-existent. Through rigorous research and experimentation, we were able to realise that every living being has DNA or genetic material, which gives that being its characteristics. It helped to explain why everyone and everything is different from each other. Everything is composed of atoms and atoms are composed of electrons, protons and neutrons. By studying their nature and reactivity with each other, we were able to provide explanations for many things and make discoveries. Therefore, there is a possibility that science can provide explanations for everything in the future.

Franklin lived in the 20th century, which means that she probably thought many things were impossible, which are possible today. Long-distance communication within seconds and travelling to space is quite possible today. Therefore, it is difficult to agree with her statement completely as science is currently progressing faster than ever.

3) Due to the advanced technology and modern treatments available in medicine today, many people believe that any disease is treatable. Routine operations are operations, which do not usually involve many complications and are relatively easy to carry out for a well-trained doctor. Death during such operations is not normal as these operations are carried out after careful planning. Since there is a very low chance that death could occur, people believe that death during routine operations is the medical staff's fault. A medical error is a preventable adverse effect of care, which could harm the patient. Medical errors could include incomplete diagnosis of disease, injury and infection.

However, this might not be entirely true. Patients, themselves, can be the cause of many complications arising during an operation. Before any operation, patients are given a guideline, which they must follow to ensure the operation goes according to plan. For example, when an operation involves the use of general anaesthesia, the patient must fast for up to 12 hours before the surgery is due. If the patients break this rule and eat just before the surgery, they can risk regurgitation. If this happens, food may enter the patient's lungs, causing difficulty in breathing and in some cases, death. This cannot be deemed as medical error.

Together with this, there is always a chance of infection during an operation, which can cause death. Doctors are supposed to inform the patients about this chance of infection and that it is not entirely preventable. If an infection occurs even after the surgery had been carried out under hygienic conditions, this is not medical error as the medical staff took all measures to prevent this from happening.

All routine operations must be carried out after careful planning. The patients should be informed about what they should do before and after a surgery as this can help to prevent any complications. If a patient dies after a routine operation due to carelessness of the medical staff, then, of course, this is deemed as a medical error. Therefore, it is difficult to come to a conclusion of whether death after a routine operation is a case of medical error as any surgery or procedure always involves risks. These risks are not entirely preventable by the medical staff.

2019 Section 1

1) C

Cost of flight previous year = $330
Booking fee last year = $50
Cost without booking fee = 330 − 50 = $280
Ratio of basic cost : taxes = 3 : 2
Total parts = 3 + 2 = 5
BASIC COST last year = (280 ÷ 5) x 3 = $168
TAXES COST last year = (280 ÷ 5) x 2 = $112

Basic cost rose by 20%. So cost now would be 100% + 20% = 120% (in decimals = 1.2)
Basic cost this year = 168 x 1.2 = $201.60

Taxes cost rose by 10%. So cost now would be 100% + 10% = 110% (in decimals = 1.1)
Basic cost this year = 112 x 1.1 = $123.20

Booking fee reduced by 50%.
Booking cost now = 50 ÷ 2 = $25

Total cost of flight = $201.60 + $123.20 + $25 = $349.80

---

2) C

The argument made by the passage is the first line "The rise of the internet-connect smartphone and similar devices poses a risk to the ties that bind us together within society."

Option A talks about previous generations where families had larger number of children. This is irrelevant to the passage as the passage talks about the interactions between people in society not number of children.

Option B states that internet-connected devices help people who struggle with face-to-face interactions. However the passage states that internet-connected devices pose risk for people. Option B weakens the argument, not strengthen it.

Option C states that younger children are entertained by smartphones and are not encouraged to have face-to-face interactions. This supports the argument as the argument states that smartphones are causing problems with face-to-face interactions which help bind us together within society.

Option D is talks about a future with robots which would be able to interact like humans.

Again, this is irrelevant to the passage as it talks about us as a society and not robots.

3) C

The only cars with both sunroof and air con together are Cornal and Elox. The only car out of these two which costs less than $160 for 7 days is Cornal. So C is the answer.

4) B

The passage states that if the internet sales tax is introduced, companies will sell fewer products and have lower profits. However, it does not take into account that the people who would have bought products online from a certain company can go to a store to buy the same products from the company at a cheaper rate. Thus, the company would not sell fewer products and hence, not pay less tax.

5) B

This question requires great spatial awareness. The only way to solve it is to visualize the 4 nets coming together to form the given shape. Only B is able to do so.

6) C

The 'model' that the passage talks about states that the value of something is determined by its cost. The passage states that some of the products and services we value most come for free. This means that the value of something cannot be determined by cost alone. There must be some other alternative we have to use to determine the value of something.

This is stated by option C.

7) E

You may think this is a tricky question because there are a lot of numbers given. However, it is quite simple!

Think of it this way.
A child is tested positive for a disease. S/he can either be true positive or false positive.
Number of true positive cases = 72
Number of false positive cases = 92

Total number of positive cases = 164

We are looking for the probability of child having the disease (true positive).
Probability of true positive out of all positives = 72 out of 164 which is 44%

---

8) E

After reading through all options, E makes most sense because the passage literally says "the analysts said that this did not mean that two-thirds of the gap must be attributable to pay discrimination by employers..." which means that we do not know how responsible discrimination is when it comes to gender pay gap.

---

9) D

The gender pay gap was 9.1% in 2017. Average weekly earnings were £550.

The solution here is to divide 9.1% by 2 first which is 4.55%.
Then subtract 4.5% of 550 from 550 to get £525.

The logic behind this solution:

To obtain an average of £550, we would have to add women's earnings and men's earnings and divide it by 2.

Let us say men earned X per week
Therefore women earned = X − 0.091X = 0.909X per week (0.091 is 9.1%)

Let us form an equation.

$$\frac{X + 0.909X}{2} = 550$$

$$\frac{1.909X}{2} = 550$$

$$1.909X = 1100$$

$$X = 1100 \div 1.909 = £576$$

So men earned around about £576.
Therefore women earned = 0.909 x £576 ≈ £525

It would not be possible to do these calculations during the exam due to time restrictions but just remember that this is how the answer is arrived at.

---

10) H

We need to look for statements that ultimately lead to men earning more money.

1) If women have longer tenures and longer tenures means more money, then women would earn more money so this is false.

2) If women have shorter tenures and longer tenures means more money, then women would earn less money so this is true.

3) If men have longer tenures and longer tenures means less money, then men would earn less money so this is false.

4) If men have shorter tenures and longer tenures means less money, then men would earn more money so this is true.

So H (statements 2 and 4) are correct.

---

11) D

This is a long calculation questions as you can see here. Please remember, whenever you are stuck on such demanding questions during the exam, please skip it and then come back to them at the end. Each question is worth the same!

Average gender pay gap in 2016 = 9.4%
Average weekly earnings in 2016 = £539
To find Average weekly earnings for men in 2016, we divide 9.4% by 2 and add it to the £539 = £539 + 4.7% = £564 (same logic used as Q9)

We know earnings for men rose by 75% from 1997.
Earnings for men in 1997 = 564 ÷ 1.75 = £322

Gender pay gap in 1997 = 17.4%
Women earned 17.4% less than men and men earned £322
So, in 1997, women earned = 322 – 17.4% = £266

We now need to find out average weekly earnings for women in 2016. Women earned 9.4% less than men and men earned £564 in 2016.
So women earned = £511

Rise in average weekly earnings for women from 1997 to 2016 = 511 − 266 = £245
% rise = (245 ÷ 266) x 100 = 92%

---

12) C

To go from X to Y, it takes 2 hours 30 minutes (2.5 hours). Then it stays for 1 hour. So we can say that the trip from X to Y takes 3 hours 30 minutes. (3.5 hrs)

From the timetable, we see that ferries set sail from each port every 1.5 hours.

Let us use an example to solve this question.

From port X, a ferry (let us call this ferry 1) leaves at 00:00. It will arrive at Y at 02:30. It will stay till 03:30. Then arrive back at X, 2 hours 30 minutes later at 06:00.

We know that from port X, ferries leave at the following times between 00:00 and 06:00:
01:30, 03:00, 04:30 and then 06:00.
At 00:00, ferry 1 departs.
At 01:30, ferry 2 would depart.
At 03:00, ferry 3 would depart.
At 04:30, ferry 4 would depart.
At 06:00, ferry 5 would depart.

Ferry 1 arrives back at X at 06:00 however, it cannot depart immediately as it has to stay for 1 hour.
Therefore, this timetable requires 5 ferries in total.

---

13) B

The conclusion of the passage is simple. Drinking culture affects the cost of coffee in different places. The conclusion is the line "it's the difference in drinking culture which has the greatest effect….". So B is the answer.

---

14) C

Total number of sales in the week = 80 + 30 + 100 + 120 + 70 = 400
This may seem tricky but remember, always try and think outside the box.

If we work out the percentage of sales for each day compared to the whole week, we will see that on Wednesday, Terence made 100 sales out of the 400 in total. This is one quarter. None of the sections in the pie chart represent ¼ of the whole pie chart. This means that Terence forgot to draw in Wednesday.

---

15) C

By reading the passage, we can see that the underlying message that is being given to us is that people do not use words such as 'umpteen' and 'zillion' randomly to describe any number. People use 'umpteen' only to describe size generally below 100 and 'gazillion' to describe size above billion or 'zillion'.
This means that there are certain rules and conditions that people follow as to when these words should be used.
e.g. people will not use 'gazillion' to describe a size below 100.

---

16) A

Total number of people tested = 50 + 50 + 200 + 150 = 450

Number of 5-17 years old females that could read the line = 28% of 50 = 14
Number of 5-17 years old males that could read the line = 32% of 50 = 16
Number of adult females that could read the line = 12% of 200 = 24
Number of adult males that could read the line = 18% of 150 = 27

Total number of people that could read the bottom line = 14 + 16 + 24 + 27 = 81

Percentage of people that could read the bottom line = (81 ÷ 450) x 100 = 18%

---

17) D

To find the assumption, we need to understand the argument made in the paragraph. The argument made is that it would not be appropriate to issue a blanket pardon for the executions that happened during the war. This is because the individual cases cannot be review fairly now since the norms have changed over the years. Therefore, a legal pardon cannot be issued.

This means that the passage is assuming that there would be individual differences between the soldiers who were executed and that some deserved deaths more than others. It does not take into consideration that those who were executed would deserve or not deserve death sentences equally.

18) D

On Monday, Jasper has maths and English before breaktime. This means he carries 4 books before breaktime. After breaktime he has history which requires 2 books. 4 + 2 = 6 Remember that he can only carry 5 books at one time. So he would need to visit the locker at break time on Mondays.

On Tuesday, Jasper has music and science before breaktime. This means he carries 3 books before breaktime. After breaktime he has geography which requires 3 books. 3 + 3 = 6 So he would need to visit the locker at break time on Tuesdays.

On Wednesday, Jasper has maths and history before breaktime. This means he carries 5 books before breaktime. After breaktime he has science which requires 2 books. 5 + 2 = 7 So he would need to visit the locker at break time on Wednesdays.

On Thursday, Jasper has music and English before breaktime. This means he carries 2 books before breaktime. After breaktime he has maths which requires 3 books. 2 + 3 = 5 So he would **not** need to visit the locker at break time on Thursdays.

19) D

Percentage change of sales of Mirror from 1992 to 2018 = -80%
Sales of mirror in 2018 = 583190 ≈ 580,000
So sales have reduced by 80% from 1992 to 2018.
Let us say sales in 1992 were X.
X – 80%X = 580,000
80% of X = 0.8X

1X – 0.8X = 580,000
0.2X = 580,000
X = 580,000 ÷ 0.2 ≈ 2.9 m

20) C

By looking at the figures for Mirror from 2000 to 2015 (in the given table), we can see the sales reduced from around 2.2 m in 2000, to around 1.7m in 2005, to around 1.2 m in 2010 and then to around 0.9 m in 2015.

The first three declines (2.2 m to 1.7 to 1.2 m) are proportional, i.e. there has been a decline of 0.5m every 5 years from 2000 to 2010. Therefore, the line should roughly be a steep straight line from 2000 to 2010.

Lines 1, 2, 4 and 5 are not completely straight between 2000 and 2010. Line 3 is the straightest so C is the answer.

---

21) D

This is quite a simple question actually. The argument presented in the second and third paragraphs is that newspapers can have an influence on the people reading them. In the third paragraph, it implies that since the 5 pro-leave newspapers had the most sales, there is "no surprise" that majority of UK population was "persuaded to vote Leave". This is a classic example of causation.
Causation in the argument – since more pro-leave newspapers were sold, majority of UK population voted leave.

The weakness in this argument is this causation. It fails to consider that people may buy newspapers which express and support the views they already have.

This is why D is the answer.

---

22) B

Statement 1: Not Supported
Decline in sales of all 9 newspapers = 6,008,137 – 5,381,969 = 626,441 (you can use estimates for quicker calculations)

Decline in percentage (use estimates for quicker calculations) =
$(620,000 \div 6,000,000) \times 100 \approx 10\%$

Statement 2: Supported
Pro leave newspapers were: Mail, Express, Star, Sun and Telegraph
Total number of sales for these 5 in 2016 (use estimates)
= 1,589,471 + 470,369 + 1,787,096 + 472,033 + 408,700 = 4,727,669 ≈ 4.7 m

Total sales in 2016 = 6,303,371 ≈ 6.3 m

Percentage = $(4.7 \div 6.3) \times 100 \approx 75\%$

So the answer is B

23) D

For explaining this easily, we will name the 3 changes that occurred to the <u>initial score</u> (initial score is the score when the person returned to the desk) as change 1, change 2 and change 3 (which is the current score).

To solve this question, we would have to use the answers given to us and work backwards. Total number of runs made by the batsmen = 4 + 6 + 4 + 6 + 6 + 4 = 30

Option A: 293
If we subtract 30 from 293, it will give us 263 (initial score). This cannot be correct as it does not correspond to the first view of the score.

Option B: 297
If we subtract 30 from 297, it will give us 267 (initial score). This cannot be correct as it does not correspond to the first view of the score.

Option C: 302
If we subtract 30 from 302, it will give us 272 (initial score). This can be the correct answer as it corresponds to the first view of the score. Let us look at the change 1.
After the first 4, the part of the score does not change. 272 + 4 = 276. This cannot be correct as 276 as the part of the score should change.

Option D: 303
If we subtract 30 from 303, it will give us 273 (initial score). This can be the correct answer as it corresponds to the first view of the score.
After the first 4, the part of the score does not change. 273 + 4 = 277.

The part of the score would not change when score changes from 273 to 277. Let us look at change 1.

After first 6, score would then be 277 + 6 = 283. This corresponds to the picture shown in change 1.

After the third 6, score would be = 283 + 4 + 6 + 6 = 299. This corresponds to the picture shown for change 2.

After last 4, score would be 299 + 4 = 303. This corresponds to the picture shown for change 3, which is the current score. So D is the answer.

If you follow the same steps for option E, you would realise that option E cannot be correct.

24) B

The paragraph explains in detail about brood parasitism noted in the three groups of birds. However, it uses brood parasitism as an example of convergent evolution. It also states this in the 4th sentence.

Option A is not correct because the main argument is not only about cuckoos, cowbirds and honeyguides avoiding raising young chicks. The argument is more about explaining convergent evolution by using brood parasitism as an example.
Similarly with option C, the main argument is not about eggs with thicker shells.

Option D is wrong because nothing is mentioned about life adaptation.

---

25) E

The question does not state how many chocolate bars Nicola has bought and whether she has bought different types of chocolate bars.

Statement 1: Incorrect
This is not necessarily true. She could have bought 8 Venus bars at 30p each which would have brought the total to £2.40

Statement 2: Incorrect
Not necessarily. Again, she could have bought 8 Venus bars at 30p each which would have brought the total to £2.40

Statement 3: Incorrect
Not necessarily. Again, she could have bought **8 Venus bars** at 30p each which would have brought the total to £2.40. This means she could have 8 bars altogether.

Statement 4: Incorrect
This is a bit tricky. Let us assume she bought one of each. This would cost her: 30p + 40p + 50p = £1.20. This is exactly half of £2.40
If she had bought two of each, this would bring her total to £2.40
So, she can have an equal number of each of the bars.

---

26) C

Statement 1 is incorrect because it makes an assumption about the future whereas nothing is mentioned about the future in the paragraph.

Statement 2 is incorrect because the paragraph does not talk about natural ability. It simply states that technology has helped the swimmers to set new world records.

Statement 3 is correct because it describes how technology has advanced over the decades and this has helped swimmers to set new world records.

So, option C is correct.

---

27) D

Although this question does not require advanced calculations, it would take time to solve it because it requires a lot of trial and errors since there are so many options given to us in terms of subscription fees and cost of newspapers.

The cheapest option for George would be to buy printed 1 printed newspaper from Times and Express each, per week.
Cost of this per week = 1.5 + 0.8 = £2.30
Cost per year = 2.3 x 52 = £119.60

We have chosen 2 newspapers, i.e. Times and Express. We need to choose a different newspaper now and the cheapest option left would be 12 month subscription of Dispatch for online and tablet (£30).

Total = 119.60 + 30.00 = £149.60

---

28) E

The argument made in the text is that the drug legalization movement is dangerous and misguided.
To support this argument, it uses the example of only one place, Colorado USA. It states that ever since marijuana has been legalized in Colorado, the rates of murder and violent crimes have increased. It assumes that legalization of marijuana has caused the increase of violent crimes. This is a flaw. So statement A is correct.

Statement B is wrong because other substances are not mentioned in the text and are irrelevant in this case.

Statement C is correct. In order to prove a correlation between two things (legalization of marijuana and increase in rate of violent crimes), it must be proven repeatedly in different places too. In this case, the text only uses the example of Colorado. Therefore, this is a flaw.

So E is the answer.

29) A

Statement 1 could be correct. If 70% swim and 40% climb, this takes the total to 110 (70 + 40 = 110%). This is not possible as the maximum can only be 100%. Therefore, at least 10% of the people would do swimming and climbing. (110% - 100% = 10%). We know therefore that some members must be doing both. This would mean 60% swim only, 10% do both and 30% climb only.

Statement 2 could be correct. We have already established that at least 10% must be doing both swimming and climbing. Some people would be swimming only and other would be climbing only. So all members are either swimming or climbing or doing both.

Statement 3 could be correct. Half of members who climb = 40% ÷ 2 = 20%
We know that there is a possibility where 30% of members climb only. So this statement can also be correct.

So A is the answer.

---

30) C

There is no mention of women seeking advice from their own mother in the text. So, we cannot make a conclusion about this. So, A is wrong.

B states that mothers who find baby care difficult buy self-help books. We do not know which mothers buy these books. This would be wrong assumption to make and hence, B cannot be a conclusion.

C is correct because the text states that some mothers had tried to implement routines of feeding and sleeping as advised by self-help books but could not do so. Therefore, this can be a conclusion.

D is not necessarily true. The text states that one in six women who used books said that the books had made them feel like a failure. We do not know whether these books helped other women or not so we cannot say that the books are doing more harm than good.

---

31) F

The questions is basically asking us to find out what the smallest amount the person can sell for and largest amount they can sell for.

Firstly we need to find the largest decrease in price and larges increase in price during this

10 day period.

Largest decrease during this 10 day period is a decrease of 10p per share (25 p to 15 p or 30 p to 20 p)

If the person bought at 25p per share and sold at 15p per share:
Number of shares bought at 25 p = 6000 ÷ 0.25 = 24,000 shares
If he sold these shares at 15p per share he would get = 24,000 x 0.15 = £3600

If the person bought at 30p per share and sold at 20p per share:
Number of shares bought at 30 p = 6000 ÷ 0.30 = 20,000 shares
If he sold these shares at 20p per share he would get = 20,000 x 0.20 = £4000

The smaller amount of these is £3600.

The largest increase is an increase of 15p per share from 15p to 30p. There is only one time this happens (day 5 to day 7)

If the person bought at 15p per share and sold at 30p per share:
Number of shares bought at 15p = 6000 ÷ 0.15 = 40,000 shares
If he sold these shares at 30p per share he would get = 40,000 x 0.30 = £12,000
Therefore, the difference between these is = 12000 – 3600 = £8400

---

32) C

The graph shows that between 5 and 10, the hazard ratio is the lowest. The only number between 5 and 10 is 6 so C is the answer.

---

33) A

The conclusion made in the first line correlates units of alcohol drunk in middle age with risk of dementia. What it fails to consider is that in middle age, people have different occupations which could cause individual differences. (e.g. some occupations may have a higher risk of dementia than others).

B is wrong because "drinking too much is defined as more than 40 units per week" is not an assumption. This can be seen from the graph that drinking 40 units of alcohol per week has the same hazard ratio as not drinking at all.

C is wrong because the main topic of the passage is dementia. It is not making any assumptions about other health risks.

D is wrong because the passage <u>does not say</u> that drinking habits ONLY in the middle age increases the risk of dementia.

E is wrong because the passage does not imply whether people can develop dementia in middle age or not.

---

34) B

Questions states that 40% of study cohort consumed 14 units per week.
Study cohort = 10,000 participants
40% of 10,000 = 4000 participants

Out of these 4000 participants, 80 went on to develop dementia.
Proportion of people out of these 4000 that developed dementia = (80 ÷ 4000) = 0.02

Now, we know that 7 glasses of wine is 14 units
1 glass of wine therefore is 2 units
3 glasses is 6 units (this is per day as per the question).
Per week, this would be 6 x 7 = 42 units
If we read the graph, 42 units corresponds to a hazard ratio of approximately 1.5

Now we use the formula given in the passage.
We need to find out the proportion of participants that consumed 42 units per week in midlife who went on to develop dementia.

We know proportion of participants that consumed 14 units per week in midlife who went on to develop dementia = 0.02

We know 42 units corresponds to a hazard ratio of approximately 1.5

$$\frac{\text{proportion of participants that consumed 42 units per week in midlife who went on to develop dementia}}{\text{proportion of participants that consumed 14 units per week in midlife who went on to develop dementia}} = 1.5$$

$$\frac{\text{proportion of participants that consumed 42 units per week in midlife who went on to develop dementia}}{0.02} = 1.5$$

proportion of participants that consumed 42 units per week in midlife who went on to develop dementia $= 1.5 \times 0.02 = 0.03$

0.03 = 3%

35) C

To answer this question, we need to look for a statement that, if true, would mean heavy drinking in midlife is more dangerous than not drinking.

The only statement that does that is statement C.

2019 Section 2

1) E

W is a section of the chromosome. It is not the entire chromosome, so it has to represent a gene.

X represents restriction enzymes that cut DNA into smaller fragments at certain specific nucleotide sequences.

Y represents plasmid which is circular DNA of bacteria.

Z represents ligase which connects the DNA taken from the chromosome and the plasmid DNA.

---

2) C

$CaCO_3$ is a salt of a strong base and weak acid, which is why it is basic in nature. In order to remove it, we need to use an acidic solution. So, statement 1 is correct.

The effervescence is caused by the release of carbon dioxide gas (which forms during the reaction) and not hydrogen gas. Statement 2 is wrong.

As the reaction proceeds, the pH does not go down as we have a base and an acid reacting. So statement 3 is wrong.

The reason we are using a cleaning agent is to remove the limescale. In order to do this, we need to convert the limescale into something more soluble. We know that a salt is formed when reacting a base and an acid. Therefore, the salt has to be more soluble than limescale so it can be removed from the bathroom surfaces. So, 4 is correct.

---

3) B

We know that the cyclist is moving forwards with acceleration 4 m/s². This means that the cyclist needs to overcome the resistive forces in order to move forwards.

So we can conclude that 600 N > 300 N + air resistance. Hence, options D and E cannot be the right answers.

Resultant force is the sum of all the forces involved. (we must remember, that force is a vector quantity, hence the resistive forces would be negative, i.e., have a negative sign in equations).

Resultant force = 600 – (300 + air resistance) = 600 – 300 – air resistance

The resultant force would be the product of the acceleration produced by the cyclist and the combined mass of cyclist and bicycle. (The equation is Force = mass x acceleration)
Resultant force = 50 x 4 = 200 N

Using the equation, we created (Resultant force = 600 – 300 – air resistance), we get:
200 N = 600 – 300 – air resistance
If we rearrange, we get:
Air resistance = 600 – 300 – 200 = 100 N

---

4) B

Let us first expand the brackets in p + q = 3 (p – q)
We get: **p + q = 3p – 3q**

We now need to think outside of the box for this question. We need to square both sides of the equation. $(p + q)^2 = (3p – 3q)^2$

So, we get
LHS: $(p + q)^2 = p^2 + q^2 + 2pq$
RHS: $(3p – 3q)^2 = 9p^2 + 9q^2 – (2 \times 3p \times 3q) = 9p^2 + 9q^2 – 18pq$

We get:
$p^2 + q^2 + 2pq = 9p^2 + 9q^2 – 18pq$
$20\ pq = 8p^2 + 8q^2$
$20pq = 8 (p^2 + q^2)$

Rearranging:

$$\frac{pq}{p2 + q2} = \frac{8}{20} = \frac{2}{5}$$

---

5) A

Active transport requires the use of energy. (represented by 1)
Diffusion and osmosis does not require the use of energy. (represented by 2 and 3)

6) D

This is a rather simple question if you know the basics of electroplating. If you wish to electroplate a certain metal with another metal, this is what you need to know:

- The **negative electrode or cathode** is the object that is going to be electroplated. (in this case, the copper rode)
- The **positive electrode or anode** is the object that is going to be used to coat the copper rod. (in this case, silver rod)
- The **electrolyte** should be a solution of the coating metal. (in this case, the electrolyte should contain silver, hence, silver nitrate solution)

---

7) C

When the object is gently lowered, here are the changes that take place:
The scale changes from 750 g to 950 g. So mass of object = 200 g

The liquid rises from 375 cm^3 to 500 cm^3.
Volume of object = 125 cm^3

Density = Mass ÷ Volume = 200 ÷ 125 = 1.6 g cm^{-3}

---

8) E

To solve this simply, we just need to not use the figures given as standard form. Using the figures as they are may confuse a bit.
E.g. $6 \times 10^2 = 600$
We get:

$$\sqrt{\frac{600 + 40}{0.012 + 0.004}} = \sqrt{\frac{640}{0.016}} = \sqrt{40,000} = 200$$

---

9) D

Statement 1 is wrong because as temperature decreased, the carbon dioxide concentration also decreased which meant that the lizard's respiratory rate also decreased. So the respiration rate of the lizard is NOT inversely proportional to the environmental temperature.

Statement 2 is wrong. We cannot determine whether the lizard is only respiring aerobically. It may also be respiring anaerobically.

Statement 3 is correct. The limewater test is a test for carbon dioxide and hence it can detect carbon dioxide in the air leaving the chamber.

---

10) H

In this question we are talking about the element with the largest atomic number in group 1. This is the one furthest down the group.

Statement 1 is correct because reactivity with water increases down group 1. Hence, it has the most vigorous reaction with cold water, as compared to

Statement 2 is correct. All elements in group 1 have one electron in their highest occupied energy level.

Statement 3 is correct. Oxidation is loss of electrons. The element furthest down group 1 will have the largest atomic radius out of the other group 1 elements. The larger the atomic radius an element has, the more readily it can lose electrons, hence the more readily it can be oxidized.

---

11) C

It is important to think about this question logically.

The smaller sphere was initially uncharged (equal number of protons and electrons). Then, when the small sphere was connected to the Earth, electrons started to flow from small sphere to Earth. This means that the small sphere started to lose electrons (i.e. started to lose negative charge). Hence when the small sphere was disconnected, its final charge would be positive. (more protons than electrons).

The larger sphere was initially negative charged (more electrons than protons). It was not connected to anything at any point in time. So, it would remain the same, i.e. negative charged and hence it would have fewer protons than electrons.

So, C is the answer.

12) H

Any straight line on a graph is governed by the formula: $y = mx + c$
This means that any point on that line has to follow this formula.
In this formula,

- Y is a function of X (you will understand as we go along to solve this question)
- M is the gradient (we are given that gradient is -3)
- C is the y-intercept (where the line crosses y-axis), in this case we know that line crosses the y-axis at (0, r). We ignore 0, and we only focus on 'r' as any point on the y-axis will have 0 for its x value.

We know points M and N are on the same straight line. Let us take point M.
X value = 6, Y value = 3p – 1, M = -3, C = r
Now we just substitute these values in the formula $y = mx + c$
$3p - 1 = -3 (6) + r$
$3p - 1 = -18 + r$
$r = 3p - 1 + 18 = 3p + 17$ (equation 1)

We do the same for point N.
X value = 1 - p, Y value = 2, M = -3, C = r
Now we just substitute these values in the formula $y = mx + c$
$2 = -3 (1 - p) + r$
$2 = -3 + 3p + r$
$r = 2 + 3 – 3p = 5 – 3p$ (equation 2)

We have two equations for 'r', we can combine them together now.

$3p + 17 = 5 – 3p$
$6p = -12$
$p = -2$

We now have the value for 'p', simply substitute this value in any of the two equations.
$r = 5 – 3p$
$r = 5 – 3 (-2)$
$r = 5 + 6 = 11$

_____

13) H

Amino acids, cellulose and lipids have carbon in them. Therefore, all 3 are part of the carbon cycle.

14) A

We know that the total volume of gas produced is lower in curve Y and the reaction takes place faster (initial line is very steep).
The steep line in curve Y shows that the reaction happened very quickly (the rate of reaction is higher than curve X). This indicates that the manganese (IV) oxide particle size would have been smaller. This is because the smaller the particle size, the more surface area is present and hence faster reaction (provided that mass of manganese (IV) oxide is same, which it is). The answer is either A, B or C.

We also know less gas is produced. This means there would be lesser number of moles of hydrogen peroxide. We use the formula, moles = volume x concentration (remember, volume should be in dm^{-3}). Moles in curve X = 0.05 x 0.1 = 0.005 mol
Moles of hydrogen peroxide in option A = 0.02 x 0.2 = 0.004 mol
Moles of hydrogen peroxide in option B = 0.025 x 0.2 = 0.005 mol
Moles of hydrogen peroxide in option C = 0.05 x 0.1 = 0.005mol

Therefore, A is the answer.

---

15) F

The only correct statement is F. Ultrasonic waves, like sound waves, are longitudinal.

---

16) D

Area of a rectangle = length x width
We can assume (7 - $\sqrt{5}$) cm can either be length or width, it does not matter.
Let us say it is the length. Let the width be W.

Area of this rectangle (66) = (7 - $\sqrt{5}$) x W
W = 66 ÷ (7 - $\sqrt{5}$)

Now we just use the formula for perimeter of rectangle. P = 2 (l + w)

$$P = 2 \left(7 - \sqrt{5} + \frac{66}{(7 - \sqrt{5})}\right)$$

By doing the addition inside the brackets, we get:

$$P = 2\left(\frac{35+\sqrt{5}}{2}\right) = 35 + \sqrt{5}$$

The two 2's cancel out to give P = 35 + √5

---

17) D

We know the pea plant is heterozygous for seed colour. The alleles for seed colour are Y and y. Therefore, the pea plant definitely has alleles Y and y.

We are only told that the pea plant is homozygous for seed shape. We are not given any information about whether it is homozygous dominant or homozygous recessive. It can either be 'RR' or 'rr' and NOT 'Rr'

Statement 1 is wrong because the pea plant cannot have both 'R' and 'r'.
Statement 2 could be correct. We know it has alleles 'Y' and 'y'. It could also have 'R'.

Statement 3 could not be correct. It cannot contain both alleles for seed shape 'R' and 'r'.

Statement 4 is correct. We know it is heterozygous for seed colour, so it's genotype for seed colour has to be 'Yy'.

Statement 5 cannot be correct. The genotype for seed colour has to be 'Yy' and not 'YY'.

Statement 6 cannot be correct. The plant is homozygous for seed shape. So it cannot be 'Rr'.

Statement 7 could be correct. Its genotype for seed shape could be 'rr'.

So D is correct.

---

18) E

We are given the concentration and volume of potassium manganate (VII). We can calculate the number of moles with this.

(convert volume to dm^3 first. $10\ cm^3 = 0.01\ dm^3$)

n = c x v = 0.05 x 0.01 = 5 x 10^{-4} mol

From the reaction equation, we can see that molar ratio of $Fe^{2+} : MnO_4^- = 5 : 1$

So, 1 mole of MnO_4^- ions reacts with 5 moles of Fe^{2+} ions.
So, 5×10^{-4} mol of MnO_4^- ions would react with $(5 \times 5 \times 10^{-4})$ moles of Fe^{2+} ions.
Moles of $Fe^{2+} = 25 \times 10^{-4}$ mol

We are given the volume of $Fe^{2+} = 25$ cm^3 = 0.025 dm^3

Concentration = moles ÷ volume

$$c = \frac{25 \times 10 - 4}{0.025} = 0.1 = 1 \times 10^{-1} \; mol \; dm^{-3}$$

---

19) A

When the universe was formed, it was filled with electromagnetic radiation in the form of intense gamma-rays. Now it is in the microwave region of the spectrum.

If you remember the electromagnetic spectrum, you will know that frequency decreases as we shift from gamma to microwave and wavelength increases. So, statements 1 and 2 are wrong.

Also, frequency is indirectly proportional to wavelength. So, statement 3 is also wrong.

---

20) E

It is best to draw a tree diagram for this.

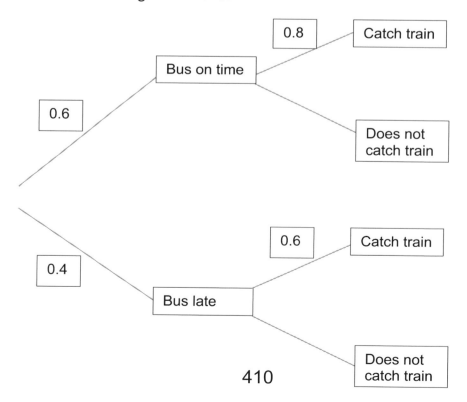

410

We know that Sylvia catches the train. There are two possibilities how this could have happened:

Bus on time:
If she had caught the train, and the bus was on time, probability that this would have happened
= 0.6 x 0.8 = 0.48

Bus late:
If she had caught the train, and the bus was late, probability that this would have happened
= 0.4 x 0.6 = 0.24

Total probability of catching the train = 0.48 + 0.24 = 0.72

Probability of catching the train with bus on time = $^{0.48}/_{0.72}$ = $^2/_3$

---

21) B

1 – Correct. Amino acids are encoded by a group of 3 bases. 166 x 3 = 498. So a gene consisting of 500 base pairs will have a maximum of 166 amino acids.

2 – Wrong. Remember, red blood cells have no nucleus, hence no nuclear chromosomes.

3 – Wrong. Adenine binds with thymine or uracil, not with guanine. So it is not necessary that the number of adenine bases in an allele must be the same as the number of guanine bases.

So, B is the answer.

---

22) D

Options A and C are wrong because they are alkenes.
Let molecular formula of alkane be C_xH_y

Ratio of volumes of alkane and CO_2 = 35 : 105 = 1 : 3

This means that number of carbons (x) = 3

Only options C and D have hydrocarbons where number of carbons are 3. We have already established that option C is wrong because it is an alkene so option D is correct.

---

23) A

Momentum = mass x velocity = 400 x 15 = 6000 kg m/s
The water ejected achieves a velocity of 15 m/s in 12 seconds.
Initial velocity = 0 m/s
Final velocity = 15 m/s
Acceleration = (final velocity – initial velocity) ÷ time = (15 – 0) ÷ 12 = 1.25 m/s^2

411

Each nozzle ejects 400 kg of water. Two nozzles eject 800 kg.
Force = mass x acceleration
Force = 800 x 1.25 = 1000 N

---

24) H

The easiest way to solve this would be to use a protractor on the pentagon diagram provided. Set the protractor in such a way that the line which represents third leg is at 110°. (such as in the diagram below)

Remember, bearings are taken from North. This means we must draw an imaginary line pointing towards north from which 110° would represent the third leg. (see diagram)

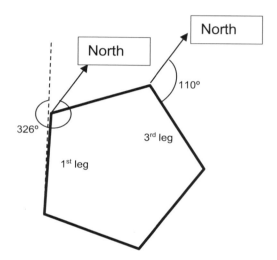

Then make a line pointing north from the end of the first leg (see diagram).
Now extend the line representing the first leg. (this extension is represented by the dashed line)
Now, using the protractor, measure the angle between the line representing North and the dashed line. (remember, we have to measure it clockwise)

We should get approximately 326°.

Please remember, if you think solving questions like these is going you take a long time, move onto the other ones and come back to these.

---

25) B

Only statement 1 is correct. If the cell membranes are damaged between the blood vessels and the Bowman's capsule, proteins can pass through the bowman's capsule and hence, be present in the urine.

The other 2 statements are wrong.

26) E

Ratio of the two isotopes = 20% : 80% = 1 : 4

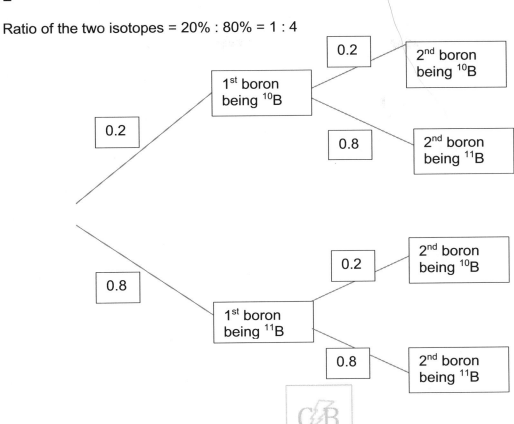

Probability of both boron being B-10 (having mass 26) = 0.2 x 0.2 = 0.04

Probability of 1 boron being B-10 and other being B-11 (having mass 27)
 = (0.2 x 0.8) + (0.2 x 0.8) = 0.32
(remember there are two ways in which it can be a mixture of B-10 and B-11)

Probability of both boron being B-11 (having mass 28) = 0.8 x 0.8 = 0.64

Ratio = 0.04 : 0.32 : 0.64 = 1 : 8 : 16

413

27) B

This question requires us to use the formula:

$$\frac{Turns\ on\ primary\ coil}{Voltage\ on\ primary\ coil} = \frac{Turns\ on\ secondary\ coil}{Voltage\ on\ secondary\ coil}$$

$$\frac{400}{240} = \frac{100}{Voltage\ on\ secondary\ coil}$$

$$voltage\ on\ seconday\ coil = \frac{100\ x\ 240}{400} = 60\ V$$

So, output voltage = 60 V

To find to input current, we use the following formula:

$$\frac{Current\ in\ primary\ coil}{current\ in\ secondary\ coil} = \frac{Voltage\ in\ secondary\ coil}{voltage\ in\ primary\ coil}$$

$$Current\ in\ primary\ coil = \frac{current\ in\ secondary\ coil\ x\ Voltage\ in\ secodnary\ coil}{voltage\ in\ primary\ coil}$$

$$Current\ in\ primary\ coil = \frac{2\ x\ 60}{240} = 0.5\ A$$

Power = Voltage x Current
Output power = 60 x 2 = 120 W

So the answer is B.

2019 Section 3

1) People may often deny the existence of certain problems if they do not disagree with the problem's solutions. This is known as solution aversion, in which, people are inclined to deny even the scientific evidence supporting the existence of the problems.

This situation usually arises when the solutions proposed to tackle a problem are going to have a negative impact on some people. Even though they know that the solutions are necessary, they will deny the problem even exists so that they would not have to face the negative impacts of the solutions. An example would be the problem of climate change. There is strong scientific evidence that suggests that climate change is real, and that urgent action needs to be taken to minimise its effects.
Even though a lot of people believe in climate change, there are some who deny its existence. This may be because some governments around the world have imposed new taxes in order to fight climate change such as the CO_2 tax. This means that people would have to pay more money to the government in order to tackle climate change. This could be one of the reasons why people refuse to believe that climate change is real as the solutions are having a negative impact on their personal lives.

On the other hand, some people may accept the solutions to a problem even though they may not necessarily agree with them. This is because even though they know they may face some difficulties because of these solutions, it is for their own good. For example, a doctor may advise the patient to abstain from eating certain foods which the patient loves. The patient may not agree with the doctor's solution but would follow the advice anyway since it would help to improve their health.

To conclude, different people have different opinions and concerns about certain problems, and it is important that these concerns are taken into consideration before coming up with a solution. There are some people (although they may be very few, compared to others) who deny the existence of major problems such as climate change because they may not agree with the solutions. In such cases, they should be provided with the scientific evidence and be educated that the solutions are necessary for the betterment of everyone.

2) Brian Cox and Jeff Forshaw present the argument that nothing is certain in science as there are no universal truths. Different people may have different views about how things work in this world and science, through scientific research and studies, helps to prove these views as false.

People usually think of science as the ultimate truth. They think that if something is proven to work by science, it definitely has to be correct and be repeatable in every situation. However, this may not necessarily be the case every time. We can take the example of medical treatments. If patients with the same disease are treated using the same method, it is not necessary that all of them would be treated successfully. The treatment may work for some, it may develop side effects for others, or it may not work at all for some. This shows that even though these treatments were proven to heal patients scientifically, it is not necessary that it may work for all patients. Therefore, this is an example of "in science, there are no universal truths".

On the contrary, others may think that some things need to be considered as 'truths' in order for science to move forward. If we come to accept that everything is uncertain in science, we may stop carrying out scientific researches, because we would be unsure of the outcome. We need to accept, that some things, if done correctly, will have predictable outcomes. We can take gravity as an example. If we throw something in the air, we can reasonably accept it to come back down because gravity is present and that is the truth. We can accept gravity as 'truth' and continue to do researches based on this 'truth'.

To conclude, science is a culmination of extensive researches and studies. When something is proven to be true by science, after extensive research has been done, it should be reasonable to accept it as a truth. If this were not true, we would not accept many medical treatments as they do not work all the time. But if they can help to heal some patients without negatively affecting others, we can accept it as a truth.

---

3) Surgical innovation refers to any advances in surgical science, technology or training which leads to improved patient healthcare and surgery outcomes. The argument made in the statement is that teamwork is more important than the skills of an individual surgeon to bring about these advances in surgical science.

Teamwork is a major aspect of medicine. To carry out a treatment successfully and effectively, a whole team of health professionals is required. This team may consist of doctors, nurses, technicians, pharmacists and even therapists. Each of these professionals plays a crucial role to provide effective treatments and improve the healthcare of their patients. A doctor cannot treat a patient by himself/herself. It is a collective effort of the medical team. This may apply to surgical innovation too. In order to progress in surgical science, opinions of nurses, physicians and other members of a surgical team may be needed before any surgical innovation is approved as safe to carry out on patients. The statement tries to convey the message that before any innovations are introduced in the field of surgery, there should be a collective agreement between members of a surgical team.

On the other hand, some may argue that a surgeon has more knowledge and experience about surgeries than the other members of the team. Therefore, the surgeon's opinions and advice should be given more importance. This may be true in cases where a surgeon wants to introduce an innovative technique or technology into their clinic or hospital. These ideas can then be discussed upon by other surgeons or medical directors. If they find it fit to introduce these innovative techniques, then in this case, the skills of the surgeon were more important for surgical progress.

To conclude, teamwork is important in every aspect of medicine, whether it is providing treatments or for surgical innovation. It would be ideal to take the opinions of every member of a surgical team into consideration before any innovative surgical technique or technology is introduced. However, the opinions of the surgeons should be given more importance as they have more knowledge about surgical procedures than others.

Printed in Great Britain
by Amazon